AF207083

LEWIS C.
SHEAFE

To order additional copies of
LEWIS C. SHEAFE, by Douglas Morgan,
call **1-800-765-6955**.

Visit us at
www.reviewandherald.com
for information on other Review and Herald® products.

ADVENTIST PIONEER SERIES
George R. Knight, Series Editor

Published volumes:
James White: Innovator and Overcomer
by Gerald Wheeler

Joseph Bates: The Real Founder of Seventh-day Adventism
by George R. Knight

John H. Kellogg: Pioneering Health Reformer
by Richard W. Schwarz

W. W. Prescott: Forgotten Giant of Adventism's Second Generation
by Gilbert Valentine

E. J. Waggoner: From the Physician of Good News to Agent of Division
by Woodrow W. Whidden II

Future volumes (partial list):

John Nevins Andrews   *LeRoy E. Froom*
W. C. White   *Alonzo T. Jones*
Ellen G. White   *William Miller*
George I. Butler   *F. D. Nichol*
Arthur G. Daniells

LEWIS C. SHEAFE

Apostle to Black America

DOUGLAS MORGAN

REVIEW AND HERALD® PUBLISHING ASSOCIATION

Since 1861 | www.reviewandherald.com

Library of Congress Cataloging-in-Publication Data
Morgan, Douglas, 1955-   .
 Lewis C. Sheafe : apostle to Black America / Douglas Morgan.
   p. cm.
 1. Sheafe, Lewis C., 1859-1938. 2. Seventh-day Adventists—United States—Clergy—Biography. 3. Seventh-day Adventist converts—United States—Biography. 4. African American Seventh-day Adventists—Biography. 5. African American civil rights workers—Biography. 6. African Americans—Social conditions—To 1964. 7. African Americans—Civil rights—History.
 I. Title.
 BX6193.S49M67 2010
 286.7'32092—dc22
 [B]
                    2009047610

ISBN 978-0-8280-2397-9

DEDICATION

To

CHARLES E. BRADFORD
empowering leader

LIST OF ABBREVIATIONS

AFB	Albion Fox Ballenger
AGD	Arthur G. Daniells
AK	Andrew Kalstrom
ATJ	Alonzo T. Jones
Bee	Washington *Bee*
CA	*Colored American*
CAR	Center for Adventist Research, Andrews University, Berrien Springs, Mich.
EGW	Ellen G. White
EGWE	Ellen G. White Estate, Silver Spring, Md.
GAI	G. A. Irwin
GCA	Archives of the General Conference of Seventh-day Adventists, Silver Spring, Md.
GCB	*General Conference Bulletin*
GCDB	*General Conference Daily Bulletin*
GCC	General Conference Committee
GIB	George I. Butler
HEO	H. E. Osborne
HWC	H. W. Cottrell
JHK	John Harvey Kellogg
JRB	James R. Buster
JSW	Judson S. Washburn
LAH	L. A. Hoopes
LCS	Lewis C. Sheafe
MCS	Matthew C. Strachan
NWA	N. W. Allee
OAO	O. A. Olsen
Review	*Advent Review and Sabbath Herald*
RMK	Robert M. Kilgore
SS	Sydney Scott
UTC	Urbana *Times Citizen*
WAS	W. A. Spicer
WCW	W. C. White
WHG	William H. Green
WP	Washington *Post*
WT	Washington *Tribune*
YB	*Seventh-day Adventist Yearbook*
YV	Youngstown *Vindicator*

CONTENTS

CONTENTS

FOREWORD

WHO IS LEWIS C. SHEAFE? And why should he be featured in the Adventist Pioneer Series? Those are excellent questions, especially since most Adventists have never heard his name and, it is probably safe to say, very few denominational historians know much about him.

That is unfortunate, because Sheafe was the first world-class preacher/leader in the African-American segment of Adventism. He not only rose to the forefront in Adventism, but had previously held a prominent position among both the Baptists and the larger North American Black community. A man with a better education than practically all of his Adventist ministerial colleagues (both White and Black), Sheafe was an outstanding speaker and a forceful leader among the various Black communities in which he worked. His public work for African-Americans in Washington, D.C., had implications for his race nationwide for those inside and those outside of the Adventist Church.

I first became alerted to the centrality of Sheafe during my research on A. T. Jones more than 20 years ago. Having collected a great deal of material, I had hoped to write a major research article on this forgotten Adventist leader. But while my intentions were good, I never managed to put my findings on paper. Thus it was that I was overjoyed when Douglas Morgan submitted a proposal for a book on Sheafe. After reading his first few chapters, I knew that we had a well-written, exhaustively researched, and perceptive book that was needed to fill a major gap in our understanding of Seventh-day Adventist history.

Douglas Morgan is well qualified for his task. With a Ph.D. in American history from the University of Chicago, he currently teaches history at Washington Adventist University. His treatment of Sheafe is significant not only because it is the only full-length biography of the man, but also because it analyzes the interactions between the Black and White races in the North American Seventh-day Adventist Church. Less than positive relationships eventually led Sheafe to leave the Adventist ministry, even though he continued to preach the denomination's beliefs. The unfortunate dynamics between the races would not end with the exiting of this powerful apostle to Black Adventism, but would continue to fracture the denomination along racial lines up through the disaffection of J. K. Humphry in the late 1920s,[1] the rise of the regional conferences in North America in the 1940s,[2] and the struggle for Black union conferences in the 1970s.[3] Thus we have in the Sheafe biography not merely the story of a person, but also the beginning of the pilgrimage of the denomination as it sought to adjust to its various racial entities within the context of a culture that was experiencing the same dynamics and challenges. As a result, Morgan's biography is meaningful on several levels. It highlights the gifts, weaknesses, and tragedy not only of Sheafe himself, but also of the denomination of which he was a part.

Lewis C. Sheafe: Apostle to Black America is the sixth volume in an unprecedented series on Adventist biography. Thus far the series has seen biographies on James White, by Gerald Wheeler; W. W. Prescott, by Gilbert Valentine; John Harvey Kellogg, by Richard Schwarz; E. J. Waggoner, by Woodrow Whidden; and my own work on Joseph Bates. Currently assigned volumes include full-length works on J. N. Andrews, Alonzo T. Jones, Uriah Smith, Dudley Canright, Ellen G. White, W. C. White, J. Edson White, Arthur G. Daniells, William Miller, George I. Butler, S. N. Haskell, Siegfried Horn, L. E. Froom, and J. N. Loughborough. Each volume will focus on the individual's major contribution to the church and will be written by a person well versed in his or her topic.

Meanwhile, we are indebted to Doug Morgan for enabling us to understand better the story of Sheafe and the racial issues that the denomination struggled with as it sought to become a church for all peoples. I trust that reading this book will be as fascinating and helpful for you as it was for me.

GEORGE R. KNIGHT
Series Editor
Rogue River, Oregon

---

[1] R. Clifford Jones, *James K. Humphrey and the Sabbath-Day Adventists* (Jackson, Miss.: University Press of Mississippi, 2006).

[2] George R. Knight, *Organizing for Mission and Growth: The Development of Adventist Church Structure* (Hagerstown, Md.: Review and Herald, 2006), pp. 145-151.

[3] *Ibid.*, pp. 153-155.

ACKNOWLEDGMENTS

L OOKING BACK ON THE CHAIN OF EVENTS culminating in this book brings pointed reminders of how much I owe to grace and the graciousness of others for a work that bears my name. Words of gratitude begin with George R. Knight, who gave warm encouragement to publication of this volume in the Review and Herald's Pioneer Series. Coming as it did from one whose monumental output over the past 25 years has placed him at the forefront among historians of Seventh-day Adventism, that endorsement was personally rewarding, beyond its significance for getting the book published. Knight not only provided affirmation toward the end of the work on the manuscript, but also, through his writing, influenced its beginning. It was in his book *From 1888 to Apostasy: The Case of A.T. Jones* that I first encountered the name Lewis C. Sheafe and became curious about his story.

That curiosity remained deep in the clutter of my mental storage closet until a phone call came out of the blue one spring day in 2001 from Mark A. McCleary, pastor of the First Seventh-day Adventist Church in Washington, D.C. We had never met and knew nothing of each other, but simply by virtue of my proximity in the History Department at Columbia Union College (now Washington Adventist University), he contacted me about completing a history of his historic congregation. That project led to the discovery of sources disclosing that Sheafe's career was a related, but separate, story that also needed telling.

The research for the book could take place only through facilities and personnel dedicated both to preserving historical materials and to continual innovation in making them more accessible. While discovery of some of the crucial sources came about only by cranking through reel after reel of unindexed microfilm and box after box of correspondence, relatively recent and remarkable advances in digitizing sources for full-text searching online greatly enhanced the gathering of evidence.

Bert Haloviak, director of Archives and Statistics at the General

Conference of Seventh-day Adventists, is at the leading edge of such developments, performing an invaluable service to researchers by overseeing the digitizing of an enormous and continually expanding body of materials from the church's heritage. Taking advantage of this resource led me, for example, to relatively brief items buried in the back pages of the *Review and Herald*, in the transcripts of General Conference sessions, and in General Conference Committee minutes that would have been easy to overlook even through hours of laborious page-by-page perusal. Especially in the case of a lesser-known figure like Sheafe, for whom sources are relatively scarce, these items were of crucial value both in filling out the narrative of his career and making the case for his historical importance despite obscurity today.

At the same time, Bert and his associate, Eucaris Galicia, responded with utmost kindness and efficiency to requests for a great deal of archival materials the old-fashioned way, even when I felt the need to revisit the same boxes a second and third time. Tim Poirier, vice director of the Ellen G. White Estate, was similarly generous with his time and expertise, enabling me to examine a wide range of unpublished correspondence. Minneola Dixon and Joyce Williams of the Oakwood University Archive and Museum went out of their way in graciously accommodating my requests for photographs, including the one used for the cover.

Emory Tolbert, chair of the History Department at Howard University, took an interest in my project, leading to fortuitous contact with one of his graduate students, Mwariama Kamau of the Washington, D.C., chapter of the Universal Negro Improvement Association and African Communities League. In remarkably generous fashion, Kamau provided documentation on Sheafe's involvement in the Marcus Garvey movement, about which I would otherwise have had no clue.

Grateful acknowledgment as well to Jim Ford and Merlin Burt of the Center for Adventist Research at Andrews University, Jane Ogora of the Weis Library at Washington Adventist University, and to the staffs of the Washingtoniana Room and Black Studies Center at the Martin Luther King, Jr., Memorial Library in Washington, D.C.; the Newspaper and Current Periodical Reading Room of the Library of Congress; the Manuscript Division of the Moorland-Spingarn Research Center at Howard University; the Schomburg Center for Research in Black Culture in Harlem, New York; the Minnesota State Historical Society; and the Ohio Historical Society.

I am also thankful for the less formal yet nonetheless meaningful support of Joan Francis, Roy Branson, and other colleagues at Columbia Union College/Washington Adventist University. Through the several years of my preoccupation with Sheafe and related research, they affirmed me with patient listening and words of encouragement, and facilitated, at their own inconvenience, fluctuations in my teaching contracts that freed time for completing the book.

Enthusiastic support for a "trial run" presentation of some of the material that went into the book at Capitol Hill Seventh-day Adventist Church in Washington, D.C., did much to energize me for completion of the task. In a wider sense, I experienced through fellowship with that congregation, led by Pastors Gene M. Donaldson and Anthony A. Medley, a kind of spiritual renewal that helped sharpen my sense of purpose for the book, which is to contribute to the upbuilding of the body of Christ through the distinctive form and discipline of historical narrative.

At the personal level, my highest gratitude goes to my wife, Barbara, for making the years of my work on this book the most joyful ones of my life. As a manifestation of her love, she recognized and honored my (duly subordinate) affection for this project and sacrificed her own interests not merely to tolerate it but to give it tangible and warm nurture.

A final word of heartfelt thankfulness for the generous spirits of three notable veterans in the cause of the "third angel's message" who took the time to speak with me about Sheafe. Clara Peterson Rock and the late Alma Montgomery Blackmon, in relating childhood experiences, made invaluable contributions to a more fully human picture of Sheafe's complex and multifaceted legacy for the Adventist community.

The third, Elder Charles E. Bradford, never knew Sheafe personally, but knew many people who did, including his own father, Robert L. Bradford, who entered the Adventist work only a few years after Sheafe did, and became part of that indomitable corps of pioneering preachers whose work established the foundations of Adventism among African-Americans. It is not only the fact of knowing several who knew Sheafe, but also the uncanny ability to draw upon an amazingly rich repository of anecdotes and insights built up over seven decades of ministry and church leadership, that makes Bradford's perspective so valuable as a historical source.

Through another grace-charged development that helped shape the context for the writing of this book, I was given the privilege of working with Elder Bradford's Sabbath in Africa study group. That positioned me to receive freely from his repository as he related to me, in numerous conversations and e-mail messages, his interactions with persons of note for the story of Lewis Sheafe and for the Black Adventist experience as a whole. I must absolve him and all others here acknowledged from any errors and shortcomings in the book, for which I bear full responsibility. But while formally cited as a source only twice in these pages, the experience and wisdom he freely shared runs behind and through them in countless ways, sometimes prompting me to see things from a different and more revealing angle, sometimes giving new leads to pursue, sometimes alerting me to connections previously unnoted, and regularly affirming the value of the work as only he can.

Therefore, I dedicate this book to one renowned for powerful preaching that both stirs the spirit and enlightens the mind, respected as a forward-thinking church leader, and recognized for pioneering scholarship on Christianity's African roots—Charles E. Bradford. This volume stands as grateful testament as well as to another of his principal gifts—that of inspiring and empowering others to exercise their gifts to the fullest, with hearts for the glory of God and the building up of God's church.

PREFACE

IN NOVEMBER 1902 one of Washington, D.C.'s African-American newspapers, the *Colored American*, reported the unusual occurrence of a minister from a different denomination scheduled to preach at the Metropolitan African Methodist Episcopal Church. Known as the "national cathedral" of African Methodism, Metropolitan AME was the site of Howard University's annual commencement exercises and, just seven years before, the funeral of Frederick Douglass. It stood at the center of Black culture in Washington, D.C., which was in turn the center of Black culture in America. The guest preacher, said the newspaper, was Lewis Sheafe, the "noted apostle of Seventh Day Adventism."[1]

A century later the once-noted apostle is virtually unknown, little more than a footnote in Adventist historical writing. As teacher of a college course in Adventist history for several years and author of a book about Adventism's interaction with American society, I knew next to nothing about Sheafe until 2002. Then, during the course of research on the history of the First Seventh-day Adventist Church in Washington, D.C., I kept coming across references to Sheafe that were as intriguing and significant as the one cited above.

I became increasingly absorbed in piecing together the story of the man who was in fact Adventism's first apostle to African-Americans in the nation's cities. Today thriving Black Adventist congregations can be found in every major city in America. But in 1903 there were next to none, until Lewis Sheafe founded the People's church in Washington, D.C. I found, from multiple sources, unanimous acclaim for Sheafe as the preeminent figure among the corps of preachers who emerged during the early years of the twentieth century to lay the foundations of Adventism among Americans of African heritage.

Also, tributes to the power and eloquence of his preaching come up again and again in the sources. Dr. John Harvey Kellogg, not a man easy to please in evaluating ministerial talent, described Sheafe to Ellen White as "an orator, a wonderfully able man." And that was not all. Elder Sheafe, said the doctor, "is a more liberally educated and cultivated man and can deliver a more forcible address than any other Seventh-day Adventist minister. We have not a white minister that can begin to stand beside him."[2] Though Kellogg's comparisons are among the most sweeping, literally dozens of similar encomiums from throughout Sheafe's career are on record. The man must truly have been an uncommonly gifted communicator of the gospel.

Even as the impulse to write a biography strengthened, the limited scope of available sources posed a formidable problem. No repository of Lewis Sheafe papers exists. No one who knew him in his prime remains alive to be interviewed. But I kept finding more, primarily in newspapers and archives. Perhaps not enough for a fully satisfactory biography—on important matters we are at times left with either a complete void or frustratingly sketchy traces. But enough to construct the story of an ardent, dramatic life as it intersects with upheavals that would transform the Seventh-day Adventist Church as well as race relations in American society.

Lewis Sheafe (1859-1938) was born just before the Civil War and died just before World War II. He grew to manhood in Massachusetts at a time when it seemed possible that the nation was moving toward racial equality. But his entry into the Baptist ministry in the late 1880s coincided with a gradual collapsing of that hope in what historian C. Vann Woodward has called a "national capitulation to racism." The defining concern of his life became the uplift of his people, already disadvantaged by the legacy of slavery, now held under the harsh and heavy hand of segregation made legal and racism made socially respectable. He grasped at every organizational lever he could find for that uplift—the Afro-American League in the 1890s, the NAACP in the 1910s and beyond, the UNIA in the 1920s, and numerous local initiatives along the way.

Yet the driving center for him was not activist organizations but the gospel of Jesus Christ, of which he was truly and thoroughly a minister. The greatest power for change, he believed, came from uncompromising biblical faith, consistently applied in all dimensions of life. In the Seventh-day Adventist Church he found a convincing commitment to biblical faith, even if it went against the grain of popular Christianity, and an impressive system for bringing that faith into the fiber of human needs for health and education. Here he saw a truth with greater potential than anything he knew to bring tangible help and ultimate liberation to his people. And with unparalleled success he put that truth on the stage of greatest possible influence—Washington, D.C.

That success, and his status as the de facto leader among Black Adventist ministers, brought him into the center of stormy conflicts buffeting the Adventist Church. There he interacted with Ellen White, John Harvey Kellogg, A. T. Jones, and, most of all, A. G. Daniells in events that would decide the church's long-term direction with regard to organization and the authority of Ellen White's writings, as well as race relations.

Here the reader should be forewarned that this is not always a happy story. In fact, it can be heartbreaking—at times almost unbearably so. Yet not without hope. Through the frequently shifting affiliations of his turbulent career, Sheafe remained anchored to two commitments: the well-being of his oppressed people and biblical truth, consistently applied to all dimensions of life.

In triumph as well as tragedy, the story of his vigorous if imperfect endeavors to fulfill those commitments enriches us. Sheafe left a lasting imprint on the church by way of both positive achievements and the leverage that his ruptures with the church provided Black Adventists who remained connected with the denomination. To dissuade others from taking his course, church leaders ended up doing much of what he had asked for in the first place.

So I have tried to tell the story as honestly and sympathetically as I can, without typecasting Sheafe in advance as a villain or apostate, or, on the other hand, as a flawless hero of truth and righteousness. The process has reaffirmed for me the value of keeping alive "the past experiences of God's people,"[3] and my hope is that readers will find in this narrative something that helps orient them on their journey to the kingdom.

---

[1] Untitled editorial comment, *Colored American*, Nov. 8, 1902, p. 8.

[2] JHK to EGW, Dec. 19, 1900.

[3] EGW to AGD, Nov. 1, 1903, in Ellen G. White, *Manuscript Releases* (Silver Spring, Md.: Ellen G. White Estate, 1990), vol. 5, p. 455.

Lewis C. Sheafe

SECTION ONE:
"Go Preach to Your People"

*"In '85 the oft-repeated call came, 'Go preach to your people.'
This he had at other times put off: now . . . [it] must be faced."*

—St. Paul *Appeal*
January 17, 1891

CHAPTER I

FROM WEST DEDHAM
TO WAYLAND SEMINARY

IN NOVEMBER 1888, while the Seventh-day Adventists were bringing to a close the momentous General Conference session held that year in Minneapolis, Minnesota, a 28-year-old newly minted graduate of Wayland Seminary in Washington, D.C., arrived in nearby St. Paul to be considered for the pastorate of Pilgrim Baptist Church. At the 1888 conference the Adventists had made a breakthrough in the struggle to ensure that their movement would be centered on Jesus Christ. In his introductory sermon on November 4, the young minister, Lewis C. Sheafe, declared to the Pilgrim Baptist congregants, "I come among you a stranger, knowing nothing but Jesus Christ and him crucified."[1] If the Adventists and Sheafe were even aware of each other then, no one would have imagined that within a decade the paths of the emerging preacher and the fledgling denomination would converge and that both would be transformed as a result.

Lewis Sheafe and the organized Adventist denomination had come into the world about the same time. On November 16, 1859, exactly a month after John Brown's raid on Harper's Ferry brought the nation to the brink of civil war, Lewis Charles Sheafe was born to Joseph and Louise Beaulette Sheafe in Baltimore, Maryland. His parents had been slaves, but before he was born they had gained their freedom—not an unusual occurrence in the border states of Maryland and Delaware.

Less than two years later a group of believers in the soon return of Jesus Christ and observance of the seventh day of the week as the Sabbath formally adopted the name Seventh-day Adventist and organized a conference—the Michigan Conference. Organization of conferences in other states followed rapidly, leading to the formation of a General Conference in 1863. Though still quite small, with a membership of about 26,000 by 1888, the Adventist Church was vigorous and growing. It had begun establishing the institutions for education, health care, and world mission that would become its hallmarks.[2]

Lewis Sheafe, meanwhile, had grown to manhood and entered gospel ministry, though it was not until his mid-20s that he responded to the call to preach. Most of the sketchy information preserved about Sheafe's early life comes from two biographical features in newspapers—the St. Paul *Appeal* (1891) and the *Colored American*, published in Washington, D.C. (1902). While they leave many questions unanswered, these articles provide glimpses of much that is of value in formulating an overall picture of his life.

Sheafe described both his parents as "strong and God-fearing people," but his mother became by far the leading influence in his upbringing.[3] In fact, when Lewis was only 5 years old, Louise Sheafe took him and his brother with her to live in Boston. His father apparently joined the Union Army,[4] but no further mention of him appears.

Among the first generation of African-Americans coming to maturity after the abolition of slavery in 1865, Lewis Sheafe enjoyed some relative advantages. Born to free parents, he was spared at least the immediate impact of the American system of slavery—"the vilest that ever saw the sun," in the words of John Wesley.[5] And he spent most of his childhood and youth in Massachusetts, one of the least racially oppressive environments to be found in the United States. Thus, Sheafe's background was similar to that of an eminent contemporary, W.E.B. DuBois, though the latter grew up in the western part of the state. In connection with DuBois' attending Fisk University in Tennessee, biographer David Levering Lewis observes that the future leader's home had been "an incomparably kinder place, racially, in which to grow up than the lynch-law backwaters and scabrous townships" that had been home to most of his fellow students.[6]

Despite enjoying a similar regional advantage, Sheafe was neither born into economic prosperity nor handed educational privilege. He worked hard from childhood onward, first as a kitchen boy, then as a waiter, errand boy, and teamster. As a young man he went into farming in West Dedham, not far from Boston.[7]

His education as a boy was sporadic. His mother taught him in the "elementary branches."[8] However, an injury to an eye sustained in 1869 made studying difficult for him during the next few years. So, he does not appear to have had any sustained formal education as a boy.[9]

Louise Sheafe impressed on her son's mind "the beauties of high principle and right living," he later recalled.[10] Lewis's own spirituality was characterized both by a transformed heart and an inquiring mind. He was converted at the age of 15, but this decisive moment in his spiritual experience left him with an unanswered question: Which of the many denominations should he join? It was only after "long and prayerful study of God's Word" over a period of several years that the young farmer reached a decision. His quest "to follow his Lord and Savior as best he knew" led him to become a Baptist.[11]

CALLED TO PREACH

Gifts of spiritual leadership rapidly became evident in the young layman's experience. His Christian endeavors led both to the winning of souls to salvation and to the cure of troubled souls—"cheering the hearts of many among the lonely and forsaken." As these signs of God's blessing on his witness appeared, he began to discern a call, "Go preach to your people." He resisted, pleading his lack of education. But the conviction kept coming back, and by 1885 the "oft-repeated call" had become irresistible. Lewis Sheafe would leave his farm to become a minister of the gospel.[12]

What we have seen thus far in Sheafe's experience fits a pattern that recurs in the careers of many of the leaders of the Adventist movement with which he would eventually connect. In William Miller and in Ellen White, just for starters, we see parallels to Sheafe in their humble circumstances, limited formal education, and immersion in Scripture, combined with critical scrutiny of established church practices and teachings as compared to the Bible. Additionally, each became conscious of a calling, initially resisted, to a large duty.

But in 1885 Sheafe's story breaks from the pattern characteristic of most of the first- and second-generation Adventist leaders: the young Baptist farmer decided to pursue a formal theological education. He responded to the call to preach by entering Wayland Seminary in

Washington, D.C., which had been recommended to him by his pastor in West Dedham, the Rev. E. S. Utford.[13]

Initially known as the National Theological Institute, Wayland Seminary was founded during the Civil War by the American Baptist Home Missionary Society to educate freedmen for ministry. George Mellen Prentiss King, president for three decades (1867-1897), led the school in establishing a high academic standard. Among its most notable students were Booker T. Washington (1878-1879) and Adam Clayton Powell, Sr. (1888-1892). The latter would go on to lead the Abyssinian Baptist Church in Harlem, New York, to become one of the nation's premiere Protestant congregations. The name of another Wayland student, Albert L. Cralle, may be more obscure, but his invention—the ice-cream scoop—is not. In 1899 Wayland Seminary moved to Richmond, Virginia, merging with the Richmond branch of the original National Theological Institute, thereby becoming part of today's Virginia Union University.[14]

In view of the illiteracy of an estimated 95 percent of Southern Blacks at the beginning of the Civil War, Wayland expanded its mission of theological education to include a program of basic and general education, known as the Normal Department. To consolidate his earlier, fragmentary education, Sheafe took the normal as well as the theological courses of study.[15]

Lewis did very well at Wayland. At the end of his first year he was one of only six students awarded a scholarship prize,[16] and he moved through both the normal and theological programs at an accelerated pace of only three years, graduating in 1888. When a group of distinguished clergy visited Wayland's campus, Lewis Sheafe was one of the students President King summoned to meet with them. King asked the visitors to give the students "an examination without a moment's notice." One of the visitors, Rev. W. W. Dawley, later a ministerial colleague of Sheafe in the Twin Cities of Minnesota, recalled being impressed with the ability of this young man.[17]

Both the newly trained preacher and Frederick Douglass, the great abolitionist and foremost national leader of the race, spoke at Sheafe's graduation ceremony on May 22, 1888. Sheafe was one of eight graduates who gave "brief addresses" to the mixed-race crowd that packed the Congregational church. Douglass sat with the Wayland faculty, and was called upon for brief remarks after the graduates received their diplomas.[18]

Beyond academic achievement, the Wayland years also proved rewarding for Lewis's personal and spiritual development. He formed a deep friendship with his roommate, W. J. Hackett, and came to feel that he owed him a debt of gratitude that would "take years to repay." "W.J.," said Lewis, "helped me not so much in the line of books, as in the line of men. He knew men, I did not. He also knew God" and "bore that Christlike spirit."[19]

ANNIE C. HOWARD—TEACHER IN MANY THINGS

In the brief recollections recorded about his Wayland years, Sheafe expressed gratitude to King, the school's president, but otherwise made little mention of the faculty. We do know, however, that he became particularly fond of one of his teachers, Miss Annie C. Howard, for she was to become his wife. Though six years younger than Lewis, Miss Howard was an instructor in the "English Branches." They married on June 6, 1888, just a few days after Lewis's graduation, at the historic Nineteenth Street Baptist Church in Washington.

After a few years of married life Lewis acknowledged that his former teacher "is still my teacher in many things."[20] A poet and, as was her husband, a talented musician, Annie became a leader with her husband in church work along the lines of benevolent service and Bible instruction.

Though W.E.B. DuBois did not coin the phrase until 1903, both Annie and Lewis Sheafe embodied the "Talented Tenth"—the educated vanguard that DuBois believed should be cultivated to lead the uplift of the Black masses. Historian Evelyn Brooks Higginbotham points out that Wayland's president was among the leading advocates for developing a "Female Talented Tenth." Slavery, said King, had deprived Black mothers of the ability to read the Bible to their children. The roles of wife, mother, church worker, and schoolteacher, he maintained, required an educated womanhood.[21]

Lewis Sheafe's first pastorate began during his final year at Wayland, when he was placed in charge of the small Beulah Baptist Church in nearby Alexandria, Virginia. During his nine months there several improvements were made on the church building, and the small debt on it retired—an early sign of the entrepreneurial energy and effectiveness that would characterize his ministry.[22]

During his time at Beulah Baptist, Sheafe's call to ministry was confirmed

by a council of ministers from Washington and Alexandria who examined
him and then ordained him "for the work of the Lord."[23] Though just beginning his ministry at close to 30 years of age, Sheafe rapidly emerged to
prominence among Northern Black American preachers. And the call "Go
preach to your people" now took him to the North Star State.

---

[1] Charles A. Allen, "In Honor of Rev. Lewis C. Sheafe, Late Pastor of Pilgrim Baptist
Church, St. Paul," *Appeal,* July 23, 1892, p. 2.

[2] For a succinct overview of the emergence of Seventh-day Adventism, see George R.
Knight, *A Brief History of Seventh-day Adventism* (Hagerstown, Md.: Review and Herald,
1999), pp. 13-96.

[3] "A New Faith Comes," *Colored American* [hereafter cited as CA], Sept. 13, 1902, p. 1.

[4] In a speech given in 1895 Sheafe referred to himself as a "son of a Republican soldier." "Rev. Sheafe Asks a 'Fair Show and a Free Fight' for His People," Urbana *Times
Citizen* [hereafter cited as UTC], Oct. 10, 1895, p. 5.

[5] Letter to William Wilberforce, quoted in Donald W. Dayton, *Discovering an
Evangelical Heritage* (Hendrickson Publishers, 1976), p. 74.

[6] David Levering Lewis, *W.E.B. DuBois: Biography of a Race, 1868-1919* (New York:
Henry Holt and Co., 1993), p. 56.

[7] "Rev. L. C. Sheafe," *Appeal,* Jan. 17, 1891, pp. 1, 2.

[8] "A New Faith Comes," p. 1.

[9] "Rev. L. C. Sheafe," p. 1.

[10] "A New Faith Comes," p. 1.

[11] "Rev. L. C. Sheafe," p. 1.

[12] *Ibid.*

[13] *Ibid.*

[14] "University History," Virginia Union University Web site, http://www.vuu.edu/about
VUU/history.htm (accessed Aug. 28, 2009). In *Up From Slavery* Booker T. Washington acknowledges that he "derived a great deal of benefit" from his studies at Wayland and "came
into contact with some strong men and women," but also cites weaknesses that he attributed to its lack of an "industrial training" program. See *Three Negro Classics,* introduction by John Hope Franklin (New York: Avon Books, 1965), pp. 75, 76.

[15] "Rev. L. C. Sheafe," p. 1. The 95 percent illiteracy figure is cited by Evelyn Brooks
Higginbotham in *Righteous Discontent: The Women's Movement in the Black Baptist Church,
1880-1920* (Cambridge, Mass.: Harvard University Press, 1993), p. 19.

[16] "Wayland Seminary, A Large Number of Pupils Graduated Last Night," Washington
Post (hereafter cited as WP), May 27, 1886, p. 2.

[17] "Rev. L. C. Sheafe, the Able Pastor of Pilgrim Baptist Church," *Appeal,* June 18, 1892,
p. 3.

[18] "Wayland Seminary, A Large Class Graduates in the Presence of an Immense
Audience," WP, May 23, 1888, p. 1.

[19] "Rev. L. C. Sheafe," p. 1.

[20] *Ibid.,* p. 2.

[21] Higginbotham, pp. 21, 22.

[22] "Rev. L. C. Sheafe," p. 2.

[23] *Ibid.,* p. 1.

CHAPTER II

PASTOR TO MINNESOTA'S
BLACK PILGRIMS

T HE "PILGRIMS" OF PILGRIM BAPTIST CHURCH in St. Paul, Minnesota, did not come over on the *Mayflower*. They came up the Mississippi River, fugitives from slavery in the middle of the Civil War. In early 1863 an intrepid group of slaves—men, women, and children—escaped from Boone County, Missouri, and set out on the Mississippi River on a makeshift raft. The Emancipation Proclamation had gone forth on January 1, but these slaves would have been among those that the proclamation had left unemancipated. President Lincoln had invoked his authority as commander in chief to issue the proclamation as a military tactic directed against the states in rebellion. Missouri was one of the slave-holding states of the Upper South that had remained in the union and to which the Emancipation Proclamation did not apply. Until the Thirteenth Amendment was ratified in 1865, slavery remained legal in Missouri.[1]

By launching into the treacherous waters of the mighty river, the Boone County fugitives emancipated themselves. It was a big risk, surely borne of a desperate desire for freedom. But it paid off when the steamboat *Northerner*, loaded with a cargo of mules, teamsters, and "contraband"[2] laborers to supply Fort Snelling in Minnesota, encountered their raft adrift near Jefferson, Missouri, and towed it the rest of the way to Minnesota. When the *Northerner* deposited them in St. Paul on May 5, the 76 souls aboard the raft boosted the Black population of the state of Minnesota—less than 300 before their arrival—by about 25 percent.[3]

These escapees formed the congregation that became Pilgrim Baptist Church. Their leader, Robert Thomas Hickman, had labored in slavery as a rail-splitter, but his master had taught him to read and gave him permission to preach to other slaves.[4] Many from this original group, including "Father Hickman," were still living when Lewis and Annie Sheafe came to lead the church a quarter century later.

Initially under the wing of the First Baptist Church of St. Paul, the believers were formally organized as a congregation affiliated with the Northern Baptist denomination in 1866.[5] Rev. Hickman retired as pastor in 1886, but not before construction of an impressive house of worship seating 500.

ST. PAUL—1888

Most of the information about the Sheafes' years in Minnesota comes from the *Appeal*, a weekly newspaper (titled the *Western Appeal* until 1889).[6] With offices in Minneapolis, Chicago, and, at times, Louisville, St. Louis, and Cincinnati, the *Appeal* styled itself "A National Afro-American Newspaper." And indeed it did have distributors in cities throughout the land, such as Boston; New York; Washington, D.C.; Birmingham; Vicksburg; Macon and Augusta, Georgia; and Gainesville, Texas, in addition to the previously mentioned.

The sustained success of this weekly newspaper reflected the stable and thriving African-American community that had developed in the Twin Cities by the late 1880s. Though still relatively small in number, about 1,400, it was comprised of mostly literate, hardworking people, linked together by churches, lodges, and other community organizations.

Though racial discrimination placed limitations on the range of employment opportunities, abundant jobs providing at least a minimally livable wage were available in St. Paul, which was booming into a major urban center with a population approaching 200,000. In addition to being on the banks of the Mississippi River, the city became a major hub for the railroad lines—the Great Northern, Northern Pacific, Milwaukee, and Canadian Pacific. Besides the railroad lines, hotels such as the Metropolitan Hotel and the Hotel Ryan provided job opportunities for Blacks, mainly as waiters, porters, and cooks.[7] Some found an opening in the skilled trades, such as bricklaying and stonecutting. Also, a small but critically important Black professional class—physicians, teachers, and lawyers—was in the making.[8]

The editor of the *Appeal*, John Q. Adams, was a significant figure in movements of the day to advance the fortunes of America's Black citizens. He hosted Booker T. Washington, W.E.B. DuBois, William Monroe Trotter, and other prominent leaders at his spacious home on St. Anthony Avenue in St. Paul.[9] The pages of his newspaper contain much that is revealing—though often frustratingly sparse—about life at Pilgrim Baptist Church with its gifted young minister and his talented wife.

The prominence of church life in the pages of a newspaper such as the *Appeal* corresponds to the central place of the church in the African-American community. "[A] proscribed people must have a social centre, and that centre for this people is the Negro church," wrote W.E.B. DuBois in 1903. DuBois' description of a typical Black church of this era is worth quoting a bit further at this point, for it sheds light on what can be pieced together about the experience of Pilgrim Baptist Church and its pastor from 1888 to 1892:

"This building is the central club-house of a community of a thousand or more Negroes. Various organizations meet here—the church proper, the Sunday school, two or three insurance societies, secret societies, and mass meetings of various kinds. Entertainments, suppers, and lectures are held besides the five or six weekly religious services. Considerable sums of money are collected and expended here, employment is found for the idle, strangers are introduced, news is disseminated and charity distributed. At the same time this social, intellectual and economic centre is a religious centre of great power."[10]

Entertainment, suppers, lectures, secret societies, mass meetings—all these and more flourished in abundance under Sheafe's pastoral leadership. However, he kept the focus on renewing the church as "a religious center of great power," and success attended his efforts.

BRIGADIER GENERALS, BUT NO PRIVATES

On the last Sunday of August in 1887 the outlook seemed brilliant for Pilgrim Baptist Church. It was a high day, filled with services of dedication for their magnificent new church building. The *Western Appeal* described it as "one of the finest and most graceful illustrations of the early Gothic style that there is in the city." A bell tower, topped by a spire reaching to a height of 120 feet, dominated the scene. "Few cities in the Union can boast of a more beautiful edifice belonging to a colored church," declared the newspaper. It was an achievement that the relatively small Pilgrim Baptist congregation could look upon with "pardonable pride."[11]

Guest speakers from Baltimore and St. Louis, along with clergy, Black and White, from the Twin Cities area, participated in the exhilarating dedicatory services. Pilgrim Baptist's founding pastor, Robert Hickman, was also among the speakers. Upon retirement, Hickman had extended the "hand of fellowship" five months earlier to a new pastor, Rev. William Gray.[12] The church's success, said the *Western Appeal*, could largely be attributed to the "indefatigable and ubiquitous" Rev. Gray.[13]

Yet, when Lewis and Annie Sheafe arrived in Minnesota a little more than a year later, they found the Pilgrim Baptist congregation in a divided, demoralized condition that sadly contrasted with the impressive new sanctuary. The church's unity had disintegrated and morale plummeted under the pressure of a very large debt of about $12,000 on the church building.

Gray had been hired as pastor with the expectation that he would "devise ways and means to meet the financial obligations," and thereby infuse the church with new vigor—"temporally" as well as spiritually.[14] His efforts got off to a spectacular start. In just three months he raised $2,000. However, despite his success at raising funds, severe opposition to Rev. Gray's leadership arose, dividing the congregation. It is unclear precisely what the disputed issues were, but they had something to do with what the *Western Appeal* called Gray's "peculiar methods."[15] By September 1888 the split in the congregation had become so severe that Gray decided to offer his resignation, effective by Christmas. When he went to the church to make his announcement, however, he found that the church trustees had locked him out of the sanctuary. He made his entry only after supporters removed the planks used to bar the door.

Gray moved his departure date up to October 5, and he was followed out by supporters who urged him to form a new congregation. In his farewell sermon at Pilgrim Baptist, Rev. Gray vented his frustration over the congregation's refusal to follow his leadership, despite his success in meeting the financial crisis and in bringing new members into the church. God would have to "create a preacher who can preside over this church," he charged. "You are not willing to accept a leader. Every member of the church wants to be a brigadier general, and there are none who will act as privates."[16]

Thus, as Sheafe put it a few years later, when he began ministry at Pilgrim Baptist, the internal dissension had reduced attendance to a "beggarly array of empty benches," averaging a mere 36 souls at Sunday services in a sanctuary that seated 500.[17] And despite what was achieved during Gray's pastorate, the congregation remained burdened with a massive debt, for which it was difficult to meet even the interest payments. Additionally, Gray and his supporters had established a rival congregation, the New Mission Baptist Church, thereby diminishing Pilgrim Baptist's financial base.[18]

The young pastor and his bride threw themselves into the challenge with an amazing energy driven by high ideals. After marrying on June 6, Lewis and Annie had gotten right down to the business of being fruitful. When they began their work in St. Paul, Annie was six months pregnant with their daughter Clara, who was born on March 20, 1889. The couple seemed to take the addition to the family in stride as they busily pursued the new horizons before them. Annie's presentation of a paper on Africa for a meeting of the Women's Foreign Missionary Society meeting came just days before Clara's birth. A little more than a month later they moved from their residence on Superior Avenue to 478 University Avenue, Suite No. 1. And only a week after moving, they hosted a large "sociable" for the church.

PREACHING THE GOSPEL FOR A DIVIDED CHURCH

To a congregation in crisis, Lewis delivered Christ-centered sermons stressing the way in which the gospel welcomes all people into one united fellowship on an equal basis. At the same time, he boldly presented the new way of life to which the gospel calls believers, and insisted on continual progress in following that way.

References to Lewis Sheafe's skill as a preacher recur with such frequency and from such a wide array of sources throughout his career that it becomes impossible to downplay them as conventional religious hyperbole. While those who heard him would sometimes use "eloquence" to describe his speaking, their testimony indicates that the power of his preaching derived from sources deeper than showmanship or dazzling rhetoric. In clear and direct words, expressed with conviction, Sheafe's messages pointed hearers to Christ and stirred them to higher spiritual development. In the words of a Pilgrim Baptist member, "his preachings were plain and true, founded upon the word of God"; "a child could understand his teachings."[19]

Yet Sheafe aimed for the head as well as the heart. He made teaching his people and challenging them to progress in their understanding of God's Word a high priority of his ministry. "Our hopes," the pastor would later say as he encapsulated the goal of his preaching and teaching at Pilgrim Baptist, "are centered in the Lord, our aim to advance Christ's kingdom, to keep the straight path, to hew to the line, regardless of where the chips fly, to preach the word for the benefit of all and not to please the ear, to know all men as sinners, Christ as Saviour to all that accept salvation."[20]

It became clear right at the start that the new pastor would not hesitate to confront his people about that which needed to be changed. The report concerning Sunday worship on December 16, 1888, declared that the worshippers had "a heavenly sitting in the Lord," but adds: "Some of our brethren that have been frozen up for years, got thawed out. Rev. Sheafe came down on the members that have fallen asleep and some of them were [awakened] by his evening sermon. He compared the church to Babylon in the time of Belteshazzar, and pointed out the things that are wanting in Pilgrim church."[21] Throughout his time in St. Paul, Sheafe would continually beckon his people to move upward and onward in righteous struggle.

Though bold, the challenge he laid before the church did not come from a severe, judgmental standpoint. Rather, Sheafe made the oneness of all humanity, both in need before God and in welcome by Christ, the controlling theme. Grounded in that truth, the church's mission was to invite all through its doors to find salvation in Christ, and to minister to the human needs of all in the community without regard to religious affiliation or social standing.

It may be that the emergence of a Black elite in St. Paul, many of whom were mulattoes, had something to do with dissensions that had divided Pilgrim Baptist prior to Sheafe's arrival. While it is difficult to be certain about this, Sheafe tried to get his congregation to see in Christ the antidote to any exclusivity in the church and its mission.

The new pastor wanted his church to move forward "with one aim in view, and that centered on Christ as our example, Christ as our elder brother, and Christ as all in all." By taking this perspective, he told his people, they would see that "the church is not a social club, not a fashionable circle that excludes a certain portion of those for whom Christ died." Rather, the gospel "puts all humanity on the same footing in the sight of God, strips a man of his righteous self, and hands him the Bible looking glass, that he may see himself as a sinner, lost and undone without Christ." This experience of the heart, he said, "should stimulate us to greater action and earnestness" in extending the appeal to all "that are out of Christ."[22] As if to underscore this all-embracing mission, he suggested that the Pilgrim church be known as "The Stranger's Sabbath House."[23]

With Lewis's eloquent, Christ-centered preaching, attendance at Sunday services surged into the hundreds. In response to his sermon on February 17, 1889, for example, "cheeks bedewed with tears" could be seen throughout congregation as he spoke on "the cry of our Saviour when He hung from the cross."[24]

Lewis and Annie also worked hard to strengthen Christian fellowship in the everyday life of the congregation. "There is between real Christians, a real brotherhood which they will neither disown, dissemble nor forget," Sheafe told the church so recently divided by bitter conflict.[25] A report in the *Appeal*, probably by the pastor himself, describes the "sociable" that he and Annie hosted at their new residence in early May 1889—a good example of their efforts to make real the ties bonding believers to one another. A report in the *Appeal* indicates that this was not a customary occasion in St. Paul and that its purpose was to strengthen the fellowship of a community of believers:

"The sociable at the home of Elder Sheafe, on Tuesday evening, was something new for St. Paul. The commodius apartments were brilliantly lighted, and everything had the stamp of home upon it. There were about 30 persons present. The evening was spent very pleasantly by all. Several solos, duets and instrumental [pieces] were rendered. After we had regaled ourselves with music, Mrs. Sheafe invited all to the dining room, where an abundant supper was served. May these gatherings bind pastor and people closer together. The pastor does not seek yours, but you."[26]

The kind of unity that Sheafe was after, though, could not be won by cheap tolerance or permissiveness. The kind of unity he talked about was itself part of a bold program based on firm principles. And that program did meet with some resistance. The opposition was serious enough for Sheafe to raise the possibility of resigning in September 1889. The specific issues are unclear, but Sheafe's determination to bring a greater measure of discipline to bear on the membership was clear enough. In March he had announced an intention to "straighten" the church's membership books[27] and in connection with the crisis in September he reiterated his resolve:

"God thinks no better of a tree for being burdened with rotten fruit, nor of a church for being swollen in numbers by base pretenders. This is our conviction and upon this we mean to live, pray and labor; only purity of heart and life can command the presence and power of our exalted Lord."[28]

An extra meeting was held on Sunday, September 15, to address the conflict. It turned out to be a memorable moment of mutual confession and reconciliation—"a sad yet happy" time during which the congregation sensed the Holy Spirit's presence making them "so truly one with each other that the occasion was hallowed."

In this early, perhaps first, major confrontation in a career that would be filled with controversy, it is noteworthy that Sheafe at least indirectly acknowledged his own role in stoking the conflict. Both "pastor and people gave way to their truer and better natures," with expressions of "grief" all around.

The pastor then declared his decision to remain with the congregation, and the meeting came to an emotional conclusion:

"Did you ever sing a hymn and feel it? We sang as never before 'Blest Be the Tie That Binds.' That tie between pastor and people was made doubly strong; we realize better than ever our relation one to the other. We request the prayers of all God's people, that we may be one until the Lord of the vineyard orders a change."[29]

---

[1] James M. McPherson, *Ordeal by Fire: The Civil War and Reconstruction*, 3rd ed. (Boston: McGraw Hill, 2001), pp. 316-321, A15-A17.

[2] This was the term that the Union Army applied to slaves who escaped during the war. *Ibid.*, p. 290.

[3] David Vassar Taylor, *African Americans in Minnesota* (St. Paul: Minnesota Historical

Society, 2002), p. 9. "History" page of the church's Web site, http://www.pilgrimbaptistchurch.org/history.htm (accessed Aug. 28, 2009).

[4] "History," Pilgrim Baptist Church.

[5] The Northern Baptists were organized as a group of regional societies. These comprised the Northern Baptist Convention, which was organized in 1907. "American Baptists: A Brief History" at the American Baptist Churches USA Web site: http://www.abc-usa.org/WhoWeAre/OurHistory/tabid/80/Default.aspx (accessed Aug. 28, 2009).

[6] Initially titled *Western Appeal*, it became simply the *Appeal* in 1889.

[7] Taylor, pp. 14-16; Yusef Mgeni, "It is because of the Rondo community that I am who I am," in *Voices of Rondo: Oral Histories of Saint Paul's Historic Black Community* (Minneapolis: Syren Book Co., 2005), pp. 309, 310.

[8] Taylor, pp. 15, 16, 22-25.

[9] *Ibid.*, p. 24.

[10] W.E.B. DuBois, *The Souls of Black Folk* (New York: New American Library, 1969), pp. 213, 214.

[11] "Pilgrim Baptist Church," *Western Appeal*, Aug. 27, 1887, pp. 1, 2.

[12] "The Installation," *Western Appeal*, May 21, 1887, p. 1.

[13] "The Dedication," *Western Appeal*, Sept. 3, 1887, pp. 4, 5.

[14] "St. Paul," *Western Appeal*, Apr. 23, 1887, p. 4. Jon Butler discusses Gray's pastorate, his fund-raising efforts, and the controversy that developed in "Communities and Congregations: The Black Church in St. Paul, 1860-1900," *Journal of Negro History* 56 (April 1971): 129-132.

[15] "Rev. W. Gray's Farewell," *Western Appeal*, Oct. 6, 1888, p. 2.

[16] Cited in Butler, p. 30.

[17] "A New Faith Comes," CA, Sept. 13, 1902, p. 1. The *Colored American* article puts the seating capacity at 900, but the *Western Appeal*'s description of the newly completed sanctuary in 1887 states the number to be 500 (Aug. 27, 1888).

[18] "The Saintly City," *Western Appeal*, Dec. 1, 1888, p. 2.

[19] Charles A. Allen, "In Honor of Rev. Lewis C. Sheafe," *Appeal*, July 23, 1892, p. 2.

[20] "Pilgrim Baptist Church," *Appeal*, Sept. 19, 1891, p. 3.

[21] "Pilgrim Baptist Church," *Western Appeal*, Dec. 22, 1888, p. 2.

[22] "Pilgrim Baptist Church," *Appeal*, Mar. 2, 1889, p. 2.

[23] "Pilgrim Baptist Church," *Appeal*, Mar. 16, 1889, p. 2.

[24] "Pilgrim Baptist Church," *Appeal*, Feb. 23, 1889, p. 2.

[25] "Pilgrim Baptist Church," *Appeal*, May 18, 1889, p. 3.

[26] "Pilgrim Baptist Church," *Appeal*, May 11, 1889, p. 2. The unnoted allusion to 2 Corinthians 12:14 ("I seek not your's, but you") illustrates the way in which Scripture unobtrusively suffused Sheafe's communication.

[27] "Pilgrim Baptist Church," *Appeal*, Mar. 16, 1889, p. 3.

[28] "Church Circles," *Appeal*, Sept. 21, 1889, p. 3.

[29] *Ibid.*

CHAPTER III

SOCIAL CENTER FOR A
PROSCRIBED PEOPLE

A S W.E.B. DU BOIS DESCRIBED IT, "five or six weekly religious services" structured the calendar for the members of Pilgrim Baptist Church. The typical week revolved around preaching services at 11:00 a.m. and 8:00 p.m. on Sundays, Sunday school at 12:45 p.m., young people's meeting Sunday afternoon, a Wednesday evening Bible class and Sunday school teachers meeting, and a general prayer meeting on Friday evening. On the many Sundays designated for an annual celebration or theme—Easter, Rally Day, Children's Day, etc.—an afternoon service at 3:00 was added.

But all of this was only part of the weekly round of church activity. On Mondays, Tuesdays, and sometimes on Thursdays the calendar filled with the meetings of various church organizations, "entertainments"— musical, dramatic, and oratorical programs—lectures, classes, suppers, and other events of mainly social function. On top of the regular weekly and monthly activities came annual events: church fairs, conventions and association meetings, celebrations of holidays, and civic anniversaries.

Annie Sheafe took a leading role in one of the church's benevolent auxiliaries—the Woman's Foreign Missionary Society. At the society's annual meeting in March 1889 she read a paper specially prepared for the occasion entitled, "What Can We Do for Africa?"[1] Later she also hosted monthly meetings of the Woman's Mission Circle in the Sheafe home.[2]

ENTERTAINMENTS, SUPPERS, LECTURES
Lyceum-style events featuring popular guest speakers and performers

was one way the church provided entertainment along with cultural and spiritual enrichment, at the same time raising money toward the church debt. In June 1889, for example, with interest in Haiti stimulated by the appointment of Frederick Douglass as the American consul general to that nation, Pilgrim Baptist scheduled a lecture by Madame O. Esparanza Luis on the subject "Hayti and the Haytiens." Madame Luis, touted as "the most eloquent oratress now before the American people," had been on the lecture circuit in the Western states and was on her way to Africa as a missionary.[3]

The following spring the church offered a phrenological lecture by Prof. G. Morris—an event that was promoted as entertaining as well as highly instructive and beneficial. Phrenology—the science of determining a person's strengths and weaknesses by analyzing the shape of the cranium—enjoyed widespread popularity in the nineteenth century. It was seen as a kind of psychological test for career and marital counseling, functioning much like the Myers-Briggs and other personality tests would a century later.

Credentialed as a graduate of the famed Fowler & Wells Institute in New York, Morris addressed such topics as "How to Read Character"; "Choice of Pursuits, or What Can I Do Best"; and "Who May and Who May Not Marry and Live Happily Together in Wedded Life." The admission charge for the lecture on April 10, 1890, was 10 cents, with individual examinations after the lecture available for 25 cents. All proceeds from the evening went to the church; however, a brief reference to the success of the event in the *Appeal* noted that "very many have since called at the office of the prof., 78 E. 7th Street, for private examinations."[4]

The annual round of entertainments and fund-raisers reached a pinnacle at the Pilgrim Baptist Fair, a weeklong event launched Thanksgiving Day. Sheafe did not view such events as the ideal way to raise money for the church. His approach was to regulate rather than abolish such endeavors, and continue using them as an expedient. Thus, while warmly promoting the fair, he cautioned: "We hope to avoid many of the evils that attend fairs and things of its nature. Would each Christian but do his duty, such things as fairs need never enter the church."[5]

The *Appeal* reported that the 1889 fair "opened in a blaze of glory Thursday night" with a dinner and opening ceremonies. Sheafe gave the opening speech, followed by remarks from attorney Frederick McGhee, Minneapolis lawyer W. R. Morris, and a "rousing speech" by Sheafe's Minneapolis colleague, Rev. J. W. Dunjee. Also, Annie Sheafe presented an original poem, "My Visit to an Almshouse," which, according to the *Appeal*, "possessed much merit and was well received."[6] The week's festivities proceeded with such activities as "Grand Auction Sale of Old Maids," a Saturday night concert, a "grand candy pulling," a drill by the Young Master Cadets using "regular army rifles," and a "Grand Baby Show and voting contest."[7] The fair generated $500 to be applied to the church debt, an outcome causing "an almost overpowering desire to shout for joy."[8]

The aftermath of the fair, and all of the time, energy, planning, and excitement that went with it, was not to be a time of relaxation but simply a return to "our regular order of work." For the coming week that meant a literary society meeting on Monday night, the choral club on Tuesday, Bible class and teachers' meeting on Wednesday, and prayer meeting on Friday, in addition to the usual Sunday services. "We are all tired," acknowledged the pastor, "but let us not stay at home."[9]

The year 1889 concluded on a positive spiritual note. On New Year's Eve things were happening at church, just like almost every other evening of the year. The sanctuary overflowed for a "watch meeting" to bring in the new year at midnight, and the people had "a joyful time."[10]

LEADERSHIP IN THE PUBLIC ARENA

In January 1892 a letter arrived at the *Appeal* newspaper office in St. Paul from Frederick Douglass, sent from his Cedar Hill home in Anacostia, Washington, D.C., to which he had recently returned after his stint as consul general to Haiti. The senior statesman of Black America commended the *Appeal* for the "skill, ability and good judgment with which it is conducted," but recommended "that greater prominence should be given to the outrages committed upon our people." A concern even deeper than discrimination and prejudice was foremost in Douglass' mind: basic security of life and limb, threatened by the appalling upsurge in lynching. In view of the murder—"fierce, bloody, and high-handed"—terrorizing Blacks throughout the South, he asked, "Where is the press or pulpit that is faithfully exposing the lawless violence"?

Having made the transition from press to pulpit, Douglass concluded his letter with a challenge to the latter: "Even our Colored preachers in presence of these hellish practices go on from Sunday to Sunday thanking God that they live in a Christian country, a land of Bibles, etc. I am sick of such cant."[11]

Douglass's letter must have struck Lewis Sheafe more as affirmation than as rebuke. Evidence from his first major pastorate points to a pattern that would hold throughout the vagaries of his entire career. In the causes of civil rights and liberation for those oppressed by social and economic injustice, Sheafe was not only a supporter but a leader who was frequently called upon to utilize his gift for eloquent and passionate oratory at "mass meetings."

Sheafe's outlook on the racial problem in America was formed during the hopeful two decades following the end of the Civil War in 1865, during which legal grounding for the equal rights of Black people as American citizens was established. In brief, the Fourteenth Amendment (1868) prohibited states from interfering with the rights of Blacks as national citizens, as provided by the U.S. Constitution. The Fifteenth Amendment (1870) prohibited the states from denying male citizens the right to vote on account of "race, color, or previous condition of servitude." The Civil Rights Act of 1875 outlawed racial segregation in transportation and public accommodations.

The Compromise of 1877 signaled the federal government's retreat from protecting those rights in the Southern states, and a series of Supreme Court rulings beginning in the 1880s eroded their legal foundation. Yet only gradually in the 1880s, 1890s, and the first decade of the 1900s did the magnitude of the backlash and the comprehensive, systematic denial of those rights unfold.

The first indications we have of Lewis Sheafe's outlook on race relations come at a time of dawning realization regarding just how vulnerable Black rights had become, and the necessity of united action to defend them. With an outrage modulated by irony, he responded in April 1889 to a widely reprinted article entitled "The Negro Problem." His commentary reveals a man fully settled in his identity as one equal in dignity and rights to all others and commanding respect as such. His approach to the racial problem was not one of submissively seeking favor from a superior class. Rather, it was to assert, in a manner regulated by the "omnipotent ruler," the reality of equal dignity and insist on recognition of it.

"It must be gratifying to every thoughtful Colored man and woman to see in every periodical of the land an elaborate article entitled, The Negro Problem. We are more than glad to know that we have ceased to be thought of as a thing and have arisen to that height where we cause the people of these United States to scratch their heads and pronounce us a problem. We are a problem because we are here to stay. We are a problem because against almost insurmountable obstacles we have advanced, and to such a degree that our friends cry, 'If we don't get rid of the Negro, he will soon take our place and nation.' This is where the problem comes in; this problem like all others has a key; this we hold, let us use it well, unlock, solve, as the omnipotent ruler would have us. Patiently, constantly, truthfully, show to the rest of mankind that we will be a people; will respect ourselves, and therefore command the respect of others."[12]

Sheafe understood the realm of his ministerial mandate to extend beyond his own congregation and into the public arena. In June 1889 he had told the church that the "Colored people of this city are finding out that we mean to do them good, regardless of whom they may be." Their goal, he said, should be to follow after Christ's example, and practice the "pure religion" that prompts one to "visit the fatherless and widows," and "then to keep unspotted."[13] With "a great many Colored people sick in the city" during the winter of 1889-1890, the pastor urged "that everyone do something for some of them." All cases for which church members could not render aid were to be reported to Elder Sheafe.[14]

For Sheafe counteracting racial oppression in society was just as much the business of the church as ministering to the sick. Using his gifts as orator and organizer in this cause became a lifetime commitment. So doing would bring him into association with several of the most notable social movements on the American scene from the 1890s to the 1920s, and bring him into contact with an impressive array of leaders.

Late in the fall of 1889 Sheafe became active in a new organization, the St. Paul Afro-American League, which came about in response to a proposal circulated by the influential publisher of the New York *Globe*, T. Thomas Fortune. The National Afro-American League became the first nationwide organization dedicated to advocacy for Black political and civil rights through legislative and judicial means. According to historian

David Levering Lewis, for a time Fortune looked to be the heir apparent to Frederick Douglass as the preeminent leader of Black Americans, but his own "brawling, hard-drinking" ways undermined him. Few tangible achievements came out of Fortune's ambitious National Afro-American Council. It did, however, create chapters in 23 states that included participation by many of the nation's leading Black citizens. Around a decade after its organization, its influence became important as part of the emerging opposition to Booker T. Washington's dominance as a Black leader.[15]

Sheafe appears to have missed the initial organizational meeting of the St. Paul chapter on November 5.[16] But a subsequent meeting on December 10 took place in the lecture room at Pilgrim Baptist, at which a revised constitution was adopted and Sheafe was added to the officers as a chaplain, joining Rev. J. C. Henderson of St. James AME.

The objectives declared by the constitution reflect the tragic patterns of racial injustice in America that had become apparent since the end of Reconstruction and would only worsen during the next two decades. The St. Paul League's objects were to:

- protest taxation without representation.
- secure a more equitable distribution of school funds.
- insist upon a fair and impartial trial by a judge and jury of peers.
- resist by all legal and reasonable means mob and lynch law.
- resist the tyrannical usage of railroad, steamboat, and other corporations, and the violent and insulting treatment of their employees.
- labor for the reformation of all penal institutions where barbarous, cruel, and unchristian treatment of convicts is practiced.
- assist healthy immigration from terror-ridden sections to other and more law-abiding sections.
- promote the industrial and moral welfare of the Colored citizens of our city.
- seek, for worthier and competent persons, access to the various industrial enterprises.
- encourage labor, frugality, and honesty.[17]

As for Sheafe, indications that the young pastor saw himself as a leader and not just a participant in the cause of racial justice and uplift began to appear. Late in December 1889 he sent a letter to the *Appeal*, exhorting the newspaper to make progress during the coming year as a means for building up the Black community and advancing its interests. "Tone up and bring the people up also, and your success is secured," he counseled. "We want you to be a power among the Colored people of the Northwest."[18]

The following April, Sheafe used the Pilgrim Baptist column in the *Appeal* to warn local officials against mistaking the outward calm in the city's Black community for contentment with existing conditions.

"We are sorry that the harmless mien of the Colored people of St. Paul has led the county and city officials to conclude that we are satisfied with the prejudice that is so strongly manifested in every section of St. Paul. Why do we not make more noise about it? Because we have found that often, calm endurance answers some questions infinitely more conclusively than the loftiest eloquence."[19]

Years later the Adventist prophet Ellen White would commend Sheafe for his tact and skill in presenting the radical claims of Adventism. Something like that quality can be seen in the preacher's endorsement of calm endurance as the most eloquent and effective response to injustice in some situations. Passionate about justice and truth, and quite capable of fiery rhetoric, Sheafe could also bridle his tongue with a strategic wisdom that enabled him to be a leader, not merely an idealistic orator, in St. Paul and beyond.

---

[1] "Pilgrim Baptist Church," *Appeal*, Mar. 16, 1889, p. 2.

[2] "Pilgrim Baptist Church," *Appeal*, Nov. 7, 1891, p. 1.

[3] "Pilgrim Baptist Church," *Appeal*, June 8, 1889, p. 2.

[4] "Phrenological Lecture," *Appeal*, Apr. 5, 1890, p. 2; "Church Circles," *Appeal*, Apr. 19, 1890, p. 1. On phrenology as an aspect of nineteenth-century health reform endorsed by many culturally prominent figures, including Henry Ward Beecher, see Ronald G. Walters, *American Reformers, 1815-1860*, rev. ed. (New York: Hill and Wang, 1997), pp. 158-165. While her husband, James, was being treated at Dr. James C. Jackson's health reform institute in Dansville, New York, in 1864, Ellen White took her sons Willie and Edson to Dr. Jackson for a phrenological reading and felt that the doctor "gave an accurate account of the disposition and organization of our children;" see Ronald L. Numbers, *Prophetess of Health: Ellen G. White and the Origins of Seventh-day Adventist Health Reform* (University of Tennessee Press, 1992), pp. 90, 91.

[5] "Pilgrim Baptist Church," *Appeal*, Nov. 16, 1889, p. 2.

[6] "Pilgrim Baptist Fair," *Appeal*, Nov. 30, 1889, p. 3.

[7] "Pilgrim Baptist Fair," *Appeal*, Nov. 23, 1889, p. 3, and Nov. 30, 1889, p. 3.

[8] "Pilgrim Baptist Church," *Appeal*, Dec. 14, 1889, p. 2.

[9] "Church Circles," *Appeal*, Dec. 7, 1889, p. 1.

[10] "Church Circles," *Appeal,* Jan. 4, 1890, p. 1.

[11] "Letter From Frederick Douglass," *Appeal,* Jan. 23, 1892, p. 2.

[12] "Pilgrim Baptist Church," *Appeal,* Apr. 20, 1889, p. 3.

[13] "Pilgrim Baptist Church," *Appeal,* June 15, 1889, p. 3.

[14] "Church Circles," *Appeal,* Jan. 11, 1890, p. 2.

[15] Lewis, pp. 38, 230.

[16] "The League," *Appeal,* Nov. 9, 1889, p. 3.

[17] "The St. Paul League," *Appeal,* Dec. 14, 1889, p. 2.

[18] "Pilgrim Baptist Church," *Appeal,* Dec. 28, 1889, p. 3.

[19] "Pilgrim Baptist Church," *Appeal,* Apr. 26, 1890, p. 2.

CHAPTER IV

FOR PROGRESS AND STRENGTH

DURING HIS FIRST YEAR OF MINISTRY IN ST. PAUL, Lewis Sheafe by and large won the support of the Pilgrim Baptist congregation. The breakaway group led by the previous pastor, William Gray, faded away, and Rev. Gray moved out of the area in the fall of 1889. More important, Sheafe could point to encouraging evidence of a new spiritual vitality and progress on an upward journey. In this first year he had also established himself in the public realm as a leader of St. Paul's overall Black community.

1890: CONSOLIDATION AND PROGRESS

As his ministry in St. Paul hit its full stride, he did not rest content with soothing the status quo. He made progress a keynote, signing letters "Yours for Progress and Strength." Sheafe challenged his congregants to progress in their understanding of biblical truth and in holiness of life, actively expressed by stepping up to new levels of service for Christ.

In February 1890 he urged believers to lift their vision beyond trivial preoccupations and join the progressive struggle against the great evils afflicting humanity:

"Where are the heroes, who resisted unto blood, striving against sin? Should we weep or laugh at the foolishness of mankind, childishly spending their indignation and force against petty evils, while SIN, the hideous parent of all evils is forever multiplying [a] brood of monsters over the world, and mankind quietly or even complacently allow it to inhabit and ravage in their midst. Let the church of God raise the standard higher and higher, day by day until the Christ has his rightful place, in both heart and life. Strike at the root, the branches will fall. We look back and we see our path has been leading upward, we look forward to greater progress. The young and vigorous life that has been added to our ranks, bespeaks for us greater achievements in the future."[1]

According to the "law of progress," in Sheafe's view, the only alternative to climbing still higher is a perilous fall to the bottom.[2] "If one citadel is achieved," he urged, "stay not, press on, for others are yet ahead." And, regarding his church, he could say: "Along this line Pilgrim is moving, it stays not for trifles, but is absorbed in the great work of leading benighted souls to Christ."[3]

Sheafe also emphasized growth in understanding truth as a vital accompaniment to progress in the development of Christian character and in advancing the cause of God. While we are left without specifics, it appears that he tried, with only partial success, to teach the congregation biblical doctrines that were new to them.

"For personal salvation, simple faith and obedience will suffice," said the pastor. But not for *progress*:

"If we stop there, how limited is our power for good and glory. The heart enlarged with heavenly love desires to do and be all that his God-given powers will admit. Knowledge is important to Christian usefulness, because it will give light and glory, surely it will give power, then work for a better means of glorifying our Redeemer."[4]

A successful five-week revival opened the year 1890 at Pilgrim Baptist, generating energy for forward movement. Forty new members joined the church during those weeks, including the 21 who "put on the complete armor of Christ" at a Sunday night service on February 9. That service, reported Sheafe, was attended by "the largest congregation that ever gathered in our church."[5]

Sheafe made ministry for young people, particularly young men, a top priority in his second year. He led the youth in forming a Young People's Society of the Christian Endeavor[6]—another indication of his progressive approach. Launched less than a decade earlier by a Congregationalist pastor in Maine, the Christian Endeavor was rapidly catching on throughout various Protestant denominations as a means for training young people to become leaders in the church and to apply Christian principles to all aspects of life. In particular, Christian Endeavor was part of the broad "social Christianity" movement for making the church a vital force in the public life of the nation's cities, where secular influences, along with population, were on the rise. It also helped launch much of what today comes under the heading "youth ministry."[7]

St. Paul's Black community included an unusually high proportion of unmarried men, most of them under age 30. These young men took advantage of the work opportunities provided by the city's hotels and wharves, as well as the railroads. Historian Jon Butler's analysis of census data and the church records indicates that relatively few of these young men joined the city's churches. While males comprised 60 percent of St. Paul's Black population in 1890, the membership at Pilgrim Baptist, as well as St. James AME, was 63 percent female.[8] Along with the "muscular Christianity" characteristic of the YPSCE, the pastor sought to reach the somewhat transient population of young Black men in St. Paul by offering a Bible class that he would teach himself on Sundays especially for them. He emphasized that "strangers are invited to come and join."[9]

Along with the churches, Black Minnesotans found opportunity for social interaction in numerous lodges and fraternal organizations.[10] In general these appear to have interacted seamlessly with the church life. For example, an afternoon service dedicated to the Mars Lodge No. 2202 of the Grand United Order of Odd Fellows on the first Sunday in March was a fixture on the annual church calendar. The account of Sheafe's first Mars Lodge sermon in 1889 may suggest some tension between lodge and church, as he pointed out both "the good and the evil sides" of the order. "Everybody was satisfied," however, and the lodge presented the elder with an unexpected honorarium of $10.45, while a general collection yielded $10.80 for the church.[11]

The Mars Lodge service the following year, 1890, provides an intriguing if opaque hint of tensions over the status of women in the community, and how Sheafe handled the issue. The report in the *Appeal* pointedly included information on the participation of the lodge's parallel organization for women, the Household of Ruth, which had gone unmentioned in the account of the previous year's event. Whether they had not participated the previous year or simply had been excluded from the report, for the service in 1890 the Household of Ruth No. 553 "turned out in good numbers," taking their place in the processional. In the sermon Sheafe paid "due regard" to the Household of Ruth, "showing how important true woman is to man's success in any noble enterprise"—a theme expressed in verse by an unidentified poet:

"They talk about a woman's sphere as though it had a limit;
There's not a place on earth or heaven,
There's not a task to mankind given,
There's not a blessing or a woe,
There's not a whisper yes or no,
There's not a life, or death, or birth,
That has a feather's weight of worth, without a woman in it."[12]

Sheafe was also in much demand as a speaker for major events held at the lodge halls. That same month an article in the *Appeal* claimed that the Twin Cities were "in a quiver of excitement" about an upcoming Knights of Pythias "grand entertainment" featuring an address by Rev. L. C. Sheafe entitled "The Religious Status of the Negro." The event, attended by "hundreds," was a joint effort by the Abraham Lodge No. 1 of St. Paul and the Nat Turner Lodge No. 2 of Minneapolis.[13] In September of the same year the Minneapolis Commandary Knight Templars, assisted by the Pioneer Commandary of St. Paul, presented a "grand prize concert" that included an oration by L. C. Sheafe, "the eminent Baptist divine of St. Paul" and music by the "world famous Iola Quartette."[14]

In the midst of a very busy March in 1890 the Sheafes were given a surprise "dry goods party," though in the message of thanks that they sent to the *Appeal*, the couple noted that "many things in the line of provisions and groceries were among the dry goods." Annie's Sunday school class presented her with a "very pretty English walking hat and a pair of kid gloves"; from "several of the ladies and gentleman" she received a "black Henrietta cloth dress very tastily made." The elder also was given a pair of kid gloves and a "beautiful white shirt." The long list of gifts for the family included tablecloths, napkins, towels, handkerchiefs, aprons, embroidery, lace, and a "blue plush bonnet" for little Clara.[15]

The Sheafes gratefully took the event as a demonstration of appreciation and esteem. Indeed, evidence from 1890 suggests that they had overwhelmingly won the hearts and support of the Pilgrim Baptist congregation, with minimal opposition. In May the *Appeal* launched a

Popular Preachers contest as a promotional device. Readers could cast votes in this unabashed popularity contest by clipping and mailing in ballots printed in each issue of the paper. Prizes would be awarded to the 10 highest vote getters among preachers in Illinois, Missouri, Kentucky, and Minnesota, the newspapers' primary circulation centers.[16]

The voting went on for months, the *Appeal* trumpeting with headlines the changes in the top vote getters and the emergence of new contenders. By the end of November Sheafe had reached the top of the list with 785 votes.[17] The *Appeal* decided finally to bring the voting to a close on December 31, 1890. After a surge of participation during the final month, Sheafe ended up finishing third with 1,816 votes, behind Rev. Charles H. Parrish of Louisville (2,524 votes) and Rev. George W. Gaines of Chicago (2,232 votes).[18]

Sheafe was not diffident about accepting his third place prize of $15 and a life-size crayon portrait. He thanked his church members and friends from many states who had come "so boldly and untiringly to the front in the preachers contest, in casting votes for me."[19]

Further evidence of a successful year of ministry, free of major controversy, came in Sheafe's annual report at the end of October. Seventy-two new members had joined the church, while one member had died and 18 had been "excluded," making a net increase of 53. Attendance averaged 300 at Sunday evening services and 100 for the morning service and Sunday school. With all of his popularity and skill, however, even Sheafe was unable to draw large numbers to the Wednesday night Bible study, which had an average attendance of only 10, while the Friday night prayer meetings drew an average of 30. Financially, the church appeared to be meeting its obligations and had $175 cash on hand. On the other hand, it had not made significant progress in reducing the principal owed for the church building loan.[20]

Overall, as the pastor put it the following January, "1890 was indeed a year of prosperity for us; progress has marked every stage in the year's work."[21]

Success in ministry, however, exacted a toll on the pastor's health, which had been tenuous since childhood. References to unspecified health issues began appearing in 1889. "Elder Sheafe has not been very well for some time," the congregation was told in June. A "short vacation" was proposed so that "he may not get down sick."[22] The following month the congregation gave him $6.80 so that he could spend a few days at the popular White Bear Lake resort.[23] Then, again in 1890 the *Appeal* reported that at services on May 18, Sheafe had managed to deliver "two sermons of power, fresh from the Spiritual fount" in spite of being in an "impaired physical condition."[24] This time, the church granted him a 30-day vacation, during which he traveled to Chicago and then to New England.[25]

Just before leaving for his vacation, however, Sheafe spoke at a gala event in St. Paul at which he shared the podium with several distinguished leaders, most notably the fiery and irrepressible antilynching crusader Ida B. Wells. The leaders of St. Paul's Black community organized a "grand reception" for the African-American educators from throughout the nation who were in town for the convention of the National Education Association. The "reception," held at Turner Hall, was truly an extravaganza—a banquet with illustrious speakers, an orchestra, vocal solos, orations both dramatic and humorous, a "grand march" of the couples in attendance, and dancing. The *Appeal* provided lavish description of all this and more, claiming that the Northwest had never before seen "a private social affair approximating in completeness of detail and in point of excellence" as that which took place July 10.[26]

Thomas H. Lyles, a successful barber and real estate agent,[27] presided over the affair. When the evening's program, following the reception proper, got underway around 10:00 p.m., Lyles introduced Sheafe, who gave a "nicely worded and nicely delivered" address of welcome. Joseph C. Price, founder and president of Livingstone College in North Carolina and president of the recently organized National Afro-American League,[28] responded to Sheafe's welcome on behalf of the visitors to the city. In the *Appeal*'s florid description Price's response "more fixedly established his right to the title of orator," and "he took his seat amid rapturous applause."

Several more speeches and performances ensued before Lyles, "with what seemed to be unusual delight introduced Miss Ida B. Wells, of Memphis, Tenn." Few in the audience had not "read from the ready pen of 'Iola,'" Lyles observed. By then, however, it was so late that Wells told the audience that she had decided against delivering the address she had prepared. Though disappointed, the applause that the audience gave her was so fervent that she was compelled to acknowledge it.

The evening was far from over, however. After comedic performances by actor Charles Winter Wood and closing remarks by lawyer Frederick McGhee, Lewis and Annie joined with the other couples as they marched to orchestral accompaniment, clad in their formal attire, from the main hall to the supper room, spectacularly decorated with a "tremendous Japanese umbrella" hanging from the top center, from which multicolored bunting ran out to the walls. Light but elegant fare was served for supper, and the dance hall opened at the same time. It was 4:00 a.m. and the sun was rising by the time carriages chauffeured the guests home.

1891-1892: CONFRONTING BARRIERS TO PROGRESS

Clearly St. Paul's Black elite had the know-how, inclination, and means to throw a spectacular party. In 1891 and 1892, however, the struggle for civil rights came to preoccupy their energies in a new way. Sheafe was in the middle of all these struggles. At the same time, his efforts to lead Pilgrim Baptist forward in understanding and practicing the Christian faith ran into new resistance. He retained strong support from the congregation as a whole, but by the fall of 1891 it became clear that his future with the church hung in the balance.

In the Sheafe household the highlight of 1891 came in March with the birth of a new addition to the family, Howard. The church family celebrated the new arrival at the Sheafe home on June 5, filling the "little cottage . . . to its uttermost." It was a "general good time" with refreshments, speeches, and the presentation of a "handsome buggy for Master Howard W. Sheafe."[29]

As for the church, the pastor's annual report at the end of October 1891 indicated addition of 20 new members to the church.[30] Though the growth rate had slowed somewhat from that of 1890, it remained impressive in view of the relatively small pool of potential new members in the Black population of St. Paul.

The church also made modest progress in reduction of the building debt, paying $500 on the remaining principal of about $10,000, in addition to keeping up with interest payments. A rebuke to the church for its apathy that appeared in the pages of the *Appeal* during July may have helped stir progress on the debt. The writer—it is unclear whether it was

Sheafe or a trustee or perhaps Annie—observed that "a scandal on the pastor or any of the officials" would draw capacity crowds to church business meetings. But since "things are done decently and in order, the major part of the members either stay at home, or, for all that we know, spend the time at the opera or dance." If the church debt was ever to be canceled, there would have to be "a pulling up all along the line," and much more done in the second half of the year than had been done in its first six months.[31]

The July 11 issue of the *Appeal* also gives evidence of conflict in the church over the manner in which worship should be conducted. The pastor's absence on the previous Sunday "made way for some whose religion consists of Ghost Dance and nothing more to parade themselves."[32] A report appearing two weeks later suggests that things settled down fairly quickly, for the people were learning "to look for sense and not for sound."[33]

While Sheafe curbed excessive emotionalism in public worship, glimmers of what would later be called "charismatic" worship can also be detected from time to time throughout his career. One influence in this direction, undoubtedly, was the African-American worship tradition, in which the presence of God's Spirit is experienced in a way so real that it makes voices shout and bodies move—and sometimes heals them. Also, it is noteworthy that during the 1890s the Holiness movement in American Protestantism was at its height, with Pentecostalism coming on its heels at the turn of the century. These movements revealed a hunger to experience the Holy Spirit in such a powerful way that transformation would result, manifested in holiness of life and physical healing.[34]

For example, worship at Pilgrim Baptist on June 2, 1889, seemed particularly Spirit-filled:

"The Lord was in his holy temple in power and great glory. The very timbers praised Jehovah's name. Everybody wanted to say a word for Jesus. Old and young . . . all were shaken. The house was well filled all day."[35]

The last Sunday of the following March was a "day of especial blessedness . . . with the power of the Lord present to heal."[36] And in the fall of 1891 Sheafe noted a consciousness of "the spirit work in our midst" and added that "we believe the Pentecostal shower is soon to descend."[37]

The absence of the pastor from Sunday services on July 5 of 1891 was because of another, and more serious, bout of poor health. While arranging for guest speakers and exchanges with other pastors to cover many of the services, Sheafe continued to attend to pastoral duties as best he could. Late in July, after starting out to make a few calls on the sick, weakness forced him to return home after he had gone only a little way. His doctor declared him "in need of absolute rest" and warned that "unless this is taken there will follow a long spell of enforced rest."[38]

He did at least some of the preaching on the next three Sundays, but the congregation granted their ailing pastor a one-month vacation.[39] He departed August 12 to seek health in the country, but it did little good, for he returned a month later without much improvement. When the first of two "surprise parties" organized by church members to welcome him back arrived at the Sheafe household on a Tuesday evening (September 8), they found the pastor sick in bed. Since he was not "dangerously ill," they remained for a short time, enjoying the refreshments they had brought. The visitors also came bearing gifts—"a large lot of chickens, hams, sugar, tea, coffee and other household necessities."[40]

These gestures must have brought, at least, a strong dose of cheer for his spirits. At any rate, Rev. Sheafe would need whatever sources of strength he could draw on, for he was about to enter the most intense season of his ministry yet that fall, facing both a dramatic flare-up of conflict in his congregation and ominous new threats to racial justice that demanded action.

Sheafe came into conflict with one of the congregation's most influential trustees, John Hickman, over the fallout from an adulterous affair that Brother Hickman had engaged in with another highly active church member, Mrs. J. W. Smith (one of the organizers of the party welcoming Sheafe back from his vacation on September 8). Both acknowledged the affair and remained with their spouses. Conflict ensued when Mrs. Smith took offense at derogatory statements that Mrs. Hickman made about her in public. Mrs. Smith took her grievance to the church, which after two meetings voted to "exclude" Mrs. Hickman for refusing to apologize for her "mischievous and malicious slander."

Hickman then aired his objections to the entire process in a lengthy letter to the *Appeal*, in which he declared that his wife had been made the "scapegoat of ill-concealed spleen." He accused Sheafe of railroading through the charges against his wife—an anonymous meeting had been held to formulate the accusation, a trial held without allowing time to "set up a defence" and the pastor had secured the verdict he wanted only by threatening to resign. Furthermore, he said, Sheafe had gone on to make Mrs. Hickman the object of a special sermon, as if to glorify the "exclusion."[41]

Sheafe, in turn, vehemently denied preaching any sermon with the Hickmans in mind or threatening to resign. The church trial process had given the Hickmans fair opportunity to present their side, he insisted, but they had been resistant to the church's guidance and procedures all along. When angry, Sheafe tended to couch his language in a smoldering indirectness for which sarcasm seems close to, but not quite, the right word. Thus, the summation of his blistering rebuttal to John Hickman:

"Mr. Hickman may be a Christian gentleman, he may be actuated by high and noble principles, he may even love truth and right; yet, I have seen men that have done as Mr. Hickman, who have acted as he has, who have spoken and written in similar strains, who have rightfully been labeled the opposite of a sincere Christian, the very reverse of a gentleman, and to say that such were cowardly would not begin to express it, and the same have been found as far from truth and righteousness, as the Mount of Transfiguration from the Valley of Hinnom."

The "Hickman trouble" does not seem to have caused serious division in the church. Yet it may have been emblematic of a broader lack of responsiveness to his leadership that Sheafe perceived, and expressed frustration about, in his annual message at the end of October. The remarkable straightforwardness of this open letter suggests a genuineness of spirit, and its balance a conscientious effort at fair-mindedness.

Warmly grateful for "generous kindness and courtesy" the congregation had shown him and his family during their three years in St. Paul, Sheafe compared the interaction of pastor and congregation with that of a healthy family made up of imperfect people. They had indeed experienced differences but in an overall atmosphere of "comparative harmony." He repeatedly stressed the purity of his aim to build up the church of Christ in truth and justice and not to serve selfish ends.

"In our efforts Christ has been all and in all. His cause and kingdom is dearer than all else to our hearts. . . . I have sought to . . . bring you more and more in the spirit and life of our Lord, to win you not to myself but to my Master."

"I have enjoyed preaching to you," Sheafe told his congregation, and he commended them for being "attentive," though he could only commend "some" for being "thoughtful, appreciative, encouraging and generous." The preacher's efforts to lead his flock to progress as disciples of Christ had met with only partial success. He chided them for not always manifesting the "Berean spirit" and thus not being able to receive some of his teaching, which, he insisted, is "all based upon the 'Grand Old Book.'"

At the same time, he felt confident that "the good and truehearted are in the majority." And he acknowledged that the learning had gone both ways: he had learned from them, and that they all had more to learn. "[You] and I know enough to know that we don't know it all yet. . . . All of life is a learning and our service to Christ is following."

Though he denied using a threat to resign to influence the outcome of the Hickman case, the conclusion of the letter indicates that the possibility of his leaving hovered closely.

"If there be strong confidence, firm friendship and real moral support from the membership, and I believe it is God's will for me to remain, I am willing to go on and do my best to share with you in every way the burdens of life. To enable me to do this I must have a band of men and women whose hearts God has touched. Then you will follow, will do, and God will bring us out more than conquerors. Let us become better acquainted one with the other."[42]

The 1891 annual letter is one of the best windows we have on Lewis Sheafe's spirituality. He is winsome and eloquent, but he cannot rest satisfied with being a popular preacher of a comfortable Christianity. He longs for close fellowship, but wants it to be the solidarity of those truly devoted to progress in learning the truths of God's Word, to following Christ fully, and to taking bold action for the cause of His kingdom. And he would not tarry long with those unwilling to join him in that restless journey.

---

[1] "Pilgrim Baptist Church," *Appeal*, Feb. 22, 1890, p. 2.

[2] "Pilgrim Baptist Church," *Appeal*, May 10, 1890, p. 2.

[3] "Pilgrim Baptist Church," *Appeal*, June 21, 1890, p. 3.

[4] "Pilgrim Baptist Church," *Appeal*, Aug. 30, 1890, p. 2.

[5] "Church Circles," *Appeal*, Feb. 15, 1890, p. 1.

[6] See, for example, the "Pilgrim Baptist Church" sections in the March 1 and 8, 1890, issues of the *Appeal*.

[7] Charles H. Lippy, "Social Christianity," in *Encyclopedia of the American Religious Experience: Studies of Traditions and Movements*, ed. Charles H. Lippy and Peter W. Williams (New York: Charles Scribner's Sons, 1988), Vol. II, pp. 923, 924.

[8] J. Butler, "Communities and Congregations," pp. 124, 125, 133, 134.

[9] "Pilgrim Baptist Church," *Appeal*, Mar. 1, 1890, p. 3.

[10] D. V. Taylor, *African Americans in Minnesota*, pp. 21, 58-60.

[11] "Pilgrim Baptist Church," *Appeal*, Mar. 23, 1889, p. 2. The financial gratuity for Sheafe is roughly equivalent to a decent weekly wage; a decade later, in a time when deflation was a greater concern than inflation, Sheafe's weekly salary from the Adventist General Conference was $13.

[12] "Pilgrim Baptist Church," *Appeal*, Mar. 8, 1890, p. 2.

[13] "The Grand K. P. Entertainment," *Appeal*, Mar. 22, 1890, p. 2; Mar. 29, 1890, p. 2.

[14] "Local News," Minneapolis *Observer*, Sept. 20, 1890, p. 3.

[15] "The Saintly City," *Appeal*, Mar. 15, 1890, p. 1.

[16] "Popular Preachers," *Appeal*, May 24, 1890, p. 1.

[17] "Top Sheafe," *Appeal*, Nov. 29, 1890, p. 1.

[18] "Parrish Wins," *Appeal*, Jan. 10, 1891, p. 1.

[19] "Card of Thanks," *Appeal*, Jan. 17, 1891, p. 3.

[20] "Pilgrim Baptist Church," *Appeal*, Nov. 1, 1890, p. 2.

[21] "Pilgrim Baptist Church," *Appeal*, Jan. 10, 1891, p. 3.

[22] "Pilgrim Baptist Church," *Appeal*, June 22, 1889, p. 2.

[23] "Pilgrim Baptist Church," *Appeal*, July 20, 1889, p. 2.

[24] "Church Circles," *Appeal*, May 24, 1890, p. 1.

[25] "Pilgrim Baptist Church," *Appeal*, July 5, 1890, p. 2; Aug. 9, 1890, p. 2.

[26] "The Reception," *Appeal*, July 12, 1890, p. 3.

[27] Taylor, pp. 20, 21.

[28] Ralph E. Luker, *The Social Gospel in Black and White: American Racial Reform, 1885-1912* (Chapel Hill: University of North Carolina Press, 1991), p. 72.

[29] "Pilgrim Baptist Church," *Appeal*, June 13, 1891, p. 3.

[30] "Pilgrim Baptist Church," *Appeal*, Oct. 31, 1891, p. 3.

[31] "Pilgrim Baptist Church," *Appeal*, July 11, 1891, p. 3.

[32] "Pilgrim Baptist Church," *Appeal*, July 11, 1891, p. 3. The tragic massacre of Sioux Indians at Wounded Knee Creek in neighboring South Dakota the previous year had been precipitated in part by misunderstandings about the Ghost Dance, which the prophet Wovoka had urged Indians to practice in order to hasten the millennial age. See Dee Brown, *Bury My Heart at Wounded Knee: An Indian History of the American West* (New York: Holt, Rinehart & Winston, 1971), pp. 389-418.

[33] "Pilgrim Baptist Church," *Appeal*, July 25, 1891, p. 3.

[34] George Marsden, *Fundamentalism and American Culture* (New York: Oxford University Press, 2006), pp. 72-80.

[35] "Pilgrim Baptist Church," *Appeal*, June 8, 1889, p. 2.

[36] "Pilgrim Baptist Church," *Appeal*, Apr. 5, 1890, p. 3.

[37] "Pilgrim Baptist Church," *Appeal*, Nov. 7, 1891, p. 1.

[38] "Pilgrim Baptist Church," *Appeal*, July 25, 1891, p. 3.

[39] "Pilgrim Baptist Church," *Appeal*, Aug. 8, 1891, p. 3.

[40] "Saint Paul," *Appeal*, Sept. 12, 1891, p. 5.

[41] "The Hickman Side of the Trouble," *Appeal*, Oct. 31, 1891, p. 2. Sheafe's reply was published the following week under the headline "Another Side of the Hickman Trouble, as Seen From the Moderator's Chair," *Appeal*, Nov. 7, 1891, p. 2.

[42] "Pilgrim Baptist Church," *Appeal*, Oct. 31, 1891, p. 3.

CHAPTER V

EARLY STRUGGLES
FOR CIVIL RIGHTS

A S TENSIONS IN CONGREGATIONAL LIFE HEIGHTENED during 1891, so did Sheafe's activity as a leader in the Black community as a whole. In May a new chapter opened in the involvement of St. Paul's Black citizens in the struggle for civil rights. The national Afro-American League formed in 1889 had come under criticism for failure to take meaningful action. In January of 1891 William A. Hazel, an articulate stained-glass artisan who later became an architect, blasted this critique home to the St. Paul chapter, which Sheafe had been involved in launching. Discrimination was alive and well in St. Paul, and the Afro-American League had not done a thing about it, charged Hazel, who claimed to know of six recent violations of civil rights and had himself sued the Clarendon Hotel in 1887 for denying him service. He denounced the national organization as a "monumental sham" and declared that among its "gaseous offspring," the St. Paul League heads the list for "bombast and vacuity." He accused the do-nothing local group of coming to life "only when there is occasion for feasting or a chance for a few individuals to emerge from their native obscurity."[1]

THE MINNESOTA CIVIL RIGHTS COMMITTEE

Despite Hazel's verbal barrage, the St. Paul League persisted, and somehow managed to get Hazel to join forces with them. Sheafe was a member of the organizing committee for a statewide Afro-American League of Minnesota Convention held in Minneapolis on May 27.[2] One of the purposes of that meeting was to select delegates for the second national convention slated for Knoxville, Tennessee, the following July. What St. Paul's delegate Samuel Hardy experienced on his journey to the convention sparked a new effort to take the kind of action for which the league's critics had called.

Just four months prior to Hardy's trip, the state of Tennessee had enacted legislation requiring racial segregation in passenger trains. Hardy purchased a first-class ticket to Knoxville, but when the train reached Tennessee, he was, in accordance with the new law, ejected from the first-class car and sent to the Jim Crow car. The St. Paul chapter decided to use the outrageous treatment of their state delegate to contest the Tennessee Jim Crow law in court, hoping thereby to strike a blow that could cripple the advance of racial repression in the South as a whole.

T. Thomas Fortune called the plans for a legal challenge "tomfoolery," pointing out that the league had no money. However, despite this discouragement from the national Afro-American League's founder and pre-eminent leader, the St. Paul activists determined to go ahead. Lacking the support of the Afro-American League, they reconstituted themselves as the Minnesota Civil Rights Committee and pursued the matter, with St. Paul attorney Fred McGhee leading the legal charge.[3]

In September the *Appeal* announced the formation of the Minnesota Civil Rights Committee in large headlines, with extensive coverage of the particulars of the case. A ringing call for support put the case in the urgent frame of the rapid erosion of the Reconstruction era's legal guarantees—a process that was rendering Black citizens vulnerable to assaults not only on their dignity and equal rights, but on their very lives.

"Without process of law, often in the absence of any well-defined charges, black men and women are sent into eternity by the torch, the bullet or the halter. The commonest civil rights are denied with impunity. To protest is to invite death; and of what avail? To submit at last to brutal cowardice, with no hope of redress, no recourse of appeal.

"We believe it is time to call a halt; and we pledge ourselves that we will not suffer our brethren in the South to cry aloud for help without making one supreme effort to succor them. We will not suffer our liberties to be imperiled without striking one blow at least in their defense. . . .

"That we are in the right is our firm belief, and in that belief we ask the assistance of all who love justice and abhor wrong."[4]

The first meeting in the campaign to generate support for the cause of "testing the validity of the separate car acts of the South" took place on Sunday evening, September 27, at Pilgrim Baptist Church. Sheafe preached a special sermon, "Rights, Civil and Otherwise," which the *Appeal* commended as "replete with sound logic and wholesome advice" and "very well received by the large audience."[5]

Soon after, Sheafe put in the Pilgrim Baptist Church section of the *Appeal* a paragraph of strong remarks—likely the gist of his September 27 sermon—on the potential of the churches as the foremost agency for Black progress in America:

"Conscious dignity makes the individual, whoever he may be, rise to heights of that dignity. It may be the dignity of manhood, of citizenship or of racial pride. Could every man and woman who has a drop of African blood coursing through his or her veins see the import of standing by the one throne of power that we have in this country, by which more of our people are reached, more influenced than by any other one thing, that is the Christian pulpit. Let the whole representation of the race in this North West combine to make the present churches more effectual by removing every hindering cause, raise the standard of Christianity and morality in our midst, and greater would be their power and usefulness. Let us not be slow to recognize the means that lift, stimulate and strengthen us as a race."[6]

These remarks suggest clues for understanding the future course of Sheafe's spiritual quest. He viewed the churches as the most powerful agency available for racial advance, but not merely because of their tactical usefulness as an existing organizational network. Rather, the churches' power in the cause of the race depended upon a renewal of genuine Christianity within their own ranks.

Despite a mass meeting in St. Paul's Market Hall on November 16 that included a vigorous speech on equal rights by John Ireland, the progressive Roman Catholic Archbishop of St. Paul,[7] the Minnesota Civil Rights Committee's legal crusade lost momentum and eventually came to nought. Sheafe's comments in the November 7 issue of the *Appeal* may imply disenchantment with the project. He warned that "to publish and cry from the housetop against the abuses of our people in the South land and ignore the needy and much neglected host at your doorstep and mine" would be a failure to live out the Christian's profession of faith. The Pilgrim Baptist pastor uplifted "the need of the church getting out and working for the masses" and pointed to "a real growth in this direction which is full of promise to all classes of our people in St. Paul."[8]

The fact that the lawsuit that Fred McGhee filed on Samuel Hardy's behalf did not lead to the "constitutional test" of separate coach laws that the Minnesota Civil Rights Committee had originally called for may have contributed to the diminished enthusiasm. When the case was called for trial in Chattanooga a year later, neither Hardy nor McGhee was present, presumably for lack of funds, and the judge dismissed the case.[9]

Though their project quickly faded, the cadre of St. Paul's leading Black citizens who spearheaded the Minnesota Civil Rights Committee did show initiative and boldness in taking a step beyond the prudent passivity of the Afro-American League's national leadership. Lewis Sheafe's wholehearted participation shows both the central importance he placed on addressing racial oppression as part of the mission of the church, and his conviction that genuine, full liberation required the power of the Christian gospel.

PRAYER AND PROTEST AGAINST LYNCHING

Late in the spring of 1892 St. Paul's Black community, with Sheafe at the forefront, endeavored once again to be as responsive as possible in joining efforts on behalf of their race. The rising menace of lynching prompted a committee formed in St. Louis to issue a call for May 31 to be devoted to a national day of fasting and prayer that "God will so work upon the hearts of the American nation that the murderous lynchings to which we are subjected may cease." While to the nonbeliever fasting and prayer may seem a mere exercise of sentiment rather than practical action, to the believer these disciplines have a value that cannot be measured by short-term, observable results alone. And even the tough-minded W. A. Hazel, so harshly critical of empty rhetoric little more than a year before, participated in this effort, giving a paper entitled "The Negro and His Critics" at the mass meeting held on the evening of May 31 in Turner Hall.[10]

Sheafe was placed in charge of the citywide evening meeting, which took place after services in all the participating churches at 11:00 p.m.

and a joint service at Pilgrim Baptist at 2:00 p.m. A background for the stage was created with life-sized portraits of Col. Robert G. Shaw, Wendell Phillips, John Brown, Frederick Douglass, and Charles Sumner "framed in evergreen over which was draped a large American flag."

"The *Appeal* reported that Sheafe's introductory address dwelt on the inequalities to which the Colored people were subjected. The persecution of which they were the objects in the South, and the prejudice to which they were generally subjected throughout the country, he condemned as contrary to the principles of a Christian nation and hostile to the spirit of emancipation."

In an address entitled "The Negro a Power in His Own Behalf" Fred McGhee raised the question of how many graves of Colored soldiers who had laid down their lives had been honored as the nation lamented its war dead the day before Memorial Day. He presented a wreath dedicated "to their common memory."

Then, after Hazel's speech, petitions to a lesser power than the Almighty were also presented and adopted. The meeting voted several resolutions, such as:

"RESOLVED, That we invoke the executive to enforce to the extent of his prerogative, such laws as already exist. We appeal to congress for that enactment of such laws as shall 'give the courts of the United States jurisdiction of offences against the lives, persons, and rights of her citizens.'"[11]

All in all, it was a meeting filled with freedom songs and speeches "brimming with the ardor of the Abolitionist movement of antebellum days," reported the St. Paul *Pioneer Press*.[12]

Just two weeks before, most of the leaders of the post-Memorial Day Fasting and Prayer observance had been part of an effort to meet a pressing problem closer at hand. While the Black population of St. Paul was not directly subjected to the terror of lynching, they did face barriers to equal opportunity for jobs. Sheafe was part of a committee with J. Q. Adams that undertook "to make an organized effort to secure the employment of some of the intelligent, capable, young African-Americans" with businesses in St. Paul.

The committee adopted the strategy of mobilizing the Black community to exert its collective economic power through united action. They circulated a statement calling for the signatures of those "who will pledge themselves to favor the houses employing Afro-American clerks, salesmen, or salesladies, with their patronage." Here was an opportunity for their community to "be a power in its own behalf" (to paraphrase the title of McGhee's May 31 address). They felt confident that if 100 heads of households signed the pledge and carried it out, their efforts would be rewarded.[13]

The *Appeal* headlined its story about this effort "A Great Movement." As with the other actions for equal rights on the part of St. Paul's Black leaders during these years, the "greatness" of this movement resided more in the nobility of their experimentation than with the very limited means available to them to effect change than in more measurable results.

"REV. SHEAFE SHOULD BE INDUCED TO REMAIN"

Lewis Sheafe, for his part, soon would no longer be in a position to carry forward this or any other endeavor in St. Paul. A conviction that he and his family should leave Minnesota grew during the early months of 1892, even while life and work continued at full throttle.

The pastor continued a new initiative begun just before Christmas—teaching a "historical class" at his home on Tuesday evenings, beginning with a series on American history.[14] On January 31 he preached the dedicatory sermon for the new church sanctuary built by Bethesda Baptist Church in Minneapolis, a sermon described in the *Appeal* as "a magnificent effort, eloquent, profound and logical."[15] In celebration of George Washington's birthday, Pilgrim Baptist held a "Martha Washington Tea Party" at which the pastor gave an address on George Washington and his wife spoke about Martha Washington. Again the following month, husband and wife both spoke at a "family supper" organized by the Mars Lodge and its female branch, the Household of Ruth. Lewis functioned as toastmaster and gave a "neat speech" entitled "The Family," after which Annie presented "a most apropos original poem entitled 'Ruth.'"[16] Fundraising "entertainments" continued, taking the "rare and novel" shape of a mock trial on March 28. Admission of 25 cents was charged to witness the murder "trial" of Joseph Ingham, with the distinguished attorney McGhee acting as judge.[17]

Then, at a business meeting of the congregation on Thursday evening, April 21, Sheafe's resignation as pastor of Pilgrim Baptist Church was accepted, effective June 1. Why did he leave at a time when all indicators pointed toward increasing success and a bright future in St. Paul?

According to an account from none other than Adam Clayton Powell, Sr., of later renown as pastor of the Abyssinian Baptist Church in Harlem, Sheafe in fact did not really want to leave. Powell's early experience paralleled that of Sheafe's, both in taking his training at Wayland Seminary and, upon graduation, receiving the recommendation of the school's president, George Mellen Prentiss King, for the pulpit of Pilgrim Baptist Church in St. Paul.

In an autobiography published some 40 years later, Powell relates that a few days after his graduation in June 1892 King sent him to St. Paul "to arrange with the Pilgrim Baptist Church to become its minister." Powell viewed it as a plum assignment, with a generous salary of $100 per month. "I wanted that church and I wanted that one hundred dollars a month," he wrote, "for only a few star preachers at that time were receiving such a munificent salary."

He could easily have had it, too, Powell claimed, but he discovered that Sheafe actually wanted to remain, even though his resignation had already been accepted. So, to avoid causing Sheafe "great embarrassment and perhaps permanent injury," Powell withdrew, an act he attributed to the principles of integrity that he learned from his esteemed teacher. He returned East, stepping off the train in Atlantic City, New Jersey, with only 40 cents in his pocket.[18]

Reports in the *Appeal* and Sheafe's own account 10 years later give us a quite different perspective, in which only the pastor's firm and repeated insistence finally brought the congregation to very reluctant acceptance of his decision. According to the *Appeal*, the official acceptance of his resignation on April 21 was more precisely a reconsideration of a previous vote to refuse it, and it came only at the "earnest solicitation" of the pastor.[19]

Furthermore, abundant evidence indicates that Sheafe left Pilgrim Baptist and the Twin Cities as a much-loved and admired pastor with a sterling reputation. He remained a month beyond the originally announced date of June 1, during which he raised an additional $500 for the church building debt. An array of fellow ministers, Black and White, paid tribute to him at a reception attended by 300 on June 13. Mrs. J. W. Smith presented Annie with a gold ring on behalf of the women of the church.

Parting gifts for the pastor included a silk umbrella and traveling satchel, both engraved, and a check for $8.[20] Editor J. Q. Adams went on record, stating, "*The Appeal* is still of the opinion that Rev. Sheafe should be induced to remain as pastor of Pilgrim church, as his place will not be easily filled."[21]

Further tribute came from Minneapolis, where Sheafe preached his last sermon in Minnesota at Bethesda Baptist Church on Sunday evening, July 3:

"Rev. L. C. Sheafe preached a most eloquent sermon at Bethesda Baptist Church last Sunday evening to a large audience. Mr. Sheafe is greatly beloved by our people and it was quite a pleasure for them to hear him before he left for the East. . . . Rev. Sheafe is a young man of great promise and we trust that a large field of usefulness may be opened up to him. He is a man of unspotted character and a fine preacher, any church in the Baptist denomination will be fortunate to obtain him as a pastor. We wish him Godspeed."[22]

The most impressive evidence that the praises for the departing pastor went well beyond the perfunctory comes in a letter from Charles Martin, president of the Pilgrim Baptist Church board of trustees. Its straightforward style and the specific details it cites testify to the genuineness of its sentiments. It also provides an invaluable, firsthand summary of Sheafe's pastoral tenure in St. Paul:

"About four years ago Pilgrim Church extended to Rev. L. C. Sheafe a call as their pastor which was accepted by him, and for nearly four years the church has prospered under his charge. There were many things for him to work against, as the church was divided and heavily in debt, but Rev. Sheafe knew that he had the Lord on his side and that He would lead him through, and he and his wife went to work, and the hindrances were moved as they came to them, so today Pilgrim Church is a power in St. Paul. Many have been added, the church brought together in peace and love. The debt placed in such condition that it can be handled, and all floating debts paid, with a balance in the bank to meet the $628.78 due on the bonded debt next September.

"The church and society have tried to retain Rev. Sheafe, but he feels that it is best for the church for him to go; however, his time was up June 1, but he consented to stay through June. During that time, he made an effort to raise $500 and the receipts for June have been over one thousand dollars. Rev. Sheafe is a model Christian preacher, an honor to our race. It is the hope of his many friends of St. Paul that he may return here, [and] if not, that he may continue his good work, for we feel that there are few such pastors as Rev. Sheafe among our Colored preachers in any denomination, and the church that gets him will be blessed by having a true and noble God-fearing minister of God."[23]

The glowing tributes and their ring of authenticity correct impressions that Powell's account, if taken alone, might leave. On the other hand, Powell's reflections also help us make sense of a fact that does not fit with the picture that a firm and irrevocable decision on Sheafe's part fully accounts for his departure from Pilgrim Baptist. For when he left St. Paul at the end of June, Sheafe had no definite place to go.

Thus, the "domestic reasons and climatic influences" that he later cited for leaving Minnesota were not the whole story. While these are plausible as contributing factors, it is also plausible that he would have preferred to remain at Pilgrim Baptist. He could well have been hoping that the congregation would make desired changes or commitments in order to induce him to remain, which they did not make, despite the generally high regard in which they held him. It is further plausible, then, that Powell would have withdrawn from a delicate and still-unresolved situation in June, even though Sheafe did leave within a matter of weeks anyway.

For the gifted young preacher and his family in July 1892 the future looked hopeful, but also highly uncertain.

---

[1] Hazel's letter to the *Appeal*, January 1891, cited in Paul D. Nelson, *Frederick L. McGhee: A Life on the Color Line, 1891-1912* (St. Paul: Minnesota Historical Society Press, 2002), pp. 30, 31.

[2] "Committee on Organization" and "Call for a State Convention of Afro-American Citizens of Minnesota," *Appeal*, May 16, 1891, p. 2.

[3] Nelson, p. 32.

[4] "Minnesota Takes the Lead!" *Appeal*, Sept. 12, 1891, p. 2.

[5] "The Jim Crow Car Must Go," *Appeal*, Oct. 3, 1891, p. 2; "Civil Rights," *Appeal*, Sept. 26, 1891, p. 2.

[6] "Pilgrim Baptist Church," *Appeal*, Oct. 10, 1891, p. 1.

[7] "Civil Rights," *Appeal*, Nov. 21, 1891, p. 1.

[8] "Pilgrim Baptist Church," *Appeal*, Nov. 7, 1891, p. 1.

[9] Nelson, pp. 33-38.

[10] "Fasting and Prayer," *Appeal*, May 28, 1892, p. 3.

[11] "Fasted and Prayed," *Appeal*, June 4, 1892, p. 4.

[12] "Cry for Liberty, Colored Citizens Passed Yesterday in Prayer and Fasting," St. Paul *Pioneer Press*, June 1, 1888, p. 8.

[13] "A Great Movement," *Appeal*, May 21, 1892, p. 2.

[14] "Pilgrim Baptist Church," *Appeal*, Dec. 5, 1891, p. 3.

[15] "Dedication of Bethesda Baptist Church," *Appeal*, Feb. 6, 1892, p. 3. The Sunday evening sermon, preached by Rev. J. F. Thomas of Chicago, received less-enthusiastic endorsement as "an acceptable sermon, urging sinners to turn from the errors of their way."

[16] "Saint Paul," *Appeal*, Mar. 26, 1892, p. 3.

[17] "The Great Mock Trial," *Appeal*, Mar. 26, 1892, p. 3.

[18] A. Clayton Powell, *Against the Tide: An Autobiography* (New York: Richard R. Smith, 1938), pp. 26, 27. Powell does not mention Sheafe by name, but the dates and other particulars mesh so as to make the identification certain.

[19] "Saint Paul," *Appeal*, Apr. 23, 1892, p. 3.

[20] "Card of Thanks," *Appeal*, July 9, 1892, p. 3; "Rev. L. C. Sheafe," *Appeal*, June 18, 1892, p. 3.

[21] "Rev. L. C. Sheafe," *Appeal*, June 18, 1892, p. 3.

[22] Untitled(?) section of Minneapolis news, *Appeal*, July 9, 1892, p. 3.

[23] "Pilgrim Baptist Church Parts With Their Pastor Rev. L. C. Sheafe With Much Regret," *Appeal*, July 9, 1892, p. 3.

SECTION TWO:
"Eminent Baptist Divine": The Ohio Years

"What the Negro needs is simply to demand his own, and cease to be a tail for any political kite. Demand proper protection and recognition, and if these are not forthcoming make the party that receives his support feel the weight of that demand, when made by the 27,000 Negro voters of Ohio."

—LEWIS C. SHEAFE
EMANCIPATION DAY SPEECH
SPRINGFIELD, OHIO
SEPTEMBER 22, 1895

CHAPTER VI

PULPIT ORATOR

"REV. LEWIS C. SHEAFE, the eloquent colored divine of Youngstown, will preach at the Methodist church on next Sunday," announced the Salem *Daily News* in its November 14, 1894, edition.[1] Though brief, the notice concerning the guest preacher for the Methodist service in the nearby community of Ellsworth points to prominent features of Sheafe's four years of Baptist ministry in Ohio.

First, the eloquence, further attested by a comment a year later in the Columbus *Dispatch*, the leading paper in the state's capital city, that "Rev. Mr. Sheafe has achieved quite a reputation here as a pulpit orator."[2] Such accolades for Sheafe's prowess in the pulpit would, of course, have come as no surprise to anyone familiar with his work in St. Paul, Minnesota.

Additionally, though, the Salem church in which the Baptist preacher was to speak was a *Methodist* church. Moreover, it was not an *African* Methodist Episcopal or AME Zion church. The "colored divine" would occupy the pulpit of a "White" Methodist church. These details reflect aspects of Sheafe's ministry that came to new prominence in Ohio and would recur throughout his entire career. As a Baptist, he took a leading role in interdenominational endeavors and agencies, thus transcending not only racial barriers but, to a remarkable degree, denominational boundaries as well.

His speaking, activism, and leadership in predominantly White settings, however, in no way diminished his outspokenness on behalf of his race. In Ohio Sheafe would take the role of advocate for racial justice even further than he did in Minnesota. While many White listeners

found Sheafe's preaching so winsome that they set aside their racial prejudices—at least for the moment—popularity with White people was not
the target at which he aimed. He indeed knew how to deploy tact and
circumspection. Yet in 1895, at the very time Booker T. Washington was
winning national acclaim for his "Atlanta Compromise" speech, Lewis C.
Sheafe would bring his eloquence to bear on racial injustice in a manner
so uncompromising as to stir denunciation from defenders of White
privilege.

YOUNGSTOWN

In mid-October Sheafe included a glowing report of how well the
Buckeye State was treating him and his family in an open letter to his former parishioners and associates in St. Paul, published in the *Appeal*. He
described Youngstown as "truly a picturesque city," set in the Mahoning
River Valley amid "a range of gently sloping hills." Jobs were plentiful, and
open to Black men, not only in the ironworks that made Youngstown a
thriving industrial city, but also in construction, masonry, and teaming.
Many Black families owned their homes.[3]

The 1890 census counted 648 Black people in Youngstown, close to
2 percent of the overall population of 33,000.[4] Fifty-five of them were
members of the Third Baptist Church when Sheafe became their pastor.

Six weeks elapsed after Sheafe's departure from St. Paul at the end of
June before the family's next location finally became definite. The
Youngstown correspondent for the Cleveland *Gazette* reported that after
Sheafe preached three times at Third Baptist on Sunday, August 14, and
generated a collection of $58, the delighted trustees of Third Baptist ex-
tended him a call.[5]

Soon after they arrived in their new home, the pastor and his wife
were awakened by a knocking late on a Monday night. It was Deacon
Walter Rose, a close neighbor, who somehow convinced Lewis and Annie
of the necessity of coming over to his house right away. They may well
have surmised what was going on by the time they stepped into the Roses'
unlit parlor. The lights suddenly came on, revealing 45 well-wishers gathered for a surprise party of welcome. Singing, prayer, and speechmaking
ensued, with remarks from Lewis, Annie, Deacon G. W. Woolidge, and
Rev. Pleasant Tucker, the retired founding pastor of the congregation.

Then, refreshments and more merriment, during which the members of Third Baptist made their welcome tangible with gifts of an "abundant supply" of groceries and provisions, a ton of coal, and a "liberal purse."[6]

Organized under Rev. Tucker's leadership in 1874, Third Baptist was Youngstown's first Black church. The congregation met in Sunday school rooms at First Baptist Church before moving in the early 1880s to a small church built on Mill Street.[7] Sheafe later described it as a "most unattractive" house of worship,[8] and indeed the church had acquired four years earlier a lot upon which to build a new structure. The new preacher set out immediately to carry the endeavor forward to culmination. "We are here to succeed, and believe we will," he declared. That determination to succeed was matched by a determination to keep attention focused on the gospel message, and to use "straightforward methods" appropriate to that message. "We simply preach the plain gospel of Jesus Christ and His Spirit does the work," he wrote.[9]

The first financial hurdle—the $128 debt remaining on the current property—was cleared within two months. A "rally day" on September 25 raised $74.88, and the net receipts from a well-received "literary entertainment" on October 12 added $16.60. By then attendance at Third Baptist's services was larger than it ever been, and the young people were "taking hold of the work."[10] With the congregation thus growing and energized, the new church building became a reality only nine months later. The "commodious structure," which seated 500, was constructed on the lot the church had purchased in 1888 on one of the city's major thoroughfares, Mahoning Avenue.[11]

A "great throng" gathered on June 18, 1893, for the dedicatory services of the new Mahoning Avenue Baptist Church, as it was now called, its interior "beautifully decorated with palms and cut flowers." During the day's three services, more than $400 was donated, thereby eliminating 17 percent of the church's overall indebtedness of $2,423.59.[12]

The array of guest ministers participating in the celebratory services for the 81-member congregation reflected the impressive range of the interdenominational and interracial ties that Sheafe rapidly forged in Youngstown. Presbyterianism had been the predominant persuasion among the original settlers of the town in the late eighteenth century,[13] and the pastors of the city's two leading Presbyterian churches lent their prestige to the occasion. Daniel H. Evans, longtime pastor of Youngtown's oldest church, First Presbyterian, was one of the speakers for the afternoon service. Another afternoon speaker, S. R. Frazier of the Tabernacle United Presbyterian Church, had also preached at a "special rally day" service on April 9 to raise money for the new church.[14] Other participating guest clergy included B. H. Lee of the AME church, and several additional pastors from Youngstown's White churches—Baptist, Methodist, Congregationalist, Lutheran, Episcopalian, and Disciples of Christ.[15]

For the first regular Sunday evening service in the new church the following week, Sheafe preached on the topic "A Greater Than the Temple," seeking to keep his people mindful of the Lord that the new physical structure was meant to serve. At the same time, diligence was needed in the practical matter of dealing with the remaining debt.

With regard to that financial challenge, the timing of the rapid movements leading to a new church building proved fortunate. Just as the congregation was getting settled in its new home on Mahoning Avenue, a harsh economic depression, triggered by the financial panic of 1893, brought Youngstown's iron mills to a standstill, resulting in massive unemployment. A new steel plant opened by the Ohio Steel Company—the beginning of Youngstown's transition from iron to steel production—brought some relief, but only to a fortunate few out of the thousands needing jobs.[16]

On the other hand, though they had built the church and occupied it before the depression hit, the hard times made the task of paying the remaining $2,000 debt much more formidable. Even so, the church made significant progress during the remaining year and a half of Sheafe's pastorate, reducing the principal to $1,500.[17]

Along with typical "rally" days, which usually featured a guest speaker for at least one of the Sunday services and often a special musical attraction, the church organized a "genuine camp meeting" held at the county fairgrounds from July 29 to August 5, 1894, as a means of raising funds. Also billed as "Rev. Lewis C. Sheafe's Great Feast of Tabernacles," the camp meeting offered three services each Sunday for which an admission fee of 10 cents was charged. Musical attractions, dramatic presentations, and some of Sheafe's most stirring sermons were on offer.[18]

An "excellent jubilee choir" was assembled for the first Sunday. Sheafe preached two of the sermons that he tended to use early in a new pastoral assignment—"The Song of Songs" in the morning service and "Esther Before the King" for the evening service. His new colleague at the AME church, Joseph M. Ross, preached for the afternoon meeting.[19] The camp meeting's final Sunday featured the "Feast of Belshazzar," a dramatic musical presentation, with the pastor himself singing "the solo of the feast." For the evening finale, the parable of the ten virgins was enacted with Oriental costumes.[20]

Abundant signs of success attended Sheafe's ministry in Youngstown. A new sanctuary with "handsome appointments" had been constructed, with strong progress toward eliminating the debt. The membership had grown dramatically.[21] As later sections of this chapter will amplify, he became highly regarded across denominational and racial lines in the Youngstown area.

It seems surprising, then, that he would leave after only two and a half years, and leave for a much smaller community, Urbana, some 40 miles west of Columbus. A year before, in December 1893, Sheafe had made public the fact that he was considering a call to the pulpit of First Baptist Church in Montgomery, West Virginia, perhaps as a way of testing just how much his Youngstown congregation desired him to stay.[22] Looking back later, he attributed his decision to leave for Urbana the following year to "a now well-digested intention never to remain with one charge long enough to inspire in its membership the faintest wish for his departure."[23] That this intention had already become "well digested" by his second pastorate and after just six years of ministry suggests that the conflicts he experienced in St. Paul, even though relatively moderate and contained, had caused him considerable pain. He may have seen a similar situation—one that he did not wish to face again—on the horizon in Youngstown.

On December 9, Sheafe's final Sunday in Youngstown, the Mill Street AME Church dismissed its evening service so that its members "could hear the last sermon of the eloquent gentleman." Many of them must have taken advantage of the opportunity, for, according to the Youngstown *Telegram*, the overflow crowd filled all the standing room as well as the staircases at Mahoning Avenue Baptist.[24]

"Rev. Sheafe was at his best last night, and he preached a sermon that all who heard him will never forget. He chose for his text Acts xx-32, 'And now, brethren, I commend you to God, and to the word of his grace, which is able to build you up, and to give you an inheritance among all them which are sanctified.' In a strong and earnest manner he pleaded with those who had not come out from the world to do so, and to take their places in the army triumphantly marching to Zion."

The singing too, by both choir and congregation, was "especially good." As the hymn "Shall We Meet Beyond the River?" was sung to close the service "the great chorus rang out until the building fairly shook under the earnestness of the singers."

The pastor did not leave his Youngstown congregation with no thought for its future. He recommended as his successor Franklin G. Warnick, a Wayland Seminary friend and classmate. Warnick was pastor of the Second Baptist Church of Matawan, New Jersey, and editor of the *Mystic Mirror*, a monthly temperance periodical that had recently been adopted as a publication of the Afro-American Baptist Association of New Jersey. He had also been considered to succeed Sheafe at Pilgrim Baptist in St. Paul in 1892,[25] but, whether by his choice or that of the congregation, did not go there. On Sheafe's final Sunday, Warnick preached a trial sermon for the 3:00 p.m. service, and was subsequently called to be the new pastor at Mahoning Avenue Baptist.[26] It would not be the last time that Warnick's ministry followed in the footsteps of Sheafe's.

URBANA

In November 1836 an old wagon carrying a woman huddled with seven children rolled into Urbana, Ohio. The two horses drawing the wagon were also old and worn-out, but they had carried Elizabeth Chavers and her children to the final destination of their trek "from a land of cruel slavery to a land where all men were supposed to be free." Urbana, a small town of barely 1,000 about 40 miles west of Columbus, was the seat of Champaign County, one of several counties in central and southern Ohio where communities of Black migrants (or refugees) from the South formed during the middle decades of the nineteenth century.[27] Just under three decades after the humble beginning represented by the Chavers wagon, several members of the heroic Massachusetts Fifty-Fourth

Regiment during the Civil War originally hailed from Urbana's small Black community.[28]

The Second Baptist Church of Urbana had its roots in the family altars of "rude log cabins" two miles east of town, where Elizabeth Chavers and her offspring settled. By conviction Baptist, but unable to find other Baptists of color nearby, Mrs. Chavers and two of her daughters covenanted to worship the Lord in accordance with their persuasion as best they could in their isolated circumstances. In 1846, nearly a decade later, Rev. Samuel Jones officially organized the little flock that now numbered six as a Baptist church, holding their services in the groves surrounding their rural dwellings.

In his history of the congregation written 50 years later, church clerk E. D. Morse recounted the disadvantages it had overcome in progressing through its early decades.[29] In the small country church "illiterateness claimed the pulpit and held it undisturbed for many years." Lack of Christian unity didn't help either, as Baptist and Methodist churches delighted in heaping abuse on one another. Looking back from the vantage point of 1896, a little more than a year after Sheafe's arrival, Morse depicted how the 136-member church had indeed come a mighty long way:

"The groves have given away to a brick building, flattened rails have given away to comfortable pews, the callow dip to chandeliers, and the quaint and weird strains of music have given away to sweet strains of anthem and chant, as are peeled forth from the organ manipulated by skilled hands and sweet voices."

The era of illiterate preachers, too, was long over. Indeed, declared Morse, with "our own Elder Sheafe"—a "peerless Christian pulpit orator"—Second Baptist's pulpit had "reached its zenith."

Morse's brief history of Second Baptist is one indicator suggesting that the Black community in the Urbana to which Sheafe arrived at the end of 1894 was progressive and vital, even if relatively small. Another is that Elmer W. B. Curry, a young Baptist minister and educator, chose Urbana as the site for establishing a training school for Black youth modeled after Booker T. Washington's Tuskegee Institute. The Curry Institute was under development while Sheafe was in Urbana and opened in 1897, not long after his departure.[30]

Qualities similar to those of the congregation may be detected in the town of Urbana itself. Though still a small town of about 7,000 in the late 1880s, Urbana supported several industries, 11 churches, four banks, and five newspapers.[31] The pages of the *Times Citizen*, its leading paper in the 1890s, convey the impression of at least moderately respectful and constructive race relations. However, the notorious lynching of a Black man accused of rape in the summer of 1897 belies perception of Urbana as an oasis of racial justice and harmony.[32]

Soon after arriving, Sheafe began a series of nightly revival meetings on January 7, 1895, that initially may have been overshadowed by other events. For one thing, a blizzard that must have reminded the Sheafes of Minnesota hit Urbana during the night of January 11, leaving nearly a foot of snow and dropping the temperature to −10°F.[33] More significantly, when Sheafe began his meetings, a 10-day revival conducted by the prominent evangelist J. Wilbur Chapman was already underway, filling to capacity the town's 1,240-seat Grace Methodist Episcopal Church. At that time Chapman, in the words of historian Sydney Ahlstrom, was "something of a class B attraction, touring only the smaller cities of the nation." But Chapman had on his team one who would soon surpass him in fame, Billy Sunday, who preached in the town's Market Square Theater on January 6.[34]

As the Chapman series came to a close, however, the *Times Citizen* observed that the nightly meetings at Second Baptist, by then in the midst of their second and final week, were "growing in interest." A large congregation had been in attendance on the evening of January 17 to hear Sheafe, "a noted divine," preach a "fine sermon" on the text "Ye must be born again."[35]

Two months later the church's forty-ninth anniversary celebration on March 24 gave Sheafe occasion both to forge ties with a fellow clergyman and position himself as a public spokesman for the Black community. His colleague from nearby Mechanicsburg, N. S. Merritt, and a contingent of the latter's congregation came to Urbana to join Second Baptist for a "grand union service" at Market Square Theater during the afternoon. Sheafe spoke to a "well-filled" house on the subject "The Status of the Negro."[36]

For 12 weeks out of his year and a half in Urbana, Sheafe repeated a series of sermons on the life of Joseph that he had presented in

Youngstown. The fifth message in that series, "Woman at Her Worst" (Potiphar's wife), received the most extensive coverage in the *Times Citizen*. Along with the by-now-familiar superlatives about the preacher's eloquence, the report gives us a small window on the themes and impact of his preaching, as well as his construal of the ever-contentious matter of gender roles.[37]

The pen "is unable to set forth the power and eloquence of the speaker as he brought forth the sublime lessons of vital truths," wrote the reporter. Flashy phrasing and sensational theatrics, however, were not the foremost qualities that made Sheafe's preaching powerful. Rather, he was "moving the city by his plain, peaceful and spiritual preaching." The reference to his impact on "the city" (not just his congregation) is reinforced by the reporter's sighting of "representative citizens" among the congregation that filled the sanctuary.

The thesis of Sheafe's entire series of sermons was that "the history of Joseph in Egypt in all its varied features is a most memorable illustration" of the "cardinal and fundamental truth that there is a superintending providence over all human action." Thus, the believer can look upon "wars and revolutions and revolting crimes" without being overcome by despair, "knowing that all things shall work together for good to those that love God."

Given that "the devil is never idle," though, the path to that resolution is never a smooth one. And that is where "woman at her worst" comes into the picture. Potiphar's wife employs her seductive wiles to bring Joseph down from the height to which he has risen at the head of her husband's estate.

The report of this sermon, as well as that of his second Mars Lodge sermon in St. Paul, contain traces suggestive of a progressive view of the equal dignity and stature of women. However, the distinctive qualities of the feminine nature—that which makes women different from men—receive much greater attention than equality.

Sheafe believed women to be endowed with unique traits enabling them to exert an almost supernatural, angelic sort of influence either on behalf of light or darkness. He spoke of "those traits that belong alone to women, and that impart to her those powers and graces that give her the touch of the angelic." In keeping with conceptions widespread in nineteenth-century America of women as "guardians of morality," Sheafe believed that these powers confer upon women a status "higher than man." It is through that difference, by occupying her own sphere rather than through "equality" with men in every sense, that woman exerts the influence of her uniquely powerful "touch of the angelic."

Conversely, when devoted to evil, the feminine powers become fearsomely demonic. Depicting the machinations of Potiphar's wife "in most picturesque and thrilling language, the Reverend painted the awful depth to which woman can go when her heart is fully set in her to do evil." Woman's "natural chances, her knowledge of hearts, her persuasiveness"—these were distinctive capacities that can make her so powerful a force for evil as to "enable her to outdevil the devil."

Many Americans in the 1890s continued to use this theory of female nature to argue that women would lose the influence of their exalted status if they lowered themselves to the male sphere by engaging in voting and party politics. Others believed that women's "angelic touch" was precisely the thing needed to reform society and that the way to apply it was for women to vote and become social activists.[38]

It seems likely that Sheafe held something like the latter view, though the sermon report is silent as to his position on controversial issues such as woman suffrage and equality in education, the professions, and the workplace. He affirmed that the woman's sphere entails an influence in the state as well as the home, and the "limitless" reach of that sphere in the verse he quoted in his 1890 sermon in St. Paul may point to a rather expansive view of the path a woman might take in exercising that influence. His closing appeal implied the possibility of a public role for a woman who will "recognize her place and power" and thereby "throw her whole heart into saving and purifying the world."

Was Annie, an educated woman and part of the faculty of Wayland Seminary before her marriage to Lewis, in harmony with him about what comprised the "woman's sphere"? Whatever she thought about it, Annie's activities during the Ohio years appear to have been almost entirely centered on the home. If, as in St. Paul, she was active in leading church-related organizations and giving occasional speeches and readings of her poetry, no written reports remain. The limitations of the available sources of information on the family for the Ohio years may be a factor,[39] but it makes sense that the demands of raising her children—Clara was 3½ and Howard was 1½ at the time of the move to Youngstown—had become even greater, thus reducing her activities outside the home. In addition, she gave birth to the couple's third child while they were in Urbana—Lewis, Jr., born in May 1896.

As for Lewis, husband and father as well as pastor, his preaching on the question of woman's place in the "gospel economy" does not appear to have been driven by desire to make a programmatic pronouncement defining the activities and occupations appropriate for women. Rather, his primary concern was to address matters of practical Christian living that his people faced day by day. Expounding on Joseph's resistance to temptation, Sheafe "urged his people with fatherly earnestness to preserve their character." It was, he told them, "better to resist temptations and suffer, than to sin and prosper." He exhorted women to use their power "to wall back the ocean of temptation that comes to the youth of today," rather than be a source of temptation.

Consistent, once again, with his work in St. Paul, the call to a higher level of holiness and the costliness of such attainment comes through in the intermittent reports about his preaching in Urbana. Under the theme "The Christian Standard," Sheafe made "earnest demands for a pure Christianity" during his Sunday morning sermon on September 8, 1895.

In his evening sermon the pastor "held a vast audience spellbound" as he brought the theme down to the question "Is there any harm in the dance?" The text he used, "The joy of our heart is ceased: our dance is turned into mourning" (Lamentations 5:15), suggests that he did in some sense answer the question in the affirmative, though we are left without further detail.

Appeals against sin and for holiness are, of course, what preachers do. However, a comment at the conclusion of the brief newspaper report on the September 8 services adds to the evidence that there was something out of the ordinary in Sheafe's efforts to promote a more rigorous and complete consecration to Christ: "Such sermons are seldom preached in our pulpits and we believe them conducive of much good." [40]

In October 1895, after only 10 months in Urbana, Sheafe informed his congregation that he had accepted a call to Xenia, Ohio, some 40 miles to the south, and that the family would move there at the beginning of

January.[41] The development of a pattern begun in St. Paul and Youngstown may be detected here. Approximately a year after his arrival, having established his effectiveness and having won enthusiastic if not always unanimous support from the congregation, Sheafe places before them the serious prospect of his leaving.

It may have simply been happenstance. It would not be surprising for a man of his ability and growing track record to receive frequent offers. No direct evidence indicates that in Youngstown and Urbana it was a matter of resistance to his leadership from a minority of the members. Indeed, Sheafe stated that the congregation in Urbana "had been kind and assisted him loyally" but that "a wider field of labor" had opened for him, which he felt duty-bound to accept. Yet it seems difficult to dismiss the possibility that he was in some sense testing or seeking to consolidate his support, for when "urgent" pleas for him to remain duly came from the church's members, he decided to do so. Whether or not it unfolded by design, the editors of the *Times Citizen* pronounced the decision "good news" for the people of Urbana, not just for Second Baptist.[42]

The unspecified call to Xenia also prompts some tantalizing what ifs. If it had been finalized, it would have brought Sheafe into the orbit of Wilberforce University, the first private college for Black students in the nation's history. And that orbit, if he had entered it, would almost certainly have brought him into contact with W.E.B. DuBois, who began his professorial career with a two-year stint at Wilberforce (1894-1896).[43] Located three miles from the AME-operated school, Xenia was about the same size as Urbana, but had a much larger Black population of about 2,000. Sheafe's call had probably come from one of the town's three Black Baptist churches.[44]

Entry to the "wider field of labor" in Xenia was not to be, though. After an extension of just six months to his ministry in Urbana, the great turning point of Sheafe's life would come, not in Xenia to the south, but much farther to the north, in Battle Creek, Michigan.

---

[1] "Ellsworth," Salem *Daily News*, Nov. 14, 1894, p. 8.

[2] "To New Fields," Columbus *Dispatch*, Oct. 17, 1895. The "here" referenced in this comment was the town of Urbana.

[3] Oct. 22, 1892, p. 3.

[4] David A. Gerber, *Black Ohio and the Color Line, 1860-1915* (Urbana: University of Illinois Press, 1976), p. 274.

[5] "Received Many Presents," Cleveland *Gazette*, Aug. 27, 1892. The *Gazette* was the leading African-American newspaper in northern Ohio during the late nineteenth century.

[6] "A Complete Surprise," Cleveland *Gazette*, Sept. 24, 1892, p. 1.

[7] Joseph G. Butler, Jr., *History of Youngstown and the Mahoning Valley, Ohio* (Chicago and New York: American Historical Society, 1921), vol. 1, pp. 316, 317; "Historical Sketch of Third Baptist Church," Third Baptist Church of Youngstown Web site, http://www.thirdbaptist-church.org/about.asp?Status=Info (accessed Dec. 9, 2008).

[8] "A New Faith Comes," CA, Sept. 13, 1902, p. 2.

[9] Letter in *Appeal*, Oct. 22, 1892, p. 3.

[10] "Buckeye Letters, Youngstown," Cleveland *Gazette*, Oct. 1, 1892, p. 1; "A New Church Building," Cleveland *Gazette*, Oct. 22, 1892, p. 1.

[11] "A New Faith Comes," p. 2; "Historical Sketch."

[12] "Hearty Rejoicing, After Years of Long Continued and Earnest Effort," Youngstown *Vindicator* (hereafter cited as YV), June 19, 1893, p. 3; "A New Church, Dedicated to the Good Work on Mahoning Avenue," Youngstown *Weekly Telegram*, June 19, 1893, p. 1.

[13] J. Butler, "Communities and Congregations," pp. 302-304.

[14] "Among the Churches," YV, Apr. 8, 1893, p. 4.

[15] Identification of the clergy has been derived from the listings for church services in various issues of the Youngstown *Vindicator*, 1892-1894. Several others whose racial identities and church affiliations I was unable to discover also participated, including the guest preachers for the morning and evening sermons, J. H. Pryor and R. S. Laws, respectively.

[16] Butler, pp. 221, 222.

[17] "A New Faith Comes," p. 2.

[18] "A Camp Meeting, One Will Be Held at the Fair Grounds Beginning Sunday," YV, July 25, 1894, p. 3; "Feast of Tabernacles," YV, July 26, 1894, p. 1; "Don't Miss the Closing," YV, Aug. 3, 1894, p. 2.

[19] "Feast of Tabernacles"; "Church Chimes," YV, July 28, 1894, p. 3.

[20] "Church Chimes," YV, Aug. 4, 1894, p. 2.

[21] According to "A New Faith Comes," the biographical feature on Sheafe in the Sept. 13, 1902, issue of the *Colored American*, the membership had increased to nearly 300, which would have been at least a third of Youngstown's Black population. However, a report on Sheafe's farewell sermon in the December 10, 1894, issue of the Youngstown *Telegram* states that "about fifty members had been added to the roll of the church," which would have doubled the membership to a little more than 100.

[22] "Church Chimes," YV, Dec. 23, 1893, p. 2.

[23] "A New Faith Comes," p. 2.

[24] "Work Closed, Rev. Lewis C. Sheafe Bade His Congregation Farewell," UTC, Dec. 21, 1894, p. 7, reprinted from the Youngstown *Telegram*, Dec. 10, 1894.

[25] "St. Paul," *Appeal*, July 30, 1892, p. 3.

[26] "Jones-Heath," Cleveland *Gazette*, Dec. 15, 1894, p. 2; "The New Pastor," Cleveland *Gazette*, Dec. 22, 1894, p. 2.

[27] Gerber, p. 275.

[28] David W. Blight, *Race and Reunion: The Civil War in American Memory* (London: Belknap Press of Harvard University Press, 2001), p. 345.

[29] E. D. Morse, "1846 to 1896, History of the Second Baptist Church of Urbana, Ohio," UTC, Mar. 30, 1896.

[30] Gerber, pp. 394-397.

[31] "Urbana," Ohio History Central, Ohio Historical Society, http://ohiohistorycentral.org/entry.php?rec=2022&nm=Urbana (accessed Dec. 8, 2008).

[32] Gerber, p. 357; Blight, p. 345.

[33] "Cold Snap, The Thermometer Takes a Sudden Tumble Downward," UTC, Jan. 12, 1895, p. 3.

[34] "Zaccheus, Make Haste and Come Down," UTC, Jan. 5, 1895, p. 3; Sydney Ahlstrom, *A Religious History of the American People* (New Haven: Yale University Press, 1972), p. 747.

[35] "Revival Services, The Churches Holding Meetings Each Night," UTC, Jan. 18, 1895, p. 2.

[36] "Sunday Services," UTC, Mar. 22, 1895, p. 4; "Fortieth Anniversary," UTC, Apr. 2, 1895, p. 4. The newspaper headline erroneously reads "Fortieth"—it was in fact the forty-ninth anniversary.

[37] "The Second Baptist, A Red Letter Day in the Church History," UTC, May 20, 1985, p. 4.

[38] For an informative discussion of the tensions over women's public role in this era, see Carolyn De Swarte Gifford, "Frances Willard and the Woman's Christian Temperance Union's Conversion to Woman Suffrage," in Marjorie Spruill Wheeler, ed., *One Woman, One Vote: Rediscovering the Woman Suffrage Movement* (Troutdale, Oreg.: NewSage Press, 1995), pp. 117-133.

[39] None of the available Ohio newspapers reported the daily life of the local Black communities in which the Sheafes lived as extensively as the *Appeal* did for St. Paul. The major Black weekly in northern Ohio, the Cleveland *Gazette*, regularly included a section on news from Youngstown, and less regularly, from Urbana, but they were very brief, and information from them on the Sheafes, while valuable, is quite sporadic and sketchy. The White-owned papers in Youngstown and Urbana give considerable coverage to Sheafe's activities and churches, but not in the intimate, almost familial manner of the Black newspapers, and thus probably would be less likely to include references to Annie.

[40] "Sabbath Services at the Second Baptist Church," UTC, Sept. 9, 1895, p. 5.

[41] "Will Leave Us: Rev. Lewis C. Sheafe Will Remove to Xenia, Ohio," UTC, Oct. 14, 1895, p. 5. The announcement was picked up by the Columbus *Dispatch* ("To New Fields," Oct. 17, 1895).

[42] "Local Notes," UTC, Nov. 15, 1895, p. 6.

[43] Lewis, pp. 151-178.

[44] R. R. Wright, Jr., "The Middle West, Ohio," in W.E.B. DuBois, ed., *The Negro Church* (Atlanta: Atlanta University Press, 1903), pp. 92-108.

CHAPTER VII

CHRISTIAN ENDEAVORER

LEWIS SHEAFE'S CREATIVE ENERGIES constantly propelled him into involvements beyond his local congregation. In Ohio such activity took place on occasion in connection with Baptist denominational agencies, but even more so with interdenominational endeavors both for evangelical proclamation and for Christian activism in society. With the chronology of the preacher's Ohio labors established, the exploration of these dimensions of his career, as well as his advocacy on behalf of his race, will move back and forth between Youngstown and Urbana.

AN APPEAL FOR A BAPTIST WILBERFORCE

One instance stands out in Sheafe's limited involvement with Baptist denominational work in Ohio. Second Baptist Church in Urbana was affiliated with the Western Association, which had its roots in the nation's earliest Black Baptist associations formed in Ohio during the 1830s.[1] In July 1895 Second Baptist hosted the twenty-third annual meeting of the Western Union Baptist Sunday school convention.[2] Along with routine functions as pastor of the host church for the three-day event and the necessity of conducting a funeral service that supplanted the morning devotional on Wednesday, the second day, Sheafe was called upon to deliver the closing address Thursday evening. Anticipation had been building, because of Sheafe's renown. Amid general admonitions, the "long-expected and -waited-for address," as summarized by convention reporter E.W.B. Curry, brought out two particularly noteworthy points.

First, the pastor's remarks seem in part to have been directed against denominational arrogance and parochialism. He exhorts his hearers to "be good Baptists," but not exhibit a "selfish disposition" toward other denominations. "We need more of the boundless love of God," he said. "It is love that causes a man to open his heart to God."

Second, Sheafe gave a ringing endorsement of the plans being developed by Curry, a young teacher from Delaware, Ohio, for taking Christian education beyond the Sunday school to the formation of a college for training Black young people. Despite his warnings against religious exclusivism, Sheafe was not above appealing to denominational (as well as regional) rivalry in rallying the Baptist gathering to escape the shadow of the Methodist achievement at Wilberforce:

"We need as a tower in this state an institution of education that will be second to none. We need one controlled by our own people. The southland points the finger of scorn at us on education.

"I am glad to know that we have one beloved young man who has the zeal to take upon himself this great work of education. I believe that the efforts of Brother Curry should be supported in his noble attempt to give his race and denomination a college of note and credit. If we, as Baptists, can hold up his arms he can and will give us a college in this state equal to Wilberforce or any other institution of this kind."[3]

By the time Curry opened his school—the Urbana Institute—in 1897, Sheafe had moved on. Later developments, though, would bear out the genuineness and depth of his interest in developing educational institutions for his people.

INTERDENOMINATIONAL AND INTERRACIAL COLLEGIALITY

Sheafe devoted far more effort in Ohio to interdenominational than to denominational activities, most notably with the Christian Endeavor. The broad spectrum of participation in the dedicatory services of the Mahoning Avenue church is in itself testimony to an amicable, supportive atmosphere among Youngstown's Protestant ministers that freely crossed lines of denomination and color. But Sheafe's interaction with White clergy in Youngstown appears to have entailed more than the occasional symbolic gesture. His service, for example, as secretary of the city's ministerial association, while Albert Frazer, rector of St. John's Episcopal Church, served as president, suggests functioning collegiality.[4]

Sheafe and S. R. Frazier, Ph.D., the pastor of the Tabernacle (First) United Presbyterian Church, collaborated in several ways. Frazier not only participated in the opening ceremonies at Mahoning Avenue Baptist but helped with the fund-raising. Sheafe reciprocated three weeks later by offering the benediction for a ceremony at which the cornerstone was laid for the Tabernacle church's new edifice.[5]

The following May, Sheafe and Frazier helped bring the Black and White Civil War veterans' associations together for joint Memorial Day observances. The Grand Army of the Republic post accepted an invitation from the Black Union Veterans Legion to Sunday morning services on May 28, 1894, at Mahoning Avenue Baptist. Sheafe extolled the patriotism and bravery of Civil War heroes in a sermon that a report in the Youngstown *Vindicator* called "one of the most patriotic and scholarly that the veterans ever listened to in this city." Then for the evening service the two veterans' groups made their way to the Tabernacle church for a service conducted by Rev. Frazier. They also participated in joint memorial services the next day at the cemetery.[6]

In August 1895 "Dr. L. C. Sheafe" was identified as one of the "eminent preachers" lined up for a 10-day "Urbana Camp Meeting." It was primarily a Methodist affair, organized by the Central Methodist Episcopal Church of Springfield, 15 miles south of Urbana. Among the other guest speakers were evangelist Anna L. Cartwright; Captain J. N. Parker of Cleveland, reputed to be "one of the most entertaining and interesting speakers in the Salvation Army"; and Dr. C. N. Sims, a former chancellor of Syracuse University and current pastor of the Meridien Street Methodist Episcopal Church in Indianapolis.[7]

Though in general received with enthusiasm, Sheafe's preaching in mainly White settings did not sit well with everyone. His sermon at the Methodist church in rural Terre Haute, Ohio, about 10 miles southwest of Urbana, on November 4 attracted a large crowd from far and near comprised of people from all denominations, curiosity seekers, and some not known to frequent divine services. However, according to the *Times Citizen* correspondent, some "good Christians" boycotted the service "because he was a colored man." Such were now sorry they did not attend, for among those who did, Sheafe's message was widely reported to be "the best sermon they ever heard." In response to those who had declared the church disgraced by Sheafe's presence, the correspondent opined that "if no greater disgrace comes on the church than Rev. Sheafe and his sermon the gates of heaven will be thrown wide open and all may enter."[8]

LEADERSHIP IN THE CHRISTIAN ENDEAVOR

The most prominent arena of all for Sheafe's interdenominational and interracial action was the Christian Endeavor society. Though begun in St. Paul and continued in Urbana, the high point of Sheafe's leadership in this organization came in Youngstown.

The main thrust of the Young People's Society of the Christian Endeavor was to energize young Christians with a vital faith and mobilize them for making it active in their lives and the society around them. The Christian Endeavor enjoyed strong support among the various Protestant churches in Mahoning County, and in 1894 it joined forces with a new movement headed by the Anti-Saloon League to confront the liquor traffic with the influence of Christianity.

Temperance and the influence of alcohol had been one of the foremost issues concerning American Protestants since at least the 1820s. The Ohio Anti-Saloon League, organized at Oberlin on May 24, 1893, was a new attempt to remove the influences in the social environment that induced people to drink and all too often made them its slaves. The movement's premise was that consumption of alcohol would decrease as opportunity to buy it decreased through legal restriction and eventual elimination of saloons. A similar league formed in Washington, D.C., later that year eventually joined forces with the Ohio league to create a national Anti-Saloon League (ASL).[9]

Temperance meetings by leaders of the ASL were conjoined with a Christian Endeavor convention in Youngstown on July 8-9, 1894. It was a presentation at the concluding meeting of this convention that propelled Lewis Sheafe to regional prominence as a Christian Endeavor leader.

The weekend convention took place in a large tent set up on the grounds of the Rayen School, with crowds filling its 3,000-seat capacity to overflowing. Howard Russell, the young Congregationalist minister and former lawyer who founded the ASL, spoke on Saturday evening about the ways the saloons ensnared children and put them "in training for hell." The great question "Who is to blame?" he said, arises when one comes face to face with a tragedy resulting from the influence of alcohol. The answer, declared Russell, is clear: "Those who make it and those who sell it are to blame." And his colleague Harry White told the crowd that if people in the numbers gathered that evening would "take a firm and aggressive stand," they "could easily crush out every saloon in this city in 60 days."

Saloons, however, were not alone culpable for the evil consequences of alcohol, Rev. Russell pointed out as he appealed for the reduction of another social inducement to drink: "In many cases young ladies are to blame. If they would say, 'The lips that touch liquor shall not touch mine,' they would help us a great deal."[10]

Sheafe was one of several speakers on the program for the Sunday evening meeting, organized by S. R. Frazier. The sides of the tent were raised to accommodate the hundreds standing, unable to find seats. The Cleveland *Gazette* gives only the general observation that Sheafe "entertained the audience with a very interesting speech,"[11] but the impression he made at the convention proved strong enough to be useful in promoting future events. An announcement for his "Feast of Tabernacles camp meeting" three weeks later billed him as "Rev. Lewis C. Sheafe, of C. E. convention fame."[12]

Throughout the remaining months of his ministry in Youngstown, Sheafe maintained a high profile of involvement with the Christian Endeavor. He occasionally penned devotional messages for a Christian Endeavor section that regularly appeared in the Youngstown *Vindicator*. These reflect his view of the Christian life as a bold, strenuous, and progressive struggle powered by faith and hope, and they convey traces of his skill as a communicator.

In one column, for example, he used the new popularity of the bicycle to illustrate the synergy between human endeavor and divine power. Mounting the bicycle, he pointed out, requires taking "a step or two" at the risk of failure. Likewise, to "get on a footing with Jesus and walk with Him you will have to step out of self and trust in Him." Then, "if you wish to stay on you must keep moving." Success in "C. E. work" comes to those who "keep everlastingly at it," for if "endeavor ceases you either have to get off or fall off."

The purpose of the persistent endeavor is not to attain salvation, but "to grow, to shine and be an instrument in the Master's hand to lead others to salvation." Nor does the striving of itself generate success. Novice cyclers are told to "sit naturally in the saddle" and "don't keep watching your feet." The advice, he suggested, "reminds us that we are to rest in the Lord, and look up to the hills from whence cometh our help."[13]

At the convention of the Mahoning County Christian Endeavor Union held in Ellsworth in October, Sheafe was the leading ministerial figure. Though most of the Protestant churches in Youngstown and throughout the county had C. E. societies, it was Sheafe whom the lay governed organization chose to deliver the convention sermon on Sunday, October 7.

Though Ellsworth was a small town, the Pennsylvania Railroad stopped there, making transportation relatively convenient. Youngstown's 50 delegates took the 10-mile train ride at the round-trip cost of 70 cents each. Others among the total of 350 delegates arrived by wagon or buggy. Hundreds more—friends, family, and other visitors—attended as well, far exceeding the capacity of the Presbyterian church that hosted the event.[14]

Along with the temperance crusade, the convention took up a wide range of topics having to do with Christian life and teachings, and devoted considerable time to organizational matters. In an open parliament session on Saturday morning, a panel concerned itself with "The Endeavorer's Relation to the Stage, the Dancing Hall, and the Card Table." An afternoon lecture dealt with "The Lord's Day, Its Use and Abuse," and the topic assigned Sheafe for his sermon at the 10:30 worship hour on Sunday was "The Bible, Its Use and Abuse."

Preaching—a 6:30 a.m. devotional on Saturday and the Sunday sermon—was not Sheafe's only contribution to the convention. He was elected to the committee on resolutions, which formulated the society's agenda for action. Since the committee had only three members, and Sheafe was the only minister, its resolutions, which the convention affirmed Saturday afternoon, must have at least come with his approval, and possibly through his initiative. When viewed in connection with other evidence, they contribute to a profile of a man for whom the anti-liquor crusade, and the broader question of Christian action in the public realm, were matters of more than casual or secondary interest.

The committee ventured into the ever-perilous territory of general principles concerning the Christian and politics in a land of religious freedom and diversity:

"Realizing that the political parties of our country do not legislate in the interest of Christian government, we believe that the time has fully come when Christian people should use the God-given right of the franchise for good government.

"We, therefore, of the C. E. Mahoning County convention, in its third annual session, at Ellsworth, Ohio, pledge ourselves to give our sympathy and support to the widespread movement for good citizenship, and recommend that all local societies hold meetings in the interest of this movement."

The phrase "Christian government" would have made Adventists squirm—as it would many in Sheafe's Baptist heritage, with its historic commitment to separation of church and state. Yet the statement did not precisely call on Christians to use the franchise to make government Christian, but rather to make it good—a goal much easier for advocates of church-state separation to support.

But what was to be the specific outcome of this support for the very general concept of good government? Along with support for an unexplained plan for mobilizing the C. E. societies outlined by one of the delegates, the committee set forth a resolution to "lend our heartiest sympathy to further the good work of the Anti-Saloon League all over our county." While still expressed in rather broad terms, the resolution represented an endeavor to get Christians in Mahoning County to shift their political commitments away from the established parties and to an issue or cause based outside the partisan system. Sheafe was chosen to serve on a five-member county temperance committee to coordinate implementation of the resolution.

By the time the 10:30 service began on Sunday the crowd overflowed the Presbyterian church, and many stood on the outside steps in order to hear Sheafe's sermon. Before the sermon he sang "Steal Away to Jesus" for the second time at the convention, repeating it by request on behalf of those who had not been present to hear it the night before. As summarized in rather workmanlike fashion by Hannah M. Brenner, the convention's correspondent for the Youngstown *Vindicator*, Sheafe's sermon on the value and proper use of the Bible contained little out of the ordinary for nineteenth-century American evangelicalism. However, her notes convey something of his facility for moving rapidly from passage to passage in the Bible, and his aptness with metaphor and literary allusion—biblical and otherwise.

The ultimate purpose of the Bible, Sheafe affirmed, is to reveal Jesus and His love. Thus, "it to us is the walk to Emmaus." And, rightly used, it has a sure power to lead others to God. "Put the flowers of the word in the path of the erring and lead them to Christ," he urged. "Let it have free course, and be glorified. Study it to see God, to see self, and the world, its needs and remedy."

A scene from the Sunday afternoon meeting appears to reflect genuine warmth of emotion flowing between Sheafe and his mainly White coendeavorers. As the "praise service" that launched the afternoon proceedings was coming to an end, Sheafe went to the front in response to requests that he sing another solo. The song he chose, "The Handwriting on the Wall," apparently was well known to the audience, for they joined him enthusiastically in the chorus. Then, needing to leave in order to preach for the evening service and celebrate the Lord's Supper with his church in Youngstown, he made his way down the aisle. As he did so, "everyone present sang 'God Be With You Till Will Meet Again.'"[15]

As it turned out, the occasion of Sheafe's next meeting with the Christian Endeavor Union would be to bid them a more permanent farewell. On his last Sunday in Youngstown two months later, he was invited to give a farewell speech for the afternoon meeting held at Plymouth Congregational Church. Here, too, a spirit of genuine fellowship seems evident. Sheafe paid tribute to the entire Christian Endeavor achievement as a *youth* movement: "The young people in church work . . . are now taking a foremost place while they were formerly kept in the background." After the meeting, "Rev. Sheafe was kept busy several minutes shaking hands and saying goodbye to the many who had worked with him in the Endeavor movement."[16]

After his move to Urbana, Sheafe may have run into a few of his Mahoning County associates at the statewide Christian Endeavor convention held at Springfield the following June. There he spoke to an audience estimated at 7,000 on Wednesday evening, June 26. At this event the music, at least in part, was pitched at a somewhat "higher" cultural level. Prior to Sheafe's speech, a 200-voice choir sang a "Gloria" by Mozart; several pieces sung by the boys' choir of Christ Episcopal Church were also part of the evening program.

In what was reported as an "admirable address," Sheafe treated the topic "The Society of the Individual." Perhaps in an effort to check the Christian Endeavor's concern for societal conditions from going to an extreme, Sheafe made the point that "society is not a substitute for an individual" and asserted that societies "rise no higher than the individuals composing them." Thus, he urged, the Christian Endeavor should "never lose sight of the individual work."[17]

THE ANTI-SALOON LEAGUE
AND THE LOCAL OPTION CAMPAIGN

The stress on the importance of the personal did not, however, represent a fundamental break from the Anti-Saloon League's approach of attacking the societal forces conspiring to destroy individual lives. Six months later, on January 26, 1896, Sheafe gave an impassioned oration in favor of a bill pending before the Ohio legislature and supported by the ASL to a crowd of more than a thousand assembled at the Opera House in Urbana.

Whereas the older Prohibition Party maintained an uncompromising line of demanding complete prohibition of the manufacture and sale of alcoholic beverages, the ASL favored more moderate measures that had a more realistic chance to succeed. Most frequently, this took the form of local option legislation—state laws authorizing local governments within the states, such as counties, municipalities, or even precincts, to close saloons within their jurisdiction. The first ASL-initiated local option bill introduced in the Ohio legislature went down to defeat in 1894. But new measures were introduced in every session, while the ASL targeted, with some success, the reelection efforts of members who opposed their bills.[18]

The meeting in Urbana had been called on short notice to demonstrate opposition to a compromise, proposed by the Liquor League of Ohio, to the Harris-Haskell local option bill that was being debated in

Columbus. By a "rising vote" the mass assembly stood unanimously in favor of sending to their two state legislators a resolution of "protest against any compromise measures which increases the tax on the saloon but will lessen the power of the people to banish the saloon itself."

Sheafe was the last of three speakers on the program, and by the time he began the pertinent information already had been thoroughly presented. Nonetheless, according to a report in the *Times Citizen*, he was given a "flattering reception" and "made a vigorous and telling speech." Along with capturing some of the vividness of Sheafe's oratory, the reporter's summary reveals a pastor sufficiently engaged and informed to provide a detailed analysis of this political issue.

Sheafe described the saloon power as a "monster" that had "its paw on every community and its teeth at the throats of the people, sucking their life's blood." Citing reports about the hundreds of thousands of dollars being raised by the Liquor League and the brewers to influence state lawmakers, Sheafe urged the citizens of Urbana to send a message that would "stiffen up the backbone of our legislators" against any compromise that would weaken the measure. "The only hope of the Liquor League," he observed, "is that there will be members [in the state legislature] who have no principle" and thus willing to give a listening ear to "the seductive voice of the briber."

As for the Liquor League's claims about saloons bringing financial benefit to the community and the proposed law leading to heavy tax increases and a ruinous devaluation of real estate, the preacher had two words: "all moonshine." The saloon increases rather than decreases the burden on a city, feeding its "insatiate appetite on our boys," he declared. "Whose boys are going to feed this monster? Your boys or mine!"

Sheafe followed the ASL line on two major points. First, he briefly laid out the necessity of shifting allegiance from a political party to the moral issue. The two major parties "bow down to policy" and the Prohibition party, with its absolutist position, "can't reach the case." Thus, "the people need to come together regardless of party and ask for this measure."

Second, he made an evocative case for getting at the problem of drink by attacking the societal influences that exploit human weakness to fuel the traffic:

"Let us remove the temptations from the weak, that they may not stumble and fall. Some men want to reform, but they must run this gauntlet of saloons. Remove the temptation—take down the bars. Disconsolate mothers, begging children, reeling drunkards—all demand that the iniquity shall cease."[19]

Sheafe never made an environmental solution to sin—a transformation of the American social order—the primary focus on his ministry. Yet his activism in the struggle against the liquor traffic shows recognition that evil can become embedded in a society's power structure, and that Christian faith cannot be silent or passive about it there any more than in individual lives. The historic oppression of his race was evidence enough of the reality and depth of societal evil. And at the very same time of his own remarkable achievement in transcending racial barriers to become a leading interdenominational voice in Ohio for combating social sin, the evil of racism in American society was becoming manifest in new and horrifying ways.

---

[1] R. R. Wright, Jr., "The Middle West, Ohio," pp. 93, 94; C. Eric Lincoln and Lawrence H. Mamiya, *The Black Church in the African-American Experience* (Durham, N.C.: Duke University Press, 1990), pp. 26, 27.

[2] The Urbana *Times Citizen* published daily reports on the convention by E.W.B. Curry, each headlined "Busy Workers, Twenty-third Annual Meeting of Sunday School Workers," July 24, 1895, p. 5; July 25, 1895; July 26, 1895, p. 7.

[3] Curry, "Busy Workers," July 26.

[4] "Ministerial Meeting," YV, Sept. 1, 1893, p. 1.

[5] "Corner Stone of the New Tabernacle U. P. Church, Impressively Laid To-Day," YV, July 6, 1893, p. 3.

[6] "Will Join in the Services, Soldiers Will Go to a Colored Church on Sunday Next," YV, May 25, 1894, p. 3; "The Departed, Sermons Preached on the Soldiers Who Are Now Sleeping, and Memorial Day Observance," YV, May 29, p. 2.

[7] Advertisement, UTC, Aug. 3, 1895, p. 4.

[8] "Terre Haute," UTC, Nov. 7, 1895, p. 8.

[9] "Ohio Anti-Saloon League," Ohio History Central, Ohio Historical Society, http://ohiohistorycentral.org/entry.php?rec=937&nm=Ohio-Anti-Saloon-League (accessed Dec. 8, 2008); Thomas R. Pegram, *Battling Demon Rum: The Struggle for a Dry America, 1800-1933* (Chicago: Ivan R. Dee, 1998), pp. 113-124.

[10] "Boys and Girls, Temperance Orators Say the Saloons Are Constantly After Them," YV, July 9, 1894, p. 2.

[11] "Buckeye Letters—Youngstown," Cleveland *Gazette*, July 14, 1894, p. 1.

[12] "Feast of Tabernacles," YV, July 26, 1894, p. 1.

[13] "Christian Endeavor, Items of Interest Communicated for Publication, Rev. L. C. Sheafe Has Evidently Been Learning to Ride a Bicycle," YV, Aug. 11, 1894, p. 4.

[14] "At Ellsworth, Third Annual Convention of the Christian Endeavor Union," YV, Sept. 29, 1894, p. 2; "In Their Hands, Ellsworth Taken Possession of by the Christian Endeavorers," YV, Oct. 6, 1894, p. 3.

[15] "The Officers, Youngstown Given Two of the Most Responsible Positions, Christian Endeavor Convention," YV, Oct. 8, 1894, p. 2.

[16] "Farewell Sermon, A Well-known Pastor Addresses Christian Endeavorers at Plymouth Church," YV, Dec. 10, 1894, p. 8.

[17] "Second Day of the Christian Endeavor Convention at Springfield," YV, June 27, 1895, p. 3.

[18] Pegram, pp. 113, 114, 117, 118.

[19] "Want It, The Urbana People Favor the Haskell Law, A Rousing Meeting Held at the Opera House Sunday Night," UTC, Jan. 28, 1896, p. 5.

CHAPTER VIII

RACE ADVOCATE

A S THE 1890S PROGRESSED, the nation's oppressive racial climate turned still more stifling. Lewis Sheafe, born in 1859, reached adulthood in Massachusetts during the 1870s and early 1880s, when hope for national fulfillment of the promise of racial equality enshrined in the Fourteenth and Fifteenth amendments to the Constitution remained very much alive. His education at Wayland and his successful interaction with White society as a minister reinforced in him a sensibility that racial equality was the expected norm, and that failures to realize it should be forthrightly addressed and corrected.

From his standpoint the developments of the 1890s were not part of a long, gradual struggle from the depths of slavery to the eventual realization of justice and equality in the far-distant future. Rather, for him they constituted a shocking betrayal of principles that the nation had already committed itself to and that had already been experienced to a substantial degree, albeit inconsistently and incompletely.

During Sheafe's Ohio years it was the lynchings, reported with ever-increasing frequency, that most horrifically signaled the regression of race relations. In 1892 Ida B. Wells, the young journalist and former school-teacher from Memphis, Tennessee, whom Sheafe had met at the teachers' convention in St. Paul in 1890, launched a courageous national crusade against lynching, wielding the weapons of voice and pen with extraordinary power. She not only exposed the extent and brutality of lynching, but also demonstrated, through in-depth investigation and analysis, that the overriding motivation behind the violence was not the heinousness of the alleged crimes, but subjugation of the Black race through terror and intimidation.[1]

Sheafe took it as his calling not only to preach *to* his people, but to speak out *for* them. And amid the unfolding crisis of the 1890s, he, like Wells, did so in a forthright and fearless manner. When, for example, the Youngstown *Vindicator* ran a report on a speech Wells gave in Chicago on September 3, 1894, detailing the lynching of six Tennessee men accused of burning barns, Sheafe entitled one of his sermons for the following Sunday "The Negro and His Murderers."[2]

A PROGRESSIVE INITIATIVE

Sheafe's involvement in racial issues became more extensive after the move to Urbana, but even in the relatively favorable environment of Youngstown he gave evidence of his dedication to race advancement. In September 1893 he set in motion a broad plan for addressing the problems faced by the city's Black population. First, to understand and document racial conditions in Youngstown more thoroughly, he sent out a questionnaire to several of the city's public officials and leading citizens. Then he would use the information in a series of sermons intended to lead his people to "loftier paths."

Nothing remains to indicate how much information he got back, what he learned from it, or exactly how he used it. Still, the questionnaire itself and the apparently respectful manner in which the Youngstown *Vindicator* reported it merits attention. One recipient of Sheafe's "circular letter" and list of questions, Police Chief John W. Cantrell, provided his copy to the *Vindicator*. Noting a recent increase in attention being given to the "mighty question" of race relations, the *Vindicator* stated, "Among the more prominent local workers who are engaged in studying the intricate question and in forwarding the cause, none are more earnest or active than the Rev. Lewis C. Sheafe, the able pastor of the Third Baptist Church on Mahoning Avenue."

In his note of introduction and request, Sheafe referred to his "desire to help my people along all lines of life" so that they might become "better men and women and more useful citizens." By responding to the questions, he said, the recipient would "confer a lasting benefit upon a race that I know you are deeply interested in." He then listed seven questions "pertaining to the Negro of Youngstown, Ohio":

"1. How do the Negro children in public schools compare with others?
"2. How many Negroes in our city?
"3. How do the Negroes compare with foreigners as citizens?
"4. What proportion of criminals are Negroes?
"5. Has the Negro made any real progress in the past 10 years? If any,
   along what lines?
"6. What are the greatest needs of the Negro today?
"7. What is the Negro's future?"[3]

The only trace of possible evidence available as to the outcome of the project is reference to a sermon Sheafe preached several months later entitled "The Negro, His Strength and Weaknesses." The Cleveland *Gazette*'s Youngstown correspondent related that it was "an excellent sermon," but provided no further detail.[4] The effort itself, though, suggests that in Youngstown, at least, Sheafe experienced a degree of productive cooperation with White people—not only in the shared agenda of the Christian Endeavor but also in regard to improving the status of the Black community. He also showed the capacity for conceiving and setting in motion a plan that tackled the tough issues, seeking White collaboration in a way that highlighted mutual benefit.

Such an approach also suggests that Sheafe was on the front edge of a progressive spirit that was gaining strength in American society. (Historians often refer to the years from the 1890s to about 1920 as the Progressive Era.) Systematic gathering of data through a survey as the first step was one of the prominent markers of the progressive approach to resolving social problems.

COMMEMORATIONS AND CONDENSED ELOQUENCE

As for the Black community's own benevolent organizations, Sheafe continued his affiliation with the Grand United Order of Odd Fellows, and was asked to serve as master of ceremonies for Youngtown's celebration of the order's fiftieth anniversary celebration on August 30, 1893. With mounted marshals, the Harmonic marching band, and a contingent of smartly uniformed, crisply drilled Cleveland Patriarchs leading the way, the lodge members marched in a "grand parade" through the center of the city and then onto the fairgrounds. A carriage transporting Sheafe and other dignitaries—including Youngtown's Mayor Miller and guest orator J. McHenry Jones of Wheeling, West Virginia—followed while smiling young women in costume cheered and waved flags from the platform of a wagon that brought up the rear. Though the crowd gathered at the fairgrounds was so "immense" that it was difficult for everyone to hear the platform proceedings, reports in the Youngstown *Vindicator* deemed the whole occasion a spectacular success that "reflected credit on all concerned."[5]

Two events in 1895, Sheafe's first and only full year in Urbana, marked the transition to a new era for Black America. Its great patriarch, Frederick Douglass, passed away on February 20. Seven months later, on September 18, Booker T. Washington gave the famous address at the Cotton States and International Exposition in Atlanta that made him Douglass' successor as the preeminent race leader. Occasions close to the time of both of these landmark events would be among the indicators of Lewis Sheafe's own rising star as a spokesman for his people in Ohio.

At a memorial service for Douglass held at the city hall in Urbana on March 10, Sheafe gave a speech praised by the *Times Citizen* for a "condensed eloquence" that made it "one of the best speeches we have listened to for some time." The fact that Sheafe was in the unenviable position of giving the last of seven speeches on the program adds significance to the observation. In his remarks, "How the Mighty Are Fallen," Sheafe focused on the moral significance of Douglass's career. For the nation Douglass "represented the commingled peoples, having helped to demonstrate that men are of a universal brotherhood and God is their common Father." For those dedicated to a righteous cause, the life of Douglass "proved that merit wins and that injustice can never quench soul-fire." For those of his own race struggling to surmount greater obstacles than others must face, Douglass's life "should be a stimulus to higher effort."[6]

In addition to serving as secretary of the ad hoc citizens' committee that organized the event, Sheafe led a three-member committee that drafted memorial resolutions for publication in the *Times Citizen* and to be sent to the Douglass family. The "colored citizens of the city of Urbana" placed on record their recognition of Douglass as a representative figure, not just in the sense of leadership, but also in the sense of embodying "the qualities and capacities with which the Creator has endowed our race."

These attributes were seen in his "patient struggle with adverse circumstance," his "self-secured freedom" from slavery, "his incalculable service in helping his fellow men to secure freedom from that slavery," and in "his career as an orator and statesman."[7]

The Douglass memorial event thus showcased Sheafe's rhetorical skills, which by now placed him in high demand as a speaker for commemorative civic occasions, such as Memorial Day services and celebrations of the Emancipation Proclamation. It was, of course, memory of the Civil War that dominated in the 1890s, and Sheafe could wax eloquent with fairly standard patriotic fervor about the nobility and bravery of its heroes and the divine blessing on the Union armies. His Memorial Day speech in 1895, for example, celebrated the advances toward freedom achieved through the war. Four months later, though, at another civic occasion in September, the emphasis would shift to critique of the nation's failure to carry forward the freedom the war was supposed to have won.

Before yet another standing-room-only crowd in a rural Ohio church—this time quite a distance from home, at the Kingston Baptist Church some 30 miles south of Columbus—Sheafe preached a Memorial Sunday sermon paralleling the armies of Israel with "the brave boys in blue." The preacher's description of God's mighty works on behalf of Israel, leading up to the battle with the Amalekites narrated in Exodus 17, are worth pausing over as one of the better of the few samples available of the actual content of his rapturously praised sermons. Even here, though, as usual, the boundary between Sheafe's actual words and the reporter's summary is blurred:

"This is Israel's first conflict with an external foe. Up to this point the Lord had fought for them. But now the word is, 'Choose us out men.' God must now fight in Israel, as before he had fought for them. This conflict began when they stood in the full power of redemption, and had tasted that spiritual meat and drunk of that spiritual rock.

"Until they met Amalek they had nothing to do. They did not cope with Pharaoh. Nor did they break the power of Egypt nor snap asunder the claims of their thralldom. Nor could they wall back the sea. Neither could they enter the commissary department of Heaven to bring bread down. Nor yet create a living fountain in the heart of the flinty rock. All this had been Jehovah's conflict for them."

Then Sheafe made the transition from the ancient battle won through the upholding of Moses' arms of intercession to the victory won under Abraham Lincoln, "our Moses." For that victory, and for those of the American Revolution, he said, "the heart of every true American" holds "a deep sense of gratitude to . . . God for the blessings of the past and present." He did not leave his listeners to rest in the glow of gratitude, though, but brought before them "the fact of our *accountability* to that same loving and just God." A true patriot "must consider his countrymen as God's creatures and himself as accountable toward them." The reason that the bloody, costly events of the Civil War were something to commemorate was that they "stamped upon the American heart the fact that humanity is one, and that liberty and freedom must be accorded to all."[8]

THE IMPERATIVE OF AN EQUAL CHANCE

An inspirational, patriotic sermon with some proddings to apply the ideals of liberty and equality to current race relations had seemed appropriate for Kingston Baptist Church on the eve of Memorial Day, but new occasions would soon bring sterner duties. First, an untitled, unattributed column in the June 24, 1895, issue of the *Times Citizen* advising "Negroes" on how to improve their status in society drew from Sheafe a swift and unsparing refutation.

The commentary was occasioned by a national controversy in 1895 over a legal challenge to a South Carolina law that in effect deprived most Black citizens of the opportunity to vote.[9] The writer's main contention was that Blacks, rather than complain about discrimination, should concentrate on working hard at whatever opportunities were available to them. They could thereby gradually build up their economic standing, which would in turn result in eventual recognition of the political rights that they sought. The White Southerners' antagonism to "social equality" between the races did not mean they desired to keep the Negro "a poor beggar," the author claimed. In fact, "the most rabid negrophobe would be glad to see every one of the race earning a good living and even laying up money." Thus, the Blacks' "worst enemy" was not White prejudice but their own "improvidence and idleness and ignorance." Their best course, then, would be to enter "the fight for financial success in such channels as are already open to them." Equality thus earned in "financial circles," placing them in the class of "heavy taxpayers," would "be quickly recognized in political circles."[10]

Sheafe responded immediately with a letter to the editor on June 26. He would not have had much time—a day at most, since it surely would need to have been at the newspaper office on June 25 in order to make the next day's paper. Additionally, prior to seeing the June 24 paper, his thoughts must have been on his trip to Springfield for the Christian Endeavor convention, where he was to speak on June 27 before what may have been the largest audience in his career to that point. Written in heated haste, the letter nevertheless contained a focused, piercing heat that exposed and decimated the specious arguments in the June 24 commentary.

"We enjoy and appreciate most heartily the general attitude of your paper toward us," affirmed Sheafe. The "article in question," though, revealed either that the editor was "not posted in regard to real conditions" or that "prejudice had gotten the better of [his] judgment." Over against the supposed favorable disposition of even the "rabid Negrophobe" toward Blacks accumulating wealth, Sheafe pointed out that the White man who created the disabilities Negroes faced "is desirous of having the conditions remain that would make the Negro a tool in his hands." He cited the "mortgage system" in the South that kept Black sharecroppers in perpetual debt peonage as evidence of "the avowed purpose of that Negrophobe, to keep the Negro poor, ignorant and dependent."

As for the commentator's identification of the Negro's "worst enemy," Sheafe simply stated, "We are not all improvident, idle or ignorant—even in South Carolina." The provisions of that state's law on voter qualifications, he contended, "were not aimed at ignorance, pure and simple, for there are too many whites that would be bound out, but you notice a loophole is left for ignorant men with white faces, and the Negro is left to the tender mercies of his enemies."

With regard to those Blacks who did "tally with" the commentator's pejorative description, Sheafe wrote:

"In the name of truth and justice, who made them what they are? Remember, sir, that it is but yesterday that the Negro emerged from being the toy, tool and thing of the white man; then the amplest opportunity has not been accorded him to rid himself of the white man's association, during slavery."

To the advice that "Negroes enter the fight for financial success in such channels as are already open to them," Sheafe countered, "Why not let them enter wherever their ability would fill the bill?" Barriers against doing so were one of the very factors repressing the Black success in the economic arena that the *Times Citizen* commentary so glibly recommended.

"Take, for example, the trade and labor unions of this country, how many of them will admit a Negro to membership? He may be a workman of the first order; that has no weight, if his face is black. Remove the barriers in the city of Urbana, give the Negro an equal chance."

What would constitute an equal chance? "We ask no favors on account of color," Sheafe said. Rather, he proposed that "if the Negro fails after he has had the opportunity of five hundred years of education and training, as the white man has, then count him inferior. But you can't in fairness overlook the long start the white man has had of the Negro, nor the fact that obstacles without number are purposely put in his path."

In response to the White South's visceral resistance to free social mingling of the races, Sheafe countered: "We are not clamoring for social equality, for to be equal with some White men, we would be obliged to lower our present standard."

He concluded with the imagery of a politician currying the favor of Blacks with promises he does not even intend to keep:

"He has long used the Negro to pull his chestnuts out of the fire, then when he has cracked and eaten the meat, gives the Negro the shell, and now you are amazed that the Negro has not gotten fat on such a diet. Just advise the White man to stand aside, and you will see that the Negro will come out all right yet."[11]

Sheafe's hard-hitting letter stirred no further controversy in the pages of the *Times Citizen*, for the editor claimed that the appearance of the objectionable column had been the result of a simple oversight in the first place. "Brother Sheafe did not notice that the article in question was '[boiler-plate]' matter" furnished by a syndicate, he said. The press foreman "rubs in" such articles when necessary to fill out a page, and sometimes they are "slipped in without the editor getting his eye on them" and "frequently just 'don't' reflect his opinion," he further explained.[12]

Sheafe's recognition of the paper's generally fair-minded approach lends credence to the editor's explanation, though it may seem a bit too tidy. Regardless, the editorial miscue was a most fortunate one from the present-day standpoint because the letter it prompted yields a fuller picture of Sheafe as an unhesitating and impassioned race advocate who spoke with forceful logic, and from a perspective well informed by history, politics, and economics.

The reference to political exploitation at the conclusion of Sheafe's letter to the *Times Citizen* foreshadows another controversy that took place in September, this time in a significantly wider forum.

RADICAL CONFRONTATION

Springfield, Ohio, was home to one of the largest concentrations of Black population in the state during the 1890s.[13] Emancipation Day celebrations had for many years been conducted in the city during September, marking President Lincoln's preliminary issuance of the Emancipation Proclamation on September 22, 1862, to go into effect January 1, 1863, if the Confederate states did not accept a final chance to return to the union and end the rebellion. Sheafe was invited to return to the city as one of three principal speakers for the celebration marking the thirty-third anniversary of the Proclamation in 1895.

With the Ohio gubernatorial election campaign in full swing, the event also functioned as something of a rally for the Republican Party, with which African-Americans identified in overwhelming numbers. The Republican nominee to replace Governor William McKinley, who would be elected president of the United States the next year, was Asa Bushnell,[14] a prominent Springfield businessman who returned home after a week of campaigning throughout the state to be at the celebration. Hoping to cement the loyalty of Black voters with his presence and a brief ceremonial speech, Bushnell was completely unprepared for what happened when Sheafe took the podium. The Cincinnati *Commercial Gazette*, a Republican newspaper, gave this account:

"Rev. Sheafe made a fiery speech, in which he denounced Lincoln, saying that he issued the emancipation proclamation only as a war measure. He said that the colored people were very little better off today than they were before the war, and frequently pointed to the flag which was above his head in scorn, and said it protected none but the White people and that the colored people could not call it their flag. His speech was frequently interrupted by cries of 'Stop' from the audience, and did not find much favor with the audience."[15]

It was a stunning moment. In the presence of the Republican candidate for governor, at an event intended to celebrate the Great Emancipator, his proclamation, and his party, Sheafe criticized all three. The degree of veneration accorded Lincoln in American culture could be matched only by that given George Washington, the father of the nation. And now Sheafe, who had himself compared Lincoln to Moses just months before, had "slurred" the martyr's memory, said the Cincinnati paper. On top of that, he was accused of heaping scorn on the flag, the most sacred icon of the American republic.

Following Sheafe to the podium, Bushnell came to Lincoln's defense with an "entirely impromptu" speech. He drew the audience's attention to the fact that he had traveled 200 miles and foregone another invitation in Dayton in order to be at Springfield's Emancipation Day celebration, as he had been every year for some time. He admonished his hearers not to "complain of Lincoln because he did not issue the emancipation proclamation earlier, as soon as the war was declared." The candidate explained that President Lincoln "had been advised against it" and "had the best of reasons for not doing so."

Bushnell also related that Lincoln had promised the Lord in prayer that "if the battle of Gettysburg was won he would free the slaves" and that the proclamation was indeed issued soon after the battle. The governor-to-be had rendered relatively brief service during the Civil War as captain of a "hundred-day" infantry company assigned to picket duty in the Shenandoah Valley in 1864.[16] However, either his grasp of the war's history had become confused or the newspaper garbled something on the way to print, for the battle of Gettysburg took place in July 1863, six months *after* the Emancipation Proclamation went into effect. Bushnell must have been thinking of the battle of Antietam, which gave Lincoln the victory—limited though it was—that he believed was needed before his emancipation plan could be announced. That preliminary issuing of the Emancipation Proclamation, which indeed took place immediately after the battle of Antietam,[17] was the event being celebrated at Springfield 33 years later.

Bushnell enumerated and congratulated the audience for Black achievements in education, journalism, and the professions. But they "must not expect to accomplish too much at once," he cautioned. "You will get all you ask in due time if you are patient and work for it," he continued, along the lines of the newspaper commentary Sheafe had protested earlier in the summer. "By being patient you will accomplish much more than if you stand still and grumble that you get nothing." In stark contrast to the cries of protest from the audience that greeted Sheafe's speech, Bushnell's was "applauded to the echo," according to the *Commercial Gazette.*[18]

How could it be that Sheafe, who had extolled patriotism and celebrated the Civil War's righteous victory over slavery at Kingston Baptist Church in May, slur Lincoln's memory and cast scorn on the flag only months later in Springfield? Or did he?

Sheafe's side of the story sheds further light not only on what happened in Springfield but also on his profile as a race advocate. His reply to the story in the *Commercial Gazette* appeared in the Urbana *Times Citizen*, at the editor's invitation.

He began by expanding on a point that he had made in previous speeches, namely, that commitment to a righteous cause must take precedence over party loyalty. A movement or interest group—in this case African-Americans—should not be subservient to a political party, but instead make support for a party depend on the party's support for their cause, and make clear to the party the cost of losing that support.[19] After declaring himself indeed to be a Republican and—in what appears to be his only extant reference to his father—"the son of a Republican soldier," Sheafe wrote:

"My position is that the Negro is not under obligation to any party but that the Republican party is under everlasting obligations to the Negro. I am not blind to the fact that no one party has a monopoly upon all the righteousness that there is in politics, even as meagre as it is. The party that has been supported so nobly by the Negro, has not discharged its obligations to him. . . .

"What the Negro needs is simply to demand his own, and cease to be a tail for any political kite. Demand proper protection and recognition, and if these are not forthcoming make the party that receives his support feel the weight of that demand, when made by the 27,000 Negro voters of Ohio."

Then Sheafe responded to three assertions made by the *Commercial Gazette*. About the claim that people in the audience had shouted "Stop" during his speech, Sheafe declared, "There never was a bolder piece of falsehood than that put in print, for no such cry was made while I occupied the floor." The vociferous denial seems convincing, particularly in view of the large number of witnesses who would not be difficult to locate. However, Sheafe moved on quickly without commenting on the newspaper's other assertion, in the very next phrase, that the speech "did not find much favor with the audience." Thus, noticeable indications of disfavor from at least a portion of the audience seem likely, as well as a cool reception overall—an unusual experience for Sheafe.

On the matter of pointing to the flag with scorn, the issue was not so much factuality as context. The *Commercial Gazette* gave the equivalent of a "sound bite." Sheafe gave the context necessary for a truthful, as opposed to narrowly factual, account:

"I recounted the valor, bravery, and sacrifice of the Negro soldiers for the flag. When the North was losing battle after battle, the Negro anxious and willing was tugging at his chains trying to get free to fight for the flag and the union, and when finally permitted to fight, who can say that he did not help by more than 200,000 soldiers to save the union, and yet, who of all the dwellers of the land is so abused, scorned, hoodwinked, and murdered as the Negro? And he finds no redress from state or central government.

"Ida B. Wells may knock at the door of the Senate chamber of these United States, seeking to present her plea for the protection of her people. No one hears or notices her or her pleas. Do with the negro as you like in this country and when he appeals to that government that is the power back of the flag there is no protection for him. Then this would look as though the flag did not protect him in this country."

The context makes possible a fuller understanding of Sheafe's references to the flag. "As lynching and lawlessness against Blacks increased in the 1890s," observes historian David W. Blight in his study of the Civil War in American memory, "discussions of progress had to share space with outrage over violence" in the presentations of Black orators and writers. Sheafe's searing logic that refused to spare America's most sacred symbol reflected Wells' hard-hitting confrontation of the nation's pretenses with the truth about its performance, requiring Americans "to swallow hard their sense of innocence."[20]

When it came to the alleged denunciation of Lincoln, Sheafe refuted the notion that he had "slurred" or disrespected the late president, or denied the debt of gratitude owed him. The name of Lincoln, he said, is one that "every negro loves and reveres," and he, for one, would not wish to dishonor it in any way. In his view, though, that honor should not bar honest and open examination of historical evidence in order to see the Emancipation Proclamation in its true light.

He then rehearsed several historical points that he had set before his audience in Springfield, including:

- The explicit statement in the Emancipation Proclamation itself that it was warranted by "military necessity."
- Lincoln's clear statement that saving the union was his overriding purpose, and that the fate of the slaves would be determined by whether that purpose was better served by freeing them or by leaving them in bondage.
- Lincoln's countermanding of Gen. John C. Fremont's emancipation policy in Missouri, ordering freed slaves back to their "so-called masters."
- The refusal to allow the Hutchinson family to sing their antislavery songs in the Army of the Potomac.[21]

"These are facts and like most of their kind are stubborn," Sheafe declared.[22] And, in all of this, Sheafe did show himself to be a resourceful and insightful historian—certainly a far better one than Bushnell. The preacher was decades ahead of the shift to a more critical assessment of Lincoln that began to gain widespread currency in the 1970s,[23] and his recognition of the crucial contribution of Black soldiers to the Union victory was likewise advanced.[24]

Lewis C. Sheafe's fiery speech in Springfield briefly stirred passions in Ohio, but soon would become all but lost to history. Five days before, Booker T. Washington had delivered a speech on race relations of incalculably greater influence—far different in character, and in a much different setting. The latter difference, especially, complicates comparison. Sheafe's message was directed to the Republican Party—the party of emancipation and the promise of equality—in a state that comprised one of its strongest bases of national power. Washington's "Atlanta Compromise" had been offered to a new order in the American South, home to 90 percent of the nation's Black people, ruled by White supremacist governments that had now firmly consolidated power, having worn down the national government's will to interfere.

Even so, the approach to race relations set forth by Washington, which came to define the era, provides a valuable reference point for assessing Sheafe's approach. *Gradualism* was a defining principle for Washington. The full privileges of the law were indeed due Black people, but for now, he said, preparation for the exercise of those privileges was vastly more important. That preparation would come mainly through taking advantage of present opportunities at the bottom of the economic scale and through industry advance to the point that their contribution to the markets of the world would inevitably bring about an end to their ostracization. Like Bushnell, albeit in a more nuanced and polished manner, Washington urged that Blacks not "permit . . . grievances to overshadow our opportunities."[25]

Immediatism, by contrast, marked Sheafe's statements. He called for immediate recognition of equal rights, based in part on contributions already made and merit already demonstrated. Equal justice and equal opportunity must be insisted upon now as the framework for the remaining progress needed to overcome the legacy of slavery, not as a future reward for that progress.

Accommodation went together with gradualism in Washington's approach. Within the forbidding reality of unyielding White political dominance, he sought to structure a productive, dignified arrangement between the races in which Black uplift would be possible. To achieve this, his speech was silent about the glaring and proliferating injustices of Jim Crow laws, denial of Black voting rights, and lynching. Washington would use his personal influence against these injustices behind the scenes, but did not undertake public campaigns for their abolition. Temporary accommodation of the indignities and injustices that went with being as "separate as the fingers" from the dominant White society would make it possible for the races to be "as one as the hand in all things essential to mutual progress." Injustice and inequality would gradually fade in the course of that mutual advance.

By 1895 *confrontation* had become more evident in Sheafe's style. He confronts instances of bigotry and injustice in a direct and uncompromising manner. He could have used his considerable oratorical skills and organizing energy on behalf of Republican Party loyalty, and thereby build up power and influence that would enable him to advance the fortunes of his people from within the political system. A crowd-pleasing speech in Springfield might have opened great opportunities toward that end. That of course, would mean keeping silent, or perhaps just speaking gently, about the betrayal and injustice that he saw. That, however, would have required an accommodation with wrong that he was not prepared to make.

These partial and unsystematic comparisons suggest only some key points of orientation in Sheafe's handling of racial issues, not a fully formed or rigidly held ideology. Though his profile as race advocate in Ohio faded almost as rapidly as it arose, he would exert a significant influence in another setting in which race relations were becoming an increasingly urgent and contested matter. Less than 10 months after the Springfield speech, the fiery civil rights orator, interdenominational activist, and eminent Baptist divine became a Seventh-day Adventist.

---

[1] Linda O. McMurry, *To Keep the Waters Troubled: The Life of Ida B. Wells* (New York: Oxford University Press, 1998); Paula J. Giddings, *Ida: A Sword Among Lions* (New York: HarperCollins, 2008), pp. 211ff.

[2] "Ida Wells, Indignant, Anti-lynching Agitatress Greatly Excited Over the Sextuplet Lynching in Tennessee," YV, Sept. 3, 1894, p. 2; "Church Chimes," YV, Sept. 8, 1894, p. 2.

[3] "Race Problem, Interesting Questions Asked of Leading Citizens, What of the Negro's Future?" YV, Sept. 11, 1893, p. 2.

[4] "Church Chimes," YV, Apr. 14, 1894, p. 3; "Flown to Parts Unknown," Cleveland *Gazette*, Apr. 21, 1894, p. 1.

[5] "Great Celebration, Parade, Speeches by the Governor and Others," YV, Aug. 26, 1893, p. 2; "Celebrating, Colored Men Gather in the City To-Day," YV, Aug. 31, 1893, p. 2; "Highly Enjoyable, The Celebration by the Colored People Yesterday," YV, Aug. 31, 1893, p. 3. Governor William McKinley was initially announced as one of the speakers for the occasion, but was unable to attend "due to other previous arrangements."

[6] "Impressive Services in Memory of the Life, Trials, and Achievements of Frederick Douglass, Who Measured Up to the Full Stature of Manhood," UTC, Mar. 11, 1895, p. 4.

[7] "Memorial Services in Honor of the Late Frederick Douglass," UTC, Mar. 9, 1895, p. 4; "Douglass Memorial Resolutions," UTC, Mar. 12, 1895, p. 2.

[8] "Memorial Sermon by Rev. Lewis C. Sheafe at Kingston Baptist Church Sunday Night," UTC, May 28, 1895, p. 4. (Emphasis supplied.)

[9] Rayford Logan, *The Negro in American Life and Thought: The Nadir, 1877-1901* (New York: Dial Press, 1954), pp. 191, 206-208.

[10] Untitled paragraph, UTC, June 24, 1895, p. 2.

[11] Lewis C. Sheafe, "The Negro Race," UTC, June 26, 1895, p. 3.

[12] Editor's note immediately following "The Negro Race."

[13] D. A. Gerber, *Black Ohio and the Color Line*, p. 274.

[14] "Asa Bushnell," Ohio History Central, http://www.ohiohistorycentral.org/entry.php?rec=14&nm=Asa-Bushnell (accessed Dec. 8, 2008).

[15] "Bushnell on Lincoln, The General Replies to an Attack on the Martyr's Memory," Cincinnati *Commercial Gazette*, Sept. 24, 1895, p. 1.

[16] "Asa Bushnell."

[17] James McPherson, *Battle Cry of Freedom: The Civil War Era* (New York: Oxford University Press, 1988), pp. 557, 558.

[18] "Bushnell on Lincoln."

[19] August Meier documents a growing disillusionment with the Republican Party and adoption of a "race first, party second" on the part of Blacks in the 1880s and 1890s. Though a large majority remained Republican, an increasing number were "uneasy Republicans," in the words of Frederick Douglass. August Meier, *Negro Thought in America, 1880-1915: Racial Ideologies in the Age of Booker T. Washington* (Ann Arbor: University of Michigan Press, 1966), pp. 26-35.

[20] D. W. Blight, *Race and Reunion,* pp. 334-337.

[21] On the role of the Hutchinson Family Singers in the abolitionist movement, see Henry W. Mayer, *All on Fire: William Lloyd Garrison and the Abolition of Slavery* (New York: St. Martin's Press, 1998), pp. 321, 328, 329, 348, 469; Scott Gac, *Singing for Freedom: The Hutchinson Family Singers and the Nineteenth Century Culture of Reform* (New Haven, Conn.: Yale University Press, 2007).

[22] "Rev. Sheafe Asks a 'Fair Show and a Free Fight' for His People," UTC, Oct. 10, 1895, p. 5.

[23] Among the numerous works on this topic, see Stephen B. Oates, "Lincoln's Journey to Emancipation" in *Our Fiery Trial: Abraham Lincoln, John Brown, and the Civil War Era* (Amherst: University of Massachusetts Press, 1979), pp. 61-85; Henry Louis Gates, Jr., and Donald Yacovone, eds., *Lincoln on Race and Slavery* (Princeton, N.J.: Princeton University Press, 2009).

[24] Joseph T. Glatthaar, "Black Glory: The African-American Role in the Union Victory," in Gabor S. Boritt, ed., *Why the Confederacy Lost* (New York: Oxford University Press, 1993), pp. 133-162.

[25] "Atlanta Exposition Address," in Cary D. Wintz, ed. (New York: M. E. Sharpe, Inc., 1996), p. 25.

SECTION THREE:
"This Message for All My People"

"I believe that Seventh-day Adventists have a truth which, if they will let it get a hold of them, can do more in this field to demonstrate the principles of the gospel of Jesus Christ than can any other people. The one thing needful is that the truth shall get hold of the individuals who profess to know it."

—Lewis C. Sheafe
1899 General Conference session
South Lancaster, Massachusetts

CHAPTER IX

OBEDIENT TO
PRESENT TRUTH

THE EVANGELISTIC TENT IN LOUISVILLE was the only place Lewis Sheafe had to lay his head in late May 1897. As he shivered through the damp nights of an unusual late spring cool spell, fighting a severe cold, he must have wondered at times what he had gotten himself into. Preaching the Adventist message that he had just embraced the previous year was bringing him into circumstances far different from the life he had known as an "eminent Baptist divine" in Minnesota and Ohio. The stability and support of an established congregation, the status and amenities, the round of entertainments, banquets and civic celebrations, were replaced by lonely travels in the daunting task of building tiny groups of believers in an obscure and demanding message. And it all had to be done with minimal resources, against much opposition, and with unreliable compensation that in any case fell short of meeting the basic needs of his wife and three small children.

Beyond all that, he was working in the South now, for the first time in his life. As he preached and traveled throughout Kentucky, Tennessee, and South Carolina over the next four and a half years, he would experience firsthand what it meant to be a Black man in the post-Reconstruction South that had been "redeemed" for White supremacy, and that had just received the Supreme Court's stamp of approval for segregation in the *Plessy v. Ferguson* decision (1896), even while "Judge Lynch" loomed as the ultimate enforcer.

The preacher could not have persisted without deep conviction that the message he had learned so much about in Battle Creek was "present truth," a message of ultimate urgency and decisive significance for America in the 1890s. And with conviction Lewis Sheafe had a vision for what the message could mean, in a particular way, for *his* people—the hope and uplift it offered a people persevering amid the unfolding betrayal of the promise of emancipation. His vision was that "this message may go to my people all over the United States," and he had rapidly begun formulating ideas on how to reach that goal.

Regarding Sheafe's potential for advancing the Adventist cause, John Harvey Kellogg, head of the Battle Creek Sanitarium, expressed with particular force what many quickly recognized:

"He is an orator, a wonderfully able man. He is a more liberally educated and cultivated man and can deliver a more forcible address than any other Seventh-day Adventist minister. We have not a White minister that can begin to stand beside him. He commands the respect of everybody wherever he goes."[1]

At the same time, in the eyes of some, Sheafe quickly became a controversial and threatening figure. To his disappointment, he soon discovered that commitment to racial equality did not run as deeply and widely throughout the church as his initial exposure to Adventism had led him to hope. Almost immediately, countervailing forces in the church drew the talented newcomer into a swirl of contention that involved many issues (including race relations) but centered on the basic question of how Adventism would define and organize its mission in the world.

In that era of turbulence Sheafe's work in the South would be a time of experimentation and learning through experience. The preacher helped nourish an Adventist mission still in its infancy in that region—particularly in reaching Black people. During these years, however, his large dreams saw only the beginnings of realization. "We are still in school, still in training," he wrote in 1899.[2] Some of the lessons he learned during these years, though, would turn out to be of critical, long-term influence—both for good and ill—in his later work of greater prominence as an Adventist leader.

"THE GREATEST AND MOST EVENTFUL CHANGE"

The General Conference Committee, taking seriously the "six days shalt thou labor" clause of the fourth commandment, resumed the work of its 1897 Spring Session in Battle Creek at 7:00 on Sunday morning, March 28. As they proceeded through "distribution of labor" matters, Elder Robert Kilgore, superintendent of the Adventist work in the South (District No. 2), moved that "Brother Lewis C. Sheafe, a colored minister from Ohio, be recommended to connect with Brother J. R. Buster in tent labor in District No. 2, under the direction of the district superintendent."[3]

A Union Army veteran who went on to become the foremost pioneer of Adventism in the South during the 1870s and 1880s, Kilgore had formulated definite convictions on how the church should handle the "color line" question.[4] If he had any concerns about the possibility that Sheafe's approach to the problem might collide with his, such did not prevent him from supporting the recent convert's assignment to the South. The committee also voted to confer on Sheafe a ministerial license, thus signaling its formal recognition that the man who just nine months before had been thriving as a widely praised Baptist preacher had now joined the ranks of Adventist ministry.

The origins of what Sheafe would call "the greatest and most eventful change"[5] in his spiritual life remain a mystery. The autobiographical information he gave in the pages of the St. Paul *Appeal* in 1892, well before he became an Adventist, reveals a conscientious seeker for truth, whose quest may not have been fully satisfied by his choice of the Baptist persuasion among the many denominational alternatives. It had not been an easy decision, but a matter of acting "as best he knew" after years of indecision and prayer. Did the Adventist teachings he later discovered provide more satisfactory answers to questions that had arisen out of his own youthful inquiry after biblical truth?[6]

During the years Sheafe was in St. Paul the Seventh-day Adventists had a chapel in which a congregation of about 50 met. A. T. Jones had visited there in 1889, and his lectures on religious liberty had been covered in the newspapers. Might Sheafe's awareness of Adventism—and fateful friendship with Jones—have originated then?[7]

Whatever the role of other influences, the Battle Creek Sanitarium played a central role in his decision to join the church. In a discussion of the medical missionary work at the 1899 General Conference session, Sheafe testified that "it was largely through benefit derived from treatment at the sanitarium, what I learned from its health foods and principles, that fully opened my eyes to present truth."[8] His statement that his eyes had been "fully opened" there seems to suggest that they had been partially opened already. But if so, surviving accounts give us no details. In a letter to Ellen White in May 1899 Sheafe stated simply that upon hearing of "present truth" three years before, he "investigated it, tried and proved, then obeyed."[9]

The new convert took a brief course of study along medical missionary lines in Battle Creek during the summer of 1896, for the *Review and Herald* reported in July that he was "at the sanitarium preparing himself for labor among his people in the South." Though his resignation from the pastorate of Second Baptist in Urbana apparently had not yet been made public, at least in the press, the new convert was invited to the pulpit of Adventism's largest church—the Battle Creek Tabernacle—on Sabbath, July 18. Taking as his topic the question of Pontius Pilate, "What shall I do then with Jesus which is called Christ?" (Matt. 27:22), he "vividly depicted" Pilate's attempts to shift responsibility away from himself, even while under the conviction that Christ was innocent. Then Sheafe "brought home with great force to every heart" the same question, "What shall *I* do then with Jesus?"[10]

Because the welfare of his race in America was ever at the forefront of Lewis Sheafe's mind, and was in fact inseparable from the gospel he was called to preach, the question of what Adventism meant for race relations was a prominent consideration as he committed himself to a new allegiance. His decision in 1896 came right amid momentous developments on race matters in Adventist history, developments that would have shaped his perceptions as to the potential this new movement held for his people.

ADVENTISM AND RACE RELATIONS:
THE OUTLOOK IN 1896

When the Seventh-day Adventists completed their formal organization as a denomination in 1863, they had no conferences, churches, or members in the South. Their movement, centered in New England, upstate New York, and then in the "Old Northwest," had emerged in a culture of radical religious and social reform that was thoroughly antislavery.

Most of these early Adventists were White, but not all. Several preachers and exhorters from the free Black population of Northern cities in the 1830s and 1840s had taken up the cause of the Millerite movement that became the springboard for Seventh-day Adventism.[11] As James and Ellen White struggled to bring coherence to the Sabbatarian Adventist movement during the 1850s, an African-American family in Michigan, the Hardys, were among their most reliable and valued friends during difficult and unstable times.[12]

Still, the number of Black Adventists, and Adventists of any kind in the South, remained negligible into the 1880s. Charles M. Kinny (1855-1951), who became the first ordained Seventh-day Adventist minister of African descent, joined the church in Reno, Nevada, in 1878. After two years of training at the new Adventist college in Healdsburg, California, Kinny spread the Adventist message amid the growing Black population in Kansas and Missouri by selling books and tracts.[13]

In 1889 Kinny was called to labor in the South under the supervision of Elder Kilgore. A few years earlier a Baptist minister named Harry Lowe had accepted Adventism and led in the formation of a small congregation in Edgefield Junction, Tennessee, that became, in 1886, the first Adventist congregation comprised of an entirely Black membership. In Louisville Alfonso Barry, who had been disfellowshipped from his Baptist church after declaring his convictions about the seventh-day Sabbath,[14] became the pastor of a new group of Black Adventists who organized as a church in 1890. Kinny's work led to the formation of small congregations in Bowling Green, Kentucky (1891), New Orleans, Louisiana (1892), and Nashville, Tennessee (1894).[15]

Taking into account the members of these congregations, the 50 or so Black members of the Washington, D.C., church, which was racially mixed, and scattered believers here and there, it is unlikely that there were more than about 150 to 200 African-Americans in the Seventh-day Adventist Church at the time Sheafe joined it in 1896. But if the Adventist Church was somewhat slow to undertake bold initiatives to reach the nation's Black population, several factors in the mid-1890s would have helped make it a viable option for a man of Sheafe's race consciousness, though we do not know for certain the extent to which any one of these may have influenced him.

First, while there was disagreement over just how to handle the problem of the color line in the church's mission work, the theological touchstone that racial prejudice is incompatible with the third angel's message and cannot be sustained in the heart of anyone who embraces the message stood out clearly—more so, it would appear, than it would in the middle decades of the twentieth century.

In the fall of 1889 Elder Kilgore, the leading advocate of pragmatic accommodation to segregation in the South, proposed that such measures as separate meetings in places where racial prejudice is strong be endorsed as policy by General Conference resolutions. At the same time, he stated that among those who "know the power of the truth in their own hearts as it is in Christ Jesus, the prejudices that once existed are gone." It was the prevailing attitudes of "those from without" that, he believed, necessitated recognition of the color line. Otherwise, Adventism would not even get a hearing among the White population.[16]

In a powerful manifesto, "Our Duty to the Colored People," delivered to 30 General Conference leaders a little more than a year later, Ellen White repudiated Kilgore's effort for resolutions from the General Conference on accommodating the color line:

"At the General Conference of 1889, resolutions were presented in regard to the color line. Such action is not called for. Let not men take the place of God, but stand aside in awe, and let God work upon human hearts, both white and black, in His own way. He will adjust all these perplexing questions. We need not prescribe a definite plan of working. Leave an opportunity for God to do something. We should be careful not to strengthen prejudices that ought to have died just as soon as Christ redeemed the soul from the bondage of sin.

"Sin rests upon us as a church because we have not made greater effort for the salvation of souls among the colored people. It will always be a difficult matter to deal with the prejudices of the white people in the South and do missionary work for the colored race. But the way this matter has been treated by some is an offense to God. We need not expect that all will be accomplished in the South that God would do until in our missionary efforts we place this question on the ground of principle, and let those who accept the truth be educated to be Bible Christians, working according to Christ's order. You have no license from God to exclude the colored people from your places of worship. Treat them as Christ's property, which they are, just as much as yourselves. They should hold membership in the church with the white brethren. Every effort should be made to wipe out the terrible wrong which has been done them."[17]

Ellen White here recognized that racial issues are "perplexing" and implied that God's leading might result in varying arrangements in different times and places. The great danger of Kilgore's approach was that expedient adjustment to the reality of racial bigotry in society could be enshrined into church policy, and thus perpetuated by the misperception that it represented the divine order of things. Thus, Ellen White set before the church, in a most emphatic and vivid way, the unchanging principle that should guide its course on race relations: "While at St. Louis a year ago, as I knelt in prayer, these words were presented to me as if written with a pen of fire: 'All ye are brethren.'"[18]

In this exhortation in 1891, and more fully in a series of articles published in the *Review and Herald* in 1895 and 1896, Ellen White envisioned a comprehensive Adventist initiative to bring liberation to the oppressed Black people of the South:

"The neglect of the colored race by the American nation is charged against them. Those who claim to be Christians have a work to do in teaching them to read and to follow various trades and engage in different business enterprises. Many among this race have noble traits of character and keen perception of mind. If they had an opportunity to develop, they would stand upon an equality with the whites."[19]

It is plausible though not certain that Lewis Sheafe would have read these articles, published just a few months before his public commitment to the Adventist cause. If he did read the articles, he would surely have seen in them a kindred spirit. Even if not, he would certainly have known of the ambitious mission only recently launched by J. Edson White, who used a steamboat, the *Morning Star*, as the base for carrying out his mother's vision for the South.[20]

The work, views, and personal support of Battle Creek's most famous personage, Dr. John Harvey Kellogg, was prominent among the influences drawing Sheafe to Adventism. The draw came from much more than the doctor's health reform principles, as important as those were to the pastor who for years had sought, with little apparent success, relief for his recurring problems. The intense idealism and seemingly boundless energy of the medical missionary and benevolent enterprises spearheaded by Kellogg were at their zenith in the Battle Creek of the mid-1890s. Well-trained, talented young people motivated by the grand purpose of bringing the healing love of Jesus in practical ways to those in most desperate need poured forth from Battle Creek to points throughout the nation and globe during those years. Many went to Chicago, where Adventist endeavors to transform lives decimated by poverty, alcohol, prostitution, or any number of other pernicious forces were most thoroughly implemented.[21]

More specific to Sheafe's foremost concerns, Kellogg brooked no compromise with the color line at Battle Creek Sanitarium and related institutions. He encouraged the training of Black physicians and nurses. In the South Dr. Kellogg joined efforts with philanthropist Almira Steele in operating an orphanage for Black children in Chattanooga. The doctor was also a valued supporter of Booker T. Washington and the Tuskegee Institute.[22]

In sum Sheafe was introduced to an Adventism that regarded racial equality as a gospel principle, anchored in biblical authority:

"In the investigation of the truth, I was taught that this people took the Bible as their guide in all questions of right and wrong, and from the Bible we were to learn our relation to God and man, and that this relation is based on principles that never change. That God is *our* Father, and *all* ye are brethren. This was good news to me, and had the ring of the gospel of Christ."[23]

PREACHING THE MESSAGE IN OHIO

Immediately upon Sheafe's joining the Adventist cause, competing church entities vied for the services of the eloquent convert. Dr. Kellogg, who took a generally dim view of the caliber of Adventist ministers, saw in Sheafe a refreshing contrast, a man more "liberally educated," more "cultivated," and more rhetorically skillful than any other Adventist minister. Additionally, Sheafe was dedicated to health reform, while, in Kellogg's view, the general run of Adventist ministry was halfhearted at best. Thus, Kellogg and Mrs. Steele, who ran a string of benevolent institutions throughout the South,[24] wanted Sheafe to connect his evangelistic ministry with these institutions, thereby advancing Adventism's wholistic gospel as a means of uplift for the region's impoverished and oppressed African-Americans. Such work would be conducted under the auspices of the increasingly influential Medical Missionary and Benevolent Association (MMBA), which operated independently of the General Conference and of local conferences.

However, General Conference president O. A. Olsen rebuffed Kellogg's initial effort to detach Sheafe from conference-based work. After Sheafe returned from Battle Creek to his home in Urbana in late July with his health "greatly improved,"[25] the Ohio Conference hired the preacher to labor "on the same plan as our other ministers." It would be best for Sheafe's future in the Adventist cause, Olsen told Kellogg in early September, that he remain, for the time being at least, under that arrangement.[26]

While the Sheafe family residence relocated to Battle Creek in August, the elder joined with W. L. Iles in conducting tent meetings at Urbana.[27] The editor of the Urbana newspaper, which in the past had given Sheafe generally favorable coverage, took a dismissive attitude toward the noted preacher's changed convictions. "Elder Sheafe, it appears, has suspended the status quo because he wants to rest on Saturday rather than Sunday," the editor observed. While the newspaperman saw nothing particularly wrong with that, he failed to grasp why the question mattered. Therefore, he preferred to "conform to the general usage" by sticking with the familiar Sunday.[28]

After the Urbana meetings concluded in September, Sheafe traveled throughout Ohio, taking advantage of his connections and reputation to gain speaking opportunities at churches of various denominations. This set a pattern for his career as an Adventist preacher. As an evangelist he preached "present truth" with full force, and in so doing sacrificed much by way of popularity and success, measured in superficial terms. At the same time, he did not burn bridges connecting him with ministerial colleagues in other denominations. This created opportunities for witness, and his influence would lead some to join him in the Adventist movement. It also kept him in a position to make common cause with them on issues of shared concern.

At Bellefontaine, some 20 miles north of Urbana, the "colored Baptist

Church" opened its doors to Sheafe for two weeks of nightly meetings in November. He reported "large congregations of both colored and white people" and expressed gratitude for the "few Sabbathkeepers" who lived there for supporting him "nobly." With plans to return and build on the interest in Bellefontaine, he went on to Ohio's capital city the following month.

In Columbus Sheafe experienced, perhaps for the first time, serious disconfirmation of his initial assumption that "all Sabbathkeepers were the same, and accepted the same truths" of biblically based racial equality that he had heard espoused in Battle Creek.[29] Dr. Kellogg reported to O. A. Olsen that while Sheafe was preaching "there suddenly appeared such a big color line that he was obliged to suspend," and that the experience had left the preacher "thoroughly discouraged." The letter relaying this incident was sent to the General Conference president in a renewed effort by Dr. Kellogg and Mrs. Steele to get Sheafe released from the Ohio Conference so that he could work under their auspices in the South. Kellogg made the further point that the conference wasn't paying Sheafe enough to support his family. During a run of very cold days in January, Annie ran out of coal and had turned to Kellogg for help. He had a ton delivered, at his expense, to the family's residence at 48 Howard Street.[30]

As for his experience in Columbus, Sheafe managed to find a positive angle for a report to the Ohio Conference paper, the *Welcome Visitor*. It was, he said, a season of "deep heart searching" in which "many confessions were made, duty blossomed into privilege, and drooping hearts were aroused." Apparently the "tithes and offerings" was another issue with which the believers in Columbus had been struggling, for Sheafe reported that the matter had been "brought forcibly home to many" and that an offering of $50-$60 had been collected.[31]

While the incident in Columbus foreshadowed larger controversies over the color line to come, a response to the work in Cleveland he began after the new year illustrated another emerging pattern. White Adventists, by and large, seemed to find Sheafe to be not only a compelling preacher and talented singer, but also a man of admirable integrity and winsome personality. In Cleveland Sheafe assisted Elder W. H. Saxby in ministering to the Adventist church and in the work of the mission on the west side of the city. He also accepted several invitations to speak at the city's Black churches of various denominations.[32]

One White Adventist in Cleveland upon whom Sheafe made a strongly favorable impression, Walter Scott Chapman, claimed descent from the famed Scottish author Sir Walter Scott.[33] What struck Chapman even more strongly than the recently converted preacher's obvious talents was his "absolute consecration." The fact that Sheafe had given up "a highly remunerative position to devote his life to the building up of a poor people, proves his sincerity," Chapman reasoned.[34]

In February Sheafe's itinerancy around Ohio in the Adventist cause took him back to the Youngstown area, the locale of his second major pastorate as a Baptist. At Ellsworth, the small town southwest of the city where he had preached for the Christian Endeavor convention two and a half years before, Sheafe conducted a three-week series of meetings in February. A report in the Salem *Daily News* commented on responses, apparently from predominantly White audiences, to the eloquent Black preacher now that he had identified with a new faith:

"Elder Sheafe holds to the doctrines and methods of the Seventh Day Adventists, and occasionally, he is given the 'cold shoulder' from the 'holier than thou sort of man,' but this prejudice is giving way as did the same feeling which was manifested toward the Friends, early Methodists, Baptists, and many other denominations."

The writer found Sheafe to be a "very instructive and entertaining teacher" whose impressive knowledge of the Bible and presentation skills enabled listeners at least to suspend racial prejudice, looking beyond the color question to "only see the man and the grand truths he so earnestly presents."[35]

Sheafe's own report in the *Welcome Visitor* stated that the "power of the Lord was present to heal the people." It is not completely clear whether he meant that physical as well as spiritual healings occurred, but here is one of the pentecostal or charismatic traces that recur occasionally through his career. As a result of the well-attended meetings, "two precious souls resolved by the Lord's help to be obedient to the truth."[36]

In Youngstown itself he preached for the AME church's Sunday evening service on March 7, and the following Friday evening met with a group at the home of Mrs. R. B. Jackson to lead what the Cleveland *Gazette* described in a vague but tantalizing way as "a very interesting meeting."[37]

Then, during its Spring Meeting in Battle Creek, the General Conference Committee made the decision to launch Sheafe beyond the

Ohio Conference, toward a broader ministry for his people. His mission to the South was about to begin, though his agenda and sponsors remained contested matters.

---

[1] JHK to EGW, Dec. 19, 1900, Ellen G. White Estate, Silver Spring, Md. (hereafter cited as EGWE).

[2] Lewis C. Sheafe, "Kentucky," *Review and Herald* (hereafter cited as *Review*), June 13, 1899, p. 15.

[3] General Conference Committee (hereafter cited as GCC) minutes, Mar. 28, 1897, Archives of the General Conference of Seventh-day Adventists (hereafter cited as GCA).

[4] Dennis Pettibone, "An Adventist Apostle to Dixie," *Adventist Heritage* 14 (Fall 1991): 4-11, 33.

[5] "A New Faith Comes," CA, p. 2.

[6] "Rev. L. C. Sheafe," *Appeal*, Jan. 17, 1891, p. 1.

[7] "Church Life in St. Paul," St. Paul *Pioneer Press*, Jan. 1, 1892, p. 12; "Origin of Sunday Laws," Saint Paul *Daily Globe*, Apr. 25, 1889.

[8] *General Conference Daily Bulletin* (hereafter cited as GCDB), Feb. 22, 1899, p. 50.

[9] LCS to EGW, May 23, 1899, EGWE.

[10] "Editorial Notes," *Review*, July 21, 1896, p. 16.

[11] Louis B. Reynolds, *We Have Tomorrow: The Story of American Seventh-day Adventists With an African Heritage* (Washington, D.C.: Review and Herald, 1984), pp. 19-27; Delbert W. Baker, *The Unknown Prophet* (Hagerstown, Md.: Review and Herald, 1987).

[12] Gerald Wheeler, *James White: Innovator and Overcomer* (Hagerstown, Md.: Review and Herald, 2003), pp. 111, 112, 167.

[13] Reynolds, pp. 173-175, 226, 227.

[14] "Bro. Barry Bounced," *Western Appeal*, June 23, 1888. The newspaper's section on happenings in Louisville gives a wry account: "Rev. J. Frank preached a powerful sermon last Sunday morning from the text 'Look to Jesus,' the effect of which was spoiled by the announcement from the pulpit that Bro. Barry had been excluded from the church for following the example of Christ while on earth and keeping the Sabbath day holy."

[15] Reynolds, p. 113; J. Michael Utzinger, "The Third Angel's Message for My People: Charles M. Kinny and the Founding of the Seventh-day Adventist Missions Among Southern African Americans, 1889-1895," *Fides et Historia*, Winter/Spring 1998, p. 39.

[16] R. M. Kilgore, "Tennessee Camp Meeting and Nashville Institute," *Review*, Oct. 29, 1889, p. 11.

[17] Ellen G. White, "Our Duty to the Colored People," manuscript dated Mar. 20, 1891, initially published as a leaflet, later published in *The Southern Work* (originally published by J. E. White in 1898 and 1901; reprinted by the Ellen G. White Estate in 1966), p. 15.

[18] *Ibid.*, p. 11.

[19] Ellen G. White, "An Example in History," *Review*, Dec. 17, 1895, pp. 1, 2; see also *The Southern Work*, p. 44.

[20] Ronald D. Graybill, *Mission to Black America: The True Story of James Edson White and the Riverboat* Morning Star (Mountain View, Calif.: Pacific Press, 1971).

[21] Richard Rice, "Adventists and Welfare Work," *Spectrum* 2 (Winter 1970): 52-63.

[22] Richard William Schwarz, "John Harvey Kellogg: American Health Reformer" (Ph.D. dissertation, University of Michigan, 1964), pp. 316-340; Gary C. Jenkins, "Almira S. Steele and the Steele Home for Needy Children," *Adventist Heritage* 11 (Fall 1986): 26-29.

[23] LCS to EGW, May 23, 1899, EGWE.

[24] Myrta B. Castle, "For Humanity's Sake," *Review*, May 26, 1896, p. 5.

[25] "Local News," Urbana *Citizen and Gazette and Champaign Republican,* July 27, 1896, p. 6.

[26] OAO to JKH, Sept. 4, 1896, GCA.

[27] Estella Houser to C.B.F. Jones and wife, Sept. 6, 1896, Ohio Tract and Missionary Society letterbook, 1896-1898, Box 3, Ohio Conference Historical Records collection 183, Center for Adventist Research, Andrews University, Berrien Springs, Michigan (hereafter cited as CAR).

[28] Untitled paragraph on the editorial page, Urbana *Citizen*, Aug. 13, 1896, p. 2.

[29] LCS to EGW, May 25,1899, EGWE.

[30] JHK to OAO, Feb. 21, 1897, EGWE.

[31] "The Work and Workers," *Welcome Visitor,* Dec. 17, 1896, p. 2; "Local Brevities," Bellefontaine *Republican,* Nov. 13, 1896, p. 3.

[32] "The Work and Workers," *Welcome Visitor,* Mar. 18, 1897, p. 3.

[33] Obituary, *Review,* Oct. 1, 1925, p. 22.

[34] W. S. Chapman to OAO, Feb. 1, 1897, GCA.

[35] "Ellsworth," Salem *Daily News,* Feb. 12, 1897, p. 8.

[36] "The Work and Workers," *Welcome Visitor,* Mar. 18, 1897, p. 3.

[37] "Good News," Cleveland *Gazette,* Mar. 20, 1897, p. 1.

CHAPTER X

INTO THE SOUTH

FOURTEEN-YEAR-OLD HATTIE WINGATE was the only one home when the fire broke out. Her mind went immediately to the huge tent that had arrived just three days before from Battle Creek to be stored at the Wingates' home until it was pitched. The courageous and quick-thinking teenager knew it had to be saved. With, no doubt, a prayer and a rush of adrenaline, she dragged the 40-foot tent to safety, even as most of the household goods were destroyed. Days later, when it was time to return the tent to storage, it took the combined strength of both of the evangelists—Lewis C. Sheafe and James R. Buster—to move it.[1]

The fire was only one of the perplexities the preachers faced in getting the evangelistic campaign underway. No sooner had they reached Louisville in early May than they received word from the General Conference secretary, L. T. Nicola, that the General Conference would not be able to supply a tent for the meetings after all. Disappointed and puzzled as to the reason for the change in plans, Elder Buster wrote back, giving assurances of financial support from the small group of Black believers in Louisville.[2] Unbeknown to Buster, and possibly to Sheafe—though the latter must at least have had an inkling—the primary issue was not money but indecision in the General Conference Committee over Sheafe's assignment.

O. A. Olsen had apparently been won over to Kellogg's view of the mission that Sheafe should take up in the South. After the General Conference session of 1897, at which G. A. Irwin was chosen as the new president, Olsen joined with Kellogg to "press the matter" of Sheafe's "engaging in more general work, and visiting these public institutions, such as Booker T. Washington's, and some of Mrs. Steele's schools, and, in a more general way, getting these more intelligent people interested in our line of work." Irwin could see some light in the proposal. He noted that "quite a number of very intelligent colored people have accepted the truth through Sister Steele's influence in getting them to the [Battle Creek] Sanitarium." It seemed plausible that Sheafe's gifts might best be used in this kind of work.[3]

So shipment of the tent to Louisville was put on hold while the General Conference officers reconsidered the matter. In the end, they decided to stay with the original plan for Louisville. Within a week after Buster and Sheafe had received the disappointing message from Battle Creek, plans were back on course, and the tent was finally on its way.[4] With regard to the more fundamental question of Sheafe's job description, a compromise arrangement apparently had been worked out. During his years of ministry in the South, Sheafe would alternate between evangelistic and pastoral work under the auspices of District No. 2 of the General Conference, and several stints of about six weeks to three months of ministry in Chattanooga in conjunction with the Steele Home and the Helping Hand Mission, affiliated with the Kellogg-led MMBA.

When their tent finally arrived, Sheafe and Buster found that it lacked a center pole and stakes. To acquire these, along with the lumber for benches, gasoline torches for lighting, and other fixtures, the preachers had to scrape together cash from what little they personally had and the believers could donate. In reporting to Battle Creek, Buster pointed out that it was impossible for them to obtain lumber on credit, as Elder J. W. Collie, who was simultaneously conducting tent meetings in Louisville for White audiences, had been able to do.[5]

Another disappointment also mingled with the joy at the tent's arrival. It was not accompanied by a "living tent"—or small tent—that the evangelists could use for their living quarters. Because a gang of 25 to 30 boys roamed the neighborhood, threatening mischief or worse, the preachers could not go elsewhere to stay and thereby leave the meeting grounds unattended overnight. So for the first two weeks of the meetings they slept in the tent, which necessitated taking their bedding and other personal items to the home of a neighbor in the morning and then bringing them back to the tent after the meeting was over and everyone had gone home.[6] By the time their "living tent" arrived in town, the preachers were too broke to pay either the freight charge or the charge for getting it hauled from the train station to their meeting site. So another mini-fund-raising campaign became necessary.[7]

EVANGELISM IN LOUISVILLE WITH J. R. BUSTER

It is the pathos-filled letters of James Buster (1858-1907), even more than Sheafe's own letters, that provide details about the struggles the two encountered during the early weeks of the Louisville meetings. A year after accepting "present truth" in 1885, Brother Buster left a good-paying job ($13 per week) as the manager of a "gentleman's café" in Chicago to take up canvassing with Adventist literature.[8] Despite intermittent successes, financial misfortune plagued his years as a colporteur. Responsibility for his aged parents, as well as for his wife and children, placed further stress on him. As a result, he became mired in debt to the Review and Herald Publishing Association, and to several individuals who had helped him, including J. N. Loughborough, G. B. Starr, and R. M. Kilgore.

Through his canvassing work, Buster had led several individuals into the Adventist Church, including a small group of White people in southern Illinois. One of these, a widow, had asked him why he was not in the ministry, preaching the Adventist message to his people. Brother Buster had to explain, with embarrassment, that his encumbrance with debt prevented him from doing so. The woman gave him $255, and later promised to assume all his debts on interest in order to free him to enter the ministry, though she could not liquidate them immediately. The General Conference Committee, however, did not see light in the proposal, and instructed Buster that he must first pay his debts.

So in May 1894 the disappointed worker turned to Ellen White, then residing in Granville, Australia. With what he could earn through canvassing, he wrote, he would probably be in debt until the Lord returns. Even with the help promised from friends, it would be at least another year or two before he could be completely free. He had waited nine years "for the privilege of working for the upbuilding of my people, and bringing the truth before them." During those years he had demonstrated ability to win people for the cause. How much longer would it have to be, he wondered, particularly when so little was being done to reach the Colored race?

"Now Sister White, as I see no organized effort made whatever, excepting the work your son has on foot to bring the truth before the colored people, my soul is made to burn almost with anguish for them. . . . Have you any light for me? Must I stay in the canvassing work a year or two longer, perhaps carrying the truth to white people, when there are already hundreds of laborers among them and none among the colored?"

After reading Buster's letter, Ellen White sent a testimony chiding the church leaders in Battle Creek for not taking a deeper or more sympathetic interest in Buster's situation and the potential he offered in doing a neglected work. She admonished them to "bear in mind that there have been times when our white brethren have had to receive substantial help, something more than the mere words, 'Be ye warmed and be ye clothed.'"[9]

In February of the following year the General Conference Committee approved an arrangement between the Illinois and Ohio conferences regarding "Brother J. R. Buster, a colored brother of Illinois, moving to Ohio to labor as the way might open."[10] A year later he went south, apparently working in Alabama and then Louisville, where he was granted a ministerial license in October 1896.[11]

At some point after 1898 Buster is reported to have become "discouraged" and left the ministry. In 1906, at tent meetings conducted by Luther Warren in Chicago, the erstwhile preacher "gave his heart anew to the Lord" and opened a "colored mission" in the city. But then, at the "height of the interest," he caught pneumonia and died on May 1, 1907.[12]

Though tragically cut short, James Buster's ministry left an enduring legacy. From the small company that formed in response to his efforts grew the Shiloh church, the largest Seventh-day Adventist congregation in Chicago, and from that a secondary school—Shiloh Academy.[13]

When the Louisville meetings opened on June 2, 1897, Buster estimated the attendance to be about 100, with the number steadily increasing during the next few meetings. According to a news note on the back page of the April 13 issue of the *Review and Herald*, Elders Sheafe and Buster had been assigned to "tent work" for "the colored people" in

Louisville,[14] and, as previously mentioned, concurrent meetings intended for the White population were being held by J. W. Collie. In his report in the *Review and Herald*, however, Buster made it clear that "so far as our tent meetings are concerned, the color line has 'gone a glimmering,' and the best class of people of all colors and shades, with their families, touch elbows on the same seats, and give the most diligent attention to the preaching of the word."[15]

In his monthly report to the General Conference secretary, Buster also made a point of declaring the approach to the race question taken at the Sheafe-Buster tent: "We do not propose to draw any color line or refer to it in any way. We firmly believe God will take care of all such things if we preach the truth in demonstration of the spirit and power."[16] By stating that both Black and White attendees "touch elbows," Buster made explicit that the races were not segregated into different seating sections within the tent.

Buster thoroughly enjoyed working with his colleague, Lewis Sheafe. "We pull together like a trained team," he said. He described his colaborer as "a most powerful and forceful speaker," and, with equal or greater emphasis, as "an earnest good man," and "a thoroughly consecrated man of keen good sense."[17]

Sheafe's perspective on the effort, while positive, seems more restrained. The preachers could report large and receptive audiences all through the summer, but little by way of decisions to join the Adventist Church. Sheafe found that individuals would approach him privately to learn more about biblical teachings, but were slow to take a public stand for "present truth." He saw a need for "personal work" that would help individuals understand and make the changes that needed to be implemented in order to live a truly Christian life. For example, he observed, "It is well-nigh impossible to have people continue in the truth as long as they are not taught to convert their surroundings."[18]

Immediately after bringing their meetings in Louisville to a close at the end of August, Sheafe and Buster headed for Lexington "to try and get matters straightened out in the church there."[19] Strife between the congregation's founding minister, Alfonso Barry, and leading members of the church had developed to the point where it seemed best that Elder Barry transfer to another assignment. In consultation with N. W. Allee, superintendent of the denomination's District No. 2 (the Southern field), it was decided that Sheafe should move to Lexington as pastor, and that Barry should take charge of the work in Covington, Kentucky.[20]

Before moving to Lexington, Sheafe spent six weeks helping develop the Adventist mission among the Black population in Chattanooga, Tennessee. The Steele Home for Needy Children provided a launching pad for his work in that city. To initiate evangelical work for the city's Black people, Sheafe held nightly meetings in a "large storeroom" that he had rented in "a thickly settled part of the city."[21] In Chattanooga, as elsewhere, the Black churches opened their pulpits to him on Sundays. He found it striking that "the Lord has led many in this city into the light, having no other teacher than the Holy Spirit." These people were clear on the truth without even knowing "the letter of the Book," having actually been "taught of God."[22]

PASTORAL MINISTRY IN LEXINGTON

Elder Charles L. Boyd of the Tennessee River Conference was not exaggerating when he described the group of believers he met with at Lexington, Kentucky, in 1894 as a "company of refined and intelligent colored people." In fact, he may have been guilty of understatement.[23] The church's charter members included Mary E. Britton (1855-1925), civil rights activist, journalist, and schoolteacher, who also became Kentucky's first African-American female physician in 1904, after graduating from the American Medical Missionary College in Battle Creek. Paul Laurence Dunbar celebrated Britton's ringing protest against a "separate coach bill" at the Kentucky state legislature in 1893 with a poem, "To Miss Mary Britton."[24]

Another member, J. Alexander Chiles, may have been Lexington's first African-American attorney when he opened his practice in 1890. Also a civil rights advocate, Chiles argued in 1910 for desegregation of railroad coaches before the Supreme Court in a case involving the Chesapeake and Ohio Railroad. The new group of believers in Lexington also included the principal of the Colored School No. 2, W. C. Taylor.[25] General Conference president G. A. Irwin referred to the congregation as "the most intelligent company of colored people we have in the South."[26]

Sheafe seemed to view his assignment to Lexington as something approximating settled parish ministry, for he decided to move his family there from Battle Creek, where they had moved after leaving Urbana. He and Annie, with their three children—Clara, 8; Howard, 6; and 18-month-old Lewis, Jr.—were "trying to keep house once more," he wrote.[27]

The source of the contention between Elder Barry and the lay leaders in Lexington is unclear, but by 1897 it had become very clear that the church was dysfunctional. After being inundated with letters and visits about the situation, G. A. Irwin felt it safe to conclude that "there is wrong all around." He described Barry as "intelligent in many ways" and able to exert "an influence even with the white people" but "inclined to be a little overbearing and dictatorial." On the other hand, Irwin viewed Attorney Chiles, whom he called the "principal disturbing element on the other side," as "rather high-spirited" and desirous of being regarded as a leader.[28]

In a report published in the *Review and Herald*, Sheafe referred to the situation only in the most general terms, stating that some of the believers "had lost heart in the struggle against sin." After his return from Chattanooga in November, a season of repentance had led to "refreshing showers of blessing" and renewed desire to do the Lord's will.[29] As their pastor, Sheafe led them to act on that desire by implementing various lines of endeavor representing the wholistic program that Adventism offered.

Health reform was one of the aspects of Adventism that Sheafe found especially appealing. He had personally benefited from treatment at Battle Creek Sanitarium and had taken brief training in health education and principles.[30] Of the revived church at Lexington he could say, "All have taken firm hold of the principles of health reform, and can testify to the benefits derived therefrom."[31]

In his evangelistic work Sheafe found presentations on health principles to be useful as "an entering wedge to open the way for presenting the truth." An incident in Lexington illustrated the point. The Sheafes' neighbors near the house they rented on Clay Street included "the principal of the schools in the city of Lexington and his wife." This couple, however, was "so prejudiced against us" that the Sheafes had little interaction with them. Around 11:00 one night, though, the wife knocked frantically on their door, crying "Elder, will you come over to see my husband—he is raving." The school administrator had become so agitated over his work problems that "his nerves were all unstrung, and he could not sleep."

Annie quickly grabbed the "Hand-book" for treatments from the shelf, but Lewis could not seem to locate the information he was looking for. So he prayed for guidance and decided to apply hot-water fomentations to the man's spine. These, along with a rubdown, had the man asleep in 10 minutes. Around 10:00 the next morning he was still sleeping, and the wife called over the fence, asking if she should wake him. No, let him sleep, replied the elder, and the man did so until noon. Later the school official said that nothing he had previously experienced had benefited him so much as that treatment. "There is now a warm place in that man's heart for our people," said Sheafe.[32]

The Lexington church also became active in "Christian Help work," which included bringing relief not only to the sick, but also to the poor, the uneducated, and all those oppressed or victimized in any way. Christian Help work became part of the denomination's program and terminology in the 1890s, the era of great medical missionary endeavors led by Dr. John Harvey Kellogg,[33] and the use would continue into the 1950s. In its January 1898 issue, published just when Sheafe was in Lexington, *The Gospel of Health* periodical urged that "every Seventh-day Adventist church ought to be an organized Christian Help band," and thus become "recognized as an uplifting force in its community, as an association of Christians who are competent to deal with every form of human need, physical, mental, and moral."[34]

At the Lexington church that winter, Christian Help work took the form of visiting the imprisoned and "homes that are darkened by sin and neglect." To meet basic needs, the women of the church made and gave away "a great many garments," and "fuel and food have been provided for many more."[35]

Sheafe also took up the cause of religious liberty while in Lexington, as did his parishioner, attorney Chiles.[36] Religious liberty, and the threat posed to it by Sunday laws and proposed constitutional amendments declaring the United States to be a Christian nation, had been a prominent theme for Seventh-day Adventists since the 1850s. It was in the 1880s, though, that Adventists became activists in the public arena to combat the danger of legislation that would give state support to religion. The church launched a periodical, the *American Sentinel*, in 1886, dedicated to preserving the U.S. Constitution with regard to religion, and to "the maintenance of human rights, both civil and religious." In 1889 the National Religious Liberty Association was organized for the same purposes.

As the Adventist work in the region gradually expanded during the 1880s and 1890s, the South became the front line of the battle against Sunday laws. Facing more rigorous enforcement and stiffer penalties than in other parts of the nation, scores of Adventists were imprisoned, and some were sentenced to chain gang labor in the South during these decades.[37]

An upsurge in sentiment for strong Sunday-closing laws stirred among the Christian clergy of Lexington just at the time of Sheafe's arrival. Near the beginning of December he attended a city ministers' meeting at which sentiment prevailed in favor of greater involvement by ministers in politics. Sheafe wrote, in an article published in the *American Sentinel*, that only one of the 10 Protestant ministers present expressed objection to the idea that preachers ought to "go into politics to purify them." He quoted one minister who supported measures against Sunday desecration as well as to "close all saloons and such places," as saying, "It is our duty to make the people stop doing wrong, and teach them what is right in politics as well as in religion."[38]

When called upon to speak, the Adventist minister said, "Brethren, you have ignored the fact that each of the many denominations would want to run the government on its own church plan, and there would be a worse muddle than we now have." He pointed to the history of "evils and cruelties" when church and state have intertwined, and to the "present attitude of the papal power toward this government."

Had Sheafe, who had been so involved with public issues as a Baptist minister, changed his view on the church's relationship to politics as a result of becoming an Adventist? Definite conclusions at this point, without the benefit of events yet to transpire over the subsequent few years, would be premature. Certainly, though, in the case of the Lexington Sunday law reform movement, he found himself in opposition to the Christian Endeavor, in which he had been so active in previous years.[39]

More noteworthy, though, is that the point Sheafe emphasized most strongly at the city ministers' meeting in Lexington in 1897 harmonizes with the main point of his sermon, "Rights, Civil and Otherwise," at the rally in St. Paul for the Minnesota Civil Rights Committee in 1891. In both instances the guiding principle he uplifted was that the church and its ministry represents a higher loyalty and a greater power than that of partisan politics. The church, therefore, must not allow itself to be reduced to the framework of human political struggle, and thereby become captive to a partisan agenda.

He told his colleagues in Lexington that "the minister of Christ had a high calling, second to none, not even to that of the president of these United States, for the minister is called and commissioned of God. His citizenship is in heaven, and his business is to preach the Word, nothing more, nothing less. He is called and separated unto the gospel of God. He must come out, be separate, touch not the unclean thing. You have all acknowledged that politics are very unclean; so, brethren, take your hands off."

Furthermore, he pointed out, in the gospel order that the church represents, freedom, not coercion, reigns.

"Then, brethren, this making people Christian by the arm of the civil law is foreign to the gospel. God leaves every man free to choose. The essence of the gospel is freedom, which voluntarily submits to absolute truth—freedom of affection, and freedom of the will."[40]

Armed with "a large budget of tracts" from the Religious Liberty Association, Sheafe and the Lexington believers countered the flurry of meetings and rallies on behalf of Sunday rest laws in January and February of 1898. By March the momentum had subsided, and Sheafe could report that the materials the Adventists had disseminated "seem to have acted like oil on the troubled waters."[41]

Interaction with the clergy of Lexington also prompted another article from Sheafe in the *American Sentinel*, this one on one of the major theological issues of the day—"higher criticism" of the Bible—which he believed was at the same time an issue of religious liberty.[42] While many of the city's preachers had become enamored with the "so-called discoveries" of "higher criticism," Sheafe pointed out that the modern scholarship was suffused with an arrogance that, like that of the medieval "papists," denied the individual believer the right of free interpretation of the Word of God. Just as the medieval church placed the authority to interpret the Bible in the hands of popes and councils and withheld it from the people of God, so "higher criticism" declared that "it is not safe for one not well versed in the languages to attempt to do much with the Bible."

Sheafe upheld Martin Luther's majestic defense at the Leipzig disputation, of the freedom of all Christians to read and interpret the Bible for themselves. Only with this Reformation principle would "the people be emancipated from the middle ages, and arise in their power and majesty, obey the voice of enlightened conscience, and be true to their convictions." As a preacher of "present truth," Sheafe warned against the new danger to religious liberty from ceding a monopoly on biblical understanding to an academic elite, thereby depriving the individual believer of access to the light for the present day shining forth from God's dynamic Word.

"Don't put the scholarship of men above the wisdom of God, for God has hid these things from the wise and the prudent and revealed them unto babes. The doubts and denials of scriptural facts, by the so-called higher critics, have gotten men into a fog, and today men and women are skeptical as to the existence of God, the moral government of the world, the truth of Christianity, and the reality of the supernatural. Now the way out of this fog is by a living faith in the living Word of God. Give it prayerful study. It has light yet to reveal for these times."

EVANGELISTIC SUCCESS IN GEORGETOWN

The varied endeavors of the Lexington church under Sheafe's leadership—health reform, Christian Help work, and advocacy for religious liberty—were all part of its overriding evangelistic mission. However, in Lexington, as in many other places, Sheafe found the lack of a church building, or even a truly suitable rented facility, to be a formidable obstacle to church growth. In March 1898 he reported that he was holding "Bible readings" with a number of people and that attendance at the church's public meetings by nonmembers was consistently good. He added, though, that "many more" would attend "if our place of worship were more suitable."[43] Whether it was primarily because of frustrations there or the urgency of invitations from surrounding locales, Sheafe would spend most of the remainder of 1898 away from Lexington, while still formally based there.

On May 1 he returned to Chattanooga and labored there for three months. Since his time in the city the previous year a Helping Hand Mission had been opened, under the supervision of O. N. Whetsel. The Chattanooga mission was one of 27 dedicated to advancing Christian Help work in cities throughout the nation, coordinated by Dr. Kellogg's Medical Missionary and Benevolent Association.[44] Sheafe conducted nightly street meetings along with the meetings conducted in the mission itself. By the end of May the work had yielded 15 "hopeful conversions."[45]

It was in Georgetown, Kentucky, though, that Sheafe experienced his first success in raising up a substantial new company of believers in the Adventist message. In late August he reunited with James Buster for an evangelistic effort in this town about 15 miles northeast of Lexington. Here the preachers succeeded in drumming up attendance by going out to the street corners to preach and sing around 7:00 each evening. Around 7:30 they would proceed to the tent, which would fill up within a few minutes. The duo continued the "no color line" policy they had followed in Louisville, and found both races well represented throughout meetings, which continued into November. "We have perfect order," Buster assured L. A. Hoopes, the General Conference secretary, adding that "the white people give expression to great surprise at the manner in which the meetings are conducted and the preaching they hear."[46]

The Georgetown meetings created such a favorable impression on Scott County officials that in October, when the weather turned too cold for tent meetings, they offered the preachers use of the county courthouse, with heat and light furnished free of charge. Elder E. H. Gates, in a supervisory visit to churches throughout Tennessee and Kentucky, found "excellent interest and attendance" at the meetings conducted by "Brethren Buster and Sheafe." At the time of Gates's visit in November, a Sabbath school had been organized, and the following month Buster indicated that the company of new believers in Georgetown numbered about 15, and was comprised of both White and Colored members.[47] According to R. Eason, a White convert from Lexington, "several of the very best white people" in Georgetown were convinced that Sheafe and Buster were preaching the truth, but "owing to their prejudices," they could not bring themselves "to step out and take their stand under colored men."[48]

Eason acknowledged that his own conversion to a new faith through the ministry of a Black preacher, Sheafe, was "a very uncommon circumstance in this Southland." But, he testified, "the truth came to me and I was compelled to yield to it." Though offered a better position if he would remain, Eason gave up his work as an agent for the Singer Sewing Machine Company to become one for the Battle Creek Sanitarium Food Company.[49]

FINANCIAL AND FAMILY STRUGGLES

While ambitious, wide-ranging endeavor and encouraging signs of success marked Sheafe's brief time as a pastor-evangelist based in Lexington, his family's situation was unsettled and financially stressed. When he received his ministerial license at the end of March 1897, Sheafe was placed on the General Conference payroll with a salary of $10 per week.

The General Conference in this era paid its workers on a "four-fifths" basis. The Battle Creek office did not automatically issue payroll checks; rather it was up to workers to write in and request payment. Under the four-fifths policy, however, they were permitted to draw only up to 80 percent of the amount credited to their account in accordance with their salary rate. The remaining 20 percent was held in the treasury so that the Conference could meet emergencies and special needs, such as illness and moving expenses.

Additionally, even payment requested by a worker within the 80 percent limit was subject to a delayed or partial fulfillment, depending upon availability of funds in the General Conference Treasury. An auditing committee met each spring to determine how much of the workers' full salary from the previous year remained due them.

Despite queries to several "brethren," Sheafe did not fully understand the system until L. A. Hoopes explained it to him in December 1897. The aspect of the plan that made Sheafe uncomfortable was that it put the worker in the somewhat-demeaning position of having to request wages due. He wrote Hoopes that he disliked nothing more than having to ask for money, and proposed that the amount due him on the four-fifths basis simply be sent him at the beginning of each month, without his having to send a letter of request.[50] Hoopes agreed to do so, but did not follow through.[51]

So, as days ticked by at the beginning of the very next month—

January 1898—the eagerly anticipated check failed to arrive, forcing Sheafe once again to ask for money. A check for $25 finally arrived on the seventeenth. The failure of Elder Hoopes to follow through on the agreed-upon plan prompted a letter from the pastor detailing the financial burdens on his family and revealing the much greater pain behind his frustrations over procedure.[52]

Sheafe made three points to preempt possible questions about the legitimacy of his claims about the family's dire needs.

First, he and his family had financially sacrificed in devoting themselves to the Adventist movement. They had "used up what little money we had before entering this work," he stated.

Second, he was devoting his full time to "the interest of the cause," and not engaging in other pursuits.

Third, he and his family were "living just as economical as we know how on grains and beans, with no extras."

Then, he laid out the circumstances they faced in Lexington:

"When we pay out of $25.00—house rent, fuel bill, and get a few groceries, you can plainly see there is little or nothing left to get clothes and shoes for my wife and three children to say nothing of myself. It seems as though I ought to earn a little more than my board. I really don't see how we are to get along if we can't get money enough to pay living expenses. . . . My wife and children are in need of clothing right now, to make them comfortable. I am wearing my summer pants that I bought three years ago, for the simple reason that they are the only respectable pair that I have, and I have no means to get others."

Conditions remained difficult for the Sheafe family throughout the remainder of the unusually rainy winter. As a result of the dampness, "my family is not so well" and "we are much in need of some money," Sheafe wrote in late February, this time directing his request to the General Conference president, G. A. Irwin.[53] A week later he asked Hoopes to send $30, adding, "We are all out of money, food and fuel, and will probably remain so until we hear from you."[54]

By summer it had become clear that Lexington was not going to work out as the family residence. In August 1898 Sheafe requested a $30 advance from the General Conference to cover the costs of moving the family to Mount Vernon, Ohio, locale of a strong Adventist school that

9-year-old Clara and 7-year-old Howard could attend. The school in
Mount Vernon, he explained in his request for the moving advance, was
the "only available school for them that is not too far away."[55] Elder
Hoopes promptly sent the $30, but wondered why the Sheafes would
look to Mount Vernon, since the school in Graysville, Tennessee, would
be nearer to Lexington. Sheafe explained that the school in Huntsville,
Alabama—farther away than Mount Vernon—was the only Seventh-day
Adventist school in the South that admitted Black students.[56]

It seems likely that the family's difficult experience in Lexington also
contributed to the desire to relocate, since lack of proximity to an
Adventist school had not prevented the move there in the first place. At
any rate, Lewis and Annie wanted their children "trained up in the knowledge of the truth as taught in our schools,"[57] and Mount Vernon was the
ideal location for that. It would be home for Annie and the children for
nearly four years. The drawback, of course, was that Lewis would be separated from them for months at a time, seeing them mainly for a just a few
weeks around the Christmas season.

---

[1] J. R. Buster, "Kentucky," *Review*, June 29, 1897, p. 10.

[2] JRB to L. T. Nicola, May 9, 1897, GCA.

[3] GAI to NWA, Apr. 18, 1897, GCA.

[4] GAI to NWA, May 11, 1897, GCA.

[5] JRB to LAH, June 14, 1897, GCA.

[6] JRB to LAH, June 2, 1897, GCA.

[7] JRB to LAH, June 14, 1897, GCA.

[8] Buster narrates his experiences after becoming an Adventist in his lengthy letter sent
to Ellen White, May 29, 1894, EGWE.

[9] Ellen G. White, *The Ellen G. White 1888 Materials* (Silver Spring, Md.: Ellen G. White
Estate, 1987), p. 1268.

[10] GCC minutes, Feb. 8, 1895.

[11] GCC minutes, Mar. 11 and Oct. 11, 1896.

[12] Obituary by J. Tabor, *Review*, June 20, 1907, p. 23.

[13] Interview, C. E. Bradford, July 11, 2007; L. B. Reynolds, *We Have Tomorrow*, pp. 213, 214.

[14] "Editorial Notes," *Review*, Apr. 13, 1897, p. 16.

[15] J. R. Buster, "Kentucky."

[16] JRB to LAH, June 2, 1897, GCA.

[17] JRB to LAH, June 14, 1897, and Sept. 2, 1898, GCA.

[18] LCS to LAH, July 20, 1897, and Aug. 13, 1897, GCA.

[19] JRB to LAH, Aug. 31, 1897, GCA.

[20] LCS to LAH, Aug. 31, 1897, and Nov. 10, 1897, GCA.

[21] LCS to LAH, Oct. 19, 1897, GCA.

[22] "A Letter," *Review*, Nov. 2, 1897, p. 13.

[23] C. L. Boyd, "Tennessee River Conference," *Review,* Feb. 20, 1894, p. 13.

[24] Paul Laurence Dunbar digital collection, Wright State University, http://www.libraries.wright.edu/special/dunbar/poems/oak_and_ivy/to_miss_mary_britton.html (accessed Aug. 30, 2009).

[25] Lexington Seventh-day Adventist Church history document, South Central Conference Web site, http://www.scc-adventist.org/forms/Lexington%20Timeline%20History.pdf (accessed Aug. 30, 2009).

[26] GAI to NWA, June 27, 1897, GCA.

[27] LCS to LAH, Nov. 10, 1897, GCA.

[28] GAI to NWA, June 27 and July 4, 1897, GCA.

[29] Lewis C. Sheafe, "Kentucky," *Review,* Mar. 29, 1898, pp. 11, 12.

[30] GCDB, Feb. 22, 1899, p. 50.

[31] Sheafe, "Kentucky," p. 11.

[32] GCDB, Feb. 22, 1899, p. 50.

[33] See J. H. Kellogg, M.D., "Work of the Medical Missionary and Benevolent Association," *General Conference Bulletin* (hereafter cited as GCB), Feb. 4, 1895, p. 4, for an explanation of "Christian Help work."

[34] Editorial introduction, *The Gospel of Health,* January 1898, pp. 1, 2.

[35] Sheafe, "Kentucky," p. 11.

[36] A note in the *American Sentinel,* Sept. 9, 1897, p. 7, quotes from a letter sent by Chiles with his remittance for several subscriptions in which the attorney declares strong interest in dissemination of the principles espoused in the periodical.

[37] See Douglas Morgan, *Adventism and the American Republic* (Knoxville: University of Tennessee Press, 2001), pp. 40-43, 47.

[38] Lewis C. Sheafe, "What Part Should a Minister of Christ Take in Politics?" *American Sentinel,* Dec. 23, 1897, p. 789.

[39] "Sunday-closing Movement in Lexington, Kentucky," *American Sentinel,* Feb. 10, 1898, p. 10.

[40] Sheafe, "What Part Should a Minister of Christ Take in Politics?" p. 791.

[41] Sheafe, "Kentucky," pp. 11, 12.

[42] Lewis C. Sheafe, "Is the Bible Equal to It?" *American Sentinel,* Feb. 17, 1898, p. 106.

[43] Sheafe, "Kentucky," p. 11.

[44] See listings in *The Life Boat,* March 1899, p. 2.

[45] LCS to LAH, May 30, 1898, GCA.

[46] JRB to LAH, Sept. 2, 1898, GCA; LCS to LAH, Oct. 2, 1898, GCA.

[47] E. H. Gates, "Cumberland Mission Field," *Review,* Dec, 6, 1898, p. 12; JRB to LAH, Dec. 16, 1898, GCA.

[48] G. A. Irwin related Eason's account in a letter to N. W. Allee, Jan. 15, 1899, GCA.

[49] R. Eason to WCW, Nov. 14, 1900, EGWE; Lillian Pierce to LAH, Dec. 21, 1898, GCA.

[50] LCS to LAH, Dec. 12, 1897, GCA.

[51] LAH to LCS, Dec. 19, 1897, GCA.

[52] LCS to LAH, Jan. 12, 1898; Jan. 17, 1898, GCA.

[53] LCS to GAI, Feb. 23, 1898, GCA.

[54] LCS to LAH, Mar. 3, 1898, GCA.

[55] LCS to LAH, Aug. 15, 1898, GCA.

[56] LAH to LCS, Aug. 17, 1898, GCA; LCS to LAH, Aug. 19, 1898, GCA. Ironically, six decades later it was Mount Vernon Academy's rejection of applications from qualified Black students that prompted a protest campaign at the 1962 General Conference session, which in turn hastened landmark measures to redress racial injustice in the Seventh-day Adventist Church and its institutions; see Frank Hale, *Out of the Trash Came Truth* (Columbus, Ohio: Frank W. Hale, Jr., Ph.D., D.Hum., 2007).

[57] LCS to LAH, Aug. 19, 1898, GCA.

CHAPTER XI

MISSION TO THE "TALENTED TENTH"

"I WRITE TO INFORM YOU that the General Conference Committee has constituted you a delegate at large, to represent the colored race at our next General Conference, to be held at South Lancaster, Mass., February 14 to March 7."[1]

Lewis Sheafe had just returned to Kentucky after spending a few weeks at home in Ohio over the holiday season when he received this summons and credential from the General Conference secretary. The thirty-third General Conference session brought the 39-year-old preacher back to his home state of Massachusetts with official recognition as the leading figure among African-American Adventists. The New England Conference hosted the session, which opened February 15, 1899, on the grounds of the church's secondary school in the village of South Lancaster, about 40 miles west of Boston.

GENERAL CONFERENCE SESSION—1899

After brief remarks of welcome from H. W. Cottrell, president of the New England Conference, and G. A. Irwin, president of the General Conference, the first meeting was opened to testimonies—"expressions of gratitude to the Most High for blessings received"—from delegates. "Pioneers" such as J. N. Loughborough, S. H. Lane, R. A. Underwood, and J. H. Morrison, who had been Adventists since the first General Conference session in 1863 and earlier, testified to what the movement meant to them. Then leaders of more recent prominence spoke, including A. T. Jones, E. J. Waggoner, L. R. Conradi, W. W. Prescott, and Mrs. S.M.I. Henry, the former "national evangelist" for the Woman's Christian Temperance Union, who, like Sheafe, had joined the church in 1896 while at the Battle Creek Sanitarium.

Sheafe waited until the testimonial period was drawing to a close to express how deeply the Adventist message had gripped his soul, his vision for what it offered his people (and indeed, the nation as a whole), and the urgency that present needs and possibilities gave to the mission of carrying the message forward.

"As I have listened to the testimonies from these brethren who have been a long time in the third angel's message, my heart has been filled with joy. I have been in the truth only about three years; and although it seems as if every day is brighter than the one preceding, I have often wondered whether this is so in the experience of those who have been in the truth for so many years, or whether they had got to the point where the truth had lost its luster and sparkle and power. I thank God that in your experience it is dearer and more precious to you every day; for this gives me courage and confidence. I am glad that he permitted this light to come to me, and that he gave me grace to accept it; and today my heart's desire and prayer is that this message may go to my people all over the United States. . . . I have asked so many times, Why is it, Lord, that this truth did not come to my people before? The fact that it has come to us at last is indicative of the near close of time, and emphasizes the importance of our giving it to those yet in ignorance. The message is now reaching out for the poor negroes of the United States of America. I praise the Lord that many of their hearts are opening to receive it."[2]

Sheafe also commented on the session's convening in Massachusetts, not far from Plymouth Rock, at "a time when religious liberty is imperiled in this country." He hoped that as a result of the conference "this portion of the truth of the third angel's message"—the principles of religious liberty—would "take a fresh start, and get a deeper hold upon the hearts and consciences of the people."

Later in the session, on February 27, Sheafe was one of the first to speak to a motion declaring the "propriety of establishing in the South a training school for medical missionaries, especially for the work in this field."[3] Through the Southern Missionary Society, set up by J. Edson White, as well as the Medical Missionary and Benevolent Association (led by J. H. Kellogg), initiatives were underway to advance the health and educational dimensions of the Adventist work in the South. However, medical missionary training was available only in Battle Creek. Thus, one of the main purposes of the motion was to make it possible for people from the South to get training and lead the work, rather than having the Southern field dependent on "outsiders" for leadership.

After a delegate raised the question of how much the proposed institution would cost and who would pay for it, Sheafe took the floor to "heartily indorse" the motion. The need for such an institution was a matter of "considerable importance" in view of the conditions faced by the people of the South, he said. He also agreed that "believers trained in a field are better fitted to do the work of that field than those who are imported." As for the cost, Sheafe declared that "if this movement is of the Lord, builders and the cost of the building will all fall into line." He appealed to the church to live up to its principles, and move forward with a program ideally suited for confronting the poverty, ignorance, and disease so prevalent in the South, with the transforming power of the gospel.

"I believe that Seventh-day Adventists have a truth which, if they will let it get a hold of them, can do more in this field to demonstrate the principles of the gospel of Jesus Christ than can any other people. The one thing needful is that the truth shall get hold of the individuals who profess to know it."

N. W. Allee, superintendent of the Adventist work throughout the South (District No. 2), followed Sheafe in supporting the motion. Allee proposed that the objective could be achieved without huge expenditures by setting up departments for medical missionary training at already-existing schools—the Oakwood Industrial School in Huntsville, Alabama, and the Southern Industrial School in Graysville, Tennessee. The motion carried, but implementation would depend on the outworking of broader issues about the future direction of the church.

A PLAN FOR REACHING THE TALENTED TENTH

The direction of Lewis Sheafe's ministry after the 1899 General Conference session was linked to these same issues. The conference marked an important transition in his career. Recognition as the preeminent spokesperson for the Adventist cause among African-Americans deepened his stake in the movement. Now the question of what specific form his own work would take as he moved forward in that leadership role converged with two larger and fundamental questions: How would the Adventist Church organize and administer its overall work, including its medical missionary and educational endeavors? And how would Adventism deal with the dilemma of race relations?

Just a week after the conference in South Lancaster closed, Sheafe presented a plan to the General Conference Committee in Battle Creek that would become the centerpiece of his work in the South over the coming two and a half years. The text of the proposal itself has not been preserved. From the committee minutes, though, it is clear that it entailed a special work focused on the educational institutions that various denominations and humanitarian concerns had established for the freedmen and their children in the South during the decades following the Civil War. It would mean moving along the lines that Dr. Kellogg and Mrs. Steele had been advocating.

"Elder L. C. Sheafe appeared before the committee to lay before them his plan with reference to the work for the colored people in the south. It is to visit the schools for the colored people, and lay before them the principles of healthful living and some features of the third angel's message, with a hope that there would be more fruitful soil in that class of people than elsewhere; also with a hope that laborers could be raised up to go out and preach the truth to others."[4]

Though W.E.B. DuBois had not yet coined the phrase, Lewis Sheafe was working with the concept: he wanted to tap into the "talented tenth" for the cause of the third angel's message. He believed that cultivating leaders for the Adventist movement from the highest caliber of individuals was of critical importance for reaching the Black masses of the South.

The General Conference leaders voted support for the plan, and sought to keep it within the conference structure by recommending that the Southern district superintendent, N. W. Allee, take responsibility, in consultation with Sheafe, for the arrangements necessary to implement the plan. From Elder Allee's point of view, however, that would not be an easy matter, because of the lack of coordination of the church's various enterprises that had perplexed him ever since he took up his responsibilities for administering District No. 2 in 1897. Agencies such as the Southern Missionary Society and the MMBA were establishing schools, medical missions, and other enterprises in the South on their own initiative, "without counsel or advice," and then demanding recognition and financial support. Allee did not object to these endeavors and praised the good they were doing, but wanted "to hear my relations defined so I would know what to do or say."[5]

G. A. Irwin, too, had been troubled by the growing trend toward independent action in the church, which he believed was destroying its unity. As the 1899 General Conference session neared, cooperation between the General Conference leadership and Dr. Kellogg and his vast sphere of influence, in particular, was in jeopardy. In a letter to Ellen White in Australia, Irwin suggested that her admonitions against arbitrary and dictatorial authority that were emphasized at the 1897 session had now led to an opposite extreme in following the "spirit of independence." He wondered if the Lord would "want our work to break up into little independent integers," which would "give the devil an opportunity to come in and separate and divide."[6]

Apprehensions were temporarily relieved when Kellogg displayed a cooperative spirit at the 1899 session. Still, the basic conflict over authority and organization remained, and it came into play in the implementation of the plan for medical missionary training schools in the South that had been voted at the conference. And the flashpoint came from the other overarching issue for the church's work in the South—race relations.

Just after the General Conference concluded in mid-March, the MMBA took up the matter of the medical missionary training programs and ended up voting to establish five of them in connection with already-existing institutions in the South: the school in Keene, Texas; the Oakwood Industrial school; the Graysville school in Tennessee; the sanitarium work beginning in Nashville; and, at a later time, the Steele Home in Chattanooga. The association also voted that admission of students into these programs be made irrespective of color.

Kellogg moved immediately to put the spotlight on the Graysville school, which the General Conference had been operating as a school exclusively for Whites, with the Oakwood school located 125 miles away designated for "colored students." Would the school now be willing to cooperate in establishment of medical missionary training on a nondiscriminatory basis?

Irwin turned to Ellen White for guidance. In describing the situation, Irwin noted that the few Colored people who were Adventists in the Graysville vicinity "attend church along with the white people, and they seem to get along all right." No issue was being made in that regard. The faculty, said Irwin, wanted to do what was right and did not wish "to sacrifice a principle to succumb to the prejudice." However, while trying to be balanced in briefing the prophet on the situation, he placed emphasis on the danger of precipitating a crisis through rash action that would stir up the prejudice of the "hot-blooded" White Southerners, and "bring suffering and distress upon the colored race." He referred to recent atrocities, such as the armed assault just months before on Wilmington, North Carolina, "in which many of the colored people were brutally shot down by the whites."[7]

While the tenor of Ellen White's counsels was already moving decidedly against open defiance of the segregationist juggernaut in the South,[8] in 1899 the issue remained very much a contested one in Adventism. The direction Sheafe's ministry took, and his own approach to the race problem, would thus have an unavoidable impact on these lines of conflict that were shaping the kind of church the Seventh-day Adventists would be in the twentieth century.

LOUISVILLE—A BREAKTHROUGH?

For the time being Sheafe returned to Louisville, where the Adventists were soon to feel moved by the power of the Holy Spirit to contest the color line. The believers in Louisville had begun calling for Sheafe to return the previous fall. At that point the preacher had his sights on going deeper into the South, possibly to Atlanta. He agreed to Louisville, however, recognizing its importance as "the gateway to the South." Thus, "the work done here will influence the work in other parts of the Southern field."[9] For the sake of Sheafe's overriding mission, the race question would have to be handled in Louisville in a way that was winsome to Black people throughout America who would be urged to consider the Adventist proclamation of "present truth."

At the time of Sheafe's return, two Adventist churches—one for

Whites and the other for Blacks—were meeting in Louisville, with Elder Willard Saxby in charge of the overall work in the city. Saxby, with whom Sheafe had briefly worked in Cleveland, had seemed anxious for his arrival. "We look for Bro. Sheafe every day now," he had written on January 5, weeks before he arrived.[10]

It was not Sheafe's preaching, however, but that of Albion Fox Ballenger that stirred momentous change in Louisville during the month following the close of the General Conference session. The 38-year-old Ballenger had been one of the church's leading advocates of religious liberty during the late 1880s and 1890s. In 1897 he began preaching a message of revival through the transforming power of the Holy Spirit. At a time when the theme of sanctification and healing through the reception of the Holy Spirit was surging through America's Protestant churches, Ballenger's preaching sparked a fervent response among Adventists. With the support of the General Conference leadership and encouragement from Ellen White, he began conducting series of revival meetings in Adventist churches throughout the nation, proclaiming, "Receive ye the Holy Ghost." Healings, sometimes physical but more often "soul healing" that brought victory over sin and despair, attended the revivals.[11]

Ballenger emphasized the power of the Holy Spirit to eradicate all sin, no matter how deeply embedded, including the sin of racial bigotry. In Louisville, and in the racially inclusive Washington, D.C., church, Ballenger's revival meetings in 1899 led to the transformation of hearts embittered by prejudice and to new patterns of behavior.[12] Sheafe's report in the *Review* testified to the impact of the Louisville meetings in April 1899:

"Brother A. F. Ballenger made us a two-weeks' visit. The Lord gave him something to tell, and power with which to tell it. The Lord blessed his word, and it was effective as a fire and a hammer. Hearts were warmed and softened, and a better mold was put upon the work here. Confessions were freely made, sins put away, and the promise of the Holy Spirit claimed. The message is onward, and we pray earnestly for the consummation."[13]

The "better mold" being put on the work was in fact a uniting of the two separate congregations into one. At the Louisville meetings Ballenger declared that "victory . . . over race prejudice" had been won, and Saxby could say that as a result of "signal victories" from the Lord during the meetings, "we have no longer two churches here."[14] Two months later Elder Saxby's wife, Bettie, testified:

"Union and harmony prevail since the union of the two churches. It is certainly a move in the Lord's way. We can but praise the good Lord every day for what he has wrought for us. The greatest victories of my life have been during and since the close of Elder Ballenger's meetings here."[15]

While he likewise rejoiced at the progress in Louisville, Sheafe's spirits were sobered by unnamed failures accompanying victories in his ministry, and by evil forces at work to counter the good. Such did not overthrow his courage, he insisted. The failures brought reminders "that we are still in school, still in training," and lessons that could be seen as part of "the unfolding of God's purpose." Despite the evil that seemed to hold down the good, "God cannot fail us, so we trust Him."[16]

---

[1] LAH to LCS, Jan. 31, 1899.

[2] GCDB, Feb. 16, 1899, p. 5.

[3] GCDB, Mar. 1, 1899, p. 114.

[4] GCC minutes, Mar. 21, 1899.

[5] NWA to LAH, Sept. 18, 1898, GCA.

[6] GAI to EGW, Jan. 20, 1899, cited in Geroge R. Knight, *Organizing to Beat the Devil* (Hagerstown, Md.: Review and Herald, 2001), pp. 94, 95.

[7] GAI to EGW, Oct. 13, 1899, EGWE.

[8] See Manuscript 118, 1899, in *Manuscript Releases* (Silver Spring, Md.: Ellen G. White Estate, 1990), vol. 4, pp. 12, 13.

[9] Lewis C. Sheafe, "Kentucky," *Review*, June 13, 1899, p. 15.

[10] W. H. Saxby to LAH, Jan. 5, 1899.

[11] Calvin W. Edwards and Gary Land, *Seeker After Light: A. F. Ballenger, Adventism, and American Christianity* (Berrien Springs, Mich.: Andrews University Press, 2000), pp. 32-64.

[12] A. F. Ballenger, "Victory!" *Review*, July 25, 1899, p. 11.

[13] Sheafe, "Kentucky."

[14] AFB to LAH, May 16, 1899, GCA; W. H. Saxby to LAH, May 2, 1899; LCS to LAH, May 1, 1899, GCA.

[15] Bettie C. Saxby to LAH, June 28, 1899, GCA.

[16] Sheafe, "Kentucky."

CHAPTER XII

**"IS THERE A PLACE IN THIS
MESSAGE FOR THE NEGRO
WITH THE WHITE MAN?"**

THOUGH THE ANCHOR OF HIS FAITH HELD, the inner turmoil Lewis Sheafe was experiencing in the late spring of 1899 was nonetheless real. His three years in the Adventist community had been a perplexing mixture of joy and disillusionment, of idealistic aspiration frustrated by lack of resources and slowness of progress. Was there, after all, a future for him in Adventism? The uncertainties pressed him to the point of seeking counsel from a woman he had never met, who lived on the other side of the world in Australia, but whom he, with his Adventist brothers and sisters, had come to regard as "a special servant of the Lord."[1]

In relating to Ellen White how he came to accept "present truth," Sheafe wrote, "My heart leaped for joy as I thought of the possible help to come to my people through the third [angel's] message." However, as he looked back over the past three years, he wrote that often "for warmth I've found coldness, for freedom bondage, and for confidence distrust." He had seen in Adventism the promise of doing what the existing denominations had largely failed to do—apply the principles of the gospel to race relations in a thorough and consistent manner. However, in the three years since he joined the Adventist cause, two things had happened. While the conditions facing African-Americans were moving from bad to worse, the Adventist Church had proven at best inconsistent and largely ineffectual in addressing the desperate need of his people.

"The caste feeling in this country is strong, it grows worse each year— it is tolerated in all the denominations; it seems that every man's hand is against us," he wrote. American Christians claim to take the Bible as their guide and declare that love is the foundation of Christianity, but with only few exceptions, "the Negro is despised by the very people who make such professions." As a result, Sheafe pointed out, "there is a host of my people today who have no faith in the God the white man serves."

The only hope for his people was in Christ, the preacher remained convinced. What they needed was "an object lesson, to see Jesus Christ manifested in the flesh." The Adventist message, with its insistence on the Bible as the only rule of faith and practice, gave promise of meeting that need. Thus, Sheafe wrote, "My people hail it with delight," but "then they say 'We will measure the depth and purity of the Christianity of SDA by their attitude toward the Negro.'"

What was disillusioning Sheafe was the frequent failure of the Adventist work to meet that test:

"Many of the workers who go among my people, act on [precedent] and not on principle. They go and inquire how other people treat us, then they do the same. . . . Some of the workers will even say in the beginning of the work . . . that God is no respecter of persons—so we can't be. But if the work grows and both races are reached, the workers are troubled and begin to ask the people what to do. And instead of teaching the people the right ways of God, and doing what they know is right, they like Pilate turn and ask an [enraged] crowd, What shall I then do with Jesus? He knew what justice demanded and ought to have done it. This treatment has weakened faith, has brought in distrust, and dried up the fountains of praise."

Some Adventist churches, Sheafe observed, draw the color line on the outside, excluding Blacks from membership altogether. In others it is drawn on the inside—Black believers are allowed into the church "but are still a side issue."

Thus, the preacher's high hopes upon embracing the Adventist message had collided with the reality that the "present methods of work among my race by us as a denomination has hardly touched the problem." And so, in the course of the letter, he posed to Ellen White several pointed and poignant questions:

"Is there a place in this message for the Negro with the white man? Then is the Negro on coming to this people to [lose] his individuality— cease to think, see or feel for himself or his people? . . .

"Now is it the mind of the Lord, that there shall be separate schools or churches for my people? Shall we have a separate organization? I am not saying that such ought or [ought] not to be, but simply desire to know what the Lord would have. . . . Is there anything definite and tangible that you would recommend for the present need, that will reach my people where they are now?"

In the Louisville church and in Georgetown, where he and Buster had raised up a small interracial company of believers the previous year, events transpired over the coming months that bore out aspects of the pattern Sheafe described in his letter to Ellen White. In November the Saxbys were transferred to a new assignment, though they had hoped to spend another year in Louisville. The new pastor, Elder Smith Sharp, took a very different view of the uniting of the Black and White believers into one church than Saxby believed had been carried out under the influence of the Holy Spirit.

In a letter to L. A. Hoopes just before going to Louisville, Sharp wrote of hearing that the Louisville church had been forced out of its meeting place "on account of the whites and blacks meeting together." Sharp cited this development as evidence of the folly of trying to bring the races together. Based on his experience in the Southern states, he wrote, "it seems to me that we are simply butting our heads against a stone wall when we attempt to ignore the social customs that have been long established." He also made a proposal—probably at least partially sarcastic:

"Elders Kilgore and Allee unite with me in requesting that Eld. Ballenger be sent to Louisville at least for a few months. He united the two elements there and are not the testimonies quite clear at least on the [principle] that leading brethren ought not to take a course that involves perplexities and then go off and leave others to bear the brunt of it?"[2]

However, Sharp's first Sabbath with the church, just a week later, was an enjoyable one, and he acknowledged that there did "not appear to be any friction" between the races. Though he maintained his views against the wisdom of bringing the churches together in the first place, he saw no reason to break up the arrangement, and pledged to do all in his power to keep things running smoothly.

That which made Sharp so suddenly amenable to the situation, though, fit precisely the pattern that so deeply disappointed Sheafe. The

Louisville church, it seems, had drawn the color line on the inside. During his visit Sharp noted with approval that the "colored brethren come in quietly and take seats in the rear and appear to know and keep their places."[3]

Whether this internal color line—apparently informal yet nonetheless real—had been part of the arrangement when the two congregations merged the previous spring or had gradually emerged over the following months is uncertain. In any case, it did not succeed in holding the church together. The following summer the church's Bible worker, Lillian Pierce, described some of the difficulties related to the two races worshipping together on a semisegregated basis.[4] Pierce, who also worked in Georgetown and had high regard for Sheafe, pointed out that while racial distinctions should not matter if a person is truly converted, the presence of Blacks in the church tended to prompt White people who had shown an interest in the Adventist message to turn away and quit the Bible studies she conducted before they could be nurtured to the point of full conversion.

Also, she observed, the racial factor put some of the church's "best members" in a tense situation. The husbands of these sisters would forbid them to attend the church if they found out that their wives were meeting with Black people each Sabbath.

As for the Black members, said Pierce, they "do not enjoy the freedom they would in their own church." She estimated that attendance by Black people was down by half from what it had been before the congregations had united. Nearly every member of the church now felt that the move had been a mistake, she claimed.

By the time Lillian Pierce expressed these observations, the yearlong union in the Louisville church was in fact unraveling. Already in April G. A. Irwin referred to the undoing of the "arrangement" that had come about under the influence of the Ballenger revival. What Ballenger, Sheafe, and the Saxbys had seen as the work of the Holy Spirit, the General Conference president now regarded as a short-lived surge of sentiment. He commented that "it takes something more than enthusiasm to ride over the customs and habits of years and successfully revolutionize things."[5] A news item in the *Review and Herald* more than a year later made clear that Louisville once again had two separate churches, both ready to move beyond the recent "discouraging circumstances," which had given evidence that "Northern principles cannot always be advantageously applied" in the South.[6]

Similarly in Georgetown, the favorable reception among both Black and White hearers to the preaching of Sheafe and Buster did not in the end lead to a lasting interracial congregation. In December 1898 Lillian Pierce was sent from Louisville to Georgetown on a temporary basis, with the mission of nurturing interests in the Adventist faith among the White population. With ministers only occasionally present, though, it fell upon her to function as pastor-teacher for the new company of Black believers, which she managed to do along with her work of conducting Bible studies with White people.

Sister Pierce found that considerable interest in the Adventist message had indeed been generated in the city. "The influence left here by Brethren Sheafe and Buster has done more for us as a denomination than anything else could do," she wrote. By the end of January she was conducting nine Bible studies among the White people. All but one or two of these were among "the best people in the town," including three "professors."[7] As time went on, though, she found it frustrating, as Sheafe had, that people would give their assent to the biblical truths being taught, but did not feel compelled to take a stand. At the same time, she observed, "most of them wish nothing more than for Eld. Sheafe to come here again or a minister just like him and they can go and listen to him."[8]

Thus, though the Bible worker had found one White Sabbathkeeper when she began her work in Georgetown, the company of those committed to the third angel's message remained all Black. "I have to take charge of the colored meetings," she wrote, and indeed the interest remained lively during the months of her work in the town. It was not possible for her to go into Black homes to conduct Bible readings with individuals or families as she wished to do, evidently because this would jeopardize her welcome into White homes. Apparently, though, leading "public readings" for a group in the home of a Black woman, Sister Redd, did not have the same stigma attached to it. Pierce held three such readings per week— on Sabbath afternoons and in the evenings on Sunday and Wednesday. These gatherings attracted new interests, including a Methodist minister who reportedly began keeping the Sabbath, and a tobacconist who traveled to the readings from Lexington, insisting that "nothing would keep him away."[9]

As for Lewis Sheafe, no direct reply to the outpouring of his heart to Ellen White is on record. In some way, though, he found sufficient hope to keep going, and the evidence of ongoing interest in the message such as seen in Georgetown must have been crucial. His work continued to sparkle with promise, though its overall direction would remain unfocused for the remainder of the year.

From Louisville Sheafe went to Camp Nelson, Kentucky, in June and then to Chattanooga in July once again to hold nightly meetings for several weeks in connection with the Helping Hand Mission.[10] In August he was called upon to assist with camp meetings. The first, held in Gadsden, Alabama, was his first preaching assignment in the Deep South. In a brief description of the camp meeting in the *Review and Herald*, N. W. Allee singled out Sheafe's presence for mention, noting that the elder's "labor and songs were enjoyed by all."[11]

Allee's report referred only in passing to a subsequent camp meeting in Knoxville, Tennessee. But at a meeting of the General Conference Committee two years later, Allee cited the Knoxville camp meeting as the point at which Sheafe's views on racial matters became controversial in the church. He did not give details. Sheafe's routine report from the camp meeting to L. A. Hoopes suggests that something problematic had indeed occurred, but he minimized it by placing it in the category of the occasional "snag" in the road, adding that "on the whole our work is good."[12]

But where would he go from here?

<hr>

[1] LCS to EGW, May 25, 1899, GCA.
[2] Smith Sharp to LAH, Nov. 8, 1899, GCA.
[3] Smith Sharp to LAH, Nov. 15, 1899, GCA.
[4] Lillian Pierce to LAH, Aug. 1, 1900, GCA.
[5] GAI to Smith Sharp, Apr. 13, 1900, GCA.
[6] Dr. and Mrs. O. C. Godsmark, "Kentucky," *Review*, Aug. 20, 1901, p. 12.
[7] Lillian Pierce to LAH, Feb. 1, 1899, GCA.
[8] Lillian Pierce to LAH, Apr. 2, 1899, GCA.
[9] Lillian Pierce to LAH, Dec. 21, 1898, Feb. 1 and Apr. 2, 1899, GCA.
[10] LCS to LAH, July 26, 1899, GCA.
[11] N. W. Allee, "The Southern Field," *Review*, Dec. 26, 1899, p. 14.
[12] LCS to LAH, Aug. 30, 1899, GCA.

CHAPTER XIII

CAMP NELSON, SCHOOL PLANS, AND SOUTH CAROLINA

SEEKING ONCE AGAIN TO CHART A COURSE for his work, Sheafe sent another proposal to General Conference president G. A. Irwin in October 1899. While related to the spring proposal to work in connection with Black educational institutions, this one introduced a major new dimension, which may have been inspired by Sheafe's interaction with John G. Fee in Camp Nelson, Kentucky.

Before the Civil War John Fee founded the first interracial and coeducational institution of higher education in the South, Berea College, in 1855. A preacher and radical reformer, Fee had been an uncompromising abolitionist in Kentucky, despite violent opposition.[1]

In 1864 Fee undertook the project of providing education for the Black soldiers whose regiments were forming at Camp Nelson, about 25 miles south of Lexington. Another need arose when some of the enlistees' wives and children, newly freed slaves with nowhere else to go, began showing up at the camp. The Union officers forced the family members out of the camp at the point of bayonet, which, Fee said, resulted in their being "exposed to the cruelty of their former masters." Taking advantage of a connection formed in the antislavery movement with the secretary of the Treasury, Salmon P. Chase, Fee arranged for the construction of 92 cottages for the families near the camp, as well as two hospital buildings, and buildings for school rooms, offices, a boarding hall, and a dormitory of teachers and school staff.[2]

Soon after the war Fee borrowed $500 that, along with the proceeds from the sale of land his wife owned in the North, he used to buy 130 acres of land at Camp Nelson. The land was divided into lots and small tracts and given to the former soldiers and their families. At the time Fee published his autobiography more than 30 years later, 42 families owned homes on the land. An academy with two buildings and 107 acres of additional land provided education for their children.[3]

When at some point in 1898 Sheafe was invited to speak at Camp Nelson, he chose the topic of health principles. Fee had been a zealous temperance reformer, and Sheafe observed that only two of the men in the 44 homes then comprising the community drank spirituous liquors, and only three used tobacco in any form. Fee had not taught other aspects of healthful living, however.

Sheafe's presentation on health reform had "aroused quite an interest," he said in remarks from the floor of the 1899 General Conference session. He said that Fee told him that he had long believed that pork was not fit to eat and admitted that Sheafe had presented "true principles" on health, though the indomitable reformer had "somehow or other . . . not dared to tell his people about them." Moreover, said Sheafe, some of the people had begun to "see the light of the Sabbath."[4]

After a return visit to Camp Nelson in June 1899 Sheafe reported to L. A. Hoopes that "this place is stirred over the message" and that four persons had "taken their stand." The preacher also expressed the hope that the way might be opened for a "wide awake" Adventist family to move into the farming community of Camp Nelson and "take hold of this school work here." With the phrase "school work" Sheafe apparently was referring to his plan to focus on Black educational institutions, using health reform as one of the primary means of gaining a foothold and creating interest in the Adventist message.[5]

Thus, what Sheafe proposed to President Irwin in October seems to have been an expansion of his earlier plan along the lines of what he observed at Camp Nelson: a cooperative community in which subjugated African-Americans could achieve economic self-sufficiency, gain an education, and learn the principles of reform—moral, physical, and religious—that Adventism offered. With only Elder Irwin's reply available, the precise details of Sheafe's proposal are unknown, but clearly it was also along the lines set forth by Ellen White in *Review and Herald* articles that appeared in early 1896 and later were published in *The Southern Work*:

"Those who love Christ will do the works of Christ. They will go forth to seek and to save that which was lost. They will not shun those who are despised, and turn aside from the colored race. They will teach them how to read and how to perform manual labor, educating them to till the soil and to follow trades of various kinds. They will put forth painstaking efforts to develop the capabilities of the people. The cotton field will not be the only resource for a livelihood to the colored people. There will be awakened in them the thought that they are of value with God, and that they are esteemed as His property. The work pointed out is a most needful missionary enterprise. It is the best restitution that can be made to those who have been robbed of their time and deprived of their education."[6] "Let farmers, financiers, builders, and those who are skilled in various arts and crafts go to this field to improve lands and to build humble cottages for themselves and their neighbors."[7]

President Irwin, however, sought to draw Sheafe away from his proposal, for several reasons.[8] First, Irwin pointed out that Ellen White had counseled the charismatic revivalist A. F. Ballenger against a similar plan he proposed at the 1899 General Conference session to aid the impoverished Colored people of the South. Ballenger also envisioned something like the Camp Nelson community—the purchase of land on which to build a school and establish a "colony" providing economic opportunity.[9] Using the same rationale Ellen White had used with Ballenger, Irwin told Sheafe the he could do more good by continuing to preach than by getting drawn into the financial and administrative matters the proposed project would require.

Irwin was also concerned that Sheafe's plan would contribute to a trend that he found more and more troubling: the growing influence and proliferating projects of the MMBA, over which Dr. Kellogg's influence, rather than that of the General Conference leadership, was preeminent. Irwin called Sheafe's attention to the fact that "the drift of the Testimonies of late" had been against starting more projects such as "orphans' homes and institutions." These "independent integers," as he had described them to Ellen White, undermined the ability of the conferences to oversee and coordinate the work of the churches.

So Irwin's principle point of concern was Sheafe's suggestion that his project be financially independent, and thus not "become a burden to the conference." A major problem with enterprises launched independently of the church's organized structure, the church president said, was that their proponents would then raise funds from church members, and thereby deplete funds available to support the denomination's regular program and agencies. If Sheafe ended up deciding to pursue his project, Irwin warned, "it would not be the proper thing" for him "to go to our own churches to attempt to raise means for this purpose."

The question of Sheafe's relationship to conference work was one of the things in the back of Irwin's mind when he, along with Elder and Mrs. Stephen N. Haskell, arrived at Mount Vernon, Ohio, in late November for a Midwest District meeting. Irwin and the Haskells had been traveling to such church gatherings that fall, presenting "straight testimonies" from Ellen White in Australia, in an effort to keep the church unified in both doctrinal and organizational matters.

"We had an excellent meeting in Mount Vernon—the best we have held in any place," he wrote to L. A. Hoopes. The church president could detect "no opposition whatever to the straight Testimonies, nor to the teaching of Brother Haskell." Irwin was also pleased that Sheafe had been in attendance, and had "paid very close attention to the reading of the Testimonies." The two men had a "good talk" after the meetings ended, Irwin said, adding that Sheafe "sees things in an entirely different light now, and he is willing to go ahead in his ministerial work."

With the question of whether Sheafe would work independently of the conference now apparently resolved, Irwin told Hoopes that he should be continued on the General Conference payroll. Sheafe "is a bright man, and it seems to me could do much good," Irwin wrote. He wanted to "try to save the man from getting into trial and perhaps losing heart entirely," and avoid a course of action that could drive him onto "the enemy's ground."[10]

SOUTH CAROLINA:
SCHOOLS AND THE PEOPLE'S GOSPEL MEETINGS

With the plan to launch a new institution deferred, Sheafe now focused on the proposal he had set forth just after the General Conference session in March. He would concentrate on building interest in the Adventist message at existing Black educational institutions, and thereby nurture talented leadership to advance the cause on a much broader scale.

After some time with his family in Mount Vernon and preaching appointments in Ohio during the Christmas season, the elder left once again for the South, with tentative plans to nurture the work in Mississippi and Alabama.[11] His first stop, though, was Graysville, Tennessee, for the Southern District meeting, at which his assignment again became a matter of discussion. Another attempt by Mrs. Steele to bring the talented preacher under her auspices was rebuffed.[12] The district meeting closed with tentative plans for Sheafe to return to Camp Nelson, but by the end of the month he was at work in South Carolina. It was there that he launched his project targeting the "schools for colored youth."[13]

At Voorhees Industrial School in Denmark, and at Claflin University and South Carolina State College in Orangeburg, Sheafe found opportunities to lecture and favorable responses to his presentations. He was unable, though, to secure a venue at which to base ongoing work in these towns. In Aiken, however, a town of around 5,000 located 25 miles east of Augusta, Georgia, his plan to reach the "talented tenth" began to show tangible evidence of success. After initially finding that "wickedness abounds on every hand," making it difficult to establish a foothold, the teacher-evangelist found doors opening at one of two schools in the town operated by Protestant denominations to educate Black young people, and at an AME church with ties to the school. Sheafe presented Bible studies at the school during the day and preached at the church in the evenings. Resonating the language of Acts of the Apostles, Sheafe claimed that "the whole city was stirred by the mighty power of God through His word" and that 75 conversions resulted.

In Sheafe's terminology, though, "conversion" meant turning from sin and to Christ as Savior and Lord. "Obeying the message" or "taking a stand for truth"—in other words, casting one's lot with the Seventh-day Adventist movement—was quite another matter.

In getting people to that latter step of accepting a message "so new and strange" to them,[14] Sheafe ran into the resistance that, by now, he knew to be inevitable. As he began setting forth more explicitly the distinctive teachings and claims of the Adventist message, his welcome from those in charge of the AME church and the school ran out. However, though church and school officials barred him from their premises, interest in hearing his message remained high among the people.

The problem now was that he no longer had a place to meet, not even a tent. Financial strains, he was told, made it impossible for the General Conference to send one.

To cut through the dilemma, Sheafe took a bold step, one with important short-term results as well as long-term ramifications:

"So we ordered a forty-foot circle and a 12 x 14 ft. tent from the Battle Creek Tent Company, for security giving the names of the Lord and Sheafe. The former moved on the hearts of a few friends and the people for whom the meetings were being held, and the tents were paid for."

Sheafe was discovering, first, that the interest in Adventism generated by his work outpaced the ability of the denomination to provide the support necessary to nurture that interest and bring its potential to full realization. Second, he found that he could succeed in raising funds outside official channels to help meet the opportunity.

When the tents arrived in July, Sheafe issued a flyer announcing "The People's Gospel Meetings," to be conducted every night, beginning July 29, at "Sheafe's Tent." He made music a prominent part of the advertising, promising that he would sing as well as preach each night, and invited attendees to bring both a Bible and the Pentecostal hymn book. On opening night not only were all 300 seats in the tent filled—the number of people standing outside the tent surpassed the crowd seated within. At the next two meetings the crowds grew even larger.[15]

While he was preaching on Tuesday night, August 1, Sheafe noticed two White men appear at the back of the tent. Who were these men, and what did they want? Disconcertingly, in the midst of his sermon they began striding down the aisle, right toward him. When they arrived at the pulpit, the men lifted their hands—but not, it turned out, to harm or threaten, but to shake the preacher's hand. When Sheafe grasped their hands—one in each of his, the men said "Pray for me" in unison, then took seats and "wept like children."[16]

Sheafe's endeavors in Aiken succeeded both in establishing a new company of believers and in recruiting workers to lead in the further spread of the Adventist movement. Two Baptist ministers "accepted the truth," he said, one of which he hired as his assistant, paying him out of his own funds, as he had done for the tents. Other talented men were also "investigating the truth," he wrote, and he considered that these, "with instruction right on the field, could become efficient workers."

At the end of September, Sheafe decided to move the tent to Graniteville, a textile manufacturing town a few miles from Aiken. He opened meetings there with three services on September 30. The audiences were large, comprised mostly of White people, and, he pointed out, "perfect order prevailed."

The progress and outcome of the Graniteville meetings are not known, but moving the tent out of Aiken did have consequences for his work in that town, which Sheafe may have intended. For those in the "valley of decision," the departure of the Sheafe tent "brought things to a head," and several took their stand for the Adventist message. And, since he was only six miles away, Sheafe could stay in touch with the Aiken company and begin holding Sabbath services with them.[17]

With a company of 12 "Sabbathkeepers" now established, a new challenge lay ahead. Many more people in Aiken were favorably disposed to the message, but, said Sheafe, were "waiting to see more proof of our sincerity in the claims we make." Likely he was referring here to the question of whether funds would be provided for a regular meeting place and pastoral leadership. "May the Lord move on hearts to assist the work in this field," he concluded.

In December he headed, as usual, for home and Ohio. The highlight of the seemingly tireless preacher's January 1901 itinerary was a return to Urbana for two weeks of revival meetings at St. Paul's AME Church. On the front page of its first edition of the new year, the Urbana *Citizen and Gazette* eagerly announced the anticipated return of the former pastor of the Second Baptist Church, describing Sheafe as "one of the most eloquent and able divines that ever paid Urbana a visit."[18] The paper subsequently characterized the series as "an unqualified success" and "a power for good in this community," with overflow crowds each evening "treated to powerful expositions of the gospel."[19]

As the "eloquent and able divine" looked ahead to 1901, his potential contribution to the Adventist cause still seemed underdeveloped. The year would bring decisive changes, both for him and for the larger cause, but it would be many years before their significance became fully evident.

[1] John Gregg Fee, *Autobiography of John G. Fee* (Chicago: National Christian Association, 1891), electronic edition at Documenting the American South, University of North Carolina at Chapel Hill, http://docsouth.unc.edu/fpn/fee/fee.html (accessed Aug. 30, 2009).

[2] *Ibid.*, pp. 174-180.

[3] *Ibid.*, pp. 182, 183.

[4] GCDB, Feb. 22, 1899, p. 50.

[5] LCS to LAH, July 2, 1899, GCA.

[6] E. G. White, *The Southern Work*, p. 53.

[7] *Ibid.*, p. 60.

[8] GAI to LCS, Nov. 2, 1899, GCA.

[9] C. W. Edwards and G. Land, *Seeker After Light*, pp. 46, 47.

[10] GAI to LAH, Nov. 29, 1899, GCA.

[11] "Briefs," *Welcome Visitor*, Jan. 4, 1900, p. 4.

[12] GAI to A. S. Steele, Jan. 14, 1900, GCA.

[13] L. C. Sheafe, "In South Carolina," *Review*, Apr. 23, 1901, p. 14. Except where otherwise noted, all of the subsequent information and quotations in the section on Sheafe's work in South Carolina during 1900 are drawn from this same article.

[14] LCS to LAH, June 1, 1899, GCA

[15] LCS to LAH, Aug. 2, 1900, GCA.

[16] *Ibid.*

[17] LCS to LAH, Oct. 1, 1900, GCA.

[18] "Coming Visit. Rev. Sheafe Will Soon Deliver a Lecture Here," Urbana *Citizen and Gazette*, Jan. 1, 1901, p. 1.

[19] "Successful Meeting, Rev. Schief Drawing Large Audiences at St. Paul's," Urbana *Citizen and Gazette*, Jan. 25, 1901, p. 1; "Meetings Closed, Rev Lewis C. Sheafe Brings His Services to an End," Urbana *Citizen and Gazette*, Jan. 29, 1901, p. 5.

CHAPTER XIV

THE 1901 GENERAL CONFERENCE SESSION AND AN UNCERTAIN AFTERMATH

THE GENERAL CONFERENCE SESSION OF 1901—a landmark in Seventh-day Adventist history because of the major reorganization of the church agreed upon—was also a landmark in Lewis Sheafe's rise to prominence in the church. He preached twice, sang several solos, and, as he had begun to do in 1899, took the role of spokesman for the interests of the Adventist work among African-Americans.

Though he was by no means a stranger to Battle Creek, the visibility given at the 1901 session to Sheafe's multiple gifts as a speaker, musician, organizer, and teacher underscored his status as the de facto leader among Black Adventist ministers. That group of preachers, though still quite small in 1901, was on the verge of rapid expansion in the decade that followed. On the other hand, while cementing Lewis Sheafe's identity with the Seventh-day Adventist movement and affirming his gifts as a leader, developments connected with the conference, and even more so its aftermath, also left deposits of mistrust and animosity.

After ministering to the Bowling Green, Kentucky, church in February and March, Sheafe made his way to Battle Creek for the General Conference session, which opened on April 2, 1901. He sang at least three solos during the three weeks of meetings, which gave opportunity to promote his compilation of hymns, *New Songs of the Gospel*. A blurb in the *General Conference Bulletin* stated that the songbook, available from the compiler at Mount Vernon for 15 cents, "contains more than 100 of the choicest songs, some of which Brother Sheafe has sung at the present conference with acceptance."[1]

164

Attendance was so large for the second Sabbath of the session on April 13 that five separate worship services were held. Sheafe's inclusion among the appointed speakers placed him in the company of some of the denomination's foremost leaders. A. T. Jones spoke for the largest gathering at the Battle Creek Tabernacle, while E. J. Waggoner spoke at the college chapel, S. N. Haskell spoke in the *Review* office chapel, and G. W. Schubert conducted a service in German in the college library. Sheafe, preaching in the Battle Creek Sanitarium chapel, presented "a very entertaining view of the life of Esther, and the history of the Jews of that time."[2]

The *General Conference Bulletin* did not include a transcript of his Sabbath sermon—Jones's message was the only one of the five that was printed—but it did include the text of Sheafe's sermon preached for the evening meeting on Thursday, April 11. Sheafe frequently drew on the narratives of the patriarchs in Genesis for his sermons, and that evening he turned to the story of Jacob and Esau. In brief, his message to this convocation of his adopted spiritual family was this: Get hold of God's promises in the midst of hard circumstances, cling to them, and then, like Jacob, go forth limping but reliant on God. and thereby empowered to face anything.

The theme of *waiting* on the Lord and trusting in the outworking of His purposes for those consecrated to Him runs through the sermon. It appears to reflect a perennial struggle in the preacher's own experience, with his tendency toward immediatism in confronting unrighteousness. In the biblical story Rebekah, "afraid that the plans of God would not carry. . . sought to help him out" by concocting the deception of Isaac so that Jacob would receive the promised birthright.

"A good many of us are in that same condition," Sheafe declared. "We are afraid that God is not equal to the emergency, and that if we do not take this thing in our hands, the thing will fail, the cause will come into disrepute, and we cannot afford to have it that way." Had not Sheafe at Lexington, Georgetown, Camp Nelson, and especially Aiken been anxious that lack of support and resources would thwart the development of hard-won results? Had he not wondered if he might be better off working independently of the conference?

"It is so hard to wait," Sheafe acknowledged, but the lesson from Jacob's night of wrestling with the angel of the Lord was to "get hold" of

God's promises, and "when we get hold, let us cling." As with Jacob, who found that with his thigh put out of joint he was able only to cling to the Lord, so today, Sheafe said, the divine blessing comes "not by might nor power, nor by the strength of your arm, the brawn of your muscle, or the sharpness of your brain or of your wit, but it is simply by the faith and love and power of your heart that you lay hold upon the eternal God and *wait*."

Yielded to God and freed from fear, Jacob, though lame and unarmed, found the courage to face Esau and his 400 warriors. The individual thus "anchored on the promises of Jehovah" can know that no "powers of earth, among men or demons" can thwart the accomplishment of God's purposes in that person's life. The one who "puts his faith and confidence in God need not hurry; he can wait on the Lord and be of good courage, for victory is surely his."

After Jacob's night of wrestling, the Lord had declared him a "prince" who had "power with God and with men." Sheafe wanted the faith to view the challenges that lay before him, and before the Adventist Church, in the light of this promise, but acknowledged that this was not an easy matter:

"As we look out on the broad field and we see humanity crying under the awful weight of sin, with condemnation resting down upon the whole human family and so little being done to bring the light of the glorious gospel of the truth of Jesus Christ to the hearts and minds of the people, we wonder at times whether or not this truth we believe is real. May the Lord help us, beloved, to come up to the help of the Lord against the mighty!"

As he neared the close of his message, the preacher drew a final point from the story about that which must characterize a people moving forward with the kind of faith that transformed Jacob. Reconciliation with God prepared Jacob to embrace his brother in reconciliation.

"Do you know tonight, beloved, that that is one of the great lessons that God is trying to teach his people in the work today—that he is the common Father of all, and we are all brethren? But we are slow to learn the lesson, and the Lord has to put us over the road, time and time again.

"But I am glad the Lord is so patient and kind and tender with us. . . .

"We can go forth from this General Conference to our work with our hearts imbued with his Spirit. Men and women will be converted and we shall be perfected as instruments in the hands of the Lord, to point them to the Lamb of God that taketh away the sins of the world."

REORGANIZATION, RACE, AND ETHNICITY

A week and a half after Sheafe's sermon a new plan for implementing the ideal of the church as bringing people from all nations, ethnicities, and races into one family of God came before the conference. In an era of heavy emigration from Europe, millions of newcomers to America spoke little or no English, and many preferred to continue worshipping in their native tongue, even as they developed a command of English.

Thus, representatives of the "German work" proposed that each of the union conferences in America appoint a minister to oversee the advancement of "present truth among the millions of Germans in this large land of America." These directors of the German work in the respective union conferences would meet together for counsel at least once a year. Additionally, this group, along with the editor of the German paper, would "constitute a committee, which shall meet with the General Conference Committee, as circumstances may demand, for the purpose of planning for the German work."[3]

While the plan addressed a compelling need, H.M.J. Richards of the Colorado Conference raised the question of whether it would be damaging to "the unity of the work." To Richards the plan looked like "a provision for the formation of a conference within a conference, or a separate German conference," and he moved to refer it back to the committee on organization. After further discussion, during which it was pointed out that the committee on organization had already approved the plan, Richards agreed to withdraw his motion, but he had raised an issue that the denomination would grapple with in changing forms throughout the century that followed.

After the delegates voted in favor of the proposal for the German work, J. M. Ericksson moved "that the same principles that have been accepted regarding the German work be also applied to the Scandinavian work." The motion carried without further discussion.

Lewis Sheafe then took the floor and moved "that this same plan be inaugurated for the colored people." The motion rapidly received two seconds, one from H. W. Cottrell, president of the new Atlantic Union

Conference, and the other from Lewis Johnson, a leader in the Scandinavian work. However, Allen Moon, who was chairing the session, expressed the view that the Southern Union Conference had been organized for "that work."

Sheafe countered, "As I understand it, the colored man comes in incidentally in the Southern Union Conference. I am also thinking of the numbers of my people who are scattered all over the North, in the Eastern, Central, and Western states, for whom very little is being done. It seems to me that some measures along that line ought to be taken."

W. C. White then cautioned that more study was needed as to whether the proposal for the work among the European immigrant communities was "well adapted" to the work for Black Americans. White proposed "a consultation between the brethren representing the Southern Union Conference, the brethren especially representing the colored work throughout the field, and the Committee on Organization" with purpose of designing a plan to accomplish "the work mentioned by Brother Sheafe."

Sheafe ended up accepting White's proposal, but not before making the point that the need for "help and aid" in bringing "this truth" to the Colored people of America was not because of their color, as such, but "because they are ostracised." In other words, like the European immigrants, an objective and clearly identifiable factor set Blacks apart from other Americans and necessitated devoting special attention and resources for ministry to them. Unlike the immigrants, though, the core factor was not language, ethnicity, or even color in itself, but systemic ostracism.

He then tried to help the delegates understand why the matter was so critical to the church's progress among Black Americans. First, to get a hearing, the church had to give real evidence of full acceptance for people of all races into one communion of faith:

"The great inquiry everywhere as I meet my people in different parts of the country is as to what body I am connected with, and whether it is a mixed body. I tell them there are all kinds of nationalities together."

Second, discerning seekers for truth in the Black population looked for racial justice in church governance and empowerment of Black leaders:

"They then ask what treatment and representation we are accorded.

These questions come, and it seems to me if an effort could be made along this line, so our people could see some of their own men who accepted the truth being put into and encouraged in the work; and if lines were marked out where they could work with freedom that they might do the work, I believe the work would wonderfully advance, and more would be coming into the truth."

The 1901 General Conference session and its aftermath brought into compressed view both the exhilarating possibilities that lay ahead for Lewis Sheafe as a champion of the Seventh-day Adventist message, and the perils poised to frustrate him. On the one hand, conference leaders gave him abundant opportunities to display his renowned eloquence—considerably more time in the limelight than many preachers of much longer experience and greater stature in the movement. Black Adventists and inquirers could thus see and draw inspiration from a gifted man of their race with the ability to lead them given public prominence. Sheafe, affirmed both by the public appearances and the conferral of full ministerial credentials, seems to have left the conference eager and energized to lead the cause of proclaiming present truth to Black America.

On the other hand, the high public visibility given him was not matched by a corresponding degree of influence in the leadership councils where decisions concerning the work among his people were made. Neither he nor any other Black Adventist had a voice on the ad hoc committee proposed by W. C. White to study Sheafe's own motion to create a leadership structure for the work among Blacks parallel to that of the German and Scandinavian work. On April 24, the day following the close of the conference session, the General Conference Committee appointed R. M. Kilgore, J. E. White, and W. C. White as a committee to make recommendations regarding the "proposition of L. C. Sheafe for special department of work for colored people."[4] The next evening the subcommittee brought back its recommendation, which was accepted:

"Your committee, after considering the proposition for the organization of a General Conference department for labor for the colored people, advises that our union conferences give due attention to this feature of our work, and suggest that it is not advisable to organize a General Conference department."[5]

No direct evidence indicates that Sheafe was particularly attached to the details of what he proposed on the floor of the General Conference session, or that the substance of the General Conference Committee's action on it caused much discontent. But he was passionately concerned about the problems that he hoped would be addressed by the measure he proposed. And to have the matter disposed of without his involvement must have caused an irritation that could fester if the underlying issues were long to remain unaddressed.

UNCERTAIN AFTERMATH

Of more immediate distress in the months following the conference was a combination of mixed signals, administrative lapses, and antagonism toward his work, leading to rumors that the denomination had cut him off from its workforce.

The 1901 session brought about both a new organizational structure and new leadership to Sheafe's field of labor, the South. The new Southern Union Conference superseded the old District No. 2. Veteran leader Robert M. Kilgore returned to the Southland as president of the Southern Union, while N. W. Allee, superintendent of the Southern district for the previous five years, became president of the Dakota Conference.

One major purpose of the denominational reorganization of 1901 was to make the union conferences stronger administrative units than the earlier districts, thus shifting responsibility away from the General Conference in Battle Creek and closer to where the church's work was taking place. In keeping with that principle the General Conference Committee voted to transfer Sheafe, who had been part of the ministerial workforce directly responsible to the General Conference, to the Southern Union, with the specifics of his assignment to be "arranged between himself and the officers of that conference."[6] This action was taken, however, without consulting the officers of the Southern Union, leaving Sheafe in an ambiguous position for several months.

For about six weeks after the close of the General Conference session, Sheafe preached at various locales in Ohio, including Bellefontaine and Waterford. A vignette from Bellefontaine provides a sense of the impact that his many short-term preaching assignments must often have made.

"Elder L. C. Sheaf and family came to this place April 26 and began holding meetings at the SDA church, continuing for ten days. Meetings were held every evening and also on Sabbath and Sunday. . . .The outside interest was very good, there being a good attendance at each meeting. On the evening of May 4 an interesting and profitable talk on temperance was given, and last evening the Lord spoke through His servant with power to the young. A large part of the people who came could not get into the church for lack of room. Some who had not been inside of a church for years attended each one of these meetings, being very much interested. . . . Many lingered to say a farewell word to Elder Sheaf and family."[7]

In June the elder bade farewell to his family, having received word from the new General Conference president, A. G. Daniells, that he was to go to the Southern Union, and, for the summer at least, would have "a rather free hand with reference to selecting your place of labor." Having just assumed office after several years overseas, and thus not thoroughly acquainted with the circumstances of Sheafe's work, Daniells felt that he could not give more definite advice. He asked Sheafe for his own view on what he felt called to do, and encouraged him to "get your orders from the Lord." And, Daniells exhorted, "push your work with all energy, with much prayer, and with tears for your benighted race; and may God greatly bless you."[8]

In reply, Sheafe set forth a tentative itinerary: a "ten-days' meeting" in Camp Nelson beginning June 20; then a return to Aiken for tent meetings, the length to be "governed by the interest"; then to Asheville, North Carolina, where he would remain for a time, "subject to the Lord's orders." Given opportunity simply to follow God's leading as to his work, Sheafe still wondered, "To whom am I to report?"[9]

As Daniells by then knew, and Sheafe would soon know if he didn't already, the leadership of the Southern Union Conference to which he had been assigned was not eager to receive his reports or have him labor in the Southern states at all. Within a day or two after the General Conference Committee action of May 22 recommending that Sheafe work in the Southern Union, Daniells received word from R. M. Kilgore that the Southern Union officers all believed that it would be better for Sheafe "to labor for his people in the Northern states."[10] With the General Conference Committee vote already on record, Daniells wrote Kilgore on May 28 of their recommendation that Sheafe conduct tent meetings in the

South, but added that they had given him the option of going to the North.[11] To Sheafe, however, Daniells wrote that the committee thought that "it might be well" for him to work in the Southern Union in consultation with Elder Kilgore, but did not urge that he do so. He did not, though, mention directly to Sheafe that the "free hand" given him included the possibility of working in the North.[12]

Moreover, in his reply to Sheafe's letter of June 17 he gave several paragraphs of devotional comments, but no answer to the preacher's query concerning the office to which he should report. When Sheafe then inquired about his compensation from the secretary of the Southern Union Conference, he was told that he should look to the General Conference.[13]

H. E. Osborne, the new General Conference secretary, explained to Sheafe that his assignment to the Southern Union had been made rather hastily by the General Conference Committee, with less than half of its members present, and that the Southern Union officers probably hadn't even been informed of it. Because Sheafe had not drawn much from the General Conference treasury that year, Osborne had no problem sending him the $50 he had requested. But the confusion over Sheafe's status was not resolved until October, when Daniells, after returning from extended travels, directed that the General Conference once again take responsibility for Sheafe's wages.[14]

The whole problem could have been attributed to the near inevitability of such mix-ups occurring in the process of a major reorganization, which Daniells indeed cited as a factor, while apologizing for the severe inconvenience to Sheafe and his family. But much greater and more long-lasting damage came from the fact that understandable administrative malfunction was accompanied by the Southern Union leadership's objection to Sheafe's ministry in that territory because of his insistence on preaching a message of racial equality.

Robert Kilgore characterized Sheafe as "unreconciled to the idea of a separation between the whites and the blacks, in the work, in the field and in the church." As a man educated in the North and who had associated with Whites there, Sheafe, said Kilgore, was among those Adventists who came to the South rejecting any adaptation to the hard and pervasive reality of color line. Such advocated that "we, as Christians, should break

down all such lines, override all such customs, and not allow these prejudices to affect us in any way in our labors for poor sinners."[15]

Kilgore's oversimplified depiction did not take into account that
Sheafe had, in fact, received his formal education in Washington, D.C.,
and by 1901 could point to four years of relatively successful evangelistic ministry at several different locales in the difficult Southern field. But
Kilgore, charged with leading the Adventist cause forward among all the
people of the South, held to the bedrock conviction he had formed more
than a decade before: crusading against the color line would defeat the
cause among both races. The White power structure (to use a phrase
coined decades later) would unleash terror and repression, making
growth among the Blacks all but impossible. White believers attempting
to interest their friends and neighbors in the faith would find it dismissed out of hand if meetings brought the races into direct social interaction.

In the basic outlines of this assessment Kilgore was far from alone. As
noted earlier in this chapter, it was similar to that of Charles Kinny,
Adventism's first ordained Black minister. J Edson White, who had seen
violence and intimidation directed against the work of the Southern
Missionary Society, held adamantly to the same position. His experiences
and observations in turn contributed to a cautionary testimony from
Adventism's most influential voice, Ellen White, who had in 1891 declared the principle of racial equality to be written with a "pen of fire."

Thus, Kilgore urged that Sheafe remain in the North, where he could
"talk out all his ideas on the color line question, and not do so much harm
as it is bound to do here." He regarded Sheafe as "a good man and an educated man, a talented man" who "should be kept where he can do the
most good and cause the least possible friction."

In the context of this controversy over race relations, then, it is not
surprising that as a result of the runaround and delays regarding his assignment and pay, "Brother Sheafe and his friends felt as though he was
cut off from the support of the General Conference," as Daniells told the
General Conference Committee.[16] In October Daniells sought to quell the
rumors, sending a check for $25 to Sheafe in South Carolina and promis-
ing him the General Conference Committee at its Fall Council later in the
month would "make some definite arrangement regarding your field." In

the meantime, though, he asked Sheafe not to make his planned preaching tour through the churches until after the council.[17]

When the General Conference Committee took up the question of Sheafe's assignment on October 27, a number of ministers buttressed Kilgore's contention that Sheafe's work had stirred up racial tensions. J. M. Rees, president of the Missouri Conference, reported in Kansas City that "the separation of the races had been delayed and greatly hindered because of [Sheafe's] instruction to the colored people there," and E. T. Russell reported a similar experience from across the border in Kansas City, Kansas. Conversely, Elders Haughey and Mitchell found that in the Ohio churches where Sheafe had labored, the color line had been built up. Speaking "upon request," N. W. Allee, the outgoing supervisor of District No. 2, stated that "the difficulty in Brother Sheafe's work" had arisen at the camp meeting in Knoxville, Tennessee, where Sheafe had asserted that "the races should be placed upon social equality." However, Allee felt that others had largely been responsible for prompting him to voice this demand.[18]

The cryptic and confusing phrases of these minutes, combined with lack of further information on the referenced events, leave a host of unanswered questions. Yet they also yield significant information. Clearly Lewis Sheafe's widely traveled ministry frequently stirred controversy regarding race relations at Seventh-day Adventist churches and gatherings. The eye of the beholder likely governed conclusions about the extent to which that impact was for good or ill.

The committee's discussion about Sheafe concluded with a suggestion from Elder Rees that the preacher be sent to cities where no Seventh-day Adventist church, "either white or colored," existed. Rees's idea received some favorable responses, but no definite action was voted. Daniells, who had assured Sheafe that a decision about his future work would come out of Fall Council, now left him hanging, with no communication at all. Sheafe continued evangelizing in South Carolina under clouds of uncertainty and controversy—an atmosphere conducive to rumors.

Daniells did not address the situation until December, when he received a letter of concern from Annie Sheafe about persisting talk that the General Conference had decided to drop her husband from the Adventist work. He thanked Annie for the "kind spirit" of her letter, and cited his nonstop travels since the Fall Council, much of the time with no stenographer, in apologizing for the delay in writing to Lewis about his field of labor.

The General Conference president emphatically denied any thought of dropping Sheafe from the work, or hearing any of "our brethren" even express such a sentiment. "When I think of the thousands upon thousands of colored people who might be helped by his labors more than almost any other person that I know of, I have an earnest desire to see him throw his life into the proclamation of this message with greater energy and devotion than ever," he wrote.[19] In A. G. Daniells, it appears, Annie Sheafe had found a listening ear.

Having responded quickly to Annie from New York City while still traveling, Daniells wrote to her husband after returning to Battle Creek a week later, finally letting him know what the committee had suggested at the October 27 meeting concerning his future work. The general consensus, he wrote, was that Sheafe should develop the Adventist work in some large northern city. He recalled Minneapolis, St. Louis, and Chicago being mentioned as possibilities. Rather than a specific recommendation, the plan that emerged out of the discussion was to bring the matter to the attention of all the conference presidents, and work with them in finalizing an assignment. The president acknowledged that if he had followed through on this right after the Fall Council, the process would have been well underway. But he had not, and matters remained where they had been on October 27.

Reassuring Sheafe of his importance to the Adventist cause, Daniells extended to him a "warm and official invitation" to an important organizational meeting of the Southern Union Conference planned for Nashville in January 1902. Not only did Daniells plan to be present, but Ellen White and W. C. White were already in Nashville, he said, and expected to remain for the meeting.[20]

In his letter a year before in which he extolled Sheafe's abilities to Ellen White, John Harvey Kellogg had commented that the gifted preacher "has not had very generous encouragement but he is hanging on and doing a good work and the Lord will, one of these days, open the way for him to do a greater work I am sure."[21] Despite Daniells' reassurances, it would be understandable if Sheafe remained skeptical during the

Christmas season of 1901 that the General Conference would be the agency for connecting him to "a greater work." Be that as it may, in this matter the doctor would prove also to be a prophet.

---

[1] "Gem of Song," GCB, Apr. 22, 1901, p. 387.

[2] "Sabbath Services," GCB, Apr. 15, 1901, p. 18.

[3] The proposal for the German work and ensuing motions and discussion are recorded in GCB, Apr. 22, 1901, pp. 388-390.

[4] GCC minutes, Apr. 24, 1901.

[5] GCC minutes, Apr. 25, 1901.

[6] GCC minutes, May 22, 1901.

[7] Ida A. Iles and Clara E. Cemer, "Tidings From the Field," Welcome Visitor, May 30, 1901, p. 4.

[8] AGD to LCS, May 16, 27, 1901, GCA.

[9] LCS to AGD, June 17, 1901, GCA.

[10] RMK to AGD, May 20, 1901, GCA.

[11] AGD to RMK, May 28, 1901, GCA.

[12] AGD to LCS, May 27, 1901, GCA.

[13] LCS to HEO, Aug. 2, 1901, GCA.

[14] HEO to LCS, Aug. 7, 1901, GCA; AGD to LCS, Oct. 16, 1901, GCA.

[15] RMK to AGD, Sept. 4, 1901, GCA.

[16] GCC minutes, Oct. 27, 1901.

[17] AGD to LCS, Oct. 16, 1901, GCA.

[18] "Labors of Elder L. C. Sheafe," GCC minutes, Oct. 27, 1901.

[19] AGD to Annie C. Sheafe, Dec. 10, 1901.

[20] AGD to LCS, Dec. 17, 1901, GCA.

[21] JHK to EGW, Dec. 19, 1900, EGWE.

SECTION FOUR:
"Noted Apostle of Seventh-day Adventism"

"His ardent temperament, his single devotion to the cause . . . his prompt and ready sympathy, his perfect familiarity with the Holy Bible, his exquisite language and extensive vocabulary . . . his scathing denunciation and ridicule of all the traditions . . . in our churches which have no biblical sanction or authority have awakened this sated city, among both the whites and blacks, to the impulses of a higher and truer Christian life."

—COLORED AMERICAN
WASHINGTON, D.C.
SEPTEMBER 13, 1902

CHAPTER XV

A NEW FAITH IN THE NATION'S CAPITAL

"REV. LEWIS C. SHEAFE STIRS WASHINGTON by His Persuasive Eloquence and Convincing Logic." The headlines beneath a striking photo of the evangelist would have immediately grabbed the attention of anyone who glanced at the front page of the September 13, 1902, issue of the *Colored American* newspaper. Most of the paper's Washington, D.C., readers would already have heard something about Lewis Sheafe by then, even if they hadn't been among the thousands attracted to his tent meetings. Just about everyone in Washington, it seemed, was talking about "the noted apostle of Seventh Day Adventism"[1] in the late summer of 1902.

The way to the "greater work" that Dr. Kellogg anticipated had indeed opened, and it was leading Sheafe to the high point of his ministry. It would also make him the central figure in a 15-year drama that would set the terms for race relations in the Adventist Church in the twentieth century. Along with race relations, two additional plot lines make the story revolving around Lewis Sheafe and Washington, D.C., an important and revealing episode in the larger story of the Seventh-day Adventist movement. The first involved the major reorganization of the denomination launched at the General Conference session of 1901. What final shape would the changes voted there take after being hammered out in reality? How strong and lasting would the new structure be?

Along with such questions about church governance in the post-1901 era came questions about the role of Ellen G. White and her writings. How would her prophetic gift function as she approached and entered her 80s? As her activity as a living messenger of the Lord to the church inevitably diminished and then ceased, to what extent and in what ways would her writings continue to be authoritative?

THE STAGE: WASHINGTON, D.C.

Washington, D.C., was a stage made for Lewis Sheafe. In the years prior to the "great migration" that brought large concentrations of African-Americans to the Northern cities, Washington had the largest Black population in the nation—nearly 100,000 in a city of just under 300,000.[2] A mostly light-skinned elite of about 400 enjoyed prestige by virtue of wealth or position in the handful of high positions in the federal government bureaucracy reserved for Blacks. A much larger middle class revolved around the employment opportunities in government offices, Howard University, and the city's outstanding Colored public school system.

A large number of Black churches, linked by numerous social and benevolent organizations, provided a sense of community and opportunities for aid and uplift to higher attainments. Culture, both high and low, thrived along the U Street corridor, the mecca for Black writers, artists, and performers in the years before the more famous Harlem Renaissance of the 1920s and 1930s. No other setting could come close to the importance of Washington to realization of Sheafe's vision that the Adventist message "go to my people all over the United States."[3]

It is not just that no Adventist was as remotely qualified as Sheafe to take that message to the intellectual and cultural capital of Black America. Even more remarkable is the fact that among its small handful of Black preachers in 1902, the Adventist Church had someone so supremely equipped as Sheafe to undertake such a mission. Along with his exceptional gifts as a communicator and years of successful experience as a pastor and race advocate, Sheafe was returning to a city he already knew. He had studied there for four years at Wayland Seminary, gaining a solid foundation in the liberal arts in addition to completing the theological curriculum. And in the course of his seminary years and his eight years of Baptist ministry he had developed a network of connections that helped him gain access to several of the leading Black churches and public forums.

Developments within the Adventist Church also went into preparation of the stage. The aspirations of a vibrant, interracial Adventist congregation that already existed in Washington and the determination of the new General Conference president, Arthur G. Daniells, to resolve the vexing color question in the denomination once and for all met in a momentous intersection that created the circumstances for Sheafe's call to the capital city. Also, the move of the General Conference headquarters from Battle Creek, Michigan, to Washington, D.C., in the summer of 1903 would add a new dimension to the significance of Sheafe's work.

WASHINGTON, D.C.'S EARLIEST ADVENTISTS

The move to Washington is indeed a landmark of Adventist history. But the intriguing origins of the movement in the nation's capital extend farther back, to the 1880s, when Washington was one of several sites in which the church established a "city mission." Out of that mission a congregation of 26 emerged in 1889, formally organized in conjunction with the Spring Council held in Washington that year by the General Conference.[4]

Denominational leaders thus were closely connected with the Washington congregation from its birth. That included Ellen White, who conducted a weeklong series of meetings just prior to the official organization of the new church. She returned a year and a half later to preach for a Week of Prayer in December 1890. While there, she and members of the growing congregation, including their enterprising young pastor, Judson S. Washburn, discussed with growing enthusiasm plans for building a church and mission center that would appropriately represent the Adventist cause in a city of such supreme importance to its world mission.[5]

The ambitious plans as they discussed them in 1890 never really got off the ground. However, in 1893 the congregation purchased from a Presbyterian congregation a modest church building located on Eighth Street Northeast, near Capitol Hill. The church continued to grow, surpassing 150 members by 1900.[6]

Though a part of the geographically vast but numerically small Atlantic Conference in the 1890s, the congregation's leaders repeatedly appealed to the General Conference for help with their church building debt, and for provision of top-quality ministers who could effectively lead evangelistic work appropriate to advancing the cause in the nation's capital. While the General Conference leaders could by no means provide everything requested by the Washington church, they did what they could, and that was enough to sustain the special relationship between the General Conference and this local church.[7]

Most remarkable of all about the Washington congregation was its interracial membership, which included the daughter of Frederick Douglass, Rosetta Douglass Sprague.[8] As the lines of racial separation hardened in America during the 1890s, and settings in which the races interacted on an equal basis became increasingly rare, the Adventist church in Washington sustained its witness to a gospel that overcomes racial barriers. To do otherwise would, in their view, contradict the very reason for their existence—to prepare a people fully dedicated to the way of Christ and prepared to meet Him at His soon return.

Albion F. Ballenger, who conducted a revival series and pastored the church in 1899 and 1900, described the Washington congregation as "a living miracle of the power of God, composed as it is of the two races." Furthermore, the "miracle" did not go unnoticed in the surrounding society, for, said Ballenger, "The harmony which prevails is a great surprise to the members of other churches."[9]

CONFUSION OVER THE COLOR LINE

The commitment of leading members of both races to the church's stand against the color line was genuine and deep. Yet even by the time of Ballenger's tribute, signs of a threat to the church's interracial witness from the phenomenon later termed "White flight" began to appear. Growth was strong among Blacks but stagnant among Whites. Additionally, a disconcerting number of White members were becoming less active or fading away entirely.[10] It was the desire to check this trend before it became irreversible, as well as to advance the church's mission in general, that prompted renewed appeals for support from the General Conference in 1901.

When A. G. Daniells, the forceful 43-year-old elected in 1901 to head the General Conference, began his administrative duties in April, one of the first items on his desk demanding attention was a letter from Andrew Kalstrom, elder of the Washington church. Equal to Daniells in strength of will and unyielding in his commitment to racial equality, Kalstrom had emigrated from Sweden as a boy and had risen to a "responsible position" in the U.S. War Department bureaucracy. His letters to Daniells marked a resumption of persistent appeals begun in 1895 urging General

Conference leaders to support a progressive program for building up the Adventist work in Washington.[11]

Since one of the principles of reorganization in 1901 was to move administrative responsibilities out of Battle Creek to more local levels, the denomination's new leader was somewhat hesitant to resume special General Conference support for the Washington church. He soon became convinced, though, that the high priority of developing a strong base for the Adventist cause in the national capital justified direct General Conference involvement. It was agreed that extra support would be provided from Battle Creek for a strong evangelistic effort that summer.[12]

Specifically, the General Conference sent John L. Brunson, rapidly becoming one of the denomination's most sought-after speakers, to work with the relatively inexperienced William A. Westworth in conducting the campaign. An imposing physical presence with his six-foot-six-inch frame, Brunson, like Sheafe, was a seminary-trained former Baptist minister whose preaching at the 1901 General Conference session elicited enthusiastic acclaim.[13] The members of the Washington church, too, were highly pleased with his work. But with regard to the goal of building up the White membership, the campaign was a signal failure.

Daniells visited Washington to assess matters in July, and when he preached for one of the services at the tent, it was to an audience that was overwhelmingly Black. The enthusiastic response of interested Black people to meetings open to any and all had the effect—sadly—of discouraging participation on the part of White people.[14]

Westworth, who remained as pastor after Brunson left for a new assignment when the series was over, tried to implement new methods for resolving the racial dilemma, such as separate services and racially segregated seating in the sanctuary. Such policies, it was thought, would allay the fears about social mingling of the races that inhibited White growth, while all members would retain membership in the one congregation. These efforts to "draw the color line on the inside" drew such vehement protests from Kalstrom that Daniells urged Westworth to accept a call to Vermont in the fall.[15]

It would not have been surprising if the travails had prompted Daniells to suspend General Conference support for the work in Washington. Instead, a strategy was forming in the General Conference president's mind for turning the race problem in Washington to advantage. If met decisively in Washington, he thought, the delicate but unavoidable problem of the color line could be resolved with the establishment of a unified policy for the entire denomination. Thus, he looked ahead to 1902 as an opportunity to get right in Washington what had gone wrong in 1901.

A haze of ambiguity, conflict, and perplexity hung over the race question in the Adventist Church at the outset of Daniells' administration. Robert Kilgore's proposal for a color-line policy in 1889 had met with a sharp rebuke from Ellen White 1891. The events of the 1890s only confirmed the conviction of Kilgore and other ministers based in the South about the necessity of such an expedient. However, the straightforward statement by Ellen White stood against implementation of an explicit policy. And other influential church leaders such as John Harvey Kellogg, A. T. Jones, E. J. Waggoner, and A. F. Ballenger firmly opposed making distinctions or separations based on race. Dr. Kellogg and Mrs. Almira Steele, allies in developing benevolent institutions in the South, actively resisted accommodations to the color line anywhere.[16]

In 1899 new counsel from Ellen White seemed to lend support to those favoring accommodation. As the prophet sojourned in faraway Australia, letters from her son Edson brought troubling news. He and his coworkers had been caught in the violent backlash of White supremacists as a result of their efforts to bring education and training in economic self-sufficiency to Black Mississippians. A mob had ransacked one of the small churches they had constructed. A Black convert had been whipped with cowhide and his wife shot in the leg. "It is 'Ku Klux' days right over and we are in the midst of it," Edson wrote to his mother.[17]

With this dangerous situation freshly in mind, Ellen White warned against injudicious rhetoric that might lead "the colored people . . . to think that they can defy their oppressors." She urged that "no spirit of resistance be encouraged" and the people be taught "to conform in all things to the laws of their state, when they can do so without conflicting with the law of God."[18]

Even in her fervent affirmation of equality and opposition to a color-line policy in 1891, Ellen White had recommended strategic flexibility in meeting varying circumstances. But facing dangerous new circumstances

at the end of the decade, had she, as some were implying, changed her position on church race relations entirely?

---

[1] The appellation given Sheafe by Edward E. Cooper, editor of the *Colored American*;
see untitled editorial comment, Nov. 8, 1902, p. 8.

[2] Constance McLaughlin Green, *Washington: Village and Capital, 1800-1878* (Princeton,
N.J.: Princeton University Press, 1962), pp. 353-355.

[3] On "Black Washington" in the first decade of the twentieth century, see Jacqueline
M. Moore, *Leading the Race: The Transformation of the Black Elite in the Nation's Capitol,
1880-1920* (Charlottesville, Va.: University Press of Virginia, 1999); Willard B. Gatewood,
Aristocrats of Color: The Black Elite, 1880-1920 (Bloomington, Ind.: Indiana University
Press, 1990), pp. 39-68; *The Black Washingtonians: The Anacostia Museum Illustrated
Chronology* (Hoboken, N.J.: John Wiley & Sons, 2005), pp. 72-76, 127-153.

[4] J. O. Corliss, "At the National Capital," *Review,* Mar. 12, 1889, p. 9; Uriah Smith,
"Visit to Washington," *Review,* Mar. 26, 1889, p. 8; Arthur L. White, *Ellen White: The
Lonely Years* (Washington, D.C.: Review and Herald, 1984), pp. 416, 417.

[5] Ellen G. White manuscript 53, 1890, EGWE.

[6] J. O. Corliss, "The Work in Washington, D.C.," *Review,* Aug. 1, 1893, p. 12; "They
Meet on Saturday, Seventh Day Adventists Secure a Church in Washington," WP, July 17,
1893, p. 5; AGD to EGW, July 12, 1901, CAR.

[7] GCC minutes, Mar. 2, 15, 16, 1899; Oct. 16, 25, 1899; Apr. 8, 1900; Oct 12, 14, 29,
1900.

[8] Louis B. Reynolds documents oral testimony concerning Mrs. Sprague's affiliation
with the Adventist Church in Washington, D.C., in *We Have Tomorrow*, pp. 270, 279.
J. S. Washburn refers to her as a prominent member of the congregation in a letter to
W. C. White, Feb. 18, 1903, EGWE.

[9] AFB to LAH, Dec. 25, 1899, GCA.

[10] AK to HWC, Sept. 3, 1900, GCA.

[11] See, for example, AGD to AK, Apr. 30, 1901; AK to AGD, May 13, 16, 1901, GCA.

[12] AGD to AK, May 21, 27, 1901, GCA.

[13] "Elder Brunson, the Seventh Day Adventist, to Conduct Gospel Meetings in the City,"
Lexington *Morning Herald,* May 12, 1900, p. 4; "Eminent Baptist Divines, They Filled
Columbia Pulpits Yesterday," Charleston *News and Courier,* Dec. 4, 1905, p. 1. In a letter
to Kalstrom written just after the General Conference session of 1901, Daniells stated that
Brunson "preached some of the most powerful sermons delivered during the conference"
(AGD to AK, May 27, 1901, GCA).

[14] AGD to WCW, July 21, 1902, GCA.

[15] W. A. Westworth to EGW, July 24, 1901, EGWE; AK to AGD, Aug. 7, 20, Sept. 21,
and Oct. 6, 1901, GCA; AGD to HWC, Oct. 2, 10, 1901; AGD to William Westworth, Oct.
7, 1901, GCA.

[16] Ronald D. Graybill, *E. G. White and Church Race Relations* (Washington, D.C.: Review
and Herald, 1970), pp. 61-64.

[17] *Ibid.,* pp. 53-62.

[18] "The Work in the South," manuscript 118, 1899, in *Manuscript Releases*, vol. 4,
p. 13.

CHAPTER XVI

THE DANIELLS PLAN

DR. JAMES HOWARD, a black physician and leading member of the Washington church, wrote Ellen White in March 1902, inquiring about reports that "the authorities of the General Conference have had explicit direction from Sister White not to try to keep the two [races] together."[1] His query reflects the lack of clarity about where the denomination stood on what W.E.B. DuBois declared to be *the* problem of the century that lay ahead—"the problem of the color line." Daniells had concluded by the end of his visit in the summer of 1901 that Washington, D.C., would be the key to clearing up the confusion.

At a total of 54, Black believers comprised a little more than a third of the Washington church's official membership list as of 1901.[2] That 54 probably made up the largest concentration of African-American Adventists meeting in a single church anywhere, since the national total at this time was only a few hundred. If for no other reason, this group would figure prominently in the progress of the Adventist movement among their race.

When the new union conferences were created in 1901, it was to the territory of the Atlantic Union Conference that Washington, D.C., was allotted initially and, as it turned out, briefly (1901-1903). But in A. G. Daniells' mind Washington's Black Adventists were bound closely with the Southern Union Conference and the "Southern work"—a phrase that Adventists at that time used as shorthand for work among the nation's Colored population. This was not because of ignorance about differing classes of Black people. Nor was it the result of failure to recognize that Washington presented a very different set of circumstances than those prevailing in the Deep South.

Rather, it was *through* recognition of the city's unique status that Daniells would also come to see its potential as a center from which the entire Adventist work among Black Americans could be shaped and advanced.

"It was the first time I was ever brought into close, serious contact" with the race question, wrote Daniells of his trip to Washington in July 1901.[3] The situation in Washington is "somewhat different . . . from what it is in the more southern states," he noted in a letter to Ellen White. In a sense that made it even "more difficult to handle," yet he expressed confidence that it could be "so managed as to build up the work, both among the white and the colored people."[4]

POINT MAN FOR THE DANIELLS PLAN?

To Willie White a few days later Daniells elaborated on the solution he believed he had hit upon by the end of his two-day visit. About the large "colored population" of Washington, Daniells observed: "As a rule they are a superior lot of people. Many of them are in government service. They have had advantages which have raised them to a higher plane than many of the poor colored people in the Southern states." In view of these facts and the lively interest in Adventism on the part of Black Washingtonians that he had witnessed, Daniells concluded that "there is constant work here for one or two of the best colored preachers we have in the denomination." And he already had Lewis Sheafe in mind—in fact, Sheafe's was the only specific name he mentioned, though it would be more than six months before he would be in a position to invite the preacher to consider it.

So, rather than fight the trend of the existing congregation toward becoming entirely "colored," which he regarded as the inevitable outcome anyway, part of Daniells' plan was to encourage the process. With "Brother Sheafe or some other good colored laborer" it would not be difficult to fill the present structure on Eighth Street with a Black congregation. Meanwhile, a White minister would hold separate meetings for the White population. Such meetings would present "no temptation for the colored people to attend" because of the other meetings being held for their race. The outcome he envisioned, then, was two racially distinct congregations, with the current church building being left with the Black congregation.

Such a solution, Daniells believed, was necessitated by the fact that for all of its differences from the deeper South, a "distinct separation between the white people and the colored people" nonetheless prevailed in Washington. Thus, separate churches would be required to accommodate the "unconverted" who would refuse Adventism a hearing if presented in a setting where that separation was violated. Evangelistic expedience, he insisted, would be the sole rationale for such a policy, for White Adventists should not "harbor the slightest prejudice against the colored, nor feel in any way uncomfortable in meeting with them."

With this plan in mind Daniells now looked toward renewal of General Conference support for Washington in 1902 with considerably greater enthusiasm than he had in 1901. As in 1901, two ministers would be assigned to evangelistic work in the city. This time, though, one would be Black and the other White, each commissioned with building up a separate church from among his own racial group. He proposed that the General Conference pay for the "colored laborer," while the local Chesapeake Conference support a White minister.[5]

During his visit to Washington, Daniells stayed in the home of the church elder, Andrew Kalstrom. The perspective through which the denominational leader filtered his observations, however, was not that of his local host. Daniells' outlook instead resembled that of Kilgore, longtime advocate of the color line as a necessary expedient for Adventist work in the South, under whose guidance Daniells began his ministry in Texas more than two decades before.[6]

Kilgore emphatically endorsed the General Conference president's plan as the only viable way forward in Washington. Despite his adamant opposition to Sheafe working in the Southern Union, Kilgore regarded the preacher as "abundantly capable" for the Washington assignment. But, he added, great care would need to be taken to ensure that Sheafe would closely stick to the plan.

"If [Sheafe] is sent to Washington he should have explicit instructions that he must labor to build up the colored church, or the colored interest in that city. And he should be made fully acquainted with the plans respecting Washington, and the work in that field. If he is not thus instructed, I fear he will put wrong ideas and principles into the heads of those for whom he labors, making it hard for a separation of the races when it is desired. You need not hope that a mixture will succeed there any more than anywhere else, if you expect to get converts from the white population."[7]

Daniells would adhere to the points affirmed by Kilgore in a most uncompromising manner over the next year and a half.

THE NASHVILLE AGREEMENT

Aboard the train to Nashville for the Southern Union organizational meeting in January 1902, Lewis Sheafe probably remained unaware of the plans for Washington that had been germinating for six months. Daniells' letter of December 17 must have brought a measure of relief from the uncertainty and suspicion under which he had labored for months, but gave him no specific assignment, and Washington was not among the cities mentioned as future possibilities.

Sheafe undoubtedly realized, though, that something of major import with regard to race relations was afoot. Simply the fact that the purpose of the Nashville meeting was to complete the basic organizational structure for the work in the South was indication enough. But Daniells had raised expectations further by going out of his way to mention the anticipated presence of Ellen White and W. C. White for the session, scheduled for January 3-13, 1902, in the chapel of the Southern Publishing Association in Nashville, Tennessee. It was a meeting that Sheafe, by informal consensus the leading spokesperson for Black Adventists, could not afford to miss.

For his part Daniells wanted to see the racial policies in his plan for Washington grounded in a broader denominational consensus before moving ahead with implementation. And he wanted to determine if Sheafe would be loyal to that consensus before sending him as Adventism's apostle to Black Washington.

The Nashville Conference was the Southern Union's first "constituency meeting" since its organization eight months before at the General Conference in Battle Creek. The agenda was a large one, with reports from eight conferences, five of which had just been formed in the months since the close of the General Conference session, and matters of the publishing, medical, and educational lines of the work to consider. Of particular importance were the two fledgling educational institutions—

the Oakwood Industrial School in Huntsville, Alabama, and the Southern Training Institute in Graysville, Tennessee.

At the session former General Conference president George I. Butler, coming out of a period of semiretirement in Florida, was elected president, replacing R. M. Kilgore, who became vice president. The names presented by the nominating committee on January 9 for the five-member board of the Huntsville Industrial School—all White men—received a unanimous vote of approval. However, at that point a motion came from the floor to add to the board "Brother L. C. Sheafe and Brother Brandon," the latter a layman from the Huntsville area.[8] The motion carried, making Sheafe and William Brandon the first persons of color to sit on the board of the historically Black institution that became today's Oakwood University.

Between the lines of the *Southern Watchman* report about the addition of Sheafe and Brandon to the Oakwood board lay the reality that "the color question" received extensive attention at the Nashville meeting, despite its absence from official reports. Sheafe and the "good representation of our colored brethren" whose presence Daniells noted in his report for the *Review and Herald*,[9] were consulted in the deliberations, but not included in the decision-making process. Daniells, W. C. White, Edson White, George I. Butler, R. M. Kilgore, Irving Keck, D. T. Shireman, and the state conference presidents constituted a committee that met several times for lengthy discussions of the issue. The committee then also met for counsel with the "colored brethren" before presenting their conclusions to the session at large.[10]

Ellen White's inability to take an active part in the Nashville conference because of a bad cold contracted at South Lancaster, Massachusetts, just before making the trip south was a disappointment to all, but particularly to Sheafe and the other Black brethren, who had largely been "shut off by themselves." They regarded Ellen White as a champion of their interests and hoped for intervention from her that never came.[11]

Whether restrained more by Ellen White's statement of opposition to a fixed color-line policy in 1891 or by general caution about stirring up an exceptionally volatile and sensitive issue, the committee "did not feel free to draft a statement of our decision," Daniells explained to H. W.

Cottrell, president of the Atlantic Union Conference. However, in letters to Cottrell and others, Daniells laid out, in clear and forceful, if somewhat unpolished, language, four points resulting from the consultations. And he made it clear that he expected the points to carry the force of operating policy. The session unanimously agreed:

"First, That the time in which we live, and the message we have to give, demand that we shall not waste our time in squabbles over the color question; but that we devote our energies to the salvation of both races.

"Second, That no effort be made to bring about an equality of the races, nor to join the popular cry of elevating the colored man.

"Third, That we advise separate meetings of the races in those parts of the country where it causes offense for them to mix.

"Fourth, That in separating the races for meeting purposes, we shall not leave the colored people to themselves, nor neglect friendly counsel and cooperation in church management."[12]

As a result of the Nashville meetings, Daniells triumphantly proclaimed, the Adventist work in the South was now solid for the accommodationist policy:

"Our brethren in the South are solid on this now, and woe be to the man who comes down from the North and advocates mixed congregations. Hereafter the brethren will desire to know from those contemplating coming to the South where they stand on this question, and if they are intending to agitate the matter of mixing up, they will be requested to remain in the North. Some of these men have done untold harm in the South, and now that a unanimous agreement has been reached, the brethren do not wish to be harassed any more in this way."

Daniells claimed that the Black Adventists present at the Nashville meetings registered "no opposition" to the agreement, though he hedged just a bit with the phrase "so far as I know." He seems to have been oblivious to the fact that the process itself, in which the "colored brethren" were brought in for a session of "friendly counsel" but were excluded from the decisive deliberations, was not one likely to elicit their true thoughts or genuine input.

It is next to impossible to conceive of Sheafe truly embracing the Nashville policy, particularly the first two points. Since no formal record was made, it may also be that in his letters to other church leaders,

Daniells was giving his own hurried summary of points presented in a less direct, explicit way to the Black representatives.

Yet it also seems clear that in his role as the leading figure among the Black representatives, Sheafe took a conciliatory, pragmatic approach in Nashville. He and Daniells had talked things over at length one-to-one, and Daniells claimed that Sheafe "seemed in harmony with the general principles laid down." The words "seemed" and "*general* principles" suggest Daniells' own recognition that he could not claim precise, definite agreement on all points. Yet no protests occurred, and the meeting resulted in apparent unity. Sheafe's motivation and reasoning are less clear, yet some underpinnings for the united front can be inferred.

When Daniells told to those assembled in Nashville that the third angel's message was "the best thing in this world for the colored race," and that "the man who will give the negro this message is bestowing upon him the greatest blessing that can come to him," Sheafe could heartily agree. He had said essentially the same thing at the General Conference session in 1899.

While highly implausible that Sheafe would have found the president's wording of the Nashville agreement satisfactory, it is plausible that he expressed concurrence with the general principle of focusing energies on raising up Black congregations rather than pushing for racially mixed ones. On the one hand, Sheafe had by then developed a considerable record of successful ministry to White people, particularly in Ohio, and he believed it was God's will that people of different races should interact freely on terms of equality and mutual respect. On the other, though, his original calling had been "Go preach to *your* people," and, after embracing Adventism, he understood his mission to be that of taking the message of present truth to his people. At the 1901 General Conference session he had advocated a separate department for the "colored work," similar to that being established for recent immigrants of various European ethnicities. And he may have taken the unfortunate aftermath of the revival-induced integration of the church in Louisville in 1899 as a caution against similar moves in the future.

So it would not be surprising if during his conversation with Daniells in Nashville, Sheafe indeed indicated that he was "perfectly willing to see the races meet at separate places for worship," and, moreover, "perfectly willing to go to any city in the United States, and give his life up to his own people."[13]

---

[1] J. H. Howard to EGW, Mar. 23, 1902, in "Letters on Racial Justice From the Louis B. Reynolds Collection," compiled by Emory J. Tolbert, in Edwin J. Humphrey (with Emory Tolbert), *My Soul Doth Magnify the Lord* (Huntsville, Ala.: Oakwood College Pub. Assn., 2001), pp. 75-78.

[2] "The Seventh Day Adventists," CA, July 5, 1902, p. 8, reports a total of 154 members, 54 of them "colored." According to Daniells' letter of July 21, 1901, cited below, the active membership was closer to 50 percent Black at that point.

[3] AGD to WCW, July 21, 1901, CAR.

[4] AGD to EGW, July 12, 1901, CAR.

[5] AGD to WCW, July 21, 1901, CAR.

[6] D. Pettibone, "An Adventist Apostle to Dixie," p. 5.

[7] RMK to AGD, Sept. 4, 1901, GCA.

[8] "Minutes of the Southern Union Conference, Held at Nashville, Tennessee, January 3-12, 1902," *Southern Watchman*, Jan. 16, 1902, pp. 1, 2.

[9] A. G. Daniells, "Southern Union Conference," *Review*, Jan. 21, 1902, p. 8.

[10] Daniells describes the proceedings in two letters to H. W. Cottrell, Jan. 21, 1902, and Feb. 3, 1902, GCA.

[11] Daniells, "Southern Union Conference." Evidence for the Black representatives' feelings about being "shut off by themselves," and lack of intervention from Ellen White is drawn from JSW to EGW, June 5, 1903, EGWE.

[12] AGD to HWC, Jan. 21, 1902, GCA.

[13] AGD to HWC, Jan. 21, 1902.

CHAPTER XVII

FROM NASHVILLE TO WASHINGTON, D.C., VIA DES MOINES

THE MOST DECISIVE FACTOR in the unlikely concordat between Sheafe and Daniells at Nashville indeed probably was a pragmatic one—a convergence of interests. For it was in Nashville that Daniells put before Sheafe the possibility of being assigned to Washington, and it is clear that both men wanted to see it happen. As they contemplated plans for Washington, D.C., both were torn between hope and fear, between grand aspirations for the cause of God and anxieties over the potential for grievous harm to race relations in the Adventist movement.

WEIGHING HOPES AND FEARS

A. G. Daniells deeply desired that his plans for Washington succeed. He wanted Adventists to establish a more powerful mission in a city of critically important influence, and he believed that only by establishing a separate congregation for each race did they stand a realistic chance of accomplishing that goal. If they did, Washington would serve as a model for resolving the race problem in the Adventist Church along the lines of the Nashville agreement, and as a center for training Black workers to take the message to their race throughout the nation.

He hoped that Lewis Sheafe would take on the challenge of leading the Black work in the city because he knew Sheafe was by far the man best fitted for the task. "Personally I like the man very much," Daniells wrote in appraising H. W. Cottrell of the situation following the Nashville conference. "He is a talented man, both as a speaker and a singer, and has the fullest confidence of all his people; so far as I know there is not a colored man among our people in the South who has the respect and confidence of the whole colored department of our people that Elder Sheafe has."[1]

To Sheafe Daniells pointed out that doors were open for him to work in other cities if he did not feel clear about undertaking the campaign in Washington on General Conference terms. However, Daniells grasped something of the unique significance of Washington for Black America and could sense that Sheafe, while well able to succeed just about anywhere, was uniquely prepared for Washington:

"Somehow I feel that you are the man for that place, and that by diligent efforts you will be able to bring many of your race in that large city to a saving knowledge of present truth.

"I do not believe there is another opportunity in the world like this for helping your people."[2]

At the same time, Daniells had misgivings about whether Sheafe would adhere to the General Conference plan that the new effort in Washington lead to separate, racially defined churches. Sheafe had, after all, developed a reputation for stirring up controversy on the race question. It was not, however, Sheafe's own intentions that concerned Daniells nearly so much as the forces in Washington, led by Andrew Kalstrom, arrayed in adamant opposition to division of the church along racial lines.

Kalstrom had set forth his position with trenchant eloquence in October 1901:

"Strong progressive work is not that which seeks to separate the believers. The world day by day is widening the breach between the races by every possible way and this separation is wrong. If this same practice is followed by the SDA it must still continue wrong. God has spoken upon this subject very clearly."

The Washington elder rejected the idea that church practices might vary in accordance with prevailing worldly practices:

"I believe that the view I hold as to the absolute oneness of all who are in Christ is right and that the principle of equality must stand alike in all places. When I see the leaders who stand in the front planning for numbers and realizing that they are taking the world as the pattern I cannot help the distress I feel."[3]

Kalstrom, said Daniells, has "a will like iron"[4] and is "most decidedly opposed to the policy enunciated in Nashville."[5] He warned Cottrell that

"Brother Kalstrom is going to make it hard for us to ever settle that race question in Washington."[6]

Daniells' great concern was that Sheafe might be induced by Kalstrom to abandon the separation plan. His worry about Sheafe's vulnerability was, in part, rooted in a racial stereotype. As with "all the rest of the colored people," it would not take much to make Sheafe feel "slighted by the white brethren," and Kalstrom could exploit this trait to his advantage.[7] So the large question troubling Daniells was Could he trust Sheafe to hold firmly to the General Conference plan for Washington?

For his part Lewis Sheafe surely found the possibility of returning to Washington exhilarating. The door through which he could reach Black America's center of influence lay open before him. For him the fear grew out of tension between his convictions about the truth of Adventism and its potential benefit for his people, on the one hand, and, on the other, mounting disillusionment over evidence of racial inequity in the church. More specifically, he was apprehensive that in his role of facilitating the plan for separate churches, he would end up being seen as the tool of an unjust system. He made clear that he did not want to be placed in the position of having to enforce the separation plans—conference officials should bear that responsibility. Daniells agreed, yet the path ahead remained anything but clear.[8]

Sheafe wanted to go to Washington, but could he do so under the terms outlined by A. G. Daniells? Could he trust Daniells and the General Conference to make good on enthusiastic expressions of support for the "colored work," so that Black people could become full participants in the Adventist movement and its institutional life on an equal, if often separate, basis?

Though both harbored apprehensions, neither was inclined to be paralyzed by them. Thus, Sheafe and Daniells parted in Nashville with plans to move forward, barring objection from the leadership of the Atlantic Union or Chesapeake conferences. Fresh evidence, however, that Andrew Kalstrom intended all-out resistance confirmed Daniells' feeling that it would be unwise to send Sheafe to Washington before a White counterpart was found and in place. If Sheafe arrived first and worked alone for a time, Kalstrom and his allies, he thought, would have opportunity to gain control of the situation much more easily in the interval before the White minister's arrival.[9]

For a few more months Sheafe was free to accept preaching invitations as he saw fit in Ohio and beyond, and with him such were never in short supply. In late February, for example, Sheafe conducted a series of revival meetings in the small town of Waterford, located near Marietta in southeastern Ohio. The place was considered "one of the worst in the state," according to George Cemer's report in the *Welcome Visitor*, and the church badly in need of revival.

"We not only invited but urged Elder L. C. Sheafe to come and spend as much time with us as possible," said Cemer. By the second meeting it was clear that the Adventist church, which could seat 150, was not going to be nearly large enough. At the offer of local citizens who were not members of the church to pay for the rental, the meetings were moved to a public hall with a somewhat larger capacity of 200 to 300. But here too, at the final service, many had to be turned away, for even the standing room was all taken. The series "revived our hearts, healed wounds, opened hearts and doors of the people, and awakened sinners in and out of Zion," reported Cemer. Indeed, he said, "a deeper spiritual interest" had never been seen in the town.[10]

THE SECOND EVANGELIST, AND SECOND THOUGHTS

Around the time of the Waterford meetings in late February, two letters from A. G. Daniells, dated a week apart, arrived at the Sheafe home in Mount Vernon with news that a White minister had been secured for the work in Washington, namely, Judson S. Washburn. As with Sheafe, the assignment meant for Washburn a return to the national capital, where he had conducted evangelistic efforts and served as pastor of the church from 1890 to 1891. Washburn, too, was an accomplished musician as well as a speaker. After leaving Washington in 1891 he spent a decade in England, and is credited with an important role in establishing a more solid foundation for the early Adventist work in that nation. An aggressive and tireless promoter, he engaged in extensive correspondence with several of Adventism's leading figures in that era, such as Ellen White and W. C. White, in addition to Daniells.

Washburn would not be able to relocate in Washington until sometime in May, said Daniells, promising more details soon so that Sheafe could plan accordingly. Things were moving forward, but the president seemed troubled by forebodings about Sheafe's level of commitment to the operational plans for Washington. "I feel exceedingly anxious, Brother Sheafe, with reference to this matter," he wrote, outlining the extent of the General Conference's investment in Washington—over the recent years, and now once again amid great scarcity of funds. "Knowing as you both do the views of the General Conference Committee, and realizing that they are making a sacrifice to support the work there," he reiterated, "I am sure you would decline to go if you could not work in harmony with our plans." He recommended that the two ministers together formulate a plan of action, winning over the church members in Washington with a firm and united front from the outset.[11]

New questions were emerging in Sheafe's mind as well, reflected in a letter, now lost, sent to Daniells in mid-March from Terre Haute, Indiana. Whether somehow prompted by Daniells' letter of February 26 or information from other sources, Sheafe now sought more details on the situation in Washington, as viewed from the General Conference perspective. The letter prompted lengthy consideration of the Washington plans by members of the General Conference Committee and "other brethren" during a meeting in Elder Daniells' office on March 20.

The committee agreed that an unambiguous meeting of minds regarding Washington should be sought at a face-to-face meeting of the principals at the time of the Northwestern Union Conference meeting scheduled for early April in Des Moines, Iowa. If that meeting did not produce a definite and mutually satisfactory agreement, "it was suggested that Elder Sheafe be invited to labor in Minneapolis."[12]

In a follow-up letter to Sheafe the next day Daniells emphatically reiterated that if the General Conference was to devote still more money to Washington, "the work must be done along the lines that our consciences approve. We do not propose to throw money away on what seems certain to us to be a fruitless effort."[13]

ATTENTION IS BEING DIRECTED TO US

As Sheafe and Daniells rethought the delicate situation, Dr. James Howard of Washington gave the most insightful analysis of it yet in a letter sent on March 23 to Ellen White in California. A physician trained at Howard University Medical School and a federal government clerk, Dr.

Howard was an uncle and mentor of the renowned Eva B. Dykes, who in 1921 became the first African-American woman to complete the requirements for a Ph.D.[14] He composed several letters to Adventist leaders over the years that were extraordinarily powerful in their penetrating, unaffected eloquence and profound spiritual depth. Regardless of whether either Daniells or Sheafe ever saw his letter of March 23, it is invaluable for understanding the scene into which Sheafe was about to plunge.

In an even fuller and more winsome manner than Kalstrom, Howard made the case for the mixed-race Washington church as a living witness to the prophetic message of Adventism, and the ruinous consequences of destroying that witness. Though Sheafe did not see establishing integrated churches as his primary calling, he so fully shared and championed the principles animating Howard's letter that he could not possibly have positioned himself in opposition to the doctor's claims about what the Washington church was accomplishing through its present racial inclusiveness.

In his letter to Ellen White, Dr. Howard explained how that inclusiveness, far from hindering the Adventist cause, drew the respect and admiration of high-minded Christians from both races:

"One of the strongest points of the Adventist cause in Washington among many white and colored people outside the church has been that with regard to the race question the Adventists were following the Christian course in that they did not separate their members on account of race."

Now, after more than a decade of standing in the name of Christ against the tide of racial oppression that surged throughout the nation in the 1890s, indications that the Adventists too were capitulating caused corresponding damage to the church's witness. And it could get much worse, for the question of how things would work out at the church on Eighth Street was becoming a matter of considerable public interest:

"But now some of these people outside the church, of both races (even some who are interested in the truth), are surprised, disappointed and even becoming hardened against the cause because a worldly spirit and prejudice against the colored people have arisen in the Adventist Church. In fact, attention is being directed to us, and there is increasing interest, outside the church and inside, to know just where the Adventists will stand now on this question at the national capital and elsewhere."

Howard denied the motivation, often attributed to Blacks in the correspondence of White church leaders, that association with White people in the church brought a prized privilege or status sought after for its own sake.

"The colored people . . . prefer and hope for union for the truth's sake, not because they seek affiliation with the opposite race. They are confident that if the spirit of separation prevail, great harm will be done to the cause here. And they pray the Lord will show their brethren their error, change the hearts of the few active spirits that are making the trouble, and save them, and enable us all to represent the truth aright."

Despite the strength of his convictions, Dr. Howard wrote in a spirit of humility and openness to prophetic guidance. He recognized that through the prophet Samuel the Lord had finally allowed Israel to have a king, even though it was contrary to the divine ideal. Thus, he and those who shared his convictions would have to be open to the possibility that something similar might happen with regard to the Washington church. He put two specific questions before Ellen White. First, did she have light "favoring the division of the Washington church"? Second, if the division took place, should the White people whose declared intention was to "go into the church with the colored people" be required instead to unite with the church formed for White people?[15]

Ellen White did not at this point give a direct response to these questions. The faithful would have to work them out on the conflicted ground that Lewis Sheafe was about to enter.

CRISIS AT OAKWOOD

Just prior to the meeting with Daniells and Washburn in Des Moines for final consultation on the plans for Washington, Sheafe was summoned to Huntsville, Alabama, in connection with his new responsibilities as a member of the board of the Oakwood school. It was an important meeting, extending over several days from March 28 to April 3. Along with urgent personnel matters, the first board meeting in the school's history in which Black members—Sheafe and William Brandon—participated, also gave extensive consideration to the question of Black involvement in the governance of the "colored school." In the past, according to board chair G. I. Butler, "some feeling with our colored brethren" had arisen "because they were not made better acquainted with the management of the school."

The board gave "careful study" to the matter over several days, and in the process Butler developed a highly favorable impression of Sheafe, calling him "by far the ablest colored preacher I have met." Sheafe had "sanctioned every step taken," which Butler, not surprisingly, called "a manly, sensible course." As the deliberations concluded, Sheafe and Brandon expressed their satisfaction by making a public statement "that they were better prepared to recommend the school among their people, and induce the young people to patronize it."[16]

The venerable church leader also felt that he and Sheafe had developed a good personal rapport. Along with his positive estimate of the preacher, Butler judged that Sheafe's "Christian experience needs deepening." Thus, "I took extra pains to get into Elder Sheafe's heart so that I might be able to help in the divine life," Butler wrote to Ellen White. No record has been found of Sheafe's own view of Butler's assumption of a position of spiritual superiority from which to help him, but Butler perceived the response as quite favorable. Sheafe "became very friendly," he wrote, "and we agreed to correspond with each other."[17]

During the time of his transition to Washington, D.C., the General Conference cleared up the question marks about Sheafe's wages left over from the misunderstandings and confusion of 1901. As rumors spread that year about a shortfall in his compensation from the General Conference, even that he had been cut off entirely, Sheafe's friends in Ohio began circulating "subscription papers" to generate support for him. While assuring the preacher that he did not believe him to be the instigator of this activity, Daniells asked Sheafe to tell his supporters to discontinue it, which Sheafe readily did.[18]

At the same time, Daniells accepted responsibility for the neglect that caused the lengthy disruption in Sheafe's wages, and the General Conference proceeded with setting its accounts with Sheafe in order. The substantial check he received buoyed Sheafe's spirits as he embarked on his new challenge.[19]

The time had finally come. Lewis and Annie, with their three growing children—Clara, 13; Howard, 11; and Lewis, Jr., 6—left Mount Vernon, Ohio, their home for four years, and settled at 2010 Third Street NW. in Washington during the second week of May.

"Be of good courage: live near to the Lord, and plan large things for your race"—that was the General Conference president's charge.[20]

"There are breakers ahead," the preacher recognized, "but Jesus is equal to them all. It is in Him we trust."[21]

------

[1] AGD to HWC, Jan. 21, 1902, GCA.

[2] AGD to LCS, Feb. 19, 1902, GCA.

[3] AK to AGD, Oct. 6, 1901, GCA.

[4] AGD to JSW, Feb. 26, 1902, GCA.

[5] AGD to GIB, Feb. 26, 1902, GCA.

[6] AGD to HWC, Jan. 21, 1902, GCA.

[7] AGD to HWC, Jan. 27, 1902, GCA.

[8] AGD to HWC, Jan. 21, 1902, GCA.

[9] AGD to HWC, Feb. 3, 1902, GCA; AGD to LCS, Feb. 7, 1902, GCA.

[10] "Tidings From the Field," *Welcome Visitor,* Mar. 13, 1902, pp. 3, 4.

[11] AGD to LCS, Feb. 26, 1902, GCA.

[12] GCC minutes, Mar. 20, 1902.

[13] AGD to LCS, Mar. 21, 1902, GCA.

[14] DeWitt S. Williams, *She Fulfilled the Impossible Dream: The Story of Eva B. Dykes* (Hagerstown, Md.: Review and Herald, 1985).

[15] J. H. Howard to EGW, Mar. 23, 1902, in *My Soul Doth Magnify the Lord,* pp. 75-77.

[16] Geo. I. Butler, "Our Training School (Colored) at Huntsville, Ala.," *Review,* June 10, 1902, p. 17; GIB to EGW, Apr. 28, 1902, EGWE.

[17] GIB to EGW, Apr. 28, 1902.

[18] AGD to LCS, Feb. 7, 19, 1902, GCA.

[19] HEO to LCS, Apr. 9, 1902; LCS to HEO, May 16, 1902, GCA.

[20] AGD to LCS, Feb. 19, 1902, GCA.

[21] LCS to HEO, May 16, 1902, GCA.

CHAPTER XVIII

THOUSANDS HEAR HIM

LEWIS C. SHEAFE AND FRED H. SEENEY, a young minister from Delaware assigned by the Chesapeake Conference to assist Sheafe, began evangelistic meetings in Washington, D.C., on June 1. Through the pages of the *Atlantic Union Gleaner* they sought the prayers of fellow believers that "the Lord may bring out a company of commandment keepers in the capital city of this nation who will have a right to the capital city of the earth when it is made new."[1] They pitched their "gospel tent" at the corner of 16th and R streets NW. Given Sheafe's track record, they likely felt hopeful about eventually seeing all 400 of its seats filled. Did they even dream, though, that before the series was over, crowds reaching 2,000 would come out to hear the messages that, in the words of the *Colored American* newspaper, "awakened this sated city, among both the whites and blacks, to the impulses of a higher and truer Christian life"?[2]

Initially attendance was not large, but the momentum rapidly built into what Sheafe later called "a movement . . . with a spirit and power that only the Lord can give."[3] By early July almost as many people were standing on the outskirts of the tent as those occupying the seats on the inside. The evangelizers set up 400 seats around the tent, so that when the weather cooperated, 800 could be accommodated. By mid-August even that was not nearly enough, with crowds reaching 1,500, the number standing again almost equaling to the number seated.[4]

Seeney, who came from the people of mixed racial heritage in Delaware identified as "Moors," conducted "Bible readings" with individuals and small groups during the day.[5] Annie Sheafe, who would later be officially employed by the denomination as a Bible worker, likely engaged in visitation and Bible readings as well during the 1902 campaign, in addition to assisting her husband with the music for the evening meetings.[6] Thirteen-year-old Clara also made a vital contribution as organist for the meetings.[7] Occasional special attractions helped boost interest. Lucinda Vance, formerly of the Fisk Jubilee Singers, sang for the evening meeting on June 28, at which Sheafe preached his dramatic sermon "The Feast of Belshazzar."[8]

The pace and extent of the campaign were nothing less than astounding. From June to October, meetings were held at the tent every night, except for Saturdays. For much of that time an additional meeting was held during the day on Sundays—at first in the afternoon, then at 11:00 a.m. later in the series. When Sabbath services at the church where he alternated with Washburn are taken into consideration, Sheafe was preaching seven to nine times per week for four months.[9]

A setback came on June 30. A dog viciously attacked Clara on her way home from the meeting that night, tearing her clothes and biting her in three places. It would be more than a month before she would recover sufficiently to resume her place at the organ.[10]

Overall, though, the meetings enjoyed spectacular success. The city's newspapers began paying attention in early July, when the *Colored American* reported that at his "well-attended meetings" Sheafe "argues his faith in an eloquent manner" and added that "he is a singer of ability."[11] It was the beginning of the highly favorable coverage given Sheafe over the next two years, particularly in the *Colored American* and in the city's other Black-owned weekly newspaper, the Washington *Bee*, but also on occasion in the White-owned dailies.

The most detailed report of a single meeting appeared in the September 1 edition of the Washington *Post*, by which time the tent had been relocated to 13th and T streets NW. That report and the laudatory profile in the September 13 edition of the *Colored American* are the richest sources available on Sheafe's preaching and on what made the attraction to his meetings so compelling.

The *Post*'s page 2 story, "Thousands Hear Him, Negro Minister Draws Large Crowds to His Tent," estimated the crowd at the meeting on August

31 at 2,000, with more than half standing throughout Sheafe's sermon on "The Marriage Supper of the Lamb." Children sat on the tent's "rude platform," around the preacher's feet.

Bearing out the *Colored American*'s reference to Sheafe's "attractive voice" and "fine musical ability," the *Post* story added an observation about the power of audience participation.

"Mr. Sheafe sings a number of songs at each meeting, the rendition of them being very effective. Usually the audience joins in the chorus, making such congregational music as is seldom heard in the churches.

"As for sermon delivery, the 'tall and angular' preacher 'drives home his texts with long-arm gestures, not altogether ungraceful, while his rich, resonant voice goes low in range or swells in volume as he brings out the points in his discourse.'"

The *Post* also generally corroborated the *Colored American*'s praise for Sheafe's "perfect familiarity with the Holy Bible, his exquisite language and extensive vocabulary," albeit less effusively. Sheafe had the ability to express familiar points in ways both fresh and memorable, the *Post* reporter observed. Sheafe had "the faculty of saying much that his hearers cannot but notice and remember," treating the basic, well-known truths of the Bible in such a way "as to appear new again."

The *Post* also detailed the way in which Sheafe demonstrated his facility with Scripture: "His sermons are extemporaneous entirely and are simply made up of Bible texts, the exposition of one leading to another, to which, as he talks, he turns with marvelous rapidity." Sheafe would raise a question and then turn to a scriptural passage for the answer, thus reading and explaining a vast number of texts in the course of a sermon.

In treating "The Marriage Supper of the Lamb," Sheafe, as he typically did, stressed the need for genuine, thorough, and even strenuous faith that truly transforms the life. He warned his hearers against expecting some kind of spiritual makeover in the grave that would prepare them for eternity. "You will be the same," he told them. So they needed *now* to "come to the station of the man in Christ Jesus." God's power can make that possible, he affirmed: "Every promise the Father makes He is able to perform." Thus: "Don't play at religion; live it. . . .You must do, more than say. . . .The life we live talks. Men may disagree with your theology, but your life tells."

Thus, he said, the garment of righteousness necessary for admittance to the great wedding feast that God has in store for the faithful cannot be a passive thing: "You can't keep the garment in a trunk or your bureau drawer. You've got to get it and wear it." For all of the emphasis on the need for human action, Sheafe typically brought the matter around to the necessity and availability of divine grace: "You can get the garment right now from the Lord."

Sheafe's sermon topics, according to the *Colored American* profile, were "not solely doctrinal or essentially religious exclusively," but dealt with "all the intricate and oft elusive questions of the day." His messages on temperance, for example, had "a most revivifying effect," leading many who had "imbibed too freely" throughout their lives to begin anew "the struggle to free themselves from liquid damnation."

The *Post*'s summary of Sheafe's August 31 sermon shows him connecting the Christian hope for the future with another "intricate" question of the day: the indignities many of his hearers faced every day of their present lives because of race:

"'To him that overcometh will I grant to sit with Me on My throne.' The color of your skin or the kink in your hair will not be counted against you if you have overcome. The Lord's table will not be a table out in the kitchen or down in the cellar. You will sit, if you are faithful, with Abraham and Isaac and Jacob, for you have the same faith as they."

The *Post* story gave high prominence to the fact that Sheafe preached "a simple gospel." Later, critics within the Adventist Church would cast doubt on whether he really preached the full range of Seventh-day Adventist doctrines. However, Sheafe's ability to express biblical teachings in simple yet vivid ways should not be confused with soothing his listeners in their present level of understanding and behavior. According to the *Colored American* his messages included "scathing denunciation and ridicule of all the traditions, fetishes and practices in our churches which have no biblical sanction or authority." And the notion that Sheafe minimized distinctive Adventist teachings gains no support from a flyer listing the topics at the "Beacon Light Gospel Tent" for the first week in September:[12]

Social Purity and Health

Law of God, Is It Binding?

The Two Laws

The Sabbath of the Lord?
Is Sunday the Lord's Day?
Prophetic America

Progress reports on the meetings give the impression that Sheafe was rather thorough and deliberate in leading prospective believers to solid understanding of the Adventist message and commitment to it before baptizing them. He also seems to have been fairly careful about distinguishing between these and the larger number who had responded favorably but not yet as fully. At the meeting on July 2 Sheafe asked those who believed the message being presented to raise their hands, and 150 to 200 did so. Of these he then asked those "willing to obey the message and step out on the promises of God" to so indicate by standing. More than 75 rose to their feet. About six weeks later in mid-August only 30 had "signed the covenant" and were "walking in the light of God's truth." Out of these, 18 had "united with the church."[13]

Many more were reading and inquiring, discussing the issues with Sheafe and Seeney and with their own ministers. As the evangelist pressed the matter of commitment to a new religious allegiance, opposition from other ministers naturally increased. In early September the *Colored American* reported:

"Baptists, Methodists, Presbyterians, and Episcopalians have helped to swell Dr. Sheafe's audiences, and have gone out heralding his wonderful command of biblical knowledge and the convincing power of his argument. . . . In fact, this Seventh Day apostle is making such a profound impression upon the members of certain churches that according to report, the pastors of the same have asked their 'regulars' to desist from Dr. Sheafe's meetings, contending that his heterodoxy will prove demoralizing to the peace and mind that orthodox Christians enjoy under normal conditions."[14]

In the months and years that followed, Sheafe would display an intriguing capacity for bringing core Adventist teachings into the arena of public debate with his fellow ministers and community leaders, without creating barriers to ongoing interaction and cooperation. As for the summer tent effort of 1902, by October it had brought a total of 60 new members into the Adventist Church, through a process that entailed much study, questioning, and discussion, leading to thorough commitment.

[1] L. C. Sheafe and F. H. Seeney, "Washington, D.C.," *Atlantic Union Gleaner,* July 9, 1902, pp. 9, 10. This report for the *Gleaner* was prepared by Seeney, who used the first person ("I") in the opening paragraph. He may have originated the quoted phrase, or he may have picked it up from Sheafe.

[2] "A New Faith Comes," CA, p. 2.

[3] Lewis C. Sheafe, "People's Seventh-day Adventist Church of Washington, D.C.," *Review,* Aug. 24, 1905, p. 15.

[4] Reports by Sheafe and Seeney, each entitled "Washington, D.C.," in *Atlantic Union Gleaner,* July 9, 1902, pp. 9, 10; *Atlantic Union Gleaner,* Aug. 20, 1902, p. 7; *Review,* Aug. 26, 1902, p. 14.

[5] *Atlantic Union Gleaner,* July 9, 1902, p. 9.

[6] "The Seventh Day Adventists," CA, July 5, 1902, p. 8.

[7] LCS to HEO, Aug. 1, 1902, GCA.

[8] "Sunday Church Services," WP, June 28, 1902, p. 11.

[9] SS to AGD, Feb. 27, 1908, GCA, indicates that Sheafe and Washburn alternated preaching duties at the church.

[10] LCS to HEO, July 1, 1902, and Aug. 1, 1902, GCA.

[11] "The Seventh Day Adventists," CA, July 5, 1902, p. 8.

[12] Flyer included with incoming correspondence from Sheafe, GCA.

[13] "Washington, D.C." reports in *Atlantic Union Gleaner,* July 9, 1902; *Atlantic Union Gleaner,* Aug. 20, 1902; *Review,* Aug. 26, 1902.

[14] "Some Afterthoughts, The Colored American's Philosopher at Work," CA, Sept. 6, 1902, p. 1.

CHAPTER XIX

COLOR LINE DRAWN
BETWEEN ADVENTISTS

SIXTY NEW BELIEVERS meant dramatic growth for the church on 8th Street, but it was offset in large measure by the departure of 40 from the existing membership to form a second Adventist church in Washington, D.C. The plan to establish a separate White church at the conclusion of the evangelistic season was implemented on September 20, 1902, amid sharp controversy. The General Conference leaders had expected opposition, but, they believed, the controversy over the plan that roiled alongside the inspiring success of Sheafe's evangelistic meetings need not have been so intense. And they placed much of the blame for the trauma on Sheafe himself for deviating from plans carefully worked out earlier in the year, a charge he stoutly denied.

In August A. G. Daniells received word from J. S. Washburn that Sheafe had abandoned the policy agreed upon in Des Moines, taking "an open and rather defiant attitude" against it.[1] Within a month of their beginning work in the capital city, said Washburn, "poor Bro. Sheafe was in the grip of Bro. Kalstrom," the church elder whose opposition to the General Conference plan had been clear from the outset. The two ministers were supposed to be working in coordination, but now Sheafe, in alignment with Kalstrom, had "made it as hard as possible for my work," said Washburn.[2]

Indeed, Washburn's tent meetings at the corner of Maryland Avenue and 13th streets NW. were greatly overshadowed by Sheafe's. Separate meetings were doing little better at drawing White people than the ones open to all the previous summer. Moreover, the number of White people in the large crowds at Sheafe's meetings in all likelihood came close to and possibly surpassed the total at Washburn's meetings.

Understandably, it was a very difficult situation for a man of considerable talent and his own record of achievement—in some ways, he said, "the most perplexing period" of his life. In the relationship between Adventism's dual evangelists for Washington, "it seemed as though he was the head and I was the tail," said Washburn, "and it is not always pleasant to be tail with such a head going on before."[3]

Washburn's personal difficulties with Sheafe went even deeper than a bruised ego. In his letters of 1902 and 1903 Washburn portrayed Sheafe as starting off with good intentions about following the plan for Washington, but then becoming a pliant tool in the "grip" of Andrew Kalstrom. In recalling events five years later, however, Washburn revealed an instantaneous, intuitive suspicion of his colleague from the outset:

"The very first time I saw Sheafe, I was somewhat startled and unfavorably disappointed when I looked at his eyes. . . .There is a peculiar, shifty, cruel, cunning look in his eyes that had made me uncomfortable, and that, I believe, is the real index of his character."[4]

Upon hearing of Washburn's difficulties, Daniells wrote to boost his spirits and urge him to press on with his tent meetings. Washburn, he pointed out, had seen at least some fruit for his labors, despite being eclipsed by Sheafe.

"You have probably not had the large attendance at your meetings that Brother Sheafe has. Your work may not be attended with all the blowing of trumpets that his is; but I believe that you are standing true to right principles, and that in the end the Lord will vindicate this, and that he will give you results that will prove abiding."[5]

RACIAL JUSTICE AND ADVENTIST MISSION:
DIVERGENT PATHS

In reports detailing his complaint that Sheafe had turned against the General Conference plan, Washburn merged the specific matter of dividing the Washington church with the more general principle of speaking out for racial justice and equality. If Daniells' earlier letters are any indication, this broader issue may have been downplayed in discussion of the specific plans for Washington. However, Sheafe's course clearly did run counter to that part of the policy promulgated at Nashville in January that renounced efforts to "bring about an equality of the races" and joining in "the popular cry of elevating the colored man."

The controversy brought into view two sharply contrasting understandings of how the race issue relates to the proclamation of the gospel and the mission of the Seventh-day Adventist Church. Daniells and Washburn held to a position, reflected in the Nashville policy, that combined a well-meaning but unmistakable paternalism in regard to race, with a strong tendency to separate the gospel from controversial public issues.

Daniells expressed the key elements of this position in his letters to Cottrell and Washburn in early 1902, briefing them about the Nashville conference and the situation in Washington. Daniells' theological touchstone was that "the best thing in this world for the colored race is the third angel's message, and that the man who will give the Negro this message is bestowing upon him the greatest blessing that can come to him. That will elevate, not the Negro as a *man*, but it will lift up the man Christ Jesus in the Negro, and the Negro with Christ."

The tactical conclusion that he drew from those principles for the mission of the church amid the worsening racial conditions in the nation was to "let this race question alone" and concentrate all energies on "the salvation of both races" through proclaiming the third angel's message. With widespread expectation of a "great crisis" approaching—even a "racial war" in which "the colored people will be butchered off like beasts," agitation for racial equality would bring only retribution that would make presentation of the third angel's message impossible. Put another way, the demand for racial justice had to be sharply distinguished from and subordinated to the spiritual blessings offered by the third angel's message.

Furthermore, expectation that world conditions would only worsen and that Christ would soon return underscored the futility of working for adjustment of race relations in society. Borrowing an often-used figure of speech from the great revivalist Dwight L. Moody, Daniells compared the world to "an old sinking ship" and declared that "the one thing resting upon us as a people is to do all in our power to rescue the people who are going down."[6]

As for the relationship between the races among those adhering to the third angel's message, said Daniells: "We have no such feeling as the world has toward the colored race. We count them as our brothers and sisters in Christ, and are as willing to lay down our lives for them as for the white people." Certain as to the virtue of his outlook, the church president appears simply to have assumed that he and the White leaders would act in the best interests of the Colored membership. Thus he regarded protests about racial inequality in the church and calls for elevating the status of the Black race as manifestations of sinful human pride and refusal to practice the self-denial required of all Christians:

"I think all this clamor on the part of either whites or blacks, for the recognition of the black people, is wrong. Jesus emptied himself. Every Christian is to repudiate self, and the black man cannot be an exception. All this loud talk about the elevation of the colored man is really doing him an injury. Our message to our colored people must be very plain and emphatic on this point. We must show them that the elevation of man is the elevation of sin; for man, as a man, is a sinner. If we can get them to see that our burden is to elevate the man Christ Jesus in the colored man, they will have very little anxiety about their recognition by the white people. I have little hope of doing very much for the colored people until we can get our own colored brethren to put away their pride, their love of recognition, and their resentment when they appear to be slighted."[7]

In sum Daniells—and Washburn—held the position that, for the sake of the third angel's message, Black Adventists should not challenge racial oppression in society. Such Christian self-denial should also be exercised within the church. Rather than indulge their sinful pride and craving for recognition by stirring up controversy over perceived slights and unfairness, they should leave such problems to be worked out by the White church leadership, under God, in the best ways and at the appropriate time.

Sheafe could wholeheartedly agree with much of the theological foundation that Daniells laid out, which gives some credence to the claims of both men that they were agreed on general principles coming out of the April meeting in Des Moines. Sheafe agreed that the third angel's message held out the greatest hope to Black America. The language of his August 31 sermon as quoted in the Washington *Post* about the necessity of coming "to the station of the man in Christ Jesus" parallels Daniells' wording with regard to the message that "will lift up the man Christ Jesus in the Negro, and the Negro with Christ." All of this, Sheafe affirmed, gave the Black believer an identity and status that far transcended anything that White society could give or take away.

The key difference that became unmistakable in Washington, if it was not obvious before, had to do with what this theology meant for the Negro "as a *man*"—in the nation and in the church, here and now. Sheafe agreed with the spokespersons for the Washington church, James Howard and Andrew Kalstrom, that racial oneness and equality in Christ was so central to the third angel's message that it required a living witness counter to the deepening racism in society, rather than accommodating it.

Sheafe apparently supported resolutions sent from the Washington church to the Chesapeake Conference in June 1902 repudiating the efforts in 1901, led by Pastor William Westworth, to segregate the races within the congregation. The date of the resolutions, June 7, fits with Washburn's claim that Sheafe abandoned the General Conference plan within three or four weeks of the two preachers' arrival in May. In the run-up to the widely anticipated division of the church in September, the *Colored American* published the Washington church's June resolutions, as follows, with explicit permission from Sheafe, and as evidence against reports in other papers that the division was indeed about to take place.

"*Resolutions passed by the Seventh Day Adventist Church at Washington, D C.*, June 7, 1902.

"Whereas, much confusion has arisen upon the subject of race distinction with this church, therefore be it

"*Resolved*, That hereby the church expresses itself before God and man, and says that the principles to which it has been committed since its organization will be followed in the future; that hence there will be no distinction, nor discrimination on account of race, and consequently that different services for the different races will not be held, nor will attempts be made to regulate the seating according to race, hereafter.

"*Resolved*, That these resolutions be entered in full on the records of the church by the clerk and that a copy be forwarded to the secretary of the Chesapeake Conference for its information."[8]

J. S. Washburn took a quite cynical view of such high-sounding pronouncements about equality from the "element" with which Sheafe had allied. While virtually every other source on record, including A. G. Daniells, testifies to the genuineness of Dr. James Howard's Christian spirit as well as his intelligence and leadership ability, Washburn spoke in a critical vein of the doctor's refusal, 12 years before, to engage in "a special work for the colored people." If Howard objected to his work being defined in this manner, he had a passion for spreading the Adventist message that few could match. Thus, Washburn's somewhat self-contradictory complaint was that the Washington church was now "filled up with colored people," the problem being that these, in turn, were "filled with [Howard's] idea" on the race question.[9]

These, Washburn said, joined the church in order to "be with white people," and were "fighting for their rights" and "for position." Kalstrom and the other White members who advocated equality did so in order to cultivate the support of the Colored members and thereby keep themselves "in a ruling position," Washburn charged.[10]

Flattery from this faction, Washburn further claimed in letters to Ellen White and W. C. White, induced Sheafe to preach a radical sermon on race matters in which "he said Moses married a colored woman and that no one had any business to interfere." Sheafe seemed unfazed by Washburn's argument "from Scripture and testimony" that Moses' wife, as a Midianite, was a descendent of Abraham.[11]

On this issue Washburn also reported a negative reaction from Rosetta Douglass Sprague to Ellen White's statement in 1891 that interracial marriage was "not the right thing to teach or to practice."[12] Frederick Douglass, Rosetta's late father, had drawn sharp criticism from both Blacks and Whites for his marriage to a White woman after the death of his first wife. Rosetta Sprague was among "the most prominent colored members" of the Washington church, according to Washburn, and he claimed that she called Ellen White's statement against intermarriage "a wicked catering to Southern prejudice."

Sheafe, in the same sermon, also made the striking assertion that "as the great testing question of the ages the Sabbath sank into insignificance beside the race question," wrote Washburn. His report should be weighed with the recognition that it came as part of an effort to gain the support of denominational leadership for his work in Washington, as opposed to that of Sheafe and his allies, which, he was seeking to prove, had gone off course. Thus it is quite possible that Washburn distorted Sheafe's message by lifting a "sound bite" out of context in order to discredit him.

Even so, it is credible, particularly in the light of later developments, that Sheafe said something in 1902 along the lines attributed to him by Washburn. Not that Sheafe would not have regarded the Sabbath itself as "insignificant." His forthright and costly advocacy of the seventh-day Sabbath, then and throughout the remainder of his life, removes any doubt as to the strength of his convictions on the matter. But as racial oppression deepened and grew more violent and, conversely, the severity of Sunday law enforcement eased in the opening decade of the new century, Sheafe apparently was coming to view the "color line" as the deeper, more rigorous, and more pressing test of authentic Christianity.

Viewing the situation primarily through information provided by Washburn, A. G. Daniells resolved not to alter his course by a single degree. The Nashville policy had to be made real in Washington. "I am just as firm in my views regarding the plans that should be followed in [Washington] as I was when we talked them over at Des Moines," he declared. "I cannot see light in any other way. Therefore I am not prepared to compromise in the least."[13]

Daniells therefore urged H. W. Cottrell, president of the Atlantic Union Conference, and O. O. Farnsworth, president of the Chesapeake Conference, to move forward decisively with the planned division of the church in Washington. W. A. Spicer, who as secretary was second to Daniells in executive authority, would be on hand representing the General Conference. As for Sheafe, said the president, in view of his evident deviation from the terms of his assignment on the General Conference payroll, he should be presented with three options: (1) come into "harmony with the wishes and plans of the conference" if he wishes to continue working in Washington; or (2) "return from that city, and go to some place where he can work in perfect unison with our desires"; or (3) "work on his own account in any way that he believes it to be his duty."[14]

Having read and taken to heart lengthy letters from Washburn critical of Sheafe's attitude, Daniells briefly resigned himself to the expectation that Sheafe would take the third option. He wrote Cottrell on September

15 that it appeared that Kalstrom and Sheafe had "gone so far that they will not agree to cooperate with us in our work in Washington." Should that happen, he said, the General Conference would simply have to withdraw its support, adding, "really I believe they will go to that length."[15]

After some reflection, as he set forth his guidance to Cottrell in a more thorough and deliberate fashion three days later, he made clear that he would "be very sorry indeed if [Sheafe] decides to cut loose from the General Conference and work on his own responsibility. This would be disastrous to himself, and to the cause of God among the colored people in Washington."[16] He also tried gently to prod the dispirited Washburn away from preoccupation with Sheafe's wrongs and focus on his own task of "preaching the gospel to the white people in that city."[17]

The more hopeful tone about resolving matters with Sheafe, though, was not meant to convey any weakening of resolve about the plan to establish separate work for the two races in Washington. "Take hold of this matter with a strong hand, and carry it through," Daniells exhorted Cottrell.[18]

THE DIVISION: IMPLEMENTED AND MADE KNOWN

"Color Line Drawn Between Adventists, The Church in Washington to Be Divided," proclaimed the prominent headlines at the top of page 3 of the Washington *Evening Times* for September 2, 1902. News of the plan to divide the local Adventist church along the color line hit the Washington papers just as the public attention given Sheafe's evangelistic meetings reached its height. Only the day before, the Washington *Post*'s major story on the services drawing extraordinarily large crowds to the tent at Thirteenth and T streets had appeared. With headlines deeply painful in retrospect, the September 2 stories accurately reflected the General Conference perspective on plans for Washington, and may well have been based on information provided by Washburn.

The *Post*'s September 2 story, "Will Form Two Churches," characterized the planned division as the resolution to a "peculiar situation" at the existing church, "concerning which wrong impressions have been created." According to the article, the congregation had not been divided heretofore because of its small numbers. No mention was made regarding principle or conviction as a factor.

The September 2 article referred to the previous day's story on Sheafe's meetings, but in so doing placed a different "spin" on an important point. In its lead sentence the September 1 story reported the presence of many White people in attendance. The September 2 article referred to the report in the previous day's paper about Sheafe's "large success in his tent services *for the colored people*" (emphasis supplied). Also, while the article on September 1 made no mention of Washburn's meetings, the briefer article on September 2 noted that they "have been largely attended and much interest manifested."

Against the backdrop of the September 2 newspaper articles, the significance of the *Colored American's* previously mentioned use of the Washington church's June 7 resolutions against "discrimination on account of race" in its September 13 cover story on Sheafe stands out more sharply. The *Colored American* regarded these resolutions as the basis for a "scoop" refuting the information that had appeared in the White owned dailies:

"We are authorized to announce that the statements in the Washington *Times* and *Post* of recent dates to the effect that an effort will be made this fall to divide the Seventh Day Adventists on race lines is utterly without foundation and we are permitted by Mr. Sheafe and greatly pleased to publish herewith a set of resolutions adopted by the Washington Church of that faith and embodying their sentiments on this question."[19]

Sheafe undoubtedly wanted to counter the damage that news stories regarding a division along the color line would cause his efforts to lead his hearers to give their allegiance to the third angel's message. Did he represent the local church's resolutions as evidence that the General Conference had rescinded its plans? If so, he misled the newspaper and its readers. It is unlikely, but not altogether implausible, that he actually believed that, in view of how circumstances had unfolded and the strength of opposition in the Washington church, Daniells and the General Conference would back down. It could also be that the newspaper did not get the story straight. Whatever the case, the conflicting news reports in themselves were indication that the division of the church would not be uncontested.

Even so, the single aspect of the controversy that most heated emotions need not have been an issue at all. Sheafe had warned Washburn that the Black members would "never go out [of the church building] while there is a shingle on the roof; the only way you can get us out is by force."[20] Thus, when Elders Cottrell, Farnsworth, and Spicer met with the Washington saints on Sabbath, September 20, to thrash out the division, the Black members and the "Kalstrom party" arrived "in thorough battle array," said Spicer, "expecting that our mission was to turn the colored folks out of the church, and take possession."[21]

Cottrell and Spicer in fact *were* hoping to come out of the September 20 meetings with the church property in General Conference control, even though Daniells had all along advised leaving the building on Eighth Street with the proposed Black congregation. As late as September 15, with it now clear that a strong contingent of Whites led by Kalstrom would remain with the Black members in defiance of General Conference plans, Daniells reiterated to Cottrell, "I should be sorry to turn them out of the building, even though they should withdraw from us. If they are willing to take the entire financial responsibility, it might be best to let them have the property, and we start anew with nothing."[22]

Cottrell and Spicer still felt that an attempt to retain control of the property was worthwhile. They researched court records and local statutes on Thursday, and discovered that the congregation had full authority to elect trustees over the property, regardless of the sources of the funds paid on it. Thus, they realized it would be futile to take a hard line on the property issue, but still hoped to win a majority to their side on September 20.[23] If the property question had been removed from contention at the outset, much of the growing antagonism might have rather quickly dissipated.

Cottrell spoke for the Sabbath morning service, taking the responsibility of setting forth the rationale for dividing the church into two companies. He felt considerable gravity about the situation, sensing that he faced "one of the largest and most difficult questions to handle that the denomination has to deal with." However, he felt "special freedom" from the Lord in making his presentation. The necessity of making cultural adaptations for the sake of mission, Cottrell declared, lay at the heart of the matter:

"The Lord holds every Christian responsible to adapt himself by practical education to circumstances and conditions as they are known in the world, that he may be, under Christ, a savior to the largest number of people."[24]

The congregation was then convened as a business meeting, with Cottrell in the chair.[25] He called upon those present who desired to form a separate congregation to so indicate by standing to their feet, but that was met by protests against the proceedings from Andrew Kalstrom, Dr. Howard, and Charles Shaffer, an outspoken literature evangelist. After about a half hour of debate, it was finally agreed that all should have a right to express their position. About 40 people then stood to their feet, signifying that they wished to be part of the new and separate congregation.

The remaining issues were addressed at an evening meeting, which went on for six hours. Outside the church people from the community listened in on the contentious proceedings, gathering around open windows and perching on the fences. After about an hour of debate, the denominational officials finally gave up efforts to get the deed to the church property turned over either to the Chesapeake or Atlantic Union Conference.

The other major point of contention was whether to grant transfer of membership letters to those wishing to form the new congregation. On this point Sheafe, who had thus far maintained a low profile, parted company with Kalstrom. The church elder, along with Charles Shaffer, argued against granting letters recommending as members in good standing those who were following what they deemed a deeply unchristian course. Sheafe, with the support of most of the Black members, supported granting the letters, thereby recognizing the freedom of those who wished to depart to act in accordance with their convictions. Spicer pointed out the inconsistency of those opposed to the granting the letters in "branding as apostates those whom they desired to hold as members of their own church." In the end, only Shaffer voted against granting the letters.

"The Lord gave us a decided victory," declared Cottrell. He and Spicer were quite pleased with the outcome of the showdown, despite the concession on the church property, and the strong minority of White members who both refused to go along with the separation and passionately denounced it as sinful. The 40 departing members organized the Second Seventh-day Adventist Church on Monday evening, with J. S. Washburn as pastor. Feelings of joy and relief ran through the group. "I think I never saw a happier group of people than the No. 2 church of Washington," Cottrell observed. They had reason to hope that 20 to 30 others who had slipped away from active church membership would join them, now that the cause of opposition from their spouses and of other social pressures had been removed.[26]

Yet the new group also faced considerable uncertainty. For the present, their only place of worship was Washburn's evangelistic tent at Nineteenth and F streets NW. Moreover, the group was far from wealthy. Their ranks did include a physician, John H. Neall, who was elected elder. But Neall was one of only six adult males, other than Washburn, in the original 40. While the members of the original congregation, which immediately took the name First church, claimed moral high ground on the race issue, the members of the Second church, and in particular its pastor, were taking the identity of exiles, cast out for their own adherence to righteous principle, and now in search of vindication.[27]

Meanwhile, at the church on Eighth Street the members' relief at not being evicted from their church home somewhat tempered the atmosphere of righteous indignation over the division. The congregation constituted itself on Saturday evening, September 27, as the First Seventh-day Adventist Church, with Andrew Kalstrom as "church elder" and Lewis Sheafe as "ministerial elder."[28]

As for the preacher's deviation from General Conference plans, the air was partially cleared in a lengthy discussion with Cottrell and Spicer on Monday, September 22. Sheafe maintained that he had not in any way violated the agreement in Des Moines. It had been agreed all along that it would not be his role to push through the separation. He had neither opposed nor condemned those desiring to separate. He had done his utmost to fulfill the mandate of taking the message to the Black population of Washington. And if the driving purpose behind the plans for Washington was to get the message before as many people of both races as possible, how could he possibly be condemned if White people, in considerable numbers, also responded to his preaching?[29]

Spicer and Cottrell countered that if Sheafe did not directly go against his word, then he must have kept his "real position" hidden from Daniells at their meeting in Des Moines. It defied common sense, they argued, that

Daniells would have sent him to Washington to "meet a situation" if the president had understood that Sheafe "stood exactly with the Kalstrom element, whose influence [Daniells] wanted to break."[30]

At any rate, the frank discussion between Sheafe, Spicer, and Cottrell resulted in better feelings between them and a more hopeful outlook. Though Spicer was not quite as fully confident, Cottrell's conclusion was that "there is a full understanding now all around," and thus "there need not be any further difficulty" over the race question in Washington.[31]

THE WATCHING WORLD

Widespread press coverage of the division proceedings bore out Dr. Howard's observation in March about increasing public interest in how Adventists in Washington would handle the race question. A generally objective and accurate report in the Washington *Post* the day after was marred by a serious exaggeration in its first paragraph that "nearly all the white members from the original church organization" were joining the new one. Corrective information that "several white families who have strenuously opposed the division will remain with the original church" did follow, but not until the final paragraph.[32]

A brief report on page 8 of the September 23 edition of the New York *Times* characterized the division as an overdue resolution to a long-standing problem: "White and Colored Members of Washington Church Finally Separate," ran the subheading. According to the *Times*, the "formal separation" resulted from the fact that the practice of both races attending the church together had "not worked well."[33]

Some Black newspapers viewed the developments quite differently. The St. Paul-based *Appeal* commented on the Adventist division in its editorial page, though it made no reference to Sheafe's pastorate in Minnesota just a decade before. Adventists of both races had been worshipping together in Washington, said the *Appeal*, "under the guidance of Rev. L. C. Sheafe, an Afro-American." It was "certain Caucasian ministers sent by the conference" who had laid down the necessity of drawing the color line. Of the White members who refused to go along, instead remaining with the original church, the *Appeal* declared, "These people are true Christians."[34]

W. Calvin Chase, the contentious attorney and Republican political operative who edited the Washington *Bee*, placed the matter in the broad historical context of the hypocrisy on race that contaminated American Christianity at the core. "Even in this new religious organization the spirit of caste is being fostered and perpetuated," Chase lamented. The sad fact further demonstrated that each "offshoot of American Christianity partakes the venom of the parent tree, race prejudice."[35] The editorial, just as Dr. Howard had warned, struck hard at Adventism's claim to be different—a faithful remnant marked by radical adherence to "the commandments of God and the faith of Jesus" in contrast to the dominant denominations that had become entrenched in compromise and conformity to the world. The racial division, said Chase, revealed Adventism to be just like all the others.

This was Chase's only comment on the division, and he made it in the September 6 edition, before the action was carried out. Edward E. Cooper, Chase's rival editor at the *Colored American*, writing after the fact in early October, took a more benign view of what the Adventists had done in Washington. In a brief report on October 4, Cooper characterized the division as a measure taken *on behalf of* the Black members. As did the White-owned papers, Cooper cited numerical growth as the precipitating factor, though unlike them he specified that the increase had resulted from Sheafe's work. To accommodate the growth, reported the *Colored American*, the White members had decided to "give" the present church building to "the colored devotees." Cooper mentioned that "a few white members will remain with the colored people," but, unlike the editor of the *Appeal*, he downplayed it. The fact that the "bulk" of the White members had joined the new congregation led by "Rev. Dr. Washburn," he wrote, had been "amicably arranged by general consent."[36]

Since Sheafe almost certainly was Cooper's principal source of information, the report suggests that Sheafe indeed was establishing a position distinct both from the unyielding idealism of the "Kalstrom element" in his congregation and the General Conference's counsels of accommodation. It suggests that while Sheafe welcomed White people in the congregation and honored their commitment to equality, he was much more readily disposed to accept the concept of a "colored church" and work primarily among the Black population, just as the General Conference plans stipulated.

In the following week's paper (October 11) Cooper devoted more extensive analysis to the situation. The Adventists had adjusted to hard social realities, and though personally opposed to racial segregation in the church or any other setting, Cooper saw no reason for particular alarm in arrangements that they had worked out. The gospel indeed proclaimed the brotherhood of all peoples, but, said Cooper, "We know that the whole thing is a polite fiction, and that the ruling sentiment of a locality fixes as irrevocably as the laws of the Medes and the Persians just who are and who are not welcome at the foot of the cross, when that cross is under control of the brother in white."

With reference to national patterns, Adventists seemed to be following the "best practices" for making racial separation more humane where it was inevitable. While churches in some parts of the North made no racial distinctions, Cooper pointed out that in other Northern locales separate churches were often urged for "social reasons." In such situations, the "parent" church typically provided generous financial support for the Black congregation's church building. In the South, where segregation was the more universal norm, the "better classes," in order to "salve their consciences," had historically given liberally as well.

"The same thing is happening here in the case of the Seventh Day Adventists. Washington is accustomed to the separate church, just as she is accustomed to the separate school, hospital, restaurant, hotel and social system; so one more separate church, where the operation is performed with a smile and the gift of a building does not aggravate the situation to any appreciable degree, in my opinion. . . . The Seventh Day people have simply done the expected, and are conforming to local sentiment—not admitting its righteousness, but accepting it as they find it."

Cooper also pointed to the positive side of racial separation—the Black church under Black leadership as an independent and empowering spiritual and social center:

"As a matter of fact, the colored followers of the Seventh Day Adventists will be better pleased to be under their own government, administered and controlled in their own way, and pastored by a man of God in whom they have confidence, and from whom they can expect sincere sympathy in every relation of life."[37]

In all of this Cooper passed over the vigorous protest of First church's lay leaders against being categorized as a "colored church." They took it precisely as their mission *not* to conform, to do the expected thing, but to demonstrate that the power of the gospel to bring all peoples together in equality at the foot of the cross did not have to be a "polite fiction" but could in fact become embodied reality. If too quick to dismiss this ideal, the *Colored American* editor nonetheless expressed insights that in the long run would serve as valuable points of reference for the Adventist experience in Washington.

FRAGILE RESOLUTION

When the dust of the church division battle settled, neither side had won a decisive victory. The "Kalstrom element" had been unable to prevent the division of the church, but the General Conference had been unable to make the division clear-cut. The larger of the two churches racially integrated on principle, and supported as such by a strong pastor whose evangelistic success accounted for nearly all of the new adherents to Adventism in the nation's capital—this was not at all how the General Conference president had envisioned implementation of the Nashville policy in Washington.

By identifying with those who saw countercultural witness to racial equality as central to the Adventist message, and by reaching Whites as well as Blacks in his evangelism, Lewis Sheafe indeed helped frustrate the General Conference plans. At the same time, he also facilitated their partial achievement by encouraging cooperation with those wishing to form a second congregation on a voluntary basis. He joined in representing the outcome of the September 20 proceedings in the most favorable light possible. In all, he assisted the denominational officials in bringing about the resolution outlined by Cottrell in the *Review*, which left believers free to follow their consciences regarding which congregation to join, and equally affirmed either choice:

"All Christians are freeborn; and this certainly involves the thought that if, under God, one believes that he can do better service by having his membership in a mixed congregation than otherwise, even though he is in a section of the country where the question is agitated, it is certainly his Christian privilege so to do; while a similar right must be conceded to those who, under the Lord, take another view of the question. We need

Christian liberty within the soul, rather than simply a form of words with-out."[38]

The way had been opened for the two congregations to move forward in a positive, even cooperative, course, functioning together under the governance of the same conference, which, for the present, was that of the Chesapeake Conference. Questions remained, though, upon which further progress would turn. Would the divisive, censorious attitudes built up on both sides during the conflict be healed or aggravated? Would decisions concerning mission priorities and funds be made in a way that was fair and equitable across racial lines? Would the fragile trust between Lewis Sheafe and the General Conference be strengthened or eroded?

About the latter, W. A. Spicer was highly uncertain. Sheafe had failed the denominational leaders. "We had hoped for just one colored man in Washington to help us; but at the last minute his courage failed him, and he turned," he wrote to Daniells. "I think he will feel better from our talk," Spicer reported, "but personally I feel that I do not know that he is true and loyal to us or not. Time only will show."[39] Sheafe had similar reservations about the General Conference's attitude toward him and the denomination's Black members, for whom he was the chief spokesperson. However, the way was now open to move forward in hope.

---

[1] AGD to HWC, Sept. 15, 1902; AGD to JSW, Aug. 21, 1902, GCA.

[2] JSW to EGW, June 5, 1903, EGWE.

[3] AGD to JSW, Aug. 21, 1902; JSW to AGD, Feb. 20, 1907, GCA.

[4] JSW to AGD, Feb. 20, 1907.

[5] AGD to JSW, Aug. 21, 1902.

[6] AGD to HCW, Jan. 21, Feb. 3, 1902.

[7] AGD to JSW, Feb. 26, 1902.

[8] "A New Faith Comes," CA, p. 2.

[9] JSW to EGW, Nov. 24, 1902, EGWE.

[10] JSW to WCW Feb. 18, 1902; JSW to EGW, June 5, 1902, EGWE.

[11] In *The Spirit of Prophecy*, volume 1, published in 1870, Ellen White wrote that Moses' wife, Zipporah, "was not black, but her complexion was somewhat darker than the Hebrews," implying that color was at least a secondary factor behind the criticism to which Miriam, Moses' sister, subjected her (pp. 286, 287). In *Patriarchs and Prophets*, published in 1890, Ellen White notes that as a Midianite, Zipporah was a descendant of Abraham. This later treatment does not include the observation that Zipporah was "not black," and draws a bit more attention to the difference of her complexion from that of the Hebrews (pp. 383, 384).

[12] E. G. White, "Our Duty to the Colored People," in *The Southern Work*, p. 15.

[13] AGD to JSW, Sept. 18, 1902, GCA.

[14] AGD to HWC, Sept. 18, 1902, GCA.

[15] AGD to HWC, Sept. 15, 1902, GCA.

[16] AGD to HWC, Sept. 18, 1902.

[17] AGD to JSW, Sept. 18, 1902.

[18] GD to HWC, Sept. 18, 1902.

[19] "A New Faith Comes," p. 2.

[20] JSW to WCW, Feb. 18, 1903.

[21] WAS to AGD, Sept. 25, 1902, GCA.

[22] AGD to HWC, Feb. 15, 1902.

[23] WAS to AGD, Sept. 25, 1902.

[24] HWC to AGD, Sept. 24, 1902, GCA. Cottrell summarized his main points in a report entitled "Washington, D.C.," published in the *Review,* Oct. 7, 1902, p. 17; the *Atlantic Union Gleaner,* Oct. 1, 1902, pp. 5, 6; and other church papers.

[25] The remaining narrative of the Sept. 20, 1902, meetings is drawn from WAS to AGD, Sept. 25, 1902.

[26] HWC to AGD, Sept. 24, 1902; WAS to AGD, Sept. 25, 1902; "New Church Elects Officers, Seventh Day Adventists Organize at Meeting Held in Tent," WP, Sept. 23, 1902, p. 7.

[27] "A New Seventh Day Adventist Church, White Members of Sect Organize Under Rev. J. S. Washburn," Washington *Times,* Sept. 23, 1902, p. 4.

[28] WAS to AGD, Sept. 25, 1902; "Adventists Elect Officers," WP, Sept. 29, 1902, p. 12.

[29] No account of the meeting by Sheafe is extant. From the letters of Cottrell and Spicer, A. T. Jones's account of July 3, 1907, and the pertinent 1902-1903 correspondence of all parties involved, the points he would have made can be inferred with high probability. The final sentence of this paragraph is more conjectural than the rest, but the likelihood is high that his argument would have included something close to this.

[30] WAS to AGD, Sept. 25, 1902.

[31] HWC to AGD, Sept. 24, 1902; WAS to AGD, Sept. 25, 1902.

[32] "Adventists Leave Church, Division in Organization Perfected by Conference Leaders," WP, Sept. 21, 1902, p. 11.

[33] "Seventh Day Adventists Split, White and Colored Members of Washington Church Finally Separate," New York *Times,* Sept. 23, 1902, p. 8.

[34] Editorial comment, *Appeal,* Sept. 27, 1902, p. 2.

[35] Editorial comment, *Bee,* Sept. 6, 1902, p. 4.

[36] Untitled paragraph, CA, Oct. 4, 1902, p. 5.

[37] "The Man-on-the-Corner," CA, Oct. 11, 1902, p. 2.

[38] "Washington, D.C."

[39] WAS to AGD, Sept. 25, 1902.

CHAPTER XX

AT THE CENTER
OF BLACK CULTURE

WASHINGTON, D.C., "churches are growing more liberal through education. . . . There was a time when the presence of a preacher of another faith in the pulpit of this church would have precipitated a riot." That was the *Colored American* editor's droll comment on the scheduled appearance of L. C. Sheafe "to expound his doctrine" in the pulpit of the Metropolitan AME Church on November 18.[1] Sheafe's ministry in 1902 indeed did not lead to any riots, but it did stir the city with a revival that seemed unprecedented: "Rev. L. C. Sheafe is attracting more attention than any minister has ever struck in this neck o' the woods," observed editor Cooper (or one of his writers) as the tent series neared conclusion at the end of September.[2]

THE WASHINGTON PREACHERS' COUNTEROFFENSIVE

Along with the widespread enthusiasm, Sheafe's work also sparked no small controversy, as the ministers of the established churches came to the defense of their doctrines and membership rolls. Remarkably, though, the vigorous debates did not lead to alienating barriers against communication and cooperation. Rather, Sheafe adroitly used the attention to gain a hearing in Black Washington's—and thus Black America's—leading centers of influence.

The Metropolitan AME Church, for example, was no ordinary church. Built under the leadership of Bishop Daniel A. Payne in 1886, it indeed functioned in many ways as a "national cathedral" for Black America. The race's most eloquent voices—such as Frederick Douglass, Ida B. Wells,

LEWIS C. SHEAFE'S
WORLD

The young preacher,
Lewis Charles Sheafe.

❧ SHEAFE'S TENT. ❧

THE PEOPLE'S

GOSPEL MEETINGS

CONDUCTED BY

ELDER LEWIS C. SHEAFE,

Every Night,

Beginning Sunday the 29th of July, 1900.

Opening service Sunday at 5.30 p. m., to which each Church, Pastor and Sunday-school of the City is cordially invited to be present and take part. Elder Sheafe will preach and sing each night. Bring your Bible and Penticostal hymn book. Let all the people come and sing.

Tent on Fairfield St. near Park Ave.

Advertisement for meetings held in Aiken, South Carolina, during the summer of 1900.

MEN OF THE HOUR.

REV. LEWIS C. SHEAFE.

Evangelist, Organizer and Financier, Who Has Been Conducting a Remarkably Successful Series of Tent Meetings in Washington Under the Auspices of the Seventh Day Adventists.

A NEW FAITH COMES.

THRILLING SUCCESS OF A SEVENTH DAY ADVENTIST

Rev. Lewis C. Sheafe Stirs Washington by his Persuasive Eloquence and Convincing Logic—Story of his Early Struggles and Triumphs—No Color Line to Local Adventist Church

Laudatory front-page feature story in The Colored American, September 13, 1902.

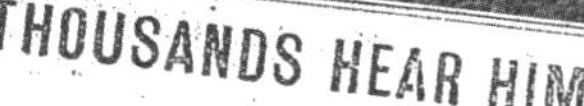

THOUSANDS HEAR HIM

Negro Minister Draws Large Crowds to His Tent.

PREACHES A SIMPLE GOSPEL

Hundreds of People Stood Last Night that They Might Listen to His Sermon on the Marriage Supper of the Lamb— Discourses Are Extemporaneous and Abound in Bible References.

Above: Washington Post, September 1, 1902.

Left: Flyer advertising the meetings.

Beacon Light Gospel Tent

COR. 13TH AND T STS., N. W.

IN CHARGE OF

Lewis C. Sheafe

ASSISTED BY

Fred H. Seeney

ENQUIRY MEETING at 7 p. m.

PREACHING at 7.45 p. m.

Subjects for the week beginning Sept 1st, 1902.

MONDAY,	Social Purity and Health.
TUESDAY,	Law of God, is it binding?
WEDNESDAY,	The Two Laws.
THURSDAY,	The Sabbath of the Lord?
FRIDAY,	Is Sunday the Lords Day?
SUNDAY,	Prophetic America.

BIBLE STUDIES on the ever-lasting GOSPEL and PROPHECY every evening.

Good Singing.   **Public Welcome.**

Above: Dr. John Harvey Kellogg, instrumental in bringing Sheafe into Adventism, later encouraged him in independence from the General Conference.

Left: J. S. Washburn, Sheafe's evangelistic colleague turned antagonist.

Above: A. G. Daniells, president of the General Conference of Seventh-day Adventists, 1901-1922.

Right: Newspapers around the nation noted the division of the Adventist Church in Washington, D.C., along racial lines.

COLOR LINE DRAWN BETWEEN ADVENTISTS

The Church in Washington to Be Divided

Decision Reached by the General Conference With Headquarters at Battle Creek.

It is the intention of the General Conference of the Seventh Day Adventists, with headquarters at Battle Creek, Mich., to divide the Seventh Day Adventist Church in this city on the color line and organize a separate church for its colored adherents in this city. Heretofore the latter have worshiped and worked with their white brothers in their church on Eighth Street northeast, between F and G Streets. The General Conference, in order to satisfactorily make the arrangement, has sent the Rev. J. S. Washburn and the Rev. Lewis C. Sheafe, both evangelists, to this city for the purpose of holding tent meetings and to divide their respective followings into two distinct followings. The Rev. Mr. Sheafe has been very successful among the colored people, while the Rev. Mr. Washburn has charge of the church.

The Seventh Day Adventists observe the seventh day of the week as the Sabbath, and believe in the doctrine of an early coming to an end of this world.

Edward E. Cooper, editor of The Colored American, which gave Sheafe extensive and favorable coverage.

Right: Francis J. Grimké, influential pastor of the Fifteenth Street Presbyterian Church, tried to refute Sheafe's preaching about the Sabbath, but also preached for a Sabbath service at First SDA Church in 1903.

Thomas J. Jones, prominent Washington, D.C., attorney who keynoted the twenty-fifth anniversary celebration of Sheafe's ministry in the city.

W. Calvin Chase, feisty editor of the Washington Bee, called Sheafe "the most learned minister in the United States among the Negroes."

The People's SDA Church building, 10th & V streets NW.

Elder J. C. Sheafe, founder of the People's Seventh-day Adventist Church, Washington, D.C.

Matthew C. Strachan, portrayed here with his wife, worked to counter Sheafe's influence among Black Adventists after the split of 1907.

Universal Negro Improvement Association

56 WEST 135th STREET   NEW YORK CITY

No. 2070

Nominal Value of Loan $ 140.00

First Payment on Loan $ 2.00

Name of Division Washington 183

Name of Ex. Sec'y L. S. Oxley

THE UNIVERSAL NEGRO IMPROVEMENT ASS'N

promises to pay to the order of Lewis C Sheafe

905 R St NW

ADDRESS

a member of this Association, all amounts appearing on account here attached. One year after date with interest at 5% per annum, payable at the office of the Association, 56 West 135th Street, New York City, or at the place of issue.

For use in the furtherance of the Industrial, Commercial and Agricultural purposes of the Association in its Construction Plans in the interest of the race.

This day of February 6 19 2

Universal Negro Improvement Association

Secretary General   President General

SPECIAL—This note must not be detached from this book.
This note is subject to the terms printed on the back

Receipt of Sheafe's investment with Marcus Garvey's UNIA.

Sydney Scott, one of the most forceful of the early Black Adventist ministers, attempted to reconcile Sheafe with the General Conference.

William Hawkins Green, a lawyer who was among the first to embrace Adventism in response to Sheafe's evangelism in Washington, D.C., later became the first Black minister to head the North American Negro Department.

WHAT doth the Lord require of thee, but to do justly, and to love mercy, and to walk humbly with thy God?
—Micah 6:8

Let not the wise man glory in his wisdom, neither let the mighty man glory in his might; let not the rich man glory in his riches: but let him that glorieth glory in this, that he understandeth and knoweth me, that I am the Lord which exerciseth loving-kindness, judgment, and righteousness in the earth: for in these things I delight, saith the Lord. —Jer. 9:23-24.

The Lord bless thee and keep thee: the Lord make his face shine upon thee and be gracious unto thee: the Lord lift up his countenance upon thee, and give thee peace —Num. 6:24-26.

FOR ENGAGEMENTS
ADDRESS

1570 W. 35TH STREET
LOS ANGELES. CAL.

Partners in ministry.

Left: J. W. Manns, with whom Sheafe allied briefly in forming a new denomination.

Bottom: A. T. Jones aligned with Sheafe and Kellogg against the Daniells-led General Conference.

SEVENTH DAY ADVENTIST LOSE RACE ELDER

Rev. Lewis C. Sheafe Withdraws From Southern California Conference on Account of Color Line Doctrine.

N. A. A. C. P. INDORSES ACT.

Cordially Invited to Pastor Berean Church of Seventh Day Adventist.

By Charles Alexander.

Los Angeles, Cal., Oct. 8.—The Rev. Lewis C. Sheafe, a valued elder of the Seventh Day Adventist denomination, demonstrated his pluck and manly courage when he withdrew from the Southern California Conference of the denomination he has served so long and faithfully, on account of its doctrine bearing upon the color line. During the past year Elder Sheafe founded in Los Angeles a splendid church. The members of this church also withdrew from the conference and passed ringing resolutions setting forth their reasons for their action.

The name of the church founded by Rev. Mr. Sheafe is the Berean Seventh Day Adventist Church. Since its severance from the conference it is now known as the Free Seventh Day Adventist Church, with Rev. Lewis C. Sheafe of 1442 West Thirty-fifth street, Los Angeles, Cal., as pastor.

The act of Rev. Sheafe and his members is regarded an an event of great historical importance. The trouble grew out of the fact that Rev. Sheafe and his members could not conscientiously subscribe to certain sentiments contained in "The Testimonies, Volume 9," bearing on the color line. This book is regarded by the elders as inspired writings. Mrs. Ellen G. White, the author, was, according to the elders of the Seventh Day Adventist Church, divinely inspired, and "The Testimonies" serve as an infalible guide to all the believers in this denomination.

NOTED NEGRO MINISTER SPEAKS IN THIS CITY

L. C. Sheafe, the famous negro evangelist of Washington, D. C., who has preached before members of congress and sung for President Taft, lectured at the A. O. U. W. hall on First street at 3 o'clock this afternoon.

and Mary Church Terrell—rang out there, and its most preeminent citizens were laid to their rest there, such as Douglass (1895) and Blanche K. Bruce (1898), the first African-American to serve a full term in the United States Senate.[3]

The Sabbath question, not surprisingly, sparked the largest flashpoint of controversy, and for a time Sheafe's preaching made it one of the leading topics of public discussion in Washington's educated and culturally discerning Black community. In fact, it became "the question of the hour around these parts," according to the *Colored American*. All the "orthodox clergy" rejected Sheafe's claims for Saturday. Rev. Walter H. Brooks of the Nineteenth Street Baptist Church, where Lewis and Annie had been married 14 years before, took the position that "any day set aside for divine worship and rest would probably satisfy the demands of Scripture" and thus preferred to stick with "the old-fashioned Sunday."[4]

St. Luke's Episcopal Church brought in a guest preacher from New York in late October for a three-sermon series on "Seventh Day Adventists." St. Luke's, the city's first independent Black Episcopal congregation, was one of the most influential churches among the Black elite, organized in 1873 under the leadership of the erudite champion of racial solidarity, Alexander Crummell.[5] The guest preacher, George Frazier Miller of St. Augustine's Episcopal Church in Brooklyn, argued along lines similar to Brooks. Miller reassured his Washington audience that "our Sunday" had been chosen as a matter of convenience, in accordance with the practice of "most nations of the earth" in "following the ancient tradition of popular gatherings for religious purposes on the first day of the week."[6]

The response of Francis J. Grimké, "the most influential minister in the city," according to biographer Mark Perry, provides an especially telling gauge of Sheafe's impact in 1902. A graduate of Princeton Theological Seminary, Grimké became pastor of the Fifteenth Street Presbyterian Church in 1877 and, except for a brief stint in Florida, served there until his death in 1937. He and his brother Archibald, an attorney, were nephews of Sarah Grimké and Angelina Grimké (Weld), renowned abolitionists and pioneers of women's equality, and the brothers in turn came to prominence in the struggle for racial justice.[7]

Rev. Grimké preached in defense of Sunday as the Christian Sabbath on September 21, 1902. However, members of the congregation who had been away that Sunday were so desirous to hear the sermon that they urged him to repeat it. The interest was so great that the pastor acceded, preaching the same sermon again six weeks later on November 2. Grimké used New Testament passages in developing his case, but in the end made the weight of tradition—in the sense of the overwhelming majority interpretation of the Bible through the centuries—the clinching argument. Referring to the many Christian scholars who have devoted intensive and prayerful study to the Bible over a period of 19 centuries, Grimké reasoned:

"The majority of them, the overwhelming majority, ninety-nine hundredths of those who have been doing this studying, who have been delving into this book, by day and by night, during all the centuries say that they believe, according to this word, that the first day of the week or Sunday is the day upon which the Christian sabbath should be kept. . . . Now is it likely that *they* are mistaken; that *they* have read this book amiss: and that the little, almost infinitesimal fraction of believers represented by the Seventh Day Baptists and the Seventh Day Adventists have alone been able to see the truth? . . . We say, we are justified in keeping Sunday by the Scriptures; the Seventh Day Adventists say we are not: and in proof that we are right, and that they are wrong, we show that ours is the view held by the great body of Christians in every age of the church, who have studied this word with the same care and earnestness as they have. . . . The probabilities are all in our favor."[8]

The Washington preachers' counteroffensive may well have helped keep some of their members from defection to the Adventist faith, but it does not seem to have altered the widespread perception that Sheafe was the premiere expositor of the Bible itself. The city's Black ministers, the Baptists in particular, "abuse him," observed Washington *Bee* editor Calvin Chase, but they had become leery of trying to refute his arguments, for "many of them have attempted but failed."[9]

THE SECOND BAPTIST LYCEUM INCIDENT

Chase's comment came in the course of an editorial about an incident that revealed the strong and conflicting attitudes toward the Adventist preacher. Sheafe had been invited to speak at the Second Baptist Lyceum on Sunday afternoon, November 23. A large crowd assembled, expecting to hear him speak on the topic "The Way and Course of True Wisdom," along with musical selections by the Capital City Orchestra. But when the president of the lyceum, the distinguished attorney Armond W. Scott, came to the podium, it was not to introduce Sheafe but to announce that the trustees of Second Baptist Church had revoked the invitation—Sheafe would not be speaking at the meeting after all.

It was an embarrassing situation for Scott, who apparently had been trying until the last minute to get the trustees to reverse their decision to revoke the invitation, which had been made the previous day but not communicated to Sheafe. Thus, the "dis-invitation" had to be announced not only to a disappointed crowd but with the announced guest speaker himself present.[10]

The *Colored American* gave a diplomatic report of the incident. The officers of Second Baptist "feared that the appearance of this wonderful biblical scholar might lead to an acrimonious discussion of a religious problem and consequent bitterness," the paper said. Attorney Scott had filled in ably with an eloquent, well-received talk entitled "The Achievements of Perseverance."[11]

Chase, however, in keeping with the Washington *Bee*'s motto— "stings for enemies; honey for friends"—landed a sharp sting on the Second Baptist trustees while lavishing honey on Sheafe (he must also have given his copy editor the day off!):

"Rev. Lewis C. Sheafe, D.D., the Seventh Day Adventist, the divine who has made all ministerial and Christian Washington to open their eyes with amazement, was invited by the president of the Second Baptist Church lyceum, to speak last Sabbath afternoon was denied admission. . . .

"The distinguished divine is the most learned minister in the United States among the Negroes, and is equal to any white. . . . [Wherever] he goes people flock to hear him. Since his advent in this city he speaks to packed houses, irrespective of creed or sex. No man has a greater knowledge of the Bible. Just why the trustees of the Second Baptist Church refused him admission it is not known. It cannot be that Rev. Sheafe does not believe in and worship the same God that the Baptists do. Rev. Sheafe has challenged anyone to meet him upon the same common level and discuss the Bible with him. Negro ministers abuse him, especially the Baptist, but they do not dare to answer his argument, many of them have attempted but failed. The action of the trustees of the Second Baptist Church committed a very small act."[12]

Though the *Colored American* was gentler on the Second Baptist trustees than the *Bee*, the coverage in both papers shows the general outlines of Sheafe's reception in the Black community of Washington, D.C. The widespread and enthusiastic response to his preaching made conflict with the city's other clergy over the controversial aspects of his message inevitable. Yet, out of Washington's Black population of 100,000, the number who fully accepted the teachings that Sheafe presented and joined the Seventh-day Adventist Church was very small, though large in relation to the existing Adventist membership. Among the vast majority who did not join the movement he represented, Sheafe retained high regard for his unsurpassed knowledge of the Bible, his impressive skill in communicating it, and for the positive impact of his work on religious, moral, and civic life.

The *Colored American*'s feature on Sheafe in its September 13 issue further illustrates this dual pattern of response. The article showers an abundance of superlatives on Sheafe and his meetings. These lead, not to a call for readers to join the preacher's movement, but an exhortation to the city's clergy to "arise from their luxurious ease" and "pursue his methods or strengthen his hands in the purely undenominational part of his work." If they did not, the paper warned, they might find that "this recent awakening in our midst will tend to the aggrandizement of the Seventh Day Adventist movement."[13]

A special Thanksgiving feature in the November 22 issue of the *Colored American* reflects the respect Sheafe gained among part of the city's Black leadership, as well as an almost friendly competition over scriptural interpretation. "Surveying the country and examining the hearts and minds of many prominent persons, our telegraphic editor discovered the paramount impulse that moved them on Thanksgiving Day," states the introduction to "Why They Are Thankful."

The brief statements attributed to well-known personages thus appear to be formulated by Cooper as commentary on current events. For example, Booker T. Washington's reason for giving thanks was "That he has given the world its most remarkable institution of learning." For Judge

Robert H. Terrell it was "That as the district political leader, he is the logical nominee for delegate to the next Republican national convention." Between the comments associated with these two men, the reason for "Rev. L. C. Sheafe" appeared: "That he has been able to set the Washington preachers to reading their Bibles early and often." The reason given for W. C. Martin, an attorney who apparently acquitted himself well in a debate with Sheafe, was "That he is in the L. C. Sheafe class as an authority upon Holy Writ."[14]

Another vignette, six months later, shows how Sheafe kept the lines of communication and collaboration open with his ministerial colleagues, amid their vigorous and public disagreements on crucial matters of biblical teaching. Despite his sharp and rather condescending refutation of the Adventist position regarding the Sabbath, Francis J. Grimké accepted an invitation to preach for the Sabbath morning divine service at the First Seventh-day Adventist Church on Saturday, April 11, 1903. The eminent Dr. Grimké made his way to the modest sanctuary on 8th Street to preach one of his best-loved sermons, an exposition on Romans 8:28 and the providential love of God. It was a sermon that he preached in several other settings as well, including the Hampton Institute in Virginia, the Union AME Church in Philadelphia, Clark University in Atlanta, and the Abyssinian Baptist Church in New York.[15]

Thus, despite the rejection at the Second Baptist Lyceum, Sheafe won widespread respect for his expertise on the Bible and his skill as a speaker in applying its message to current issues. That respect opened frequent opportunities for him to speak at public occasions and in the pulpits of other churches to audiences filled with representatives of Washington's large sector of well-educated and forward-thinking Black citizens. He did not use these events to gain further adulation by speaking about topics guaranteed to cause no controversy. Rather, he improved on the opportunities before him with regard to the cause that he was commissioned to advance.

THE BETHEL LITERARY AND HISTORICAL SOCIETY

On November 18 Sheafe spoke to a "large audience" at the Bethel Literary and Historical Society on the subject "Is the Seventh Day the Sabbath of the Christian, According to the Bible?" The Bethel Society was, in the words of historian Jacqueline Moore, "the center of black intellectual life in the capital" from the 1880s to the 1920s. Howard University historian Rayford Logan called it "the most important lyceum of colored people at the turn of the century [where] some of the most noted colored men and women of the day spoke to large audiences."[16] In speaking there, Sheafe took turns with the likes of Booker T. Washington and W.E.B. DuBois, and his presentation to the society on November 18 was only the first of several over the years.

Again at Bethel Literary in the fall of 1904, the week after a season-opening lecture by the distinguished activist Mary Church Terrell,[17] Sheafe sparked a lively debate with a presentation on the history of world powers in prophetic perspective.

"Rev. Sheafe spoke for an hour on the 'Rise and Fall of Nations in the Light of Scripture.' He endeavored to trace the prophecies concerning the leading nations of the world, and showed their decay because of sin. He discussed America, and told of the prophecy concerning it and how it pretended to stand for liberty and equality, but at the same time pampered oppression."

Three respondents—Shelby J. Davidson, Dr. S. L. Corrothers of the Galbraith AME Zion Church, and a Dr. Funnell of King Hall—discussed Sheafe's presentation at length. Dr. Funnell was quite critical, dismissing Sheafe's argument as "obsolete, sixteenth-century theology." The ensuing discussion "waxed warm and was full of excitement." If some denounced Sheafe's theology of history, his vocal solo, "Asleep in the Deep," sung "with magnificent basso voice" was received with warm enthusiasm. Indeed, the preacher's singing voice was in as much demand as his speaking at these occasions dedicated to the display of high culture and intellect.[18]

Sheafe accomplished something truly noteworthy through these presentations at Bethel Literary and similar settings.[19] He succeeded in placing the Seventh-day Adventist message concerning the Sabbath, prophecy, and what prophecy discloses about the role of the United States in the culmination of history before the most influential forums in the culture he was seeking to reach. Rarely, if ever, has an Adventist preacher in America so successfully taken the message beyond the church building and evangelistic meeting and into the broader cultural arena.

RACE ADVOCATE IN THE NATION'S CAPITAL

As a Seventh-day Adventist minister in Washington, Sheafe took on the role of race advocate, as he had done as a Baptist minister in Minnesota and Ohio. He joined organizations dedicated to bringing about racial justice and spoke at their meetings. And he was also called upon to speak at commemorative events of particular interest to African-Americans.

The most striking instance of such an event was the Washington, D.C., celebration of the fortieth anniversary of President Lincoln's issuance of the Emancipation Proclamation. The *Colored American* called upon the citizens of Washington to turn out en masse for the celebration at 8:00 p.m. on the evening of January 1 at the Metropolitan AME Church.

An impressive lineup of speakers had been "selected by reason of their familiarity with the history of the epoch" to discuss the "several phases of race progress since the birth of freedom": P.B.S. Pinchback, former governor of Louisiana and prominent among the Black politicians who attained high office soon after the Civil War ("Fruits of Reconstruction"); Mary Church Terrell, the leading figure among the women activists in Washington's Black elite ("Woman's Contribution"); George H. White of North Carolina, the last of the Reconstruction era Black congressmen ("Present Political Perils"); Major Charles R. Douglass, son of Frederick Douglass and veteran of the famed 54th Massachusetts Regiment ("Emancipation as a Military Necessity"); Armond W. Scott, a successful young attorney ("The Youth and the Hope of the Race"); and Kelly Miller, a prominent Howard University scholar who combined the roles of academic and activist, addressing the role of education in advancing the race. Among the list of dignitaries, the speaker called upon to address the religious dimension of the experience of emancipation and beyond was L. C. Sheafe.[20]

The event, carefully planned by a committee of Washington's leading Black citizens, ended up falling short of expectations. A crowd of only 200 or 300—a "fair audience," in the *Colored American*'s assessment—assembled at Metropolitan AME, which could seat 2,500. Word may have gotten out that the more prominent of the advertised speakers had either declined or withdrawn, which may in turn reflect a rift of some kind in the Black community over the celebration. At any rate, Pinchback, White,

Terrell, and Douglass sent letters of regret, the latter indicating that he had been detained by the serious illness of his brother, Lewis H. Douglass.[21]

The ambiguous success of the event does not diminish the significance of Sheafe's being chosen from Washington's many eminent Black clerics to speak from the standpoint of religion. Indeed, many of those leading ministers, including Grimké, Brooks, and Corrothers, were part of the committee of prominent citizens that planned the celebration.

The speech given by "the well-known evangelist"—as the Washington *Post* identified Sheafe in its brief notice of the event[22]—drew upon the same historical analysis he had presented in Springfield, Ohio, in 1895. Now, however, he linked the history in a more thorough and definite way with divine providence, using the title "God's Hand in the Work of Emancipation." No evidence indicates that this speech stirred the kind of controversy that the one in Springfield had. Yet Sheafe did not shrink from a clear-eyed characterization of President Lincoln's course in connection with the event for which he is most remembered and honored.

Not even a disposition to interfere with slavery had been in "the plans and purposes of President Lincoln." But, said the evangelist, "military necessity caused him . . . to fall in with the master purposes of the Almighty."[23]

Later that year Sheafe was part of a movement for a new national organization for defense of Black rights that would eventually contribute to the formation of the National Association for the Advancement of Colored People (NAACP) in 1909.

It was in 1903 that W.E.B. DuBois published, in *The Souls of Black Folk*, his call to the "black men of America" to perform the "stern and delicate" duty of opposing the generally acknowledged leader of their race, Booker T. Washington, insofar as he "apologizes for injustice, North or South, does not rightly value the privilege and duty of voting, belittles the emasculating effects of caste distinctions, and opposes the higher training and ambition of our brighter minds."[24]

The success of "Bookerite" forces in gaining control of the Afro-American Council at a meeting in Louisville in July 1903 contributed to the escalating conflict between DuBois and Washington. In the aftermath of the Louisville meeting, Washington *Bee* editor W. Calvin Chase spearheaded formation of the Negro Suffrage League of the District of

Columbia, with a view toward its becoming part of a new national organization for bold advocacy of Black civil and political rights.[25]

Lewis Sheafe was one of the speakers at the initial meeting of the D.C. Suffrage League on September 25 who urged "united and systematic resistance" to the increasing restriction of Black rights. The meeting passed resolutions protesting the breakdown in the South of the rights to equal citizenship and the vote established by the Fourteenth and Fifteenth amendments, and requesting President Theodore Roosevelt to take action against "the rank and flagrant discriminations" practiced in the District of Columbia.

A "large and enthusiastic crowd" that included "some of the most prominent Negroes of this city" attended the meeting, held at Plymouth Congregational Church. Chase gave the main address, while Sheafe and several others, including his attorney friend and Wayland classmate, Thomas L. Jones, gave short speeches. Opposition to some of Booker T. Washington's policies was aired, and in general the rhetoric took on a militant tone—according to the Washington *Post*, anyway. "All the speeches dwelt on the fact that the time had now come for the Negro to take up arms in his own defense and work out his own salvation," said the paper.[26]

Calls for self-determination and self-defense should not be confused with inciting aggressive violence. Even so, the oratory irritated nerves at the editorial office of the *Post*. An editorial in the Sunday paper for September 27 advised "our colored friends" to stop "their speech-making and their tiresome demands for recognition" as a class and concentrate on developing individual worth. Thoroughly weary of hearing about the meetings for organizing race advocacy, with "the inevitable harangue and protestations," the editorialist exclaimed: "Negroes, Negroes, this and that—there is no end to their complaints."[27]

On the editorial page of the *Bee*, Chase responded that "our orators . . . are not demanding recognition but justice."[28]

---

[1] Untitled editorial comment, CA, Nov. 8, 1902, p. 8.

[2] "The-Man-on-the-Corner," CA, Sept. 27, 1902, p. 4.

[3] "Bishop Johnson to Preach at Metropolitan," WT, Feb. 10, 1928, p. 5; Sandra Fitzpatrick and Maria R. Goodwin, *The Guide to Black Washington* (New York: Hippocrene Books, Inc., 1999), pp. 189-191.

[4] "The Man-on-the-Corner," CA, Oct. 4, 1902, p. 10.

[5] Fitzpatrick and Goodwin, p. 153.

[6] "Sunday, Our Day of Worship," CA, Nov. 1, 1902, p. 4.

[7] The sisters were from a prominent slaveholding family in South Carolina. After the death of his wife, their brother, Henry Grimké, lived openly with a slave, Nancy Weston, as husband and wife, a union that produced Francis, Archibald, and another son, John. Mark Perry tells the family story in *Lift Up Thy Voice: The Grimké Family's Journey From Slaveholders to Civil Rights Leaders* (New York: Viking, 2001).

[8] "Exodus 20:8," sermon manuscript, Francis J. Grimké Papers, Box 40-18, Folder 788, Manuscript Division, Moorland-Spingarn Research Center, Howard University.

[9] "A Small Thing," *Bee,* Nov. 29, 1902, p. 1.

[10] "A Small Thing"; "Lecture Before the Second Baptist Lyceum," *Bee,* Nov. 22, 1902, p. 8.

[11] "At Second Baptist Lyceum," CA, Nov. 29, 1902, p. 9.

[12] "A Small Thing."

[13] "A New Faith Comes," CA, p. 2.

[14] "Why They Are Thankful," CA, Nov. 29, 1902, p. 3.

[15] "Romans 8:28," sermon manuscript and back page notations, Francis J. Grimké Papers, Box 40-18, Folder 788, Manuscript Division, Moorland-Spingarn Research Center, Howard University.

[16] Jacqueline M. Moore, *Leading the Race,* pp. 66-69. Logan quoted in *Black Washingtonians,* p. 132.

[17] "The Bethel Literary," *Bee,* Oct. 1, 1904, p. 1.

[18] "The Bethel Literary," *Bee,* Oct. 15, 1904, p. 4.

[19] He also spoke, to give one further example, on the subject "God's Hand in the Rise and Fall of Nations," at the People's Literary, sponsored by the People's Congregational Church in December of 1902. "City Paragraphs," CA, Dec. 20, 1902, p. 16.

[20] "Emancipation Celebration," CA, Jan. 3, 1903, p. 9. Speaker topics identified in "Date of Emancipation," Washington *Evening Star,* Jan. 2, 1903, p. 6.

[21] "City in Brief," CA, Jan. 10, 1903, p. 4; "Date of Emancipation."

[22] "Celebration of Lincoln's Proclamation," WP, Jan. 1, 1903, p. 3.

[23] "Date of Emancipation."

[24] *The Souls of Black Folk* (1903), p. 42.

[25] D. L. Lewis, *W.E.B. DuBois,* pp. 298, 299; P. D. Nelson, *Frederick L. McGhee,* pp. 109-111; Hal Scripps Chase, "'Honey for Friends, Stings for Enemies,' William Calvin Chase and *The Washington Bee,* 1882-1921" (Ph.D. diss., University of Pennsylvania, 1973), pp. 251-254.

[26] "Negro's Status Here, District Suffrage League Appeals to President," WP, Sept. 26, 1903, p. 4.

[27] "Why Don't the Negroes Stop It?" WP, Sept. 27, 1903, p. E6.

[28] "Why Don't the Negroes Stop It?" *Bee,* Oct. 3, 1903, p. 4.

CHAPTER XXI

THE "RIGHT MOLD"
FOR WASHINGTON

T HOUGH THEY USED LESS HARSH LANGUAGE, the letters of Adventist Church leaders sometimes echoed the Washington *Post*'s irritation with the seemingly continual "clamoring for recognition" from the Black people, of which the Washington First church was a major source. Following the division that took place in September 1902, the members of the First church worked hard to demonstrate their value to the cause of God through sacrificial commitment. In the swirl of exciting progress and profound change between October 1902 and June 1903, however, perceptions of injustice with racial overtones once again accumulated.

FINANCIAL TENSIONS

Their pastor's communications with the General Conference during these months generally focused on the positive developments, the major exception being the financial stresses he and his family faced trying to live on his allotted wages. Sheafe found immediately after moving in May that with the high cost of living in Washington his family of five would barely be able to subsist on his salary of $15 per week[1]—standard for Adventist ministers at the time. The inadequacy of the wage was one topic on which he and Washburn saw eye to eye. A few years later Washburn recalled struggling along in Washington on $15 per week until the General Conference moved there in 1903, and then the "salaries of the brethren were raised at once."[2]

Sheafe's problems were compounded by the city's increasingly harsh racial climate in a time when, says historian Constance Green, successful,

well-educated Blacks "discovered that each passing year made it harder
for them to purchase or rent comfortable houses without paying exorbi-
tant prices."[3] Sheafe put it this way in a letter to E. R. Palmer at the
General Conference office: "The rule of this city is to give the Negro less
and charge him more than others."[4]

On top of that, a protracted coal miners' strike dragged on into the fall
of 1902, driving up the cost of coal and just about everything else, including rents. "We are in the midst of the pressure," wrote Sheafe to H. E.
Osborne, the General Conference secretary, at the end of September.[5]

These factors contributed to the very high rent on the small home at
324 Spruce Street Northwest that Sheafe had secured by September. The
house was in LeDroit Park, a formerly all-White neighborhood near
Howard University that was in the midst of a transition to becoming "one
of the city's political and cultural black residential centers during the first
decades of the twentieth century." Here, in a residence described in the
Colored American both as "cozy" and "handsome," the Sheafes lived just two
or three blocks from the famed poet Paul Laurence Dunbar and other
prominent Washingtonians such as Robert H. Terrell, the District of
Columbia's first Black judge, and his activist wife, Mary Church Terrell.[6] At
$25.50 per month, though, the rent absorbed nearly half of Sheafe's salary.

In these circumstances the preacher found himself perpetually in debt
just to meet basic living expenses. He disliked having to ask for money,
but finally, after several allusions to the high costs in his monthly reports,
he decided to put the matter directly to Osborne on December 1: "I am
not able to meet the running expense of living in this city at the present
salary." With his success in bringing a large number of new members into
the church to back up his request, he asked that the brethren of the
General Conference consider giving him an increase in salary.[7]

Osborne responded with encouragement and understanding. "It
seems very certain that the brethren will not expect you to live in
Washington, D.C., on the same wages you were given in 1902," he wrote,
with a view to the upcoming year. The matter would not formally be decided until the annual "audit" in the spring, he explained. But he encouraged Sheafe to go ahead with asking, in his monthly requests, for the
amount he needed.[8]

Accordingly, in January Sheafe began asking for and receiving $70 per month, which would average around $17.50 per week. Also in March the family moved to 83 L Street Northwest in the North Capitol Street area, near the renowned M Street High School, where the rent was a much more favorable $17.30 per month.

The worst of the financial pressure had thus been relieved, but no formal action had been taken to raise the preacher's salary. Not wishing to be perceived as constantly holding out his hand for money, Sheafe waited in hope that the matter "would be adjusted without my saying anything about it." Meanwhile he kept requesting $70 per month, thereby steadily increasing the amount drawn on his account over and above what would normally be due at his $15-per-week pay rate.

When Palmer questioned him in June about the growing discrepancy, Sheafe explained that he had acted on the advice of Osborne and that he was now able to pay his bills as they came, rather than having to borrow just to meet the cost-of-living necessities. "It does seem to me that one ought to be able to earn enough to pay his current expenses," wrote Sheafe, adding, "that is, when they are within reason, and he works all the time."

Palmer's inquiry, though, may have at least implied suspicion as to whether in fact Sheafe was keeping his expenses "within reason." In his reply, dispassionate in tone overall, Sheafe defended himself against any such insinuation by telling Palmer that "the brethren" who had "condescended to look in on us at my home" on a recent visit to Washington could "testify as to whether I am living in splendor or extravagance."[9]

The General Conference move to Washington, which began shortly after this exchange of letters, helped ameliorate Sheafe's financial pressures as it did for Washburn. Yet the financial question would continue to generate an undercurrent of tension, as it had almost from the beginning of Sheafe's work as an Adventist minister.

Outside of the problem of the preacher's salary, the First church in Washington was vibrant with growth, joy, and hope-filled dedication to carrying forward the mighty movement launched in the summer of 1902. After the tent was taken down, evangelistic meetings continued on Sundays at the Cadets Armory Hall at 708 O Street Northwest. Baptisms also continued, so that by February 1903 a total of 75 new members was attributed to the work begun in June. Attendance at Sabbath worship and

Sunday evangelistic services strained seating accommodations. Financial support was strong, and sacrificial commitment was in evidence as eager anticipation built for a new tent effort in 1903.[10]

Alongside these happy developments, however, a new crisis was brewing over just what kind of faith Adventists would put on display on the national—and international—stage of Washington, D.C. The conflict emerged without reference to a possible move of the General Conference headquarters, but when the move happened, the conflict took on heightened significance.

The reports in the Black press emphasizing the positive aspects of the division of the church and characterizing the First church's retention of the building on Eighth Street as a "gift" from the departing White members suggest effort on Sheafe's part to foster, at minimum, peaceful coexistence between the two congregations. Yet conviction ran deep in both congregations that they had followed the course of truth and righteousness while the other congregation had departed from it. Both believed the other had gone against divine admonitions conveyed by the Lord's messenger, Ellen White.

The embers of opposing conviction flared into direct conflict in connection with the Second church's drive for a church building of its own. For J. S. Washburn that effort was not merely a fund-raising campaign, but a righteous crusade to vindicate the course that he and his congregation had taken, at General Conference direction, in forming a separate, White church.

Despite the reports indicating that a large majority of the active White members of the original congregation had gone into the Second church, and that a sizable contingent of those who had become inactive would soon join them, the new congregation's viability was shaky during its first few weeks. With no place to meet other than the evangelistic tent and then a rented hall, the church "wandered without a home."[11] The membership included only six men, other than Washburn and his son Forest, nearly all of them poor, according to the pastor. "Everyone was down low," said Washburn, and in fact "the whole thing here" was "at death's door."[12] He himself had at times come to the point of feeling that he would be "forced to leave the city entirely, and the work must fall into the hands of Bro. Kalstrom, Dr. Howard and Bro. Sheafe."[13]

Washburn's discouragement, however, did not overwhelm his formidable skill as a promoter and fund-raiser. When the Central Methodist Church building at Twelfth and M streets Northwest came up for sale, Washburn saw an opportunity to turn Second church from "death's door" to a bright future, and he seized it without asking permission from headquarters. For a down payment of $500 the attractive 14-year-old edifice could be theirs, and they could take possession right away. Equivalent to half of a decent annual salary, $500 was not an insignificant sum. But Washburn came up with it, perhaps with the help of Dr. B. Ashbourne Capehart, a physician strongly interested in the Adventist message,[14] and put the money down on November 1, 1902.

The further catch, though, was that another $2,500 toward the total price of $12,900 would be due in 90 days, at the end of January 1903. To meet this obligation created by his unilateral action, Washburn turned to the General Conference brethren for help. "It was pretty risky for you to purchase that place with the expectation that the General Conference would take the burden of raising the money," chided A. G. Daniells, concerned about setting a precedent for pleas from cities all over the country to the General Conference for help in paying for church buildings.[15]

Washburn countered that "the providence was so clear and bright I dared not refuse to make this move." And he had felt confident that the conference leadership would support his action once they realized that the very life of the Second church, and with it the "principle" that the General Conference had sent him to Washington to carry out, were at stake. If the General Conference was serious about the plan for establishing racially separate congregations in Washington as a model for the South and anywhere else where the color line was contentious, it was going to take a major new infusion of support to keep the White church alive.[16]

By the time of this exchange of letters in early December, the General Conference Committee and A. G. Daniells, despite his reluctance, had already acknowledged, implicitly at least, the force of that argument. On November 23 the committee approved use of denominational channels to raise up to $10,000 for Washington on the grounds that the capital of the nation "is deserving of respectable places of worship, where our people can assemble with those interested in the third angel's message."[17]

Seemingly unremarkable on the surface, the phrase was code for "churches where potential White converts who would be driven away by a sizable Black presence could attend."

The permission to appeal for funds in the *Review and Herald*, union papers, and other union and local conference channels may have been more than half the battle, but the money still had to be raised. Washburn was given the opportunity to set forth his appeal with a lengthy article published in the January 13, 1903, issue of the *Review*, which also featured photos of the new church building on the cover.

In his bid for support, Washburn framed the situation in apocalyptic terms. A strong church in Washington, he contended, was key to nothing less than the rapid completion of Adventism's mission to the world and the second coming of Jesus. The turn away from religious freedom to oppression that Adventists believed the United States would finally take could not take place until a strong witness for biblical truth had been set before the lawmakers, government officials, and other people of influence in the capital city. "I am certain the great consummation, the glorious coming of the King, cannot take place until the work is rightly represented here in Washington," he wrote.

That "right representation" required "a respectable, comfortable house of worship, so situated that we can reach the men who make Washington what it is." In explaining why that work could not be accomplished through the existing Washington church, Washburn began with a somewhat dubious geographical rationale. The location of the small church on 8th Street in the Northeast sector of the city, he claimed, put it "practically out of the reach of the Washington that is Washington." The newly acquired church on M Street Northwest was indeed situated in the city's leading commercial section, and close to governmental departmental buildings, foreign embassies, and the White House. But Washburn failed to mention that the 8th Street church was only a mile from the U.S. Capitol building, the Supreme Court, and Union Station—twice as close to these and other important sites as the M Street church. He also avoided direct mention of the racial issue, though he referred readers to H. W. Cottrell's article in the October 7, 1902, issue, which addressed it with relative candor.[18]

Most significant, of course, was the glaringly obvious implication that the First church was at best marginal to the truly important work in Washington, which was only now beginning under the auspices of the Second church. The numerous additional reports and appeals from denominational leaders that appeared in church publications repeatedly referred to the fund-raising campaign for the Second church as being for "the Washington work" or "the Washington church." The First church was simply left out of the picture, even though nearly all the additions to the church from the dual tent campaign of 1902 had been generated by Sheafe's effort, and the number of White members claimed by First church (46 out of a total of 168) was not drastically less than the total membership of 66 now claimed by Second church.

Thus, despite the conciliatory gestures made by Sheafe during the division of the church and in following weeks, Washburn found it necessary to use, in printed appeals, thinly veiled denigration of the work of First church. In correspondence with church leaders, including Ellen White, he used direct attacks centered on the racial issue.

Seeking the prophet's own endorsement of the Second church fund-raising campaign, Washburn warned that the Adventist work in Washington could not be left under the dominance of Sheafe and the First church, for they were stamping upon it a "wrong mold." The phrase came from a manuscript Ellen White wrote while in Australia on April 27, 1899, published in the 1901 edition of *The Southern Work*. In this manuscript, which apparently originated as a draft of a letter to an unidentified denominational leader, Ellen White wrote that "incorrect methods have given a wrong mold to the work" in the South. Such methods had to do with "breaking down of distinctions between the white and colored races," which, she wrote, "unfits the blacks to work for their own class, and exerts a wrong influence upon the whites."[19]

This statement "has been exactly fulfilled here in Washington," Washburn declared, referring to the work of Dr. Howard and others at the First church. It was only now, after the formation of a second congregation by the White members in September, followed by the "wonderful providence" in which "the Lord suddenly placed in our hands" the church at 12th and M, Washburn explained, that Adventism could "reach Washington as never before." The work, he wrote in this letter of November 24, "is just now commencing in Washington," for only now was the way open for a "strong church here as a living witness."[20]

In quoting Ellen White's own words to her, Washburn ignored the driving concern of her original document, which was that more must be done on behalf of the oppressed race and that it must be done with the wisdom and sound judgment required by increasingly difficult and dangerous circumstances. He also turned her statement about something that had already occurred—"incorrect methods *have given* a wrong mold to the work" in some parts of the South—into a *forecast* now being fulfilled in Washington, D.C.

Washburn claimed, in his letter to A. G. Daniells three weeks later, that Ellen White had agreed to support his cause,[21] but weeks turned into months without an endorsement from her pen appearing. The initial phase of the fund-raising campaign succeeded quite well without it. The needed $2,500 and more came in by the end of January. But that was still a very long way from the total of $10,000, and by the end of February 1903 Washburn became anxious about the promised appeal for donations from Elmshaven.

He expressed his concern to W. C. White on February 25 that the "stream of money" coming in was likely to "dry up" soon because of the indifference and even opposition from "several leading men in some conferences." The resistance, he said, was based partly on "misunderstanding of the color line" and partly on the question of whether it was appropriate for the General Conference to have become involved in meeting the church's debt. "Several are waiting to see what Sister White will say in regard to the Washington matter" before deciding whether or not to give, he wrote.[22]

A. G. Daniells, too, was concerned about the delay in publication of Ellen White's appeal on behalf of the new church in Washington. W. C. White had shown him a copy in January when the two had been at a meeting in Nashville, mentioning that he felt it needed some editing. But, Daniells wrote to Ellen White on February 24, he had, to his chagrin, seen nothing of it since. Despite his concern about setting a precedent that could be abused and his discomfort with Washburn's unauthorized initiative in acquiring the church, Daniells had swung fully behind the fund-raising project. He agreed that the new building was indispensable to bringing his entire plan for Washington to fruition, and seconded

Washburn's reports of "unmistakable evidences of the Lord's blessing" on the endeavor. Physicians and senators had attended services at the new church, he reported to Ellen White, something that "could never have been brought about with the mixed congregation in the old church."[23]

It turned out that by the time Washburn and Daniells had posted their letters to Elmshaven on February 24 and 25, the much-anticipated appeal from Ellen White had just been sent on its way from California to the *Review* office. The brief message, which appeared in the March 10 issue, warmly endorsed the call for funds on behalf of the new church in Washington. A house of worship was needed in that section of the city, Ellen White wrote. It would "provide a suitable place in which witness can be borne to the truths we advocate" and thus would "stand as a memorial for God." She affirmed the purchase as "a wise step," and desired that all in a position to help liquidate the indebtedness would "be constrained to do so by their love for Christ." Sacrificial support for "the Lord's cause in Washington," she assured believers, "will bring you into harmony with the beneficent purposes of the gospel."[24]

Washburn could not have hoped for a more emphatic endorsement. Yet while the text of Ellen White's appeal made explicit that it was on behalf of "the *Second* Seventh-day Adventist Church of that city," the misleading title under which it appeared in the *Review* carried connotations that she did not intend. The heading, "An Appeal in Behalf of the Washington (D.C.) Church," suggested that the Second church was *the* Washington church, and thus implied acceptance of the "either/or" terms in which Washburn depicted the work in Washington. *Either* his work would prosper as the truly important, definitive Adventist work in Washington, with the rebellious First church relegated to the margins, *or* the Sheafe-Kalstrom-Howard nexus would define Adventism in the city, and efforts to reach influential and White Washington would be doomed to failure.

In reality, Ellen White, along with A. G. Daniells, viewed the situation in "both/and" terms. They firmly supported *both* the establishment of a predominantly White church as an instrument for broadening the reach of the Adventist message among the White residents of the nation's capital *and* the work led by Sheafe that was rapidly swelling the ranks of the mixed-race congregation at First church. From Sheafe's perspective, though, questions about how that support was expressed would recur as the story unfolded: How forceful? How public? How tangible? How timely?

------

[1] LCS to HEO, June 2, 1902, GCA.

[2] JSW to WCW, Feb. 19, 1915, EGWE.

[3] Constance McLaughlin Green, *The Secret City: A History of Race Relations in the Nation's Capital* (Princeton, N.J.: Princeton University Press, 1967), p. 127.

[4] LCS to E. R. Palmer, June 12, 1903, GCA.

[5] LCS to HEO, Sept. 29, 1902, GCA.

[6] S. Fitzpatrick and M. R. Goodwin, *The Guide to Black Washingtion,* pp. 84-99; "Washington Under the Calcium," CA, Oct. 25, 1902, p. 4; "City Paragraphs," CA, Dec. 6, 1902, p. 16.

[7] LCS to HEO, Dec. 1, 1902, GCA.

[8] HEO to LCS, Dec. 4, 1902, GCA.

[9] LCS to E. R. Palmer, June 12, 1902.

[10] LCS to AGD, Feb. 13, 1903, GCA; LCS to HEO, Mar. 31, 1903, GCA.

[11] JSW to EGW, Nov. 24, 1902, EGWE.

[12] JSW to AGD, Dec. 12, 1902, GCA; "A New Seventh Day Adventist Church" Washington *Times,* Sept. 23, 1902, p. 4.

[13] JSW to EGW, Nov. 17, 1903, EGWE.

[14] Washburn made much of the interest of Dr. Capehart and his wife in his reports and fund-raising appeals. Capehart died suddenly at the age of 39 in 1904, and Washburn gave a summary of his life and connection with the Second church in a lengthy obituary published in the *Review,* Jan. 26, 1905, p. 23.

[15] AGD to JSW, Dec. 4, 1902, GCA.

[16] JSW to AGD, Dec. 12, 1902, GCA.

[17] GCC, Nov. 24, 1902.

[18] J. S. Washburn, "Washington's Appeal to Every Seventh-Day Adventist in the United States," *Review,* Jan. 13, 1903, pp. 12-14.

[19] E. G. White, *The Southern Work,* pp. 95, 96.

[20] JSW to EGW, Nov. 24, 1902, EGWE.

[21] JSW to AGD, Dec. 12, 1902. No correspondence from either Ellen White or W. C. White to Washburn is on file in or near this time frame.

[22] JSW to WCW, Feb. 25, 1903, EGWE.

[23] AGD to EGW, Feb. 24, 1903, GCA.

[24] Ellen G. White, "An Appeal in Behalf of the Washington (D.C.) Church," *Review,* Mar. 10, 1903, p. 17.

CHAPTER XXII

TO STAND UNITED
BEFORE THE WORLD

IT DID NOT TAKE A. G. DANIELLS LONG to get past his anger at Lewis Sheafe for the apparent betrayal of the Washington plan in the summer of 1902, though a residue of mistrust remained. Sheafe's ultimate cooperation with the division of the church and the reports of his evangelistic success gradually worked a change in the General Conference president's attitude. After Sheafe sent him a "pleasant letter" in late November reporting positive developments and making no complaints, Daniells determined to write him a "good friendly letter of counsel" and made a point of letting Washburn know that he was going to do so.[1]

The reports of the interest in the tent meetings and the additions to the church were indeed "encouraging and cheering," Daniells told Sheafe. The church president had, on the other hand, been "surprised and grieved" by the troubles reported, but acknowledged that everyone had tried to do what they believed was right and had looked to the Lord for help and blessing. The Lord "is a friend who never forsakes us," Daniells affirmed. "If we err and repent, he pardons and saves our error from wrecking either us or his blessed cause."

At the same time Daniells reiterated the core conviction about the relationship between Adventism and the race problem that he had expressed to Sheafe when they met months before in Des Moines:

"I believe, Brother Sheafe, that the only thing that will truly elevate and bless the colored race is the threefold message of Revelation 14. In fact, this is the only hope there is for the white race. We all stand in need of this one remedy, and it will prove an effectual remedy to all who will put their trust in it."[2]

On this basic point the two leaders shared a genuine conviction that made them brothers, despite significant differences over how the principles of the three angels' messages should be worked out in practice.

RAPPROCHEMENT THROUGH RESULTS

As the spring of 1903 approached, Sheafe and the First church looked eagerly ahead to an even more ambitious tent effort to build on the interest generated the previous year. In order to lay plans, they needed to know how the General Conference would relate to the effort, the most basic issue being whether the conference planned for Sheafe to continue working on salary in Washington.

Sheafe put the question to Daniells in a letter of February 13, after summarizing the progress of the church's work since his arrival the previous May. Altogether, 75 new members had been added, bringing the church's total membership to 160. Tithe was running about $125 per month. In addition to also meeting church expenses and various calls for aid, $332 had been contributed to reduce the church building debt since the division in late September. Sheafe believed it would be best for him to remain for the new evangelistic season, but desired to know the president's thinking.[3]

Daniells had just survived an attempt by John Harvey Kellogg to have him ousted from office in November 1902 and knew that another major battle over leadership lay ahead at the 1903 General Conference session that was to begin the following month in Oakland. Thus, he cautioned that the uncertainty of his own position made it impossible for him to make firm commitments about anything beyond the session. But he assured Sheafe that the General Conference Committee had not even considered the possibility of withdrawing support for his work in Washington. As for his own view, Daniells stated emphatically that "it would be suicidal to break off at the present."[4]

On the same day Daniells also replied to Dr. James Howard, who had also written to inquire about the General Conference's intentions. In this somewhat longer letter, which he asked Howard to share with Sheafe, Daniells acknowledged that in all of the recent fund-raising calls for Washington nothing had been said about the remaining debt on the First church. If faithful progress continued at First church, Daniells believed, then "in due time it will be possible for something to be done for your church building," though he hastened to add that this was only a personal opinion and not a pledge on the part of the General Conference, particularly in view of the uncertainties just ahead.[5]

In Daniells' view Sheafe's assignment in Washington continued to be that of establishing a strong work among the city's Colored population. But the president's unequivocal expression of support now came at a time when he was well aware that First church remained a genuinely interracial, if Black majority, church. And he was almost certainly aware that some of the new members joining through Sheafe's ministry were White. In his letter of February 13 Sheafe indicated that his work was stirring interest among "all classes of people." More explicitly, in his monthly report sent just a few days earlier to H. E. Osborne, Sheafe stated that the almost weekly accessions to the church came "from both races." In fact, he added, a number from both races would be baptized the next Sabbath.

Strictly speaking, then, Sheafe remained out of harmony with the plan for Washington and, although now held in check, antagonism at First church toward the General Conference over the division remained high. But Daniells was no longer interested in fighting on that point, especially when things were going well. In his letter of February 24 to Ellen White, in which he reminded her about the importance of raising funds for the Second church, he also reported, with warm enthusiasm, the growth in membership and giving at First church under Sheafe's leadership. He also made a special point of commending Dr. Howard "as a very intelligent colored man" and "a sincere, humble Christian"—particularly noteworthy in view of Dr. Howard's strong opposition to Daniells' racial policies.

Development of the Black work in Washington remained sharply in focus as the goal, but for the present at least Daniells was willing to regard the mixed-race church, with its strong-willed proponents of racial equality, as an acceptable base from which to build, and seemed confident in Sheafe as the leader. "We must not withdraw this help from the colored work in Washington," he declared. He went on to suggest, in a very general way, that Washington, given its unique status in Black America, become a center for training Black workers for the church's mission in the South.

"There are over one hundred thousand colored people in that city.

They are the best educated and strongest class of dark people in the United States. They hold many professional and official positions in the government. Can we not raise up a good strong class of Bible workers and ministers in Washington for the colored people farther South?"[6]

The sentiment for a "both/and" approach was real enough, but in the coming months—and years, in a broader sense—its strength would face the stern test of hard choices and ordering of priorities.

FIRST CHURCH'S CASE FOR INCLUSION

Spurred, perhaps, by the misleading title of Ellen White's appeal for the Second church in the March 10 *Review*, the leaders of First church decided they could not afford to sit back and wait for denominational leaders to work out, in their own good time, a financially equitable implementation of the "both/and" approach. Much more than getting an equal piece of the pie was at stake. The aggressive fund-raising for "Washington" but exclusively on behalf of the Second church reheated the core conflict over the meaning of the gospel. How, on the stage of national influence that was Washington, D.C., would Adventists work out the implications of the gospel for race relations?

As one prong of the First church offensive, Sheafe carefully crafted a report on the progress of First church for the *Review* that summarized the story that had gone untold in the sweeping references to the work in Washington appearing in recent months. Published under the title "The First Washington Church" in the April 7 issue, the report took the high road, making no complaints or pleas. That approach made the comparative references to the campaign for the Second church that Sheafe left between the lines all the more telling.

He reported that the interest generated the previous summer had been sustained, with consistently large attendance at Sabbath services at the church in Northeast, at numerous Bible studies, and "at the large hall Sunday nights, in the northwest." All told, 80 persons had been added to the church through his work in the city. Washburn's much longer article of January 13, by contrast, had contained no references to a specific number of additions, though he did refer to a physician (Dr. Capehart) who had opened his home to Bible readings that other doctors were attending with avid interest.

First church had been giving special attention to the importance of two things in its services—"a true conversion and consecration to God and his work," wrote Sheafe. And his report specified some of the financial sacrifices the church members were making to advance the cause. First, after the Chesapeake Conference had turned down its request for a Bible worker because of shortness of funds, Sheafe explained, the church had decided to hire and pay the wages for one on its own until the conference was able to do so. Second, progress was being made on the long-standing church debt. Third, the congregation had pledged to support and raise funds for the purchase of a new evangelistic tent that would seat 1,000, though the acquisition was not yet certain.

It all added up to First church carrying forward a strong and effective evangelistic program, entirely on its own financial resources, save for Sheafe's salary. "We ask at least your sincere prayers that God may grant us wisdom and strength to carry forward this long-neglected work for God and the people," he concluded. He stopped short of an explicit appeal for funds, which would not have been allowed at this juncture anyway. Yet, for those with ears to hear, he had put forth a powerful rationale for support, especially when considered alongside the large sum being raised for the Second church, which had yet to demonstrate any comparable evangelistic success.[7]

Meanwhile the congregation, through its elder, Andrew Kalstrom, *was* making an appeal to the denominational leadership. Not for new funds, mainly, but for an allocation of the resources devoted to Washington in a manner that would be more evenhanded and demonstrate genuine support for First church's convictions about how best to advance the gospel cause in Washington. Specifically, the church petitioned the General Conference to do two things:

First, appropriate $3,500 of the $10,000 fund for Washington to the First church toward liquidation of its building debt. A request from the church in 1900 for General Conference help in paying off its mortgage, he pointed out, had been rebuffed on the grounds that it would set a dangerous precedent. Now that concern had been set aside in the denominational fund-raising campaign for the Second church in Washington. The fund-raising appeals had been made in such a way that "the impression has been made that that church was the only SDA church in this city," he noted. But they also opened the precedent for First church to make its case anew.[8]

Second, assign a White minister to work alongside Sheafe in carrying out the plan advocated by the leaders of First church for evangelical work in harmony with the gospel. Like Daniells, the spokesmen for First church recognized that deeply rooted prejudice and deepening entrenchment of racial barriers necessitated special measures. And, like Daniells, they believed those measures including a biracial ministerial team. They believed, wrote Kalstrom, "that the preliminary work up to joining the church can be done most successfully by workers of the same race or nationality as the convert." Unlike Daniells, though, they did not believe that such work should lead to racially divided congregations but rather to the integration of new members into a racially unified church.

"Our church consists of forty-six white and one hundred and twenty-two colored members, and we are fully convinced that God's people should stand united before the world so as to show by actual facts and real lives that God has real power to convert men and women wherever they are born or to whatever position in society they have attained, from any wrong thing—yes, even race prejudices which are lodged deeper than some other [evil] habits."

With much interest already stirring in the resumption of Sheafe's tent evangelism, the addition of a White minister—"thoroughly consecrated to God, of first-rate ability as a speaker and general worker and entirely free from race prejudices"—would "give the work a power it has never had" and "go a long way toward warming all the people here," Kalstrom contended.[9]

The appeal or "memorial" from First church was presented at the final meeting of the 1903 General Conference session on April 22. It was referred to the General Conference Committee, which in turn referred it on May 1 to an ad hoc subcommittee comprised of H. W. Cottrell, I. H. Evans, and A. G. Daniells "for such favorable action as the committee may be able to devise."[10]

BRIDGE TO THE SOUTH

J. S. Washburn lobbied hard against the First church proposal. At the same time, his protestations on this issue became intertwined with his aggressive advocacy on another matter of considerable significance in denominational history. After the fiery destruction of the Review and Herald publishing plant on December 30, 1902, which came on the heels of a similar conflagration of the Battle Creek Sanitarium only 10 months before, church leaders resolved to break up the conglomeration of Adventist institutions in Battle Creek. Admonitions from Ellen White had for several years pointed in this direction, and now, along with reelecting A. G. Daniells, the 1903 General Conference mandated that the denominational headquarters and the Review and Herald plant move out of Battle Creek.[11]

The question of where to move remained unresolved at that point, but Washburn had already been pushing his proposal for months. In fact, on the very same day that he heard about the Review and Herald fire, Washburn quickly moved from shock to strategy: he began a letter-writing campaign on behalf of Washington, D.C., as the new locale for the publishing house and the General Conference headquarters.[12]

The prospect of General Conference relocation magnified the significance of how the racial question was handled in Washington. In March Washburn thanked Ellen White for her message of appeal on behalf of the Second church, commenting that it would "do much to vindicate a great principle"—the principle upon which they had "come out of the mixed church to form a white church." With the General Conference move in view, Washburn cited, as one of the advantages Washington had to offer, that it "is the very bridge between the North and the South." Thus, if Washington became the General Conference headquarters, a proper handling of the race problem there would, in an even more decisive way than before, settle it for the entire denomination.

"We meet the Southern questions, the Southern people, here; Southern customs; but there is also Northern energy, Northern enlightenment, here, to meet it. The true way of dealing with the Southern question, the race question, once settled here, will set a precedent for all the nation, all the South."[13]

As did the First church leaders, Washburn, now more than ever, believed that the Seventh-day Adventist witness to the entire nation concerning race relations was at stake in Washington. First church believed that witness should be a living demonstration of the power of the gospel to overcome racial barriers. Washburn believed that it should roughly parallel the national rapprochement between the White North and White South just then being consolidated: acceptance of racial segregation where it is a pre-vailing social pattern in an overall framework of White supremacy—benev-olent in intention, to be sure, but supremacy nonetheless.

In Washburn's view that principle had emerged victorious in the con-flict over dividing the church and had been resoundingly confirmed by providential leading in acquiring an attractive church building, and by the denomination-wide financial support, endorsed by Ellen White, to pay for it. But now, First church's bid for a portion of the funds and its solidify-ing plans for another high-profile evangelistic effort in a brand-new tent, along with scant evidence of tangible growth in his own congregation, placed that vindication in jeopardy. If Sheafe once again grabbed the headlines and won a large number of converts, Washburn's plan, in which a General Conference move to Washington, the flourishing of the Second church, and a denomination-wide resolution of the race problem all fit to-gether, would be frustrated.

He warned Ellen White in early June that "a mold that is terrible" was being placed on the work in Washington by Kalstrom, Sheafe, and their supporters at First church "who preach a political gospel which brings in many colored people." The church was indeed growing impressively, he acknowledged, and likely would experience more success that summer. But all of that, he feared, would only strengthen the "terrible" mold and make it something that "will take a long time to change."[14]

He put the matter even more starkly to A. G. Daniells: the success of Sheafe and First church served only to harm the success of the authentic and truly important Adventist work in Washington. Upset by rumors that a decision had already been made for New York as the new location for the Review and Herald, Washburn, in a testy letter of May 27, reminded Daniells of what was at stake in Washington. After months of exuberant reports about the providential successes of the Second church, Washburn now again pronounced his work to be "near to the death." And he put the blame squarely on Sheafe and the "self-constituted martyrs" at First church, who "spare no pains to make the work hard for me."

"Brother Sheafe will have a big tent and do a big work this summer," he wrote, but "the greater the success that work has the greater harm it will do." He reminded Daniells of the clear set of alternatives that had been set out for Sheafe after he had "gone over to Kalstrom" the previous summer:

(1) work along separate racial lines in accordance with the General Conference plan; or (2) leave Washington; or (3) "leave the work" (what Daniells actually wrote was "work on his own account"). As Washburn saw it, Sheafe had not met the terms of the first option, and thus should have been confronted with the necessity of choosing one of the latter two. Instead, with the support of a salary and a degree of encouragement from the General Conference, he was "building up a work that makes it hard for us and will work sorrow and trouble for our work all through the South."

Washburn was further peeved by a suggestion from Chesapeake Conference president O. O. Farnsworth that since Sheafe had acquired a new tent for his 1903 effort, Washburn should use Sheafe's old tent for his meetings. Noting that the tent "was down several times" the previous summer and "torn up," Washburn declared: "I do not like to see the work that should be the real work crippled so it must play second to that which is built upon a principle that will work ruin."[15]

Despite the fact that his work did not fully comply with the terms of Daniells' ultimatum in September 1902, Sheafe had in fact won renewed confidence from the General Conference president. Washburn's complaints not only failed to shake Daniells from that confidence—they were starting to exasperate him. "Oh, drop all this controversy over the race question," he said to Washburn during a visit to Washington soon after receiving the May 27 letter.[16]

Yet Daniells' commitment to a "both/and" approach did not mean he had been won over to the First church ideal of a racially integrated congregation. His vision for the way in which race relations in the church should be molded in Washington, D.C., as a model both for the denomination and for its public evangelistic work remained essentially the same as Washburn's, and not that of Kalstrom and Howard.

The fact that Sheafe would be working in 1903 in cooperation with the latter made it unlikely that Daniells would favor requests for support from First church beyond the pastor's salary. Thus, the General Conference Committee, meeting at College View, Nebraska, on June 18, flatly rejected the First church "memorial" for "a white preacher to labor with Elder Sheafe." No response to the request for a portion of the $10,000 fund is on record.[17]

Another action by the committee on the same day was hardly calculated to encourage Sheafe. Despite the assurances from H. E. Osborne in December that the General Conference would take into account the high cost of living in Washington when reviewing Sheafe's salary in the spring, and Sheafe's detailed explanation of June 12 to E. R. Palmer as to why, based on Osborne's word, he had been drawing funds at a higher rate, the committee voted to keep his salary right where it was at $15 per week. In context, that action at best signaled minimal, begrudging support for the preacher who was stirring Washington on behalf of the third angel's message.

"BROTHER DANIELLS, YOU ARE GRIEVOUSLY WRONG"

The rejection of First church's request prompted two lengthy letters of protest from Dr. Howard, one each to Ellen White and A. G. Daniells. With extraordinary eloquence the doctor laid out the issues at stake in the struggle to define Adventism's answer to the racial dilemma.

While his characteristic spirit of Christian kindness and humility was not abandoned, the impassioned truth-telling equally characteristic of Howard predominates in this letter: "I tell you plainly, Brother Daniells, with all respect, that you and your committee are grievously wrong in your cause and policy on the race question."

In the first place they were wrong, astoundingly so, Dr. Howard believed, in turning their backs on "a splendid opportunity." Despite past failings, Adventism remained exceptionally well positioned "to present the pure gospel here both in practice and precept" by making a concerted effort to reach both races, and then "making no distinction between the races in the church." Where Washburn saw a "terrible" mold in the making, leading to long-term disaster, Dr. Howard saw the hand of God shaping events in preparation for a broad and powerful witness. The attention drawn to the interracial character of the church, and the great magnification of interest brought about by Sheafe's meetings, constituted "openings and opportunities made by Providence and the Holy Spirit."

Further, he said to Daniells, "you are wrong at a time when the world is growing worse in this respect and so much needs your wise and corrective influence." Rather than justifying accommodation to evil, Howard contended that the deteriorating racial situation in America made all the more necessary a forthright witness to truth:

"The compromising plea of expediency, policy, the demands of the world and doing the thing that good may come, is too weak and unworthy of our cause. . . . It would seem that while the people of the world will disregard each other more and more because of national differences, the people of the Savior would be all the more careful not to seem to justify the others in their wicked discriminations."

As Dr. Howard saw it, their mission of proclaiming the last message of warning and rescue for a dying world made it all the more imperative that Adventists stand for gospel principles in human relations:

"It is difficult to see why it is necessary to make a race line in the Adventist denomination in face of the fact that the truth involves a positive protest against any such thing in the church. . . .

"Such a policy not only discredits the body of people who profess to be getting ready to meet the Lord at his coming and be translated, but it deceives the world as the true standard of righteousness, seduces and perverts the conscience and heart of the church and renders obtuse its spiritual discernment.

"I plead not for any fanatical affiliation of the races. That is not desired by either party. But in the name of Heaven, the message and righteousness I plead for a pure and correct standard and practice in this denomination, or church, which professes to be the last."

This was a matter of immediate urgency, he stressed. The series of tent meetings launched by Sheafe on June 28 presented the opportunity for a course correction that would bring at least partial recovery from the damage to the Adventist cause from the mistakes of 1901 and 1902. These mistakes had "produced a woeful effect upon people of both races, to whom the truth now appears less important and less sanctifying, because of what has been done." But now, he exhorted the church president, "you have no such opportunity anywhere else on earth to demonstrate a correct gospel principle than just now at our tent," situated in the national capital, from which "a profound and extensive influence will go out to all the world."[18]

Howard made similar points in a letter, also dated July 10, seeking an authoritative word from Ellen White. Adherence to the "testimonies" was one of the disputed issues in the Washington race controversy. Washburn impugned First church for "fulfilling" Sister White's warning about going too far in the "breaking down of distinctions between the white and colored races." But First church took its stand firmly on her strong message of equality in 1891, "Our Duty to the Colored People," and its clear, specific statement that Black believers should not be excluded from membership in the same congregation as Whites.

Claims made by some ministers that changing conditions over the past decade required modification of the counsel given in 1891 "served to unsettle minds as to the testimonies and discredit the Spirit of Prophecy to a grievous degree here," said Dr. Howard.[19] At this point, however, Ellen White did not feel that the Lord had given her any light beyond what she had already written. Her assistant, Sara McEnterfer, replied to Dr. Howard on Ellen White's behalf, writing that "she says they will have to take what the Lord has been pleased to give her already . . . and with the help of the Lord work this question out for themselves unless the Lord sees fit to put the burden again upon her and give her words for the people."[20]

Despite the power of Dr. Howard's case, it effected no change. The overall episode of the $10,000 campaign for the Second church and the controversy over distribution of church resources in Washington during 1903 had a devastating impact. It represented a second major setback to the opportunity created for Adventism when the emergence of a mixed-race congregation in the nation's capital intersected with the arrival of an evangelist whose exceptional gifts were exceptionally well suited for Washington, D.C. That opportunity involved nothing less than becoming a beacon of light for the entire nation during its darkest hour of racial oppression, a light showing how humanity's deepest antagonisms could be healed and restoration begun when people take seriously the gospel of a crucified, risen, and soon-returning Savior.

As with the first blow that came with the acrimonious division of the Washington church, the second blow did not crush the life out that opportunity. But it aggravated the wounds inflicted by the first blow, and also created new ones. Unless attended to, these threatened to debilitate and perhaps destroy the hopeful possibilities. And as the drama over whether those wounds would heal or fester played out, in the summer of 1903 the arena became even more significant for the future of Adventism. Based on guidance sent from Ellen White on June 26, the denominational leadership finally settled on the Washington, D.C., area as the new locale for the General Conference offices and the Review and Herald Publishing

Association. They executed the move swiftly, locating in temporary quarters rented at 222 North Capitol Street in mid-August.[21]

Meanwhile, a two-month series of meetings at the Beacon Light Gospel Tent, located once again at 13th and T streets, opened on June 28. With the tent crowded, Lewis Sheafe preached on the subject "Christ the Theme of the Bible." According to the Washington *Post*, the Adventist evangelist said that "the great result of Christ's teaching is to make all brothers in the great human family."[22]

---

[1] AGD to JSW, Dec. 4, 1902, GCA.

[2] AGD to LCS, Dec. 11, 1902, GCA.

[3] LCS to AGD, Feb. 13, 1902, GCA.

[4] AGD to LCS, Feb. 20, 1902, GCA.

[5] AGD to James H. Howard, Feb. 20, 1902, GCA.

[6] AGD to EGW, Feb. 24, 1902, GCA.

[7] [Lewis C.] Sheafe, "The First Washington Church," *Review*, Apr. 7, 1903, pp. 19, 20.

[8] The proposed amount of $3,500 was based on a claim that Kalstrom had been making for years that the purchase of the building in 1893 had proceeded on the basis of a promise made by John O. Corliss of $5,000 from the General Conference, which had been only partially fulfilled.

[9] AK to AGD, Mar. 30, 1903, GCA.

[10] The last meeting of the 1903 General Conference session in Oakland was adjourned on April 13 to resume for a final meeting in Battle Creek on April 22, at which the First church memorial was presented. "General Conference Proceedings," *Review*, May 5, 1903, p. 16; GCC minutes, May 1, 1903.

[11] Gary Land, ed., *Adventism in America* (Grand Rapids: Wm. B. Eerdmans, 1986), pp. 131, 132.

[12] JSW to WAS, Dec. 31, 1902, GCA; numerous letters to E. G. White, W. C. White, A. G. Daniells, and other denominational leaders during the first half of 1903, EGWE and GCA.

[13] JSW to EGW, Mar. 2, 1903.

[14] JSW to EGW, June 5, 1903, EGWE.

[15] JSW to AGD, May 27, 1903, GCA.

[16] Washburn recalled the comment in his letter to Daniells of Feb. 20, 1907.

[17] GCC minutes, June 18, 1903.

[18] J. H. Howard to AGD, July 10, 1903, GCA.

[19] J. H. Howard to EGW, July 10, 1903, excerpt printed in *My Soul Doth Magnify the Lord*, pp. 80-83. See also the excerpt of Howard's letter to E. G. White of Mar. 23, 1902, in the same volume, pp. 75-77.

[20] Sara McEnterfer to James H. Howard, July 17, 1903, EGWE.

[21] Arthur L. White, *Ellen G. White: The Early Elmshaven Years* (Washington, D.C.: Review and Herald, 1981), vol. 5, pp. 271-277.

[22] "Tent Meetings Are Begun, First of Beacon Light Gospel Services Held Last Night," WP, June 29, 1903, p. 4.

CHAPTER XXIII

DELICATE HARMONY
AND RENEWED OPPORTUNITY

LEWIS SHEAFE'S PASTORAL DUTIES took him to Takoma Park on a late April day in 1904. More specifically, to the temporary residence of Ellen White—the Carroll Manor House on the campus of the new Washington Training College that was under construction. He asked her if she would be willing to preach the Sabbath sermon at First church.

"I was only too glad to promise that I would speak in the church next Sabbath," she wrote in a letter to Mrs. M. J. Nelson, one of her assistants at her Elmshaven home in California. She noted that it was "the church here in which both white and colored people assemble," and that "some little difficulty in regard to the color line exists here, but we hope that by the grace of God things will be kept in peace."

Sheafe likely took the opportunity to update her on his work. "Under the labors of Elder Sheafe, many colored people in this city have accepted the truth," she also related to Sister Nelson. "Sixteen were baptized the Sabbath before last, and seven last Sabbath."[1]

Ellen White was on an extended visit to Washington to help nurture the institutions being planted there.[2] Sheafe's first opportunity to meet the prophet would have been at the 1901 General Conference session in Battle Creek. They both were in Nashville for the Southern Union meetings held in January 1902, but because of her illness it is unlikely that they had any significant interaction there. The visit in Takoma Park on April 27, 1904, probably lasted only a few minutes, but it was the most substantial and likely the last personal encounter they had.[3]

Though she spoke of "next Sabbath" in her letter of April 28 to Mrs. Nelson, it was not until May 14 that Ellen White spoke at First church. Sheafe had told her that he would invite the members of the new, mainly Black congregation he had established four months before to be present when she spoke to the church on 8th Street. He may well have done this, but was not himself present, perhaps because of a scheduling shift. It was J. S. Washburn who accompanied Ellen White to the First church on May 14, her son Willie desiring to have the morning to "study and rest his mind."

In her summary of the event Ellen White observed that the "house was filled" and the "singing was good." Also, "there were white people and dark people seated together, there being more dark than white." To this congregation, which was becoming increasingly countercultural week by week simply by virtue of being a public assembly where the races freely interacted, with no restrictions or barriers for separate seating, she spoke on the final prayer of Christ for the unity of His disciples.

"I spoke to the people from John 17. I told them I wished them to have that precious last prayer of Christ before He left His disciples to pass through His great agony in the garden of Gethsemane, prior to His crucifixion. There seemed to be a most earnest interest and many felt deeply and showed that their hearts were touched. . . .

"There were many outsiders at the meeting, and all seemed to listen with intensity of interest. I tried to impress upon the people that we had no time and no vital powers to devote to criticizing each other. Our great work is to keep our own souls in the love of God, to learn of Christ His meekness and lowliness of heart, if we would find that rest we desire. . . . We may seek to relieve the soul-burdened one, but we have no permission from the word of God to gather up reports and tell them to hurt the influence of another. We need to keep our own souls in the love of God, that in social conversation we . . . give words of courage and hope."[4]

The spirit of mutual upbuilding for which Ellen White pleaded in her sermon had, by then, begun taking fragile hold among the Adventist churches of Washington, D.C. In fact, for nearly three years following the move of the General Conference in the summer of 1903, antagonisms were submerged, and the congregations, though largely defined and separated by race, interacted regularly under the leadership of a committee appointed by the General Conference.

During these years Sheafe enjoyed a relatively harmonious, in some ways close, working relationship with A. G. Daniells and other church leaders. Even he and Washburn maintained, at the least, a cease-fire.

Soon after it was decided to make Washington the denominational headquarters, Sheafe, along with Andrew Kalstrom and Dr. Howard, represented First church on a committee that met on July 19 to decide how the "evangelical work" of the local churches would be administered. They joined Washburn and Dr. Neall, representing the Second church, and representatives of the Chesapeake Conference, Atlantic Union Conference, and General Conference.[5]

The committee unanimously supported a recommendation making the District of Columbia and Takoma Park a territory directly under the General Conference, rather than remaining part of the Chesapeake Conference and Atlantic Union. Washburn had proposed such a move a month before, citing, in support of the idea, the analogy to the District as federal government territory. When the recommendation came to the Autumn Council in October, A. T. Jones, whose opposition to Daniells' leadership was hardening, cited the same parallel in objecting to the arrangement. The General Conference, he said, would be "a patterning after the United States government, which is headed toward Rome, and is to make an image to the beast." Jones withdrew his objection after Daniells pointed out that the churches in the District and the conferences involved had been consulted and consented to the plan.[6]

Sheafe was one of the five members of the executive committee set up under the arrangement. W. T. Bland, assistant treasurer of the General Conference, was named chair of the committee in 1903 and 1904,[7] but in fact Daniells himself closely supervised matters. Sheafe dealt directly with the General Conference president on a regular basis.

The Autumn Council of 1903 also confirmed another recommendation of the committee that Sheafe had been part of during the summer— the purchase of 50 acres of land in Takoma Park for the sum of $6,000. The General Conference offices, a sanitarium, and a school were to be built on this land, and the council approved establishment of a $100,000 fund to be raised from church members worldwide to pay for these institutions.[8]

A SNAPSHOT OF COMMUNITY AND FAMILY LIFE

While the General Conference move brought him more directly into the orbit of the denominational organization, Sheafe remained a widely recognized and respected figure in the Washington community. After bursting onto the scene in such spectacular fashion in 1902, his public profile gradually receded somewhat, but he remained in frequent demand as a speaker and singer, and active in the civic concerns of the Black community. The most significant of these events have already been discussed, but one further instance deserves mention, both for the way it associated Sheafe with other figures of prominence, and because it was something of a family affair.

The Jones School, where two of the Sheafe children attended, was part of the city's segregated but high-caliber Black public school system. Sheafe was one of the speakers for the school's Easter program in 1904, which unabashedly celebrated the religious meaning of the holiday. The Thursday afternoon event, to which parents were invited, took place in a school "transformed into a veritable tropical scene, with palms, ferns, rubber plants, and bowers of Easter lilies and roses." Kelly Miller, an influential Howard University scholar and activist, preceded Sheafe on the program with "an instructive talk on seed life and gardening."

Connecting nicely with Miller's topic, as well as 1 Corinthians 15, Sheafe "gave a most thrilling and eloquent talk on the meaning of the Resurrection to us—starting with that of the [vegetable] kingdom, he soared, in his remarks to the kingdom of the risen Lord." The account, which appeared on the front page of the Washington *Bee*, also noted that Sheafe "preaches to crowded houses every night." Sheafe's message was followed by exhortations to parent-teacher cooperation by Dr. W. S. Montgomery, assistant superintendent of the D.C. public schools and head of the Colored system, and by James H. Hayes of Richmond, one of the primary organizers of the Negro Suffrage League.

After the dignitaries had said their pieces, it was time for the children to come into the spotlight. Miss Clara Sheafe was noted for her contribution to the musical program, while 8-year-old Lewis gave a recitation.[9]

With her children well into their schooling—Howard was, or soon would be, away at Tuskegee Institute in Alabama—Annie had more time for involvements outside the home. Sometime later that year or in 1905, she was officially made part of the denominational workforce and given a part-time salary as a Bible worker.[10]

A BLACK TRAINING SCHOOL: WASHINGTON'S NEED AND ADVENTISM'S OPPORTUNITY

In 1907 a committee chaired by Charles Douglass formed in the interests of establishing in the District of Columbia a national training and industrial school for Colored youths. The school was to be modeled after the Tuskegee and Hampton institutes, providing training in trades and practical skills. In addition to the main campus in the District, the plans envisioned a "farm school" nearby in Maryland. Though "nonsectarian," the school would be "conducted on a high plane of morality, temperance, economy, and religious teaching." Advanced students would do "practical and intelligent missionary work" in the city. The esteemed educator and community leader Anna J. Cooper, who had been principal of M Street High School from 1901 to 1906, took a leading role among planners. The Rev. S. Geriah Lamkins, pastor of the Tenth Street Baptist Church, headed the drive to raise $50,000 for the project.[11]

The plans never materialized as such, but another school, generally similar in ethos and goals, soon did when Nannie Helen Burroughs established the National Training School for Women and Girls in Washington in 1909, with the support of the National Baptist Convention. Instruction at the new school centered on the "three B's: Bible, bath, and broom."[12]

The strong interest in such institutions in the nation's largest center of African-American population during the first decade of the twentieth century sheds light on the rich opportunity that remained open for Adventism in Washington, despite the divisive turmoil of 1902-1903. The strong gains in membership and public awareness through Sheafe's ministry, combined with the public hunger for the type of education Adventism could offer, made the time ripe for locating an Adventist training school for Black youth in Washington. Such a school would provide a base for implementation of Sheafe's animating vision: a movement carrying Adventism's message of hope for the whole person to his people throughout the entire nation.

Not just Sheafe, but White Adventist leaders as well, had possibilities along these lines in mind in 1903 as they looked toward developing Adventist institutions in Washington. No one expected it to happen immediately. But over the next two years events would move, albeit somewhat fitfully, in the direction of that tantalizing possibility.

A NEW CHURCH AT TRUE REFORMERS' HALL

Four days before Sheafe attended the July 19 committee meeting that considered plans for planting Adventist institutions in Washington, thousands gathered to celebrate the planting of an impressive monument to Black achievement in the national capital. The stately, five-story brick building at 12th and U streets Northwest, dedicated with a full day of ceremonies on July 15, 1903, had been designed and constructed entirely with Black expertise and labor, and financed by the United Order of True Reformers, a Black-operated mutual aid organization based in Richmond, Virginia. Its 28-year-old architect, John A. Langford, was a graduate of Booker T. Washington's Tuskegee Institute.[13]

True Reformers' Hall came to anchor the center of Black culture and enterprise that was developing along U Street and surrounding blocks. In addition to a dance hall destined to host Duke Ellington's first public performance, the building provided rental space for offices and meetings. And one of its earliest tenants was the Adventist preacher Lewis Sheafe, who began conducting his "off-season" Sunday evangelistic meetings there in October. The evening services typically drew crowds of 400 to 500 people.[14]

The meetings at True Reformers' Hall signaled a new phase in Sheafe's endeavor to plant Adventism in the cultural center of Black Washington. His willingness to focus on a Black-oriented ministry made for tension with the leaders of First church who remained deeply dedicated to seeing the congregation embody a gospel-based ideal of racial integration. The difference was a matter of priorities rather than a conflict over deep-seated principles. Sheafe certainly welcomed White people who responded to his preaching and at times took care to point out that he was baptizing members of both races. Yet he did not seem interested in special measures to ensure an ongoing racial mixture, such as hiring a White copastor, and, in fact, may have been a little offended by that proposal.[15]

This tension may have contributed to Sheafe's receptiveness when A. G. Daniells encouraged him to start a new congregation, this one specifically intended for Black believers, with a promise of General Conference help if he would do so. Over the objections of the officers at First church, Sheafe proceeded with organizing the additional congregation, which began meeting on Sabbaths at True Reformers' Hall on November 21, 1903.[16]

Two weeks later a congregation of 51, soon to be known as the People's Seventh-day Adventist Church, was officially organized, with the General Conference president preaching the sermon of dedication. Daniells was about two thirds of the way through his sermon when scores of people started pouring into the rented auditorium. They were the members of First church, who closed their service early in order to come across town as a church body to express goodwill toward the new congregation and the pastor they now shared with it.

WORKING TOGETHER:
THE CHURCHES, THE RACES, AND THE BRETHREN

The warmhearted gesture came as a pleasant surprise to Daniells and Sheafe, given the disagreements, and it bolstered hopes that a new era of cooperation and progress lay ahead for the Adventist cause in the Washington area. "The colored membership is growing very rapidly, and we have some of the nicest colored people in the city," Daniells wrote W. C. White with a touch of pride. It seemed that the "color question" was under control at last, even if not precisely in the way he had envisioned it.

"As the matter is now arranged, I think we can please anybody and everybody on the color question. We have a white church for those who want an unmixed white congregation; we have a church for the colored people, and we have a mixed church where the white and black can both unite. I think this is ideal, and we shall do all we can to build up the interests of all three. The brethren all seem to be coming into harmony."[17]

The interests of harmony probably gained from Andrew Kalstrom's resignation as church elder. Because of a serious decline in health, to which nearly a decade of intense negotiations and conflict with the General Conference brethren over a variety of matters may have contributed, Kalstrom moved out of the city, to Berwyn, Maryland, about six miles east of Takoma Park. Brother Kalstrom, Daniells once commented, had a will like iron. Yet the embattled elder seems to have come through it all more mellowed than embittered. His actions had been driven by a heart that "ached for the needs of this great and influential city," he wrote Daniells. He acknowledged that the denominational leadership's plans for the work in Washington "have much that is practical in them," and assured Daniells that "nowhere will you have a heartier support than at and through the First church." Kalstrom urged the church president to become better acquainted with the congregation, for he would find it "a body of brothers and sisters who love you and live out faithfully the truth."[18]

Within a year the 54-year-old elder who stood like iron for what he saw as the course of truth and righteousness went to his final rest, his death attributed to "acute indigestion." Along with the main sermon by Volney H. Lucas of Baltimore, Sheafe spoke at Kalstrom's funeral, using as his text 2 Samuel 3:38: "And the king said unto his servants, Know ye not that there is a prince and a great man fallen this day in Israel?"[19]

As the dust from the General Conference move began to settle, some glimpses of the Washington-area Adventist churches working cooperatively across racial lines came into view. K. C. Russell, head of the Religious Liberty Bureau (as the General Conference's department for the work on behalf of religious liberty was then called), was given the added responsibility of chairing the District of Columbia Evangelical Committee in 1905. By then a fourth church, Takoma Park, had been established.

Sheafe was the leadoff speaker for a two-day "midsummer convention" that Russell organized for the District churches on August 1 and 2, 1905. The purpose was to provide for the interchange of ideas and experiences concerning evangelistic work that typically took place at the camp meetings and conference sessions, but which the Washington churches missed out on by reason of not being connected with a local conference.

The Memorial church, as the Second church at 12th and M had been rechristened in 1904, hosted the first day of meetings. Sheafe opened the convention with an "enthusiastic address" on the subject "How to Keep

Our Churches Alive in the District." He made two straightforward points: first, that "all the members should be connected with Christ, the great source of life"; and, second, that "all should be given something to do." A "lively discussion bringing out many practical points" ensued, Russell reported.

Several other talks addressing how-to topics followed that day and the next, presented by General Conference workers, and by Washburn, whose topic was "How to Create and Hold an Interest in Our Public Meetings." The venue shifted to the People's church on the second day, where Sheafe again gave one of the talks, this one entitled "How to Bind Off a Public Effort and Establish the Believers in the Faith."[20]

Collaboration between Sheafe and A. G. Daniells also gave evidence of movement toward a hopeful future and restoration of the trust damaged by the conflict of 1902. Daniells' support for Sheafe sometimes extended to details of day-to-day church life. For his Sunday evening evangelistic service at True Reformers' Hall on the first Sunday of February 1905 Sheafe was scheduled to speak on the subject "God's Chamber of Mysteries: or, the Sealed Book." He took ill, however, and turned to Daniells for last-minute help. In a note sent on Sunday morning, Daniells promised the indisposed preacher that he would "make the best possible arrangements for your services tonight" and that he or some other brother would "run in and see you." And in response to a previous request from Sheafe, he agreed to be present for an upcoming service in which the church elder and several deacons and deaconesses were to be ordained.[21]

The most significant aspect of Sheafe's working relationship with Daniells had to do with the development of Black workers for the Adventist cause. Daniells looked to Sheafe for information and advice concerning men he had met or had recommended to him as potential ministers. One of these, J. Marion Campbell, would eventually succeed Sheafe at People's church and altogether render more than four decades of productive service as an Adventist minister.[22]

Conversely, Sheafe recommended promising individuals to Daniells, seeking his support in finding a place for them in denominational work. Sheafe was particularly insistent about a young attorney, William H. Green, who had studied for ministry at Shaw University, a Baptist school in North Carolina. After beginning his legal career in Charlotte and then

Elizabeth City, North Carolina, Green moved to Washington, where he was admitted to practice before the Supreme Court of the United States. He and his partner, J. E. Collins, represented Rufus Bingon, convicted of murder in the Indian Territory (Oklahoma). They succeeded in gaining on behalf their client a "writ of error" from Supreme Court Justice David Brewer, directing that the case be reexamined in the Court of Appeals of the Indian Territory.[23]

While he harbored political aspirations, Green remained a man of deep dedication and principle concerning the cause of God. His disgust with the practices of many of the Baptist ministers put him on a search for something better that culminated in his acceptance of the Adventist message through Sheafe's evangelism. Convicted that he should give up his legal practice for ministry, he expressed willingness to go anywhere to spread the message. He closed his practice in 1905 and, after some delays in the church's decision-making process, was formally added to the denomination's salaried ministerial ranks that summer, and assigned to begin work in Pittsburgh.[24]

------

[1] EGW to Mrs. M. J. Nelson, Apr. 28, 1904, in *Manuscript Releases*, vol. 4, p. 24.

[2] A. L. White, *Ellen G. White*, vol. 5, pp. 318-328.

[3] Both were at the 1905 General Conference session in Takoma Park a year later, but nothing indicates that they met there.

[4] Ellen G. White, "That They All May Be One," manuscript 45, 1904, EGWE.

[5] Minutes of the July 19, 1903, meeting included with GCC minutes; AGD to GCC, Aug. 7, 1903, GCA.

[6] GCC minutes, Oct. 18, 19, 1903.

[7] YB, 1904 and 1905.

[8] A. G. Daniells, "Washington (D.C.) Medical and Sanitarium Interests," *Review*, Feb. 4, 1904, pp. 6, 7.

[9] "Parents Meet—Teachers and Friends," *Bee*, Apr. 16, 1904, p. 1.

[10] Mrs. A. C. Sheafe was among those given a missionary license by vote of the 1905 General Conference; see "Credentials and Licenses," *Review*, June 8, 1905, p. 21.

[11] "Washington to Have Training and Industrial School," New York *Age*, June 20, 1907, p. 3; "Colored Training School" *Bee*, Oct. 13, 1907, p. 7.

[12] *The Black Washingtonians*, pp. 141, 42.

[13] S. Fitzpatrick and M. R. Goodwin, *The Guide to Black Washingtion*, pp. 168-170; "True Reformers' Hall," at "Duke Ellington's Washington," http://www.pbs.org/ellingtonsdc/vtTheaters.htm#Reformers (accessed June 26, 2009).

[14] A. G. Daniells, "Development of the Work in Washington," *Review*, Dec. 31, 1903, pp. 5, 6.

[15] AGD to SS, Feb. 4, 1907. Daniells here states that the leaders of First church became dissatisfied with Sheafe because he was drawing "mainly colored people" and thus "wished

to get rid of him," which "hurt his feelings very much." In narrating events leading up to the breach in 1907 between Sheafe and the General Conference, Daniells was seeking to show Scott, a promising young Black minister, all that he had done to stand by Sheafe when other members of the General Conference Committee and even the leaders of Sheafe's own congregation did not. It is likely that Daniells blurred the call for a White minister to work with Sheafe into a desire to "get rid of him." The observation that this hurt Sheafe's feelings very much may likewise be an exaggeration, though it is plausible that Sheafe would have taken offense from a proposal implying that his ministerial leadership was inadequate.

[16] "Sunday Church Services," WP, Nov. 21, 1903, p. 14.

[17] AGD to WCW, Dec. 6, 1903, CAR.

[18] AK to AGD, Dec. 3, 1903, GCA.

[19] Obituary, *Review*, Nov. 3, 1904, p. 23.

[20] K. C. Russell, "District of Columbia Midsummer Convention," *Review*, Aug. 10, 1905, p. 18.

[21] AGD to LCS, Feb. 5, 1905, GCA; LCS to AGD, Feb. 2, 1905, GCA; "Sunday Church Services," WP, Feb. 4, 1905, p. 11.

[22] AGD to LCS, Sept. 2, 1904, GCA; LCS to AGD, Feb. 15, 1905, GCA; obituary, *North American Informant*, February-March 1959, p. 9.

[23] "Washington Scored a Hit," New York *Age*, June 22, 1905, p. 1; obituary, *Review*, Dec. 27, 1928, p. 22; "City Paragraphs," CA, Jan. 2, 1904, p. 4.

[24] LCS to AGD, Aug. 3, 1904, June 21, 28, 1905, GCA.

CHAPTER XXIV

THE PEOPLE'S CHURCH: PROFOUND POSSIBILITIES AND HARD QUESTIONS

DESPITE DEEP DISAPPOINTMENTS over the contrast between Adventism's performance on race relations and the high expectations he had formed when he joined the church in 1896, Sheafe now staked his hopes on a basic fairness in the allocation of church funds, within the framework of ministry along separate racial lines. Events unfolded in Washington so as to set up a test of that fairness.

As it raised funds for the institutions of its new headquarters, would the denomination devote resources in an equitable and expeditious manner for the development of a strong institutional base in Washington for its work on behalf of African-Americans in the South and throughout the nation? The power attending Sheafe's evangelism in the city had thrown open doors to vast opportunity. Would the denominational leadership move in tandem with him through those doors, and to the untold possibilities beyond?

He had some basis for hope. Daniells had promised General Conference support if he established a new congregation. And in his response to Sheafe's query in February 1904 about a permanent home for the growing congregation meeting in True Reformers' Hall, Daniells indicated that both he and W. C. White favored starting "a colored training school near Washington." After he and White returned from a medical convention in New York the following week, Daniells suggested to Sheafe that the three of them meet for counsel on the matter. At the same time, he cautioned that providing funds for such a project "would tax us very much," and thus was noncommittal when it came to specifics.[1]

Whether the meeting ever took place, it soon became clear enough, if it was not already, that a training school for Black youth would have to await completion of the large task of establishing the institutions planned for Takoma Park—the headquarters office, publishing house, sanitarium, and college, rather than being considered part of the overarching project for establishing the new denominational base. That summer, though, the General Conference did take an initial step toward acquisition of a building for the People's church.

"DOES THE CONFERENCE
REALLY MEAN TO DO ANYTHING?"

The congregation continued to grow as Sheafe pushed forward with seemingly perpetual evangelism. The weekly evangelistic meetings on Sundays, along with Sabbath services, continued through the winter and early spring at True Reformers' Hall. He launched the 1904 summer effort by pitching the Beacon Light Gospel Tent for nightly services at a new location, 1st and K streets Southwest. Sheafe also preached one Sunday each month at the D.C. jail. Along with the inmates, some 200 to 300 visitors typically attended these meetings, many of whom were thereby drawn to the evangelistic meetings. By July the membership of the People's church surpassed 80.[2]

Meanwhile, Sheafe remained on the lookout for promising real estate. In July he located property on 12th Street Northwest that held good prospects, and Daniells agreed to form a committee to investigate and take counsel on the details. W. C. White, who along with his mother had returned for a final month in Washington after meetings in Michigan and a trip to the South, was placed on the committee along with Sheafe, Joseph Gillis, a successful Black businessman and prominent member of the First church, and A. P. Needham, business manager of the incipient Washington Sanitarium.

White's participation on the committee was of considerable potential significance. As his mother's trusted confidant and recognized spokesman, and a close colleague and advisor to A. G. Daniells since their years together in Australasia during the 1890s, W. C. White was the connecting link between the charismatic and administrative authority that combined to lead the Adventist Church.[3] His appraisal and recommendations would carry great weight with both the prophet and the president.

Unfortunately, despite persistent efforts by Sheafe to make arrangements, the Takoma Park-based members never seemed able to work into their schedules a trip into the city to see the property and meet with the owner. Then on August 11 the Whites departed on the cross-country trip back to California. Daniells later acknowledged that the brethren appointed to the committee may not have devoted the attention to it that they should have.[4]

In November, after a year of renting at True Reformers' Hall, Sheafe sought specific and decisive action with a written proposal to Daniells. The document reflects frustration—albeit restrained—as Sheafe attempted to impress upon Daniells the urgency of swift action while the window of a unique opportunity was still open. And if, on the other hand, the General Conference was *not* going to come through with tangible support any time soon, the congregation needed to know that, too.

The People's church membership had now reached 103, but Sheafe contended that the lack of a church building impeded much greater growth. Many who attended Sheafe's meetings and were impressed with the truth of his message had deep, all-encompassing ties to one of Washington's many great Black churches. To cut those ties and connect with a previously unknown and rather odd movement that required radical, inconvenient changes in how one lived was daunting enough. Question marks about the movement's lasting viability that remained because of the lack of a church building added a barrier to the pull of the message. And then there were some who refused to attend services at True Reformers' Hall because of its "associations" and uses made of it for "dances and such things" during the week.

Removal of that barrier "while the interest is still up," Sheafe contended, would bring a significant breakthrough in winning new members. After major evangelistic campaigns for three summers in a row and weekly evangelistic meetings the rest of the year, Sheafe was still attracting large and eager crowds. But that could not last forever, so to delay would be to lose much.

Before getting to specific actions steps, Sheafe laid before Daniells the gauntlet of commitment: "Now do you think that the conference really means to do any thing to aid us in securing a place of worship, and if so when? and to what extent?"

Sheafe proposed that the General Conference appropriate $2,000 and lend an additional amounted as needed to make the purchase. What he and his congregation most wanted, though, was clear, definite answers, so that "we may know how to arrange our work."

Daniells, who replied after discussing Sheafe's letter with Spicer, the General Conference secretary, and W. W. Prescott, the *Review and Herald* editor, strongly affirmed the General Conference's intention to support the People's church project. Regarding the "when?" and "to what extent?" he was no doubt less specific than Sheafe desired, though he did put forward a tentative proposal.

That proposal, though, came only after a rundown of the "avalanche of demands" then pressing on the denomination, making definite commitments difficult. In language likely more revealing of the racial differentiation in his outlook than he intended, Daniells cited the endeavor "to raise $100,000 for *our* Washington enterprise" as foremost among the circumstances making it impossible just then to undertake raising "a few thousand for *your* enterprise" (italics supplied). Acknowledging that Sheafe might view it as a "dangerous delay," Daniells suggested that the General Conference's "Fourth of July call for missions" in 1905 could include "a church for the colored people of Washington" among the needs to be met.[5]

In some ways this reply did give Sheafe important information on how to arrange the work that was placed in his charge. If the People's church waited for funds from the General Conference, it would be, at minimum, close to another year before they could expect to move into a building of their own, and even that prospect would be highly uncertain. By the same token, if they were to move quickly so as to take full advantage of the current high level of interest, they would have to act on their own initiative and resources.

WONDERFUL BUILDING, GREAT PRICE, IDEAL LOCATION

Accordingly, the People's church established a building fund and by February 1905 had raised $1,000 for it. They continued to pray, watch, and work, and, as Sheafe put it, experienced "much trial, perplexity, and difficulty in looking for a location for our church house." Then, suddenly, an unexpected opportunity opened. The New Jerusalem Society offered for sale its elegant, three-story brick church on the corner of 10th and V streets Northwest.[6]

The structure and location both were wonderfully suited to the needs and mission of the People's church. The property at 10th and V had been the site of an African-American church ever since the Abyssinian Baptist Church had moved there in 1879. By 1896 it was in the hands of the First African New Church Society, as the New Jerusalem Society was also known, who transformed the existing one-story structure by adding two floors and a corner tower. The architect for the new structure, Paul J. Pelz, and his partner, John L. Smithmeyer, were the original architects of the Library of Congress.[7]

When completed in 1896, the building was worth $10,000 and the property $7,000. Sheafe and the People's church acquired the building and the lot for a total of $10,000 on May 4, 1905. By that time their building fund balance had reached $1,500. They financed the rest with five bank notes of $500 each at 5 percent interest, and a mortgage with a 6 percent interest rate on the remaining $6,000. By July, not long after taking possession, the congregation had repaid one of the $500 notes, leaving a remaining principal of $8,000. The church came with no pews or any other furniture, necessitating the purchase of 350 chairs, as well as tables and an organ, all of which were paid for completely during their first summer of occupancy.

With an auditorium on the top floor that could seat 250, two large rooms on the second floor divided by folding doors, and a lower level in which a printing office and a large kitchen were set up, the building provided ample facilities for the various aspects of Adventism's ministry to the whole person. "It is admirably adapted for the general work of a training school for young men and women," wrote Sheafe, and already plans had been formulated to use the kitchen on the lower level for a cooking school.[8]

The location, "a thickly populated section of the city near the car lines," was ideal for reaching people. It was just a block from the U Street corridor, the cultural and commercial center of Black Washington. Leading centers of community life such as the congregation's former, temporary home, True Reformers' Hall, as well as the 12th Street YMCA, the

Phyllis Wheatley YWCA, and the MuSoLit Club, were all within walking distance. Many of the city's most prominent Black churches also were within a few blocks, such as Shiloh Baptist, John Wesley AME Zion, St. Luke's Episcopal, and 15th Street Presbyterian.[9]

The evidence of providential workings seemed abundant, leading Sheafe to declare, "The Lord's hand was surely in the movement to secure the property." Indeed, he looked back to his first evangelistic meetings in the city three years earlier as the beginning of "a movement that has continued to the present, with a spirit and power that only the Lord can give."[10]

Along with the First church, members of the Memorial and Takoma Park churches crowded into their sister congregation's new sanctuary to join the 130 or so members of People's church for dedicatory Sabbath services on June 10. Sheafe preached on Acts 28, which depicts the apostle Paul preaching the kingdom of God freely in Caesar's capital city, even while under house arrest. Dr. Howard, of First church; G. B. Thompson, representing the General Conference; and K. C. Russell, chair of the D.C. Committee for Evangelical Work, joined Sheafe on the podium.[11]

In the summer of 1905 signs of hope still pointed to the bright possibility that the Adventist message might go forward in the American capital city with minimal hindrance from racial discord among the messengers. Now in his fourth consecutive summer of evangelistic meetings in this city, Sheafe continued drawing large crowds that eagerly received "the glorious message," resulting in steady additions to the church.

A series at 22nd and M streets Northwest concluded in mid-August with an overflow crowd on the final evening. The meetings continued, though, with the tent now pitched on the lot outside the new church property. The 500 seats set up in and around the tent could not accommodate the crowds, which, on Sunday nights, spilled onto the streets. Sixteen candidates initiated the church's new baptistry on Sabbath, September 9, bringing the number of new members resulting from that summer's effort to 26.[12]

J. S. Washburn had words of praise for the work of his old nemesis in the reports he published in the *Review* in his capacity as "fund-raising agent" for the $100,000 Second church. Also, in an article promoting the annual offering for the work among "the colored people" in the South, he acknowledged the importance of Sheafe's work in reaching "a most excellent class" among the city's influential Black population.[13]

Positive interactions seemed in evidence at the previously noted Midsummer Convention for the District of Columbia churches, as well as at the General Conference session held in May in Takoma Park. Sheafe responded warmly to Daniells' invitation for the People's church (as well as the other two Washington churches) to join the conference for Sabbath services on May 13. Sheafe was also called upon to offer prayer or sing at other meetings during the conference.[14]

Most significant of all, as the campaigns to raise large amounts for the Takoma Park projects proceeded, denominational leaders continued to hold out the possibility of a Black training school of some kind in the Washington area. A statement made by W. C. White in this regard alludes to the practice that emerged in the course of the $100,000 campaign of a "Surprise Party" in which delegates to the General Conference session presented a special offering as a "surprise" gift. A particularly poignant "surprise," for example, came on May 12 at the 1905 session, when O. R. Staines presented $87.55 contributed from the "colored training school" in Huntsville, Alabama. Those in attendance "recognized that it was indeed out of deep poverty and need that the young people and workers in that place had joined in this offering."[15]

In material sent out from Elmshaven to conference and union conference papers in support of the October offering for the "colored work," White called upon readers to "surprise the managers of the Huntsville training school" and to do similarly for others engaged in Adventist work directed toward African-Americans, among them Lewis Sheafe. "Let us surprise Brother Sheafe by helping to provide the means for the opening of a workers' institute in the V Street meeting-house in Washington, D.C." An excerpt from the *Testimonies*, volume 7, by Ellen White, entitled "An Appeal for the Colored Race," accompanied her son's appeal.[16] The development of a strong center in Washington, D.C., for the Adventist mission to the nation's Black population was on the agenda for which the prophet and her son worked in a carefully unified way.

STUBBORN FACTS

Yet along with these signs of comity, certain facts remained stubborn in the autumn of 1905. In 1903 a denomination-wide campaign had raised $10,000 to house a newly created all-White congregation in Washington. In 1904 and 1905 more than $100,000 had been raised for new and transplanted denominational institutions in Washington. During this time the evangelistic efforts led by Sheafe added at least 150 new members to the church rolls, a substantial minority of them White, with every prospect of a great many more soon to come. No specific numbers of new members from the concurrent Whites-only efforts appear to have been reported. But despite the talk of what ought to happen someday, the total amount appropriated or even specifically pledged for the Black-oriented work Sheafe was charged with leading remained $0.

"We hope that definite steps may be taken to give this branch of the work some financial help," Sheafe appealed in concluding his report on the People's church in the August 24 issue of the *Review and Herald*. On the back page the editors briefly endorsed consideration of "the needs of this effort on behalf of the truth." A few individuals responded, including one of the denomination's great pioneers, J. N. Loughborough, who donated $5.00.[17] But the leading brethren took no definite steps.

Daniells, it appears, quietly dropped his offer to make the People's church building fund a prominently identified recipient of funds contributed in the Fourth of July mission offering. J. S. Washburn, in his role as "financial agent" for the Washington work, informed W. C. White in July that he would be glad to help raise money for the church recently purchased by "Brother Sheafe and his congregation," but added, "I cannot do this just now."[18] W. C. White's own appeal in connection with the October offering for the "colored work" did indicate that the proposal for a Black training school in Washington had not been forgotten, but listed it, with no particular emphasis, as but one among many pressing needs in that category.

As delay in addressing the disparity continued, the pressure on Sheafe mounted. Even amid the rejoicing over the new and hopeful chapter opened by the acquisition of the church at 10th and V, growing concern and frustration became evident in Sheafe's communication with Daniells. While acknowledging the many demands on the church president's time, Sheafe made a special plea for Daniells' participation in at least one of the services of dedication for the newly purchased building that were held on

June 10 and 11. "[The] people ask me questions that are hard to answer, relative to the interest that the conference has in our work here, so please try to come," he urged.[19] Daniells, however, did not find it possible to be there, and the conference representatives on hand were not in a position to resolve the questions.

A minor dispute about the same time, perhaps a misunderstanding, over the employment of W. H. Green as a minister illumines Sheafe's increasing exasperation. "Pardon me for annoying you so often," he began a letter in which he pointed out that Green, based on Daniells' encouragement, had closed his business on April 1 to enter the ministry. It was now nearly the end of June, and Green had yet to hear anything regarding his assignment. In Sheafe's view the conference should take responsibility for Green's time since April 1.

"Now will you kindly let him know personally what the conference means to do—in order that he may regulate himself accordingly," Sheafe concluded. "I am not saying what you shall do, but please don't keep the man in uncertainty any longer."[20]

Daniells agreed to see Green, but denied making a specific commitment as to his employment. "You surely told me to have him close out his business and be ready to work by April 1," Sheafe insisted in reply. Daniells also asked whether Sheafe needed help with the work in Washington, raising the possibility of Green being assigned that role. "I think Brother G. would be able to render good service" in assisting him with tent meetings, Sheafe said, adding, "At all events the experience would be helpful to him." But it also irritated Sheafe that Daniells would even ask if he could use assistance. "I supposed you knew that I have no one to assist me at all; I have asked help so often and have not gotten it that I made my mind not to say any more about it."[21] The matter was soon resolved with Green's assignment to Pittsburgh, but the exchange suggests that Sheafe's reservoir of trust in the denomination's leadership had reached a low level.

As work on the sanitarium in Takoma Park moved toward completion, the medical missionary aspect of the work for Black Washington came to the forefront. At a "workers' council" for the District of Columbia held at the Memorial church on October 11, an "urgent appeal" was presented for immediate consideration of "treatment rooms for the colored people of Washington," in view of the "very great demand for this kind of work among a number of influential citizens." Daniells and other top General Conference leaders such as W. A. Spicer and G. A. Irwin attended the meeting, along with Sheafe and the other ministers and Bible workers working in the District.[22] Here, too, though, no "definite steps" in response to the urgent appeal are in evidence.

The window of unique opportunity opened through the convergence of the widening witness of Washington's original Adventist congregation with Sheafe's charismatic leadership was beginning to close.

VACATION?

The preacher had thrown himself into three and a half years of intense, nearly nonstop evangelistic and pastoral labor. The signs of divine favor upon his efforts had indeed been abundant, and it was beyond question that he now deserved—and needed—a good vacation. According to a brief notice in the October 19 issue of the *Review*, the People's church was taking care of the expenses for their pastor to spend "a few weeks in some quiet place where he could secure needed rest."

Whether and where Sheafe found such a place, and if so, how much time he spent there, is unclear. It is clear that the ensuing weeks were by no means entirely devoted to secluded relaxation. In his column on Washington news for the New York *Age*, Edward E. Cooper, formerly editor of the now-defunct *Colored American* newspaper, reported in early November that Sheafe was on a "lecture tour in the Carolinas." Sheafe's eloquence and singing ability had drawn "large throngs" in Washington, and the preacher was "unusually conversant with the Bible and apt at repartee at public meetings," Cooper informed readers of the *Age*. His lectures in Charleston and Columbia, South Carolina, the previous week had been attended by "large and enthusiastic audiences."[23]

While on a visit to Chicago during the last week of November, according to the society column of the Washington *Bee*, Sheafe was a guest of J. R. Buster, his early partner in Adventist ministry.[24] It was also around this time, in all likelihood, that he paid a visit to a young preacher from Jamaica, James K. Humphrey, who was developing a promising work in New York City. What was Sheafe doing with his "vacation"?

---

[1] LCS to AGD, Feb. 2, 1904, GCA; AGD to LCS, Feb. 5, 1904, GCA.

[2] A. G. Daniells, "The Work in Washington, D.C.," *Review,* July 7, 1904, p. 24.

[3] See Jerry Allen Moon, *W. C. White and Ellen G. White: The Relationship Between the Prophet and the Son* (Berrien Springs, Mich.: Andrews University Press, 1993), p. 264, and throughout chapters 4 and 5.

[4] LCS to WCW and A. P. Needham, July 18, 21, 27, 28, 1904, EGWE; AGD to SS, Feb. 4, 1907, GCA.

[5] AGD to LCS, Nov. 10, 1904, GCA.

[6] Lewis C. Sheafe, "People's Seventh-day Adventist Church of Washington, D.C.," *Review,* Aug. 24, 1905, pp. 15, 16. This article states the church deposited $1,000 in a building fund account in February 1904. However, in a letter of Feb. 8, 1905, Sheafe informed Daniells that the church had at that point almost raised $1,000 for the building fund (GCA).

[7] Paul Kelsey Williams, "Scenes From the Past," *The InTowner,* July 2006, p. 12; "Chronology of the Thomas Jefferson Building," virtual tour of the Library of Congress, http://www.loc.gov/jefftour/chronology.html (accessed Apr. 6, 2009). In 1873 Smithmeyer and Pelz were awarded first prize in the competition for design plans authorized by Congress, and they were the first two architects, respectively, during construction. Williams indicates that the First African New Church was listed in the city directory as "Swedenborgian-Colored." The New church was the small denomination of adherents to the highly spiritualized biblical interpretations of the eigthteenth-century mystic Emmanuel Swedenborg; see Sydney E. Ahlstrom, *A Religious History of the American People* (New Haven, Conn.: Yale University Press, 1972), pp. 483-486.

[8] Sheafe, "People's Seventh-day Adventist Church," p. 15.

[9] S. Fitzpatrick and M. R. Goodwin, *The Guide to Black Washingtion,* pp. 117-160.

[10] Sheafe, "People's Seventh-day Adventist Church," p. 15.

[11] K. C. Russell, "Dedicatory Service," *Review,* June 15, 1905, p. 24.

[12] Sheafe, "People's Seventh-day Adventist Church," pp. 15, 16; K. C. Russell, "A Workers' Council," *Review,* Oct. 19, 1905, p. 20; Lewis C. Sheafe, "Washington, D.C.," *Review,* Sept. 21, 1905, p. 24.

[13] J. S. Washburn, "Washington, D.C.," *Review,* July 27, 1905, p. 24; and Aug. 3, 1905, p. 24; J. S. Washburn, "The Voice of Thy Brother's Blood," *Review,* Sept. 14, 1905, pp. 5, 6.

[14] LCS to AGD, May 7, 1905, GCA; "Fourth Meeting," *Review,* May 18, 1905, p. 28; "Sixteenth Meeting," *Review,* June 1, 1905, p. 8.

[15] "Third Meeting," *Review,* May 18, 1905, p. 27.

[16] W. C. White, "Another Surprise," New York *Indicator,* Oct. 4, 1905, pp. 1, 2; see also *Welcome Visitor,* Oct. 4, 1905, p. 3, and *Atlantic Union Gleaner,* Oct. 4, 1905, p. 1.

[17] Sheafe, "Washington, D.C.," *Review,* Sept. 21, 1905, p. 24.

[18] JSW to WCW, July 7, 1905, EGWE.

[19] LCS to AGD, June 4, 1905, GCA.

[20] LCS to AGD, June 21, 1905, GCA.

[21] LCS to AGD, June 26, 1905, GCA.

[22] Russell, "A Workers' Council."

[23] "The Week's News in Washington," New York *Age,* Nov. 9, 1905, p. 7.

[24] "This Week in Society," *Bee,* Dec. 1, 1905, p. 5.

SECTION FIVE:
"The Separation Was a Sad Mistake"

"Then as the children of God are one in Christ, how does Jesus look upon caste, upon society distinctions, upon the division of man from his fellow man, because of color, race, position, wealth, birth, or attainments? The secret of unity is found in the equality of believers in Christ. The reason of all division, discord, and difference is found in separation from Christ." (Emphasis supplied.)

—ELLEN G. WHITE
REVIEW AND HERALD
DECEMBER 22, 1891

CHAPTER XXV

CONFRONTATION OVER RACIAL INJUSTICE

JAMES K. HUMPHREY was in the middle of his sermon at the 1922 General Conference session in San Francisco when he recalled an experience exemplifying his determination not to allow anything to separate him from the love of God. In 1905, said the pastor of the 600-member Harlem Seventh-day Adventist Church, "a brother"—his senior by about 20 years—came to his home in New York and "urged me to cut loose from this denomination." The unnamed brother almost certainly was Lewis C. Sheafe. Beyond the fact that Sheafe was born 18 years before Humphrey, no one else seems remotely plausible. And New York could easily have been one of the several locales on Sheafe's "vacation" itinerary in November 1905.

As effective speakers sometimes must, Humphrey oversimplified the incident to make a point, namely, that he "flatly refused" then, and refused "now" (in 1922) to "turn aside from God's organized plan." Humphrey did not interject this solemn, forceful declaration into his message before the assembled leaders of the world church simply to illustrate a sermonic point. Much had happened during the 17 years since 1905 that had turned the 43-year-old preacher's formerly black hair almost completely white, and caused some people to wonder about his future with the denomination. He wanted to clear the air, and according to biographer R. Clifford Jones, the endeavor was so emotion-laden that he had to grip the pulpit to help prevent tears from flowing.[1]

In 1905, though, it was not at all clear, and in fact quite unlikely, that Sheafe had made a definite decision to "cut loose" from the denomination.

Yet he did make a fateful decision that fall. It was a decision that set him on a course in which he was willing to risk separation from the General Conference. The General Conference's failure to support the People's church project even while investing heavily in segregated institutions in Takoma Park led him to resolve that the denominational leadership must face up squarely to the issue of racial inequity, and do so swiftly. If it did not, or did not do so satisfactorily, he would lead his congregation and other Black Adventists to self-governance and freedom from the dominance of White church leaders. Sheafe's plans do not seem to have been precise at this point, but he wanted to sound out and gain support from other Black ministers should a break become necessary.

Put another way, his loyalty to church organization became decidedly provisional. And that meant that the possibility of a denomination or association of Black Seventh-day Adventists separate from the existing denomination was now on the table.

Sheafe's decision to push the race question to the point of resolution came just as the most profound crisis of authority in the denomination's history was reaching its climax. Race relations intertwined with issues involving organization and the gift of prophecy in a period of dramatic conflict that would set the denomination's trajectory into the century that followed. On the one hand, the conflict surrounding Sheafe contributed to the severity of the overall crisis. On the other hand, the sharply polarized atmosphere likely made Sheafe's actions appear more threatening and the disputes he raised more intractable than they would have in less tumultuous times.

By 1905 the chasm between Dr. John Harvey Kellogg's medical and humanitarian empire centered in Battle Creek and the reorganized denominational authority structure headed by A. G. Daniells in Takoma Park had at last become unbridgeable. Also, through a protracted process in which partial reconciliation alternated with renewed antagonism, Kellogg ultimately refused to submit his judgment to the prophetic guidance from Ellen White, though he continued to profess respect for her spiritual gift.[2]

For Alonzo T. Jones the main problem was that Daniells' aggressive leadership had taken reorganization in a direction precisely opposite the one intended in 1901. In Jones's view the main purpose was to break up the exercise of domineering authority by a few individuals. While dispersing much of the burden of administration to the new union conferences, Daniells had, in effect, created a more efficient system for the exercise of dynamic leadership from the center. After a narrow reelection victory in 1903 gave Daniells the green light to move forward with his program of centralized coordination, Jones became increasingly antagonistic and increasingly radical in advocating a doctrine of no authority above that of the individual Christian. In 1906 Jones too went public with doubts about whether all of Ellen White's messages could be trusted as a word from the Lord.[3]

Though at times on opposite sides in previous disputes, Kellogg and Jones, united by shared resistance to Daniells and the new organizational system, sought to establish an alternative Adventism in the denomination's old hometown, Battle Creek. They posed a formidable threat. During the 1890s, while Ellen White ministered in Australia, Jones and Kellogg were easily the most influential Adventist leaders in America. Kellogg towered over Adventism's growing medical and health reform work. The International Medical Missionary and Benevolent Association that he directed had, as of 1901, 2,000 employees, while the total number under the General Conference umbrella was only 1,500.[4] Jones had been coleader of the righteousness-by-faith revival that emerged out of the 1888 General Conference and had enjoyed Ellen White's warm endorsement and enthusiastic participation. A powerful speaker and prolific writer, he became Adventism's most influential theological voice in the 1890s. Longtime editor or coeditor of the *American Sentinel* (predecessor to *Liberty*), he also coedited the *Review and Herald* from 1897 to 1901.[5]

Another notable, Albion F. Ballenger, joined the ranks of the disaffected in 1905. Associated with Jones in the work for religious liberty in the 1890s, Ballenger stirred the denomination in the late 1890s with his "Receive Ye the Holy Ghost" revivals. However, he began teaching an alternative interpretation of Christ's ministry in the heavenly sanctuary as it relates to 1844, which put him at odds with church leadership and led to his dismissal from the ministry.[6]

Sheafe had strong personal affinities with these men. It was through the ministry of Battle Creek Sanitarium that Sheafe learned and embraced the Adventist message in 1896. Dr. Kellogg had been a strong patron of his early ministry and had generously provided critical financial support for his family during the time of transition. Ballenger and Sheafe had worked well together in Louisville in 1899. Sheafe's most important links with Jones lay in the future, but like the other two, Jones was known for his strong stand on racial equality as a gospel principle. Given these connections, it is not surprising that as his confidence in the General Conference administration diminished, Sheafe felt the pull of the anti-Daniells alliance in Battle Creek.

Sheafe's travels in November 1905 may also have contained signs of another source of turbulence. Apparently he traveled alone. No references bring Annie or the children into the picture, suggesting a family vacation. Absence of such references in itself could be explained any number of ways. However, a deteriorating relationship at home would soon surface that paralleled and contributed to the crisis in his relationship with the denomination.

THE PEOPLE'S CHURCH PETITION

The year 1906 opened with no signs of tangible support from the General Conference yet visible. A. G. Daniells favored making a sizable appropriation for the People's church building debt, but other members of the General Conference Committee opposed it. Rumors of Sheafe's discontent aroused suspicion that he planned to break with the denomination after getting its help to pay for the building, and Daniells acceded to the resistance from his brethren.[7] The small sanitarium that operated in a house formerly owned by Ulysses S. Grant on Iowa Circle (later renamed Logan Circle) prior to completion of the new facility in Takoma Park in 1907 did not welcome Black patients or students in its Nurses Training School.[8] The "urgent appeal" in October for treatment rooms to serve the Colored population had not produced action. The outlook was equally forbidding at the Washington Training School near completion of its second year of operation in Takoma Park.

Thus, the time for patience and deference was over. Lewis Sheafe and his congregation swiftly embarked on a course of confrontation. The People's church, on February 26, petitioned the General Conference, in courteous but formal language, for information that would clear the way toward resolution of an intolerable situation: "We desire to give the whole message in our day, and generation; but we find ourselves handicapped in that we have no schools, hospitals, or sanitariums under our control, or to the best of our knowledge, for our use."

Thus, while the race problem created the handicap, the distinctive imperative of Adventist mission, not a mere demand for equality, drove the petition's urgency. The third angel's message was to be given in *our* day, *this* generation, and the People's church wanted to get on with it.

One solution, of course, would simply be to remove racial barriers to the institutions currently operating or under development. This was highly unlikely, the petitioners recognized, given "the doctrine of expediency by which the Seventh-day Adventist churches in this city were separated on racial grounds." Still, that was the first matter needing clarification for the record:

"The People's Seventh-day Adventist Church, 10th and V streets NW., in convention assembled, hereby requests to be informed, specifically and unequivocally, whether its members are privileged to accept the services and benefits of the schools, hospitals, and sanitariums, either or all of them, now under the control of or operated by the General Conference of the Seventh-day Adventist churches, located at Takoma Park, D.C., or by any district, state, or local conference subordinate thereto or in ecclesiastical fellowship therewith, or by any person or persons acting under or deriving or possessing power or authority from either or all of the directing, controlling or supervisory bodies hereinbefore mentioned."

A request followed for specific information on any institutions that might exist in which members of the People's church could receive treatment for their ailments and its young people "may be educated along God's appointed lines."

If the formal, legal terminology seems excessive, it underscored the serious intent behind the petition. It grew out of "urgent and immediate needs," stated the petitioners, requesting that the General Conference meet a deadline of March 15 in giving its response. Indefinite delays and vague assurances would not suffice.

While the entire document, in its assertiveness and formality, was unusual in Adventist practice, it was not until its next-to-last paragraph that it ventured into territory that denominational leaders would regard as truly foreign and dangerous. Should the prompt provision of specific information on institutions open to its members not be deemed "expedient," the People's church "suggested" that it "be granted the privilege of using its tithes and offerings for the purpose of creating such facilities as its work may demand from time to time."[9]

Since provision of a satisfactory answer on access to existing institutions seemed a practical impossibility, it was only with this concluding suggestion that the petition reached its central point. Yet it too amounted to a practical impossibility in the Adventist setting, for it cut at the heart of the denomination's centralized, connectional system of church governance. Church leaders could not entertain a proposal for local church authority over all its funds—the essence of congregationalism—especially in the midst of an epic struggle over loyalty to the newly restructured organizational plan.

Against the airtight logic of church policy, though, Lewis Sheafe and the People's church brought the compelling logic of basic fairness in the real world. Though racial segregation violated their ideals and dignity, they were willing to adapt to an arrangement that amounted to "separate but equal." But after two years of giving their tithes and offerings in sacrificial support of the denominational program, funding major and dramatically successful evangelistic campaigns, and shouldering the complete financial burden of the church building, fairness still seemed a long way off. Not only barred from White institutions, they saw little credible evidence on the horizon for comparable Black institutions materializing. The "separate" was there, but where was the "equal"? Viewed from that standpoint, control over their own funds and thus responsibility for their own institutions, in the context of fervent dedication to the Adventist message and mission, made eminent sense.

TWO TURBULENT MEETINGS

The two perspectives clashed in a series of stormy encounters in April, following the return of A. G. Daniells and General Conference vice president G. A. Irwin to Washington after a lengthy trip to the West Coast. Because of that trip, they did not even see the petition until nearly two weeks after the requested March 15 deadline for a reply. Then a two-week Spring Council began immediately after their return. Thus the leadership's written response did not appear until late May.

In the meantime Sheafe arranged with the other General Conference officers for the denominational leaders to meet with the People's church on Sunday, April 1, right after the president's return to Takoma Park on the evening of March 28. I. H. Evans, the General Conference treasurer; K. C. Russell, religious liberty leader and chair of the District Committee; and B. G. Wilkinson, temporarily assigned to the Memorial church, were among the leaders who joined Daniells and Irwin.

The meeting did not go well. The church members came with the expectation of a specific and substantive response to the points raised by their petition of February 26, and would be satisfied with nothing less. Daniells spent considerable time rehearsing all that the denomination was doing to reach the African race, both on the native continent and in the American South, as well as its rapidly expanding missionary work throughout the globe. He affirmed that Washington "should be made a center for the education and training of colored people for the work." Church schools, an intermediate school, and a training school for workers, including training for nurses, all should be established as soon as possible, he said. "But it will take time to develop all these interests," he tried to explain, especially in view of the "enormous burden" of the church's vast range of current commitments in Takoma Park.

General sentiments about what should happen, combined with admonition to wait rather than specific commitment—that was precisely what Sheafe's flock was tired of hearing. The whole point of their petition had been to get beyond such rhetoric, and they would not have more of it.

A "spirited discussion" ensued, Russell reported in the *Review*, but it went nowhere. The meeting was "a very unpleasant and unsatisfactory one indeed," Daniells told W. C. White, and in the end the only thing that could be done was to schedule another try on April 22, after the close of Spring Council.[10]

Sheafe kept a low profile at the meeting, and in an effort to draw him out more fully, Daniells summoned him to Takoma Park for an individual conference with himself and other General Conference officers. Sheafe, however, determined to maintain his reserve. "We did our very best to get his position, but failed," Daniells acknowledged.[11]

Perhaps Sheafe was "keeping his powder dry" for the April 22 meeting at the church. Daniells, Irwin, and Evans occupied the first two hours, reviewing the denomination's endeavors to reach both the White and Black populations in Washington and throughout the South, and reiterating that the cause would not advance among either race unless conducted along separate lines.[12]

Sheafe then took the podium, delivering a speech that "fairly set the congregation wild." He told the General Conference brethren that he knew they were considering removal of his ministerial credentials. But with a snap of his fingers he dismissed the threat, saying that his commission did not come from them and that they could not take it away. He declared that he could not accept seeing his people neglected while their tithes and offerings went to educate White people who already enjoyed so many advantages. He sought no special favors, he told them—just a fair deal.[13]

According to Charles Shaffer, the First church elder, "the fire burned" when Sheafe spoke, making the "G. C. folks" visibly uncomfortable. Daniells, said Shaffer, interrupted several times, to defend his course of action and point out Sheafe's shortcomings.[14]

Shaffer followed Sheafe with a speech setting forth the First church position that no racial distinctions should be made in church institutions, after which the people "broke loose" in expressing approval. The role of the White elder of the mixed race church in the controversy especially irritated Daniells. He regarded Shaffer's position as "unreasonable and extravagant." In their replies he and his colleagues made clear that the People's church could not expect General Conference support if they held to that position, but were unable to get them to repudiate it. Some of the people expressed derision toward Daniells, and "he began to quarrel with them from the desk" before finally sitting down, according to Shaffer. In his report to W. C. White, Daniells complained that while there were "a lot of nice people" in the People's and First churches, their tendency to be "rather difficult people to deal with" was made considerably worse "by the fanatical white people who are continually unsettling their minds, and creating dissatisfaction."[15]

Establishment of the People's church in 1903 had both brought Sheafe into a closer working relationship with Daniells and distanced him somewhat from First church. It had pleased Daniells that with the People's church, Sheafe's focus now was on a more specifically Black-oriented ministry. The church president had invested time and effort in cultivating his ties with the congregation and its pastor. But the April 22 meeting revealed that Sheafe was moving back into alignment with the radical idealists at First church, forming an opposition front against the General Conference.

So the second meeting with the People's church had, in Daniells' words, turned out "worse than the first one." In addition to the signs of an anti-General Conference confederacy between the People's and First churches, Sheafe's defiant rhetoric brought out into the open his willingness to withdraw from the denomination and take his church with him if their demands were not met.[16]

The question of authority and loyalty itself had now come to the forefront, along with the disputed racial issues. Daniells still hoped to salvage the situation: "I love these people, and am anxious to see them saved," he told W. C. White. But it would have to be on General Conference terms. The April 1906 confrontations reinforced his resolve that "we must hold this colored element with a stiff rein," and not allow them to "frighten us and press us to their terms."[17]

With the atmosphere only made more contentious by the April meetings, Daniells undertook a written response to the February 26 petition from the People's church, hoping to meet the twin goals of making clear the General Conference's firm position while restoring the loyalty of the Black believers in Washington to the greatest extent possible.

Daniells' lengthy statement expanded on the points formulated in Nashville in 1902. Seventh-day Adventists, he affirmed, "more especially" than any people, should not harbor "prejudice against any of our fellowmen because of nationality, race, or color." At the same time, all must be willing to set aside personal rights and privileges in order to advance the cause of making the Adventist message known to "anxious, suffering, lost humanity." In some settings, he pointed out, "this principle of self-sacrifice" makes necessary "separation of the races in school and church associations." Where this is so, "suitable provision should be made to instruct and encourage believers of all classes, and to strengthen and develop the work and workers among them." Application of that principle, he specified, meant that "our colored young people" in the District of Columbia should have opportunity for training "broad and varied enough to prepare them for the ministry, Bible work, canvassing, school teaching, and nursing." Furthermore, he recognized that the resources for providing such education would have to come "very largely" from the denomination as a whole, not just the Washington believers themselves.

Unresolved dilemmas remained, however, at the next level of specificity. Having acknowledged the legitimacy and importance of the concerns expressed in the People's church petition about the lack of educational and health facilities, Daniells' statement offered no specific commitments as to funding, an action plan, or timetable for developing the "colored" institutions envisioned for Washington. He could only express the General Conference Committee's desire to assist, and indicate that while they were doing their best, they were simply unable to provide all the help for separate ethnic work—he included in this the German and Scandinavian as well as the Colored—as promptly as it was needed.

Regarding admission to institutions already existing or being built, Daniells' reply took an evasive route, probably in order to avoid putting an official "color line" policy on record. The question of admittance, he pointed out, would have to be decided by the boards of the institutions, which were not directly under General Conference management. It is difficult to imagine this casuistic distinction impressing many people, for Daniells himself was "president" of the Washington Training College Board of Trustees, and most of the other trustees were General Conference officials. G. A. Irwin, vice president of the General Conference, headed the Washington Sanitarium board, on which General Conference men, including Daniells, also held a majority.[18]

Daniells recommended that the People's church appoint a committee to confer with the boards of these institutions with regard to Black youth in the District of Columbia who might wish to enroll in these institutions. The statement's very next sentence, however, seemed to undercut the value of such conferrals by anticipating their outcome: "After careful consideration, should it be deemed unwise, on account of existing circumstances," for them to enter the Takoma Park institutions, Daniells identified Adventist institutions to the north and west that would be open to them, the closest being South Lancaster Academy in Massachusetts.

In conclusion Daniells again suggested the People's church appoint a committee, this one "to confer with the District Committee and General Conference officers regarding the question of educating the colored young people of the District of Columbia for missionary work."[19]

TURBULENCE AT HOME AND AN UNEASY STANDSTILL

By the time Daniells presented the statement in another meeting at People's church on May 29, Sheafe had pulled back from the brink of confrontation. His course may have been influenced by a serious incident with Annie earlier in the month that jeopardized his standing with his congregation. Emotional distance between the couple had been increasing since their move to Washington. On that evening in early May 1906 the tension erupted in a fierce quarrel. Feelings became so enflamed that Sheafe threatened his wife with violence. This he acknowledged, though those who heard both sides of the story were uncertain as to whether he physically struck Annie.

At any rate, the incident was so frightening to Annie that she reported it to Elders Russell and Evans. Daniells was attending a meeting of the Lake Union Conference (May 8-18) at the time, but after he returned, he and the couple talked the matter through for five hours in his office on May 23.

Word also spread quickly to the members of the People's church. The pastor issued a public apology, which the church board accepted. Unfortunately, the process not only failed to reconcile Annie to her husband—it alienated her from the congregation. She began attending services at First church.[20]

Though restored to good standing with his church, Sheafe's base of support for a risky challenge to the General Conference may have been weakened temporarily. Whether or not that was a factor, A. G. Daniells found a much less hostile atmosphere at People's church on May 29 when he presented to a full house the reply to the church's petition that he drafted on behalf of the General Conference.

The people gave "very calm, respectful attention" to his presentation. Daniells gave opportunity for questions afterward, but Sheafe quickly intervened, stating that the church board would give the written document careful attention, and thus a discussion that evening would be of no particular value. Though it was not necessarily a sign of positive reception, Daniells welcomed the pastor's directive, perhaps relieved that the meeting would end without the unpleasantness that had marked the proceedings on April 1 and 22. Several members greeted him in a "very warm, brotherly fashion" after the meeting closed.[21]

An uneasy calm held over the next few months. Sheafe carried forward with his fifth consecutive summer series of evangelistic tent meetings in the city, with an average attendance of about 300 on weeknights and considerably more on Sunday evenings. At the quarterly meeting of the Evangelical Committee for the District of Columbia on July 15, he reported on the success of some innovations. Since Monday tended to be a "dull evening," he had decided to devote it to health and temperance topics, and that worked well in holding his congregation. Also, prior to the preaching service each evening, his associate and tentmaster, W. S. Connolly, led an "inquiry meeting," or question-and-answer session, and the people took an active interest, making it a very strong feature of the meetings.[22]

Daniells believed he had successfully placed the ball in Sheafe's court with his suggestion about the formation of a committee at the conclusion of his reply to the People's church petition. The church now had an opportunity to show cooperation by proceeding along the lines he suggested. If they refused to do so, he reasoned, "the onus of independence and rebellion (if it comes to that) will rest on them."[23] Also, Sheafe's public display of an independent attitude at the April 22 meeting, along with reports from Annie that her husband was laying plans to withdraw from the conference,[24] hardened opposition on the General Conference Committee to making a major appropriation for the church building debt or educational development without convincing demonstration of a changed disposition and renewed loyalty.

Thus, from the General Conference standpoint, nothing was going to happen without an initiative from the People's church giving definite indication of loyalty to church organization. From the standpoint of the People's church, though, the status quo meant that their grievances remained unaddressed in a meaningful way.

---

[1] J. K. Humphrey, "The Evening Sermon," GCB, May 25, 1922, pp. 253, 254; R. Clifford Jones, *James K. Humphrey and the Sabbath-Day Adventists* (Jackson: University Press of Mississippi, 2006), pp. 3, 9.

[2] G. Land, ed. *Adventism in America*, pp. 133-136, 155, 156.

[3] *Ibid.*, pp. 153, 154; George R. Knight, *Organizing to Beat the Devil* (Hagerstown, Md.: Review and Herald, 2001), pp. 109-125.

[4] Knight, *Organizing to Beat the Devil*, p. 110.

[5] George R. Knight, *From 1888 to Apostasy* (Hagerstown, Md.: Review and Herald, 1987), pp. 75-88, 159-177.

[6] C. W. Edwards and G. Land, *Seeker After Light,* pp. 10-31, 131-146.

[7] AGD to SS, Feb. 4, 1907, GCA.

[8] ATJ to unidentified, July 3, 1907, GCA.

[9] GCC minutes, May 28, 1906.

[10] K. C. Russell, "The Work Among the Colored People," *Review,* Apr. 12, 1906, p. 18, 19; AGD to WCW, May 25, 1906, EGWE.

[11] AGD to WCW, May 25, 1906, EGWE.

[12] AGD to WCW, May 25, 1906; Charles T. Shaffer to an unidentified recipient in Battle Creek, Apr. 22, 1906, J. H. Kellogg Papers (C. MacIvor Collection), CAR.

[13] AGD to WCW, May 25, 1906; Shaffer letter, Apr. 22, 1906.

[14] Shaffer letter, Apr. 22, 1906.

[15] Shaffer letter, Apr. 22, 1906; AGD to WCW, May 25, 1906.

[16] AGD to WCW, May 25, 1906.

[17] AGD to WCW, May 25, 1906; AGD to WCW, May 30, 1906, EGWE.

[18] YB 1906, pp. 97, 119.

[19] Letter to the People's Seventh-day Adventist Church, May 28, 1906, included in GCC minutes.

[20] Daniells relates the incident and events surrounding it in two letters to W. C. White, May 25, 1906, and Jan. 18, 1907, EGWE.

[21] AGD to WCW, May 30, 1906.

[22] K. C. Russell, "An Interesting Meeting," *Review,* Aug. 2, 1906, p. 19.

[23] AGD to WCW, May 30, 1906.

[24] AGD to WCW, Jan. 18, 1907.

CHAPTER XXVI

THE PEOPLE'S CHURCH
DECLARES INDEPENDENCE

THE STANDSTILL LINGERED UNTIL NOVEMBER, when Sheafe made a 10-day visit to Battle Creek, which within three years had gone from being the General Conference headquarters to being the headquarters of the anti-General Conference camp forming at the Battle Creek Sanitarium around John Harvey Kellogg and Alonzo T. Jones.

Adventism's health message had figured prominently in attracting Sheafe to the movement and his conviction about the comprehensive redemption it offered his people. In Battle Creek he had found help for his recurring health problems and took a brief course in application of basic remedies along with learning about the Adventist message as a whole. Thus, the denomination's failure to act promptly to help make it possible for his people to experience this central feature of Adventist life and mission just as White people did was a very serious matter to him. With their pastor's emphasis on health reform, it is no surprise that young people in the People's church desired training along medical missionary lines. Also, the winter of 1904-1905 had struck hard, causing widespread illness in the congregation, underscoring the people's experiential need both for treatment and education in healthful living.[1]

AN ANTI-GENERAL CONFERENCE AXIS

Unsatisfied with the General Conference response to the People's church petition, Sheafe wrote Dr. Kellogg about the possibility of his young people being accepted for training in Battle Creek and received a favorable reply.[2] This fateful turn to Battle Creek now set Sheafe on a collision course with testimonies from Ellen White, not just with the denominational leadership.

Since 1903 Ellen White had been sending forth warnings about the dangerous spiritual and intellectual atmosphere at the Battle Creek Sanitarium, rebuilt, against her counsel, on a grand scale after the fire of 1901. She also disapproved of the new Battle Creek College that opened in the fall of 1903; the original institution had moved to Berrien Springs in 1901 under the leadership of educational reformers Edward A. Sutherland and Percy T. Magan. A. T. Jones's decision to accept the presidency of the new institution went against forceful admonitions from Ellen White, and marked a decisive shift away from his formerly close relationship with her.[3]

Thus, Ellen White, in testimonies brought together in pamphlet form as Series B, No. 6 and No. 7, warned that Dr. Kellogg's campaign to undermine the General Conference leadership and the deceptive "science of human sophistry" he promoted made Battle Creek an unsafe place to send Adventist young people for education. Bearing a cautionary tone in 1903, by November of 1905 her messages became urgent, all-out warnings: "God does not accept Dr. Kellogg as His laborer, unless he will now break with Satan. . . . 'Come,' I call, 'come ye out and be separate from him and his associates whom he has leavened.'"[4]

Sheafe later claimed that he had not read these testimonies, but he must at least have heard them quoted in the warnings about Kellogg, Jones, and Battle Creek that repeatedly cropped up in talks given by General Conference leaders. Indeed, it was these warnings and the questions they raised among his people that prompted Sheafe to make the trip to Battle Creek in November 1906 and conduct his own investigation.

He preached and sang several times while there, receiving the typical warmly favorable responses. On Sabbath, November 10, he spoke for a Sabbath morning worship service at the sanitarium chapel, with unintended consequences for a power struggle at the denomination's former flagship church, the Battle Creek Tabernacle. Key leaders of the tabernacle's "pro-sanitarium" faction went to hear Sheafe that Sabbath. To the General Conference loyalists in the majority at the tabernacle and their new pastor, M. N. Campbell, this seemed like a good time to elect the nominating committee that would in turn recommend church officers for the coming year. A church business meeting was convened immediately after the worship hour, which elected a committee safely dominated by members loyal to denominational leadership. After getting word of this favorable turn of events, Daniells commented, "Now if the Lord will favor us in this way when election time comes, we shall get through very well, I think, for another year."[5]

Somewhat ironically, Sheafe was invited to speak for the young people's meeting at the tabernacle later that same afternoon. A large congregation turned out to hear him. He did not address the controversy, but instead gave a message of practical spirituality based on the text "There went with [Saul] a band of men, whose hearts God had touched" (1 Sam. 10:26).[6]

The sanitarium periodical, the *Medical Missionary*, reported only briefly on Sheafe's visit, but in its few words touched on critical aspects of Sheafe's work in Washington and the conflict over it. By adding to its commendation of his "good work in the national capital for the colored race" the observation that "his audiences are composed of both races," the report both nicely captured the complexity of the racial dimensions of his ministry and affirmed the inclusive aspect that disrupted the General Conference plan of work.[7]

Kellogg and Jones warmly welcomed the preacher and his investigation, empathizing with his reports of unfair treatment from the General Conference and encouraging his resistant stand. On the street one day Dr. Kellogg told the aging Adventist pioneer George W. Amadon of the "wicked and oppressive" way in which the General Conference was treating Sheafe and his people in Washington, "making a color line where it is needless." By way of tangible support, Kellogg sent a donation of $100 from the sanitarium for the work of the People's church in Washington.[8]

For his part, Sheafe, in a letter from Battle Creek reporting his findings to the People's church, gave a glowing appraisal of Kellogg and the sanitarium. He endorsed Kellogg's perspective on the controversy with the denomination, attributing the difficulty to a campaign of persecution from the General Conference officers.[9]

A copy made its way into the hands of A. G. Daniells, and in that context of all-out ecclesiastical warfare, nothing could have more thoroughly provoked the ire of the General Conference president. Upon his return to Washington, Sheafe was summoned to Daniells' office in Takoma Park on December 4 for an "interview" about the letter, in which he was asked to read it out loud. When Daniells asked him to explain his letter in the light of Ellen White's pointed testimonies about the dangers at Battle Creek and who was responsible for them, Sheafe protested that he had never read these messages. Daniells then gave him a copy of Series B, Nos. 6 and 7, along with some related documents, and urged him to study them carefully.[10]

Sheafe, however, had chosen his course and was not inclined to rethink it at this point. The following week he sent Daniells a succinct note, stating that the many demands on his attention since his return from Michigan left him no time for the material the president had given him to read. He added that such a reading "would necessarily demand the same for the other side." Then, as if to make sure that he left no implication of promise to study the material as soon as the hectic period died down, he concluded, "I have nothing more to say than what has been said, therefore do not see the need of my coming to the Park again on this matter."[11]

If Sheafe was unwilling to present the warnings of the Spirit of Prophecy to his congregation, Daniells was determined to do it himself, and to present the rationale for General Conference actions—information Sheafe had not included in his report to the church on the Battle Creek situation. Daniells requested to speak to the People's church on Sunday, December 16, and asked K. C. Russell, as chair of the District Committee, to finalize the arrangements with the People's church. Sheafe agreed, but imposed a condition unacceptable to Daniells—that someone "present the Battle Creek side of the question." Lacking this, he refused to announce the meeting to the People's church. To Daniells, this was tantamount to denying him opportunity to speak to the congregation.[12]

ABOVE THE PASTOR, ONLY CHRIST

By this time Sheafe had thoroughly flaunted the authority of church leadership in several ways. In April he had, with a snap of his fingers, dramatically signaled his lack of regard for denominational credentials. In October the steadily declining tithe receipts from the People's church had come to a complete stop.[13] In November he had openly sided with the opponents of the General Conference in the most severe struggle for church unity in the denomination's history. In December he had refused to find time to read Ellen White's testimonies on the matter, and hindered the scheduling of a meeting with his congregation requested by the General Conference president.

Yet when Daniells, in a meeting right after the beginning of the new year, pointed to a pattern of action that seemed clearly to indicate an intention to lead the People's church away from denominational organization and place it under his own control, Sheafe forcefully denied any such intent.[14] And when it was pointed out to him by other members of the District Committee that in the Adventist system no pastor had authority to deny conference officers opportunity to meet with his congregation, Sheafe finally acknowledged his mistake. He agreed that Daniells and the General Conference officers were free to announce and hold a meeting with his church at any time.[15]

Despite this concession, Sheafe had in fact already done just about everything but formally announce his church's independence from denominational control, and Daniells was now thoroughly convinced of his settled determination to take the final step. In addition to the pastor's own actions, Daniells received through Annie information that Kellogg was continuing to urge the pastor to stay his course toward independence. Sometime after Lewis returned from Battle Creek, a telegram arrived at the Sheafe home, which Annie assumed was from their son Howard, who was attending Tuskegee Institute in Alabama. When she opened it, she discovered it was from Dr. Kellogg, who encouraged Sheafe to stand firm, for he was in the right. She passed it on to Daniells.[16]

So long as Sheafe professed loyalty, though, Daniells had been hesitant to take further corrective action. He did not want the General Conference to be perceived as the aggressor, driving the People's church out of denominational fellowship. But he also recognized the force of the argument made by some, such as George I. Butler, that the longer the General Conference paid Sheafe to build up a congregation that would eventually turn independent, the more damaging it would be.

"My dear Arthur, I think you will have to do some amputating right in Washington," advised Butler. More specifically, "I think you will have to cut Sheafe adrift." In attacking "organization," Butler maintained, the Battle Creek faction was attacking a "cardinal doctrine," and Sheafe was "right with them," advocating their position to Black believers all around the nation. "I have not been able to see for a long time the consistency of supporting a man to fight us or create his conduit among our people," he added.[17]

Daniells, though, had held off, not wishing to give the People's church, whose members, he thought, were "so excitable and fanatical" any "opportunity to cry persecution." Then, in mid-January 1907, just as the

General Conference officers had concluded they could wait no longer and were on the verge of initiating the kind of action Butler recommended, Daniells received a letter that, just as he had hoped, made Sheafe and the People's church the initiators of the severed relationship.[18]

"The People's SDA Church, assembled Wednesday evening, Jan. 9, 1907, to study conditions pertaining to its welfare, and to transact [business].

"A very important matter which came before us for consideration was that pertaining to the rights and privileges of the individual church of Christ.

"We learn from scriptures that it is the right and privilege of the individual church to take part directly in all lines of missionary work, at home and abroad; to ordain persons for special work, at home or abroad; to exercise self-government, under the guidance of its exalted head, the Lord Jesus Christ; to collect and expend its means, such as tithes and offerings, furnished by its members; being subject to no foreign tribunal or court of review, the only recognized head of this church, above the pastor, is the Lord Jesus Christ.

"This church by [unanimous] voice decided to at once enjoy these and other scriptural rights and privileges,

"We therefore very respectfully notify you of our action,

"Done by order of the church.

"(signed) Lewis C. Sheafe, Pastor.

"(signed) Elmira B. Greene, Clerk"[19]

THE CONGREGATIONAL SOVEREIGNTY PRINCIPLE

The congregationalism asserted in the People's church "declaration of independence" was the principle of church governance that Sheafe had known as a Baptist minister. Though in the present crisis church organization had assumed special prominence as a touchstone of loyalty, even, in Butler's words, a "cardinal doctrine," it probably never held particular significance in Sheafe's mind among the biblical truths of Adventism that corrected or advanced beyond the teachings and practices of his previous denominational affiliation.

Also, his formative years in Adventist ministry (1896-1901) came at a time of considerable flux in the church's organizational structures. Dr. Kellogg and Almira Steele had attempted to have his ministry come under their auspices, rather than the denominational conference system, albeit with only marginal success. Most significant of all, on more than one occasion during those years he had reason to feel that he was being left to his own devices, whether resulting from administrative neglect or design.

So, in taking this drastic and momentous step, Sheafe was not merely being swept along by influential antagonists of the General Conference. A pattern of inequality building over several years drove his action. Yet align with them he did. Thus Daniells and other denominational loyalists interpreted his actions first and foremost in the light of that all-or-nothing conflict with the Battle Creek rebellion. Some gave a degree of weight to the issues of racial injustice that led to his loss of hope in the current denominational governance. But at best such concerns had to be submerged far into the background when it came to a choice between the organizational authority of God's last-day church and the foes who would rend it asunder.

The action of the People's church, Daniells believed, came as part of a conspiracy orchestrated in Battle Creek to destroy the denomination, and that frame of reference dominated his thinking about it. A tract by an otherwise obscure Philadelphia dentist, W. L. Winner, entitled "Gospel Simplicity: the Need of the Hour" had appeared in late 1906, setting forth in a clear and relatively succinct way the position A. T. Jones had taken on the supreme authority of the local congregation. The publisher of the tract was not clearly identified, but Daniells had received word that the Battle Creek Sanitarium was promoting its circulation. The Winner tract and the People's church withdrawal, Daniells believed, represented a new phase in the sanitarium faction's fight against church organization. Having failed to break up the denominational body with one heavy blow, they were now trying to do it piecemeal—stirring dissent and encouraging individual congregations to defect one at a time.[20]

Regarding Sheafe as pretty much a lost cause, Daniells now planned to win the loyalty of as many individual members of the People's church as possible. He began sending out inquiries about other Black ministers who might be brought to Washington to counter Sheafe's influence and form a loyal Black congregation. He asked C. H. Edwards, president of the Greater New York Conference, about the promising young Jamaican James K. Humphrey, and G. I. Butler about possibilities from the Southern Union, such as Sydney Scott.[21]

Meanwhile, matters with Sheafe and the People's church would also have to be brought to final resolution. Daniells wanted to reply in person to the notice sent him by the church on January 15, hoping to make clear the tragic consequences he saw in the decision, and stir the hearts of at least some to draw back from it. A meeting was scheduled for Wednesday evening, January 30, but when a matter arose that called Daniells out of town, it was postponed until February 13.

------

[1] LCS to AGD, Feb. 2, 1905, GCA.

[2] ATJ to unidentified, July 3, 1907.

[3] G. R. Knight, *From 1888 to Apostasy*, pp. 208-211.

[4] Ellen G. White, *Testimonies for the Church Containing Messages of Warning and Instruction to Seventh-day Adventists*, Series B, No. 7, 1906.

[5] George W. Amadon to AGD, Nov 10, 1906, EGWE; AGD to WCW, Nov. 22, 1906, EGWE.

[6] Amadon to AGD, Nov. 10, 1906.

[7] Untitled news note, *Medical Missionary*, Nov. 28, 1906, p. 192.

[8] George W. Amadon to AGD, Nov. 26, 1906, EGWE (copy from original in General Conference Secretariat vault); ATJ to unidentified, July 3, 1907.

[9] Sheafe's letter, apparently, is lost. We have only Daniells' summary in AGD to WCW, Jan. 18, 1907.

[10] AGD to People's Seventh-day Adventist Church Board, Jan. 18, 1907, GCA; AGD to WCW, Jan. 18, 1907.

[11] LCS to AGD, Dec. 10, 1906, GCA.

[12] LCS to AGD, Dec. 14, 1906, GCA; AGD to LCS, Dec. 14, 1906, GCA; AGD to People's Church Board, Jan. 18, 1907. Daniells' January 18 letter to the People's church board came in reply to a letter of December 24, 1906, signed by the church clerk, Elmira B. Greene, on behalf of the board, stating that Sheafe had presented them with Daniells' request "to present the Battle Creek controversy" to the church, but that board voted unanimously to deny the request since most of the "elders" assigned to preach for them while their pastor was away had already spoken about the matter. It is uncertain when Daniells first saw the December 24 letter, but his response came on the very day that he received the People's church letter of January 15, 1907, announcing even more drastic action.

[13] Daniells' letter of January 18, 1907, to W. C. White indicates that until that date he had only heard that Sheafe was laying plans to have his church control its tithes and offerings, not that remittances to the conference had already ceased. However, in a letter to Sydney Scott of February 8, 1907, Daniells states that no tithe had been received from the People's church since October 1906.

[14] AGD to WCW, Jan. 18, 1907.

[15] AGD to People's Church Board, Jan. 18, 1907.

[16] AGD to WCW, Jan. 18, 1907.

[17] GIB to AGD, Jan. 11, 1907, GCA.

[18] AGD to WCW, Jan. 18, 1907.

[19] People's S.D.A. Church to AGD, Jan. 15, 1907.

[20] AGD to HWC, Jan. 20, 1907, GCA.

[21] AGD to C. H. Edwards, Jan. 26, 1907, GCA. This letter to Edwards also mentions his communication with Butler about Scott.

CHAPTER XXVII

"STOP RIGHT WHERE YOU ARE"

A S THE APPOINTED EVENING NEARED for A. G. Daniells to address the People's church, a letter from Ellen G. White in Sanitarium, California, dated February 4 and addressed to Elder L. C. Sheafe, arrived at 2021 Eighth Street Northwest.[1]

"I am writing to you in the early morning. In the night season I have had representations of your case, and have been conversing with some of the brethren in Washington, D.C., in regard to the work to be done in that city.

"Elder Sheafe, Satan has been at work upon your mind, and for a long time you have been entertaining his suggestions. . . .

"The Lord has given you tact and skill in knowledge to proclaim the last message of mercy to our world, that you might become a great blessing in Washington, D.C., but you have entered into temptation. . . . And the enemy is working through you to spoil the flock of God. The Lord bids me say to you, Stop right where you are."

In one sense, though not the one Ellen White meant, Sheafe was right where all the leaders of the movement had been at one time or another. Not just Kellogg and Jones, but Daniells, Prescott, Irwin, Butler—all of them had been on the receiving end of messages of stern rebuke and sharp warning, messages that stopped them short and cut through their self-justifications. Now it was Lewis Sheafe's turn. Receipt of such a testimony, even in its exposure of satanic influence, did not place him outside the pale of the Adventist family or in some category of especially shameful and defective persons any more than it did the others. Instead it showed that even if A. G. Daniells had all but given up on Sheafe, Ellen White had not. Despite his recent assertion of freedom from General Conference authority, the message treated him as a gifted but erring brother, a leader who had accomplished great things for God and would do even more if he would yield and accept a course correction.

Though the testimony contains some general warnings about doctrines that were leading people in the wrong direction, Ellen White made no pronouncements on the specific issues in the dispute between the People's church and the General Conference. Nor did she criticize Sheafe's involvement with civil rights organizations. He had "lost [his] bearings concerning many things," she said, and this placed in jeopardy the work so effectively begun in Washington. But when it came to specifics, her focus was on the strife in the Sheafe home, the dangers of his dalliance with Battle Creek, and the underlying "spiritual pride" he had allowed into his heart.

The lengthy letter weaves back and forth through these themes, but the preacher's course of action in his home and the injury it caused himself and the cause of God was the first "for instance" that Sister White cited. Both Lewis and Annie needed to be converted anew, she said. Otherwise, "you will, in the madness of your deceived souls, take some rash and dreadful step." The naming of the evil was not to stigmatize or vilify, but to open the way for spiritual counsel to a struggling couple from the depths of the prophet's maternal heart.

"The Father calls you to live the life of Christ, to put away the passionate temper, and henceforth to walk in meekness and lowliness of mind. He desires that you and Sister Sheafe shall become a son and daughter in the heavenly family.

"Your heavenly Father, the God of heaven and earth, gave everything into the hands of Christ for those who will give up their hereditary and cultivated tendencies to evil, and become the children of light. He did all this to make you and your wife patient and kind to one another. Will you not be convinced of your wrong, and be renewed in the spirit of your mind? . . .

"When men or women are under the temptations of Satan, let them look constantly to Jesus for aid, and not utter words of passion that dishonor Christ. If the husband speaks unkindly, let the wife not speak a word in response, for at such times silence is eloquence. This is the best way to meet the words that are prompted by the tempter. Let husband and wife treat each other kindly under all circumstances, then the children will learn from them lessons of forbearance. Never, never give your children an education in faultfinding. Set them an example that will help them to prepare for the future immortal life."

With regard to his public course of action, it was in turning to Battle Creek, not in his work in Washington, that Sheafe triggered spiritual alarms from Ellen White. Even his reasons for establishing the Battle Creek ties are neither censured nor praised. Her concern is quite simply that he has turned to the wrong place for help:

"I do not want you to destroy yourself. Battle Creek is not the place where you will get light. The work being done there does not bear the signature of the Divine. Another spirit has come in and taken possession of human minds."

Ellen White does not simplistically pin a "Battle Creek theology" label on Sheafe or imply that he is an impressionable minion of Kellogg or Jones. Yet she perceives that some of Sheafe's views "bear the same mark of spiritual disease that has led to the disaffection at Battle Creek." Thus, she sees him as vulnerable to greater deception if he does not stop and change course:

"The warning is given us in the Word, 'Some shall depart from the faith, giving heed to seducing spirits, and doctrines of devils.' Brother Sheafe, is not this warning fulfilled in what we see in Battle Creek? . . .

"Let no man unsettle your faith. The Lord is greatly dishonored by those in Battle Creek who are turning away from the truth. I am sorry for them, and sorry that you are becoming confused by the doctrines that are being presented to lead souls from the true faith. May the Lord help you not to spoil your record. In the name of the Lord I say to you, Humble your heart before God, and practice the life of Christ, else you will lose your soul."

Her central purpose in writing, of course, was precisely that Sheafe not "lose his soul." Thus, Ellen White concluded her testimony by uplifting the possibility of a future bright with renewed promise, if Sheafe would turn in the right direction for help.

"My brother, look unto Jesus. You need not look to any human agency for the supply of grace that you can find in its perfection in Christ. . . .

"Through His sacrifice, Christ has made provision for you that you may become sweet in disposition, meek and lowly of heart. . . . Do not, I beg of you, turn aside to strange doctrines.

"In the visions of the night I am charged by the Lord to warn you against this. I want you to be a happy man in this life, a representation of what a minister of Christ should be. Work diligently to make your calling and election sure. Bring peace into your heart, even the peace of Christ. . . . The Lord Jesus is to be your Pattern. No man is to please himself. I want you to know what the grace of Christ can do for you. I want you to speak sound words, with true, eloquent utterance. Serve the Lord Jesus Christ with the whole heart. . . . You need to be converted every day in order to be a vessel unto honor, one who can teach others. Do not make a mistake. Your soul is precious, and Christ will save you if you will be saved by purifying your soul through obedience to the truth."

While it is possible that the exhortation "Stop right where you are" may have given him pause about moving further away from the main body of Adventism than he already had, the testimony clearly did not prompt a fundamental change in Sheafe's direction. Questions about *process* troubled him—questions that he may have been predisposed to raise by things Kellogg and Jones had been saying. Just how and from where did Sister White receive the information upon which her testimony was based?

"In the night season I have had representations of your case, and have been conversing with some of the brethren in Washington, D.C." Was this not an acknowledgment that the information she had about him came in part through communication with "the brethren in Washington"? Elements of the content indeed seemed to reflect Daniells' point of view. Should not Sheafe's side of the story have been heard? He would raise these questions later, when Daniells queried him about his response to the testimony. However, the testimony was not an issue at the February 13 meeting, for though Sheafe had likely received it by then, a copy had not yet been sent to Daniells.[2]

WELL-MARSHALED RESISTANCE

"The church acted like a well-trained company of soldiers," Sheafe ex-
ulted after the meeting held with A. G. Daniells at the People's church on
Wednesday evening, February 13.[3] He anticipated that Daniells would
summon to the fullest his rhetorical powers and whatever spiritual authority his office and the testimonies of Ellen White still held in the hearts
of the people, in a final effort to turn their loyalty back to the denomination. So Sheafe developed a strategy for keeping firm control over the proceedings, and carefully prepared his congregation.

Daniells indeed viewed the February 13 meeting as something far
more than a final processing of a breakaway church's severance from the
denomination. Despite the sharp opposition he had encountered at the
meetings held the previous spring, he had received some positive individual feedback from well-spoken members who seemed to carry influence. He felt confident that he could win over a significant portion of the
congregation with a clear and forceful presentation of the weighty issues
at stake. His spirits gained a further boost on Monday, February 11, when
correspondence from W. C. White arrived enclosing a copy of a testimony
entitled "Individual Responsibility and Christian Unity" that Ellen White
had presented at a meeting of the California Conference in January. It contained fresh and compelling material perfectly suited for the situation he
was to meet on Wednesday evening.[4]

Accompanied by several other General Conference officers, and with a
large contingent from Takoma Park and the Memorial church in the audience, Daniells arrived ready to take charge of the meeting scheduled to
begin at 7:30. However, Sheafe announced that the usual prayer meeting
would be conducted first, after which Elder Daniells would be given time
to make his statement. Though taken by surprise, Daniells could hardy object, and he, W. A. Spicer, and K. C. Russell all participated in the service.

Sheafe ended the service promptly at 8:30, and then sprang another
surprise on the visitors. Elder Daniells had a statement to make, he said,
but it was an item of business for members of the People's church only.
He encouraged all members to remain after the prayer meeting was dismissed, but requested all visitors to leave promptly.

For a few moments following the benediction, no one moved, seemingly stunned by this unexpected turn of events. Russell had been pro-

moting attendance among area Adventists (except at First church, presumably!) for days, and now they were being dismissed from the showdown they had come to witness. After a couple of moments a few of the visitors departed, but most remained. Deacons began moving through the congregation inviting nonmembers to be dismissed. This prompted a few more to leave.

Sheafe then repeated in a direct but calm manner that the presentation by Elder Daniells was for members only. The visitors still present, he said, were only delaying the proceedings, for Elder Daniells could not begin speaking until they left. Daniells protested from the podium that everything he had to say would be appropriate for all to hear and that he had no objections to nonmembers being present. He tried to argue the point for a few minutes, but Sheafe refused to budge from the announced decision or even debate the point.

After the singing of a hymn, Sheafe pulled out his pocket watch, which showed that it was seven minutes before 9:00. To the visitors who remained firmly planted in their seats, he declared that if they were not gone by 9:00 he would dismiss the meeting entirely, without Elder Daniells being able to deliver his remarks. At this, many left, but some still remained. One member of the People's church suggested that the meeting be rescheduled so that it could then proceed with better understanding all around. But Sheafe insisted that Daniells would either speak that evening to members only or not at all. This "cleared the house," but the final holdouts did not go quietly. According to Sheafe, "it was like the demon going out of the boy," and, in particular, "the women acted shamefully."

Satisfied that with the exception of the "conference brethren" only members remained, Sheafe placed further strictures on the proceedings. He read the communication sent to Daniells by the People's church on January 15, and stated that the present meeting had been arranged because Elder Daniells wished to give his reply in person.

In regard to the action taken by the church in January, he stated, "We believe it was right when it was taken; we believe it is right since we took it; and we will believe it is right after we are dismissed." Their only purpose in this meeting, he made explicit, was to listen respectfully to what Daniells had to say.

"We are not here to answer back. I want every member to keep his seat. When Elder Daniells is through, we are ready to dismiss the meeting. We do not propose to have any discussion at all from anybody. Elder Daniells has the time to speak, and we want to not interrupt him in any way by asking questions or answering questions, or making statements."

Disheartened by the way the evening was unfolding and feeling that now, because of the lateness of the hour, he would have to condense his lengthy prepared statement, Daniells floundered slightly at first. He quickly warmed to the task, though, and ended up speaking for more than an hour, setting forth two central reasons the church was making a "fatal mistake" in withdrawing from the conference.

First, he declared, their action was "entirely contrary to the instruction that has come to this people through the Spirit of prophecy these forty years." He read several quotations from the "testimonies" affirming that the denomination's system of organization must "stand, strengthened, and established, and settled."[5] In no uncertain terms he declared, "Every true Seventh-day Adventist believes that God is speaking to his people, to this remnant people, in prophecy by the Spirit of prophecy, through one that he has chosen and placed in the church." Since their action was out of harmony with the instruction of the Spirit of Prophecy, he asked, appealing with all the fervor he could muster, "How can it be right, brethren and sisters, how is it possible?"

Second, he argued that in the entire history of the movement, no church that separated from the organizational structure had long sustained Seventh-day Adventist beliefs or identity. Many churches through the decades had indeed taken a step similar to theirs, he told the People's church. But today, he said, not a single one of the churches that had withdrawn from the conference organization "holds together as a Seventh-day Adventist church . . . not one."

Yet, despite his reasoning, despite his passion, despite his effort to be pleasant and winsome, despite trying every means he could think of to establish favorable rapport with his audience, Daniells, by his own admission, failed, except with three or four individuals. Immediately after Sheafe gave his opening instructions, Daniells later complained, "The whole congregation immediately assumed an insolent, defiant attitude."[6]

Sheafe put it this way: "Everybody was as still as the grave; he tried to arouse them, but failed every time."

When Daniells completed his remarks, Sheafe asked the congregation to disperse quickly and quietly after the dismissal. Noting that someone had predicted that "there would be five or six of us on the floor at once tonight talking," the pastor then quipped, "I do not think that report can truthfully go out." After giving brief reminders about upcoming meetings and the singing of "Blest Be the Tie That Binds," Sheafe pronounced the benediction.

"You never saw men more badly beaten in all your life," gloated Sheafe about his triumph over the General Conference brethren.

"I have never seen one of our ministers pursue such a high-handed, autocratic course as Elder Sheafe took last night," Daniells fumed to W. C. White. He kept his people under "complete command" with an influence that seemed "almost hypnotic in character." Even in the confrontational meetings of recent years held in Battle Creek, he said, "I have never witnessed the insolent and insulting behavior shown by the church in the meeting that evening."[7]

As he promised to do at the meeting, Daniells sent Sheafe a copy of all the quotations from the writings of the Spirit of Prophecy that he had read. In an accompanying note he declared, "This cause can move on without you or the church of which you are pastor, but you and those poor people cannot get on without this cause." He acknowledged that Sheafe saw things differently and commented that time would have to demonstrate which of them was right.[8]

Sheafe replied, "My Brother, your believing I am wrong does not make me wrong, nor my believing that I am right does not make me right, but by the Word of God, the Bible, we stand or fall, Acts 5:39."[9]

EXPRESSIONS OF OUTRAGE, COUNSELS OF PATIENCE

The February 13 meeting ratified the independence declared by the People's church on January 15. "We shall revoke Sheafe's credentials, and withdraw his support," declared Daniells the next day. No alternative remained. The General Conference would bring in another Black minister to hold meetings—probably in True Reformers' Hall, in an effort to recoup some of the damage and make a fresh start. They would probably print up something on the issues to distribute among the members of the People's church, and perhaps visit them in their homes. But the church as a whole, the building, and the pastor were now lost to the denomination.[10]

It was a painful outcome for Daniells. As a church administrator, a decision he had made and stuck with contrary to the advice of some of his brethren had ended in costly failure. He also felt a sense of personal betrayal. Even after Sheafe's return in December from his provocative visit to Battle Creek, Daniells "very earnestly" urged a resistant General Conference Committee to appropriate $2,000 for the People's church building, contending that taking "a very liberal attitude" might win Sheafe's renewed loyalty.[11] "I trusted Sheafe, and stood by him as a true friend for four years," Daniells lamented. "I cannot understand how a man can be so cruelly ungrateful."[12]

As Daniells' account of the February 13 meeting and Sheafe's unrepentant defiance spread among church leaders, some who had already been critical of Sheafe now chimed in with even more scathing denunciations that brought the racial element of their attitudes to the surface.

He is "so bombastic, and bigheaded and self-confident, and has so much of the negro independence in him, that I have no confidence in him," groused G. I. Butler, who, five years earlier had warmed to Sheafe at the extended Oakwood board meeting.[13]

J. S. Washburn, now at the Southern Union office in Nashville, took the opportunity to ventilate deeply seated antagonisms he had muted since 1903 when it became clear that Daniells was committed to working with Sheafe. He reminded Daniells that he had warned him soon after the General Conference move that Sheafe was "a dangerous man," who "attends the meetings of the colored agitators in Washington" and, Washburn thought, "believed in arming and fighting to kill when his people were threatened with lynchings."

With regard to church organization, said Washburn, "I believe that he has been a traitor ever since he came to Washington." Almost from the beginning, he had suspected Sheafe of plotting to build up a following while on the denominational payroll and then breaking away at the opportune time.

Sympathizing with the church president's sense of betrayal,

Washburn affirmed that Daniells had been Sheafe's "best and truest friend! You held to him when some of the rest of us thought it would be safer to drop him." As he went on to commiserate with Daniells about that ingratitude and the "arbitrary, tyrannical procedure" at the February 13 meeting, Washburn revealed his growing sympathy for the imposition of White supremacy in the South following the Civil War:

"The weaker you are, the more you realize what a terrible thing it would be to be under black government, under colored dominion. . . . The more one knows of the colored people, the less he feels to blame the Southern white people, who feel that it will not do to let the colored man get on top, and it would be a terribly dangerous thing."[14]

Correspondence from California, however, displayed a very different attitude toward Sheafe. On February 14 W. C. White responded, less promptly than usual, to Daniells' letter of January 18 regarding Sheafe's assertion of congregational independence and marital strife. White noted that two copies of his mother's February 4 letter of admonition had been forwarded "a couple of days ago" to Daniells. "I think we should deal very patiently with Brother Sheafe, giving him every possible opportunity to repent and correct his ways," White advised.[15] At that point White had not yet seen Daniells' account of how Sheafe and his church had resisted his effort to regain their loyalty, which was crossing his letter in the mail. Still, it was *after* they both had read Daniells' letter of January 18, with its news that Sheafe and the People's church had already taken the drastic step of seceding from denominational authority, that Willie White sent his counsel of patience to Daniells and Ellen White sent her testimony to Sheafe.

Even in the light of the information in Daniells' letter, both communications regarded Sheafe as a valued if erring participant in the Adventist cause. Rather than regard him as a traitorous manipulator who should be cut off as soon as possible to prevent further damage, Ellen and Willie White wanted to see every possible effort made to reconcile him and encourage him back into unity; they did not want to see such efforts cut short by undue haste.

ABOUT THE TESTIMONY, QUESTIONS OF PROCESS

With Ellen White's testimony to Sheafe now before him, Daniells would give the preacher one more opportunity to change course. He and

K. C. Russell would meet with him to talk about the message from Ellen White and the matters dividing them overall. "If he still manifests the high-handed, overbearing spirit that he has of late," said Daniells, there would be no point in waiting any longer to withdraw his credentials. With probable reference to White's sentiment for forbearance, Daniells told him that they had given Sheafe every possible opportunity, but they could not wait indefinitely, for the dissident preacher and his followers would take advantage of the delay.[16]

Sheafe was ready when the brethren called on him that Friday evening, February 22. Since Ellen White began her letter with a straightforward acknowledgment that she had "been conversing with some of the brethren in Washington, D.C.," he should have been given opportunity to see what they said about him and then give his perspective, said Sheafe. Both Russell and Daniells denied having written to Ellen White about him. "But I think you *have*," Sheafe insisted. To him it seemed self-evident. But Daniells remained adamant, finally declaring, "I tell you as a man and a Christian, I have not written one line to Mrs. White concerning this matter."[17]

Here, among other instances, Daniells used narrow fact to obscure wider truth. True, he had not written to Ellen White about it, but he had written at length to W. C. White and in that letter stated, "If you think best, I would be glad to have you let your mother read this letter. We shall greatly appreciate any advice that either you or Sister White can give us at this time."[18] Moreover, Ellen White, writing Daniells on the same date that she wrote Sheafe confirmed that she had read Daniells' letter of January 18 to her son.[19]

Yet the phrasing of the critical second sentence of Ellen White's testimony to Sheafe contained just enough ambiguity to allow Daniells to contend, however improbably, that his report was not the source of her information. In a letter to Ellen White after the February 22 meeting with Sheafe Daniells indicated his understanding that her "conversations with some of the brethren" had not been ordinary communication at all but "took place in the night season when the views of his work were given you." Ellen White did not reply directly to this letter, and evidently neither she nor W. C. White, to whom Daniells had written similarly, ever made any direct comment on his interpretation of the Sheafe testimony.[20]

Thus, with regard to the testimony's impact on Sheafe, questions about process seem to have overshadowed the content. At the February 22 meeting Sheafe gave no indication of a disposition to change course. In accordance with Daniells' suggestion, he returned his ministerial credentials the following week.[21]

That action brought to an end Lewis Sheafe's decade of ministry in the employ of the General Conference of Seventh-day Adventists. If it had ended up marking the final end to his connection with the denominational work, his experience during those dramatic 10 and a half years would remain a fascinating and revealing episode in Seventh-day Adventist history. However, it would have been a little easier to view Sheafe as something of a short-lived aberration in Adventism, and Adventism but one of the numerous organizations with which he affiliated in his 50 years of ministry. An interpretation along the lines of George I. Butler's, which regarded Sheafe as more akin to a Seventh Day Baptist than a deeply rooted Seventh-day Adventist, and thus relatively rapidly swept away from loyalty to the cause by racial and administrative grievances, might be more credible.

But it was not the end. In fact, in retrospect it seems unclear that either side in the "separation" of 1907 ever really let go.

---

[1] The full text of the letter is published in *Manuscript Releases* (Washington, D.C.: Ellen G. White Estate, 1990), vol. 13, pp. 159-165.

[2] Correspondence from California appears typically to have taken about a week to reach Washington, D.C., so if mailed on the February 4 date given in the letter, it would likely have reached Sheafe before the thirteenth. W. C. White sent copies of the testimony to A. G. Daniells on February 14; WCW to AGD, Feb. 14, 1907, EGWE.

[3] Except where otherwise noted, information on the Februay 13, 1907, meeting at the People's church is drawn from the following sources: "Report by Elder Sheafe of a Meeting Held in His Church," n.d., J. H. Kellogg Papers (C. MacIvor Collection), CAR; "Statement of L. C. Sheafe to the members of the church known as the People's SDA Church, Washington, D.C., Feb. 13, 1907, GCA; "Remarks of Elder A. G. Daniells to the People's SDA Church," Feb. 14, 1907, GCA.

[4] AGD to WCW, Feb. 11, 1907, GCA.

[5] This sentence comes from Daniells' detailed account of the meeting in AGD to WCW, Feb. 14, 1907, GCA.

[6] AGD to WCW, Feb. 14, 1907.

[7] AGD to WCW, Feb. 14, 1907.

[8] AGD to LCS, Feb. 15, 1907, GCA.

[9] LCS to AGD, Feb. 17, 1907, GCA.

[10] AGD to WCW, Feb. 14, 1907.

[11] Daniells made this claim at least twice in letters defending his course to other leading Black Adventist ministers (AGD to SS, Feb. 4, 1907; AGD to WHG, Oct. 28, 1908). It is difficult to ascertain just how forceful the General Conference president was in advocating the appropriation, and would be particularly surprising if he had done so wholeheartedly just as Sheafe's disaffection was becoming increasingly open. Also, if the matter was of highest priority to him, it seems plausible that he, as a strong leader, could have cajoled the committee into agreement. On the other hand, correspondence from Washburn and Butler corroborates that Daniells took a more favorable view of Sheafe and his motives than did other denominational leaders.

[12] AGD to WCW, Feb. 14, 1907.

[13] GIB to AGD, Mar. 3, 1907, GCA.

[14] JSW to AGD, Feb. 20, 1907, GCA.

[15] WCW to AGD, Feb. 14, 1907, EGWE.

[16] AGD to WCW, Feb. 22, 1907, GCA.

[17] Daniells reports on the February 22 meeting with Sheafe in letters to Ellen White and W. C. White, both dated Feb. 28, 1907, EGWE. Further details of the interchange come from an account by an unidentified author, "The Worst Kind of Lying," *Gathering Call* (November 1932): pp. 12-15. The article is said to be "contributed," and thus apparently not written by E. S. Ballenger, brother of the by-then-deceased A. F. Ballenger, and editor of the periodical that was devoted to criticism of the denomination on matters having to do with organization, the authority of Ellen White's writings, and interpretations of prophecy and the sanctuary doctrine. This particular article may have been written by W. A. Colcord, who, not long before the article appeared, had just reconciled with the denomination after several years of alienation over issues having to do with the authority and use of Ellen White's writings. Colcord was in Washington in 1907 and wrote letters indicating close acquaintance with developments involving Sheafe and the People's church. The article's criticism is directed toward A. G. Daniells' handling of the situation, rather than Ellen White.

[18] AGD to WCW, Jan. 18, 1907.

[19] EGW to AGD, Feb. 4, 1907, EGWE. In this letter Ellen White does not refer specifically to Sheafe, but does mention other matters having to do with organization and A. T. Jones that Daniells brought up in the lengthy letter of January 18 to W. C. White. The latter, too, virtually states that he had shown the letter to Ellen White, and that she had taken cognizance of it, including the part on Sheafe: "Your letter of January 18 regarding the attitude of Elder Sheafe to the subject of organization was diligently studied by us and when I learned that Mother was writing to Elder Sheafe, I was glad" (WCW to AGD, Feb. 14, 1907, EGWE).

[20] AGD to EGW, Feb. 28, 1907, and AGD to WCW, Feb. 28, 1907. Ellen White did not reply to Daniells' letter of February 28. WCW acknowledges the two letters to him bearing the same date in a letter of Mar. 9, 1907, but makes no mention of the testimony sent to Sheafe.

[21] LCS to AGD, Feb. 26, 1907, GCA.

CHAPTER XXVIII

EQUIVOCAL FREEDOM

LEWIS SHEAFE EXUDED CONFIDENCE in February 1907, exhilarated by the feeling that he had taken a bold stand for truth and righteousness, throwing off the shackles of an oppressive ecclesiastical hierarchy. "We are all right," he wrote to a sympathizer in Battle Creek. "God is surely leading," he declared, "and we stand free from the domination of the General Conference; stand where we can hear the voice of God and do his will."[1]

On the other hand, Daniells and the denominational loyalists had utter confidence that despite the setback, their cause remained God's and would fully triumph without Lewis Sheafe and the People's church, who would not only fail but risk their eternal destiny if they set themselves against it. Yet alongside the respective expressions of confidence, and in spite of the intense feelings generating the conflict and occasional acrimony of verbal barrages across the divide, efforts toward reconciliation began almost immediately after the separation, and recurred over the next six years.

Sheafe proved quite willing to use the possibility of reuniting in the same way that he had used the threat of separation—as leverage for tangible action from the General Conference toward a center for Black education and health ministry in Washington. He decried the denomination's racial policies, but, in sharp contrast to D. M. Canright, for example, continued to preach Adventist doctrines. He and his church members laid full claim on Seventh-day Adventist identity and continued using the Sabbath school quarterly and other denominational publications. The issue was not the content of the message but the respect and just treatment due each member of the church body.

The General Conference stood to gain much from a genuine return to loyalty on Sheafe's part. At minimum, his withdrawal caused confusion and doubt throughout the fledgling Adventist work among African-Americans, creating an obstacle to further growth. The gifted preacher, not yet 50 years old, still had much to offer in advancing the cause, not to mention the excellent property his church had acquired. And, of foremost importance in the thinking of denominational leaders throughout 1907, regaining Sheafe would set back the oppositional forces gathering around Jones and Kellogg.

Between Sheafe and the General Conference, a third force emerged to take an influential role in grappling with the dilemma. As of 1907 Sheafe enjoyed undisputed recognition as the "greatest colored man in the cause."[2] However, the Black Adventist ministerial force had grown considerably since 1896, when Sheafe brought the total to three by joining the movement.[3] A little more than a decade later the number had reached 45.[4] None of them, as yet, rivaled Sheafe, but several were of outstanding ability—forward-thinking, well-spoken, vigorous leaders supremely dedicated to the daunting mission of taking the Adventist message to the nation's 12 million souls of African descent. Among them, Sydney Scott, Matthew C. Strachan, and William H. Green stepped forward to offer leadership in the crisis surrounding Sheafe.

Each recognized the racial inequities that Sheafe protested and how these hindered the progress of the message among Black Americans, but chose to address them with their feet planted firmly on the ground of loyalty to the organized work led by the General Conference. From that standpoint they worked along the dual lines of countering Sheafe's influence while at the same time seeking to mediate his reconciliation with the denomination.[5]

The unifying purpose behind the dual approach was advancement of the Adventist cause among Black Americans. Reconciliation of Sheafe would surely be advantageous, but either way, they would seek to impress upon denominational leadership the genuineness and severity of the root causes of the disaffection, and the necessity of strong action to counteract its spread.

AN ALLIANCE WITH A. T. JONES?

While Sheafe was in Battle Creek during the fall of 1906, word spread that A. T. Jones was arranging for Sheafe and E. E. Franke, another renowned evangelist now at odds with denominational leadership, to join him for a grand tent series the following year in Battle Creek. That series did not materialize, but when Jones toured the East the following spring, holding meetings in cooperation with Franke in Newark, New Jersey, and then with Sheafe in Washington, D.C., it did appear that an alliance between the three dissident preachers was firming up.

Sheafe issued a flyer inviting the public to a series of lectures by Jones entitled "The World's Greatest Issues," at the People's SDA Church, April 3 through 14. Good-sized audiences, sometimes filling the church, with a large portion of non-Adventists from the community, assembled to hear Jones speak on such topics as "The Eastern Question," "Church Federation," "Creation or Evolution, Which?" and "The Church of Christ." Jones claimed that the entire series consisted of positive, evangelistic messages, in which he made no reference to any controversy in connection with the General Conference.[6]

W. A. Colcord, of the denomination's Religious Liberty office, agreed, for the most part, based on his attendance at most of the meetings. However, said Colcord, on the crucial matter of the organization of the church, Jones "began to shoot wildly, and go to extremes." While Colcord caught only one direct reference to the denomination, he thought that Jones "put things in such a way as to really cast slurs and insinuations on the General Conference and its management." Ridiculing the role of "presidents" and "committees" in gospel work, Jones, according to Colcord, "made some very bold assertions in regard to each individual being absolutely independent of every other individual in all religious matters."

Some members of the People's church found Jones's radical views on organization unconvincing. One of the church members debated the issue with Jones during question-and-answer time until finally, after about 10 minutes, Sheafe intervened. Colcord did not attend that night, but the reports given him indicated that "the colored brother had the best of the argument."[7]

Future events would bring Sheafe and Jones into collusion at least once more, but no ongoing, cooperative relationship developed between the two. No Battle Creek-People's church axis formed.

A "COLORED CONFERENCE"?

However, another question of church unity and organization hovered over the scene. Would Sheafe attempt to draw Black Seventh-day Adventists into some kind of association or affiliation independent of the General Conference? More broadly, in retrospect, would racial discord lead to a separate Black Adventist denomination, as it had led to separate Methodist, Baptist, and soon thereafter, Pentecostal denominations?

According to A. G. Daniells, Sheafe, in January 1907, had already been engaged for several months in "missionary efforts" among Black Adventists in various states.[8] Sheafe had been writing ministers and churches throughout the South, "laying foundations for a work of opposition and defection," said G. I. Butler. The "whole colored work is in jeopardy from this new movement," Butler declared, and he predicted Sheafe would try to form "a colored conference." Only a month later Butler was considerably less alarmed over the sway that Sheafe might exert in the South.[9] Yet Sydney Scott, one of the leading Black ministers in the South, warned in January 1908 that "all the colored people are looking to the Sheafe movement."[10] And the following summer General Conference treasurer I. H. Evans expressed renewed concern that Black Adventists throughout the nation might coalesce around Sheafe in independence from the denomination.[11]

The question of whether other churches would align with the People's church met its first test across town at the First church. Just days after the People's church issued its statement of congregational independence on January 15, Charles Shaffer announced that Sheafe would preach at First church on January 26 and would be accompanied by a large portion of his own congregation. This gesture, along with a pattern of collusion over the past year, led Daniells to observe, "I shall not be surprised if the 8th Street church follows the action of the People's church." At that point, in the heat of crisis and wearied by five years of recurring contention with First church, Daniells frankly told H. W. Cottrell that the loss of both churches "would not be the worst thing that could happen to us."

Daniells' actions would demonstrate greater diplomacy and patience than this remark reflects. But the outcome that on that day he seemed almost ready to welcome—the loss of First church along with People's— would have greatly increased the already-seismic impact of the crisis on the denomination's Black membership. Together the two congregations accounted for at least 200 of the total African-American membership, estimated at 1,300.[12] If the First church had indeed followed People's, it is easy to imagine momentum building from the nation's capital toward consequences much more divisive and difficult to reverse at this early and very critical stage in the development of the Black Adventist work.

Though the exact nature of such consequences can only be conjectured, it is safe to say that a very great deal was at stake on March 30, 1907, when 25 leading members of First church met to consider whether they would follow the lead of Sheafe and the People's church. The voice carrying the greatest influence in the deliberations was that of Dr. James Howard, whose eloquence in defending racial equality as a principle of Adventist faith remains unsurpassed to this day. As they weighed the momentous decision, Dr. Howard urged that the current failures in meeting that ideal not be the decisive consideration.

"No condition brought about by the errors of our conference brethren would justify Brother Sheafe in taking the extreme position that he did.

"Don't separate from the cause. Men don't own the cause nor the denomination. Don't let us move one peg from the organized work. I shall not move, even if all others move."[13]

It deserves consideration as one of the foremost defining moments in Black Adventist history, both for its direct consequences and as a precedent that has, by and large, prevailed down to the present. Through the following decades some would follow Sheafe's approach of making loyalty to the denomination conditional upon its performance. A large majority, however, have adopted Howard's stance of bedrock conviction that the organized Adventist work is ordained of God as the instrument through which His final message is to be taken to the world. For them, the shortcomings, even evils, of particular policies or leaders do not alter that reality of faith. While pointing to the credentials of their unshaken loyalty and evangelistic zeal, they would persistently press the denomination toward greater realization of its much-professed ideal of the equality of all people in Christ.

As for the more immediate impact, the March 30 decision did not yet fully end the drama over First church's relationship with the denomination, but it did keep the tenuous connection intact during a time of crisis. And it stalled the possible spread of the "Sheafe movement" to other congregations.

How persistently and systematically Sheafe himself worked to bring other Adventist ministers and churches into his "movement" is unclear. It is clear that in the run-up to the People's church withdrawal in 1907, and from then into 1910, he made some efforts to cultivate support and establish some form of connection between the like-minded. Yet the direct evidence on just how and to what extent is sketchy.

ECCLESIASTICAL POPULIST

The varied and somewhat contradictory role of Sheafe's views on church governance provides one window on his ambivalence toward a counterorganization project. The complexity stems in part from the fact that in announcing its independence, the People's church put forth the procedural grounds for its action without stating the reasons behind it. The January 15 letter stated the principle of congregational freedom under Christ from any other "tribunal or court of review" as authorization for assumption of complete control over tithes and offerings, as well as other church functions. But it did not state the reasons driving them to make that assertion, which centered on the lack of satisfying response to their petition of February 1906 for racial parity in the health and educational dimensions of the Adventist work. The matter of organization thus took on a prominence, at a time when denominational leaders were highly sensitive to it, that far outstripped the actual importance that Sheafe attached to it.

That said, Sheafe did have genuine affinities for the concept of congregational freedom from domination by higher ecclesiastical authorities. The choice of the name "People's" for the church in itself reflects its significance in his outlook. Commonly utilized by shops, banks, and insurance companies as well as churches, that single word evoked the cherished American ideal of government "of the people, by the people, and for the people." But for Sheafe it also, almost surely, had a more specific resonance. During his years in Minnesota (1888-1892) the People's Party, eventually better known as the Populist Party, emerged as a transforming force in American politics, with the Midwest as one of its primary centers of strength. In brief, the Populists used highly emotive rhetoric to champion the interests of the common people against the powerful corporate interests that corrupted the entire political system, including both major political parties. Partially absorbed by the Democratic Party, with which it jointly nominated William Jennings Bryan for president in the 1896 election, the Populists faded as a party, but populism remained an important strand in the nation's political fabric.[14]

In declaring his church to be "for the people," then, Sheafe reflected a kind of spiritual populism. He wanted a church open to all regardless of race or social class, a church that empowered its people rather than any privileged interest group or priestly hierarchy. And, in his setting, that meant an all-White church governance structure should not be allowed to subordinate and unfairly treat his people—Black believers whose standing in Christ made them the equal of all others.

So Sheafe was well disposed to congregationalist ideas when set forth by those, such as Jones, who also had a record of standing for racial equality in the church. He seized the concept as a way of asserting freedom from the racially oppressive exercise of "kingly authority" that he saw at work in the actions of the General Conference leadership. He also showed some interest in linking with those who had similar concerns.

However, he did not hold to a rigid concept of congregationalism as the line of division from the General Conference of Seventh-day Adventists. He did not have a deep interest in rallying other Adventists together under the congregationalist principle of organization. Rather, his overriding concern was to make the Seventh-day Adventist message work better for his people in real life. And he remained open to the possibility that it could happen within the existing denominational framework.

The decentering impulse in the congregational concept and the forceful personalities of the men who were espousing it may also have militated against any efforts Sheafe undertook at this juncture toward forming a new organizational connection. In a system in which cooperation is voluntary, preachers with strong convictions and leadership traits may find little incentive to defer to others when differences arise. Colcord commented that if Sheafe, Jones, Ballenger, Franke, "and a few more of this sort, should get together, they would make a pretty strong team, in a way."[15] However, to use more recent terminology, a collection of individual superstars does not necessarily make a great team.

"ALWAYS A FAVORITE SPEAKER"

In Washington the People's church, though it remained strong, did not make the kind of advances that would have met the hopes raised either by its founding in 1903 or by the recent initial excitement of being free from denominational fetters. Issues left unspecified by the sources caused the loss of some members and some resignations from the church board in 1907 and 1908. On the other hand, Sheafe continued to attract some new members, in part by making the "color question" central to Adventism's message of reform for the last days.

Sheafe took the position that because of developments in church and society during the past decade, race had become a decisive test of Christian integrity, surpassing the Sabbath in significance. He reportedly preached that because of their failures on this issue, Seventh-day Adventists had lost their standing as "true descendents of the apostolic churches." Thus, he called the denomination to reform, with uncompromising adherence to racial justice and equality in all its churches and institutions. Faithfulness to the gospel requires a radical stand, he maintained, even at the cost of death. Sheafe "preaches that thing with power, and it leaves a deep impression on the mind," said one observer.[16]

Overall, the People's church experienced little net change in membership. It did make considerable progress in reducing the debt on the church property, while also making some physical improvements. The pastor enjoyed a substantial increase in salary from $16.50 to $25 per week under the new arrangement, though when the wages paid Annie as a Bible worker and Clara as a church musician are included, the family's weekly income from the conference had been $22.[17]

In Washington's Black society Sheafe seems to have become something of a well-recognized fixture—"always a favorite speaker," in the words of a brief report mentioning an address he gave in February 1911 that "captivated the men" at the 12th Street YMCA.[18] His name surfaces occasionally in press reports, and his denominational affiliation, when given, is identified as Seventh-day Adventist. In the late fall of 1907, for example, Sheafe participated in two interdenominational series of meetings conducted by two of the more prominent Black preachers in the city. He preached for a "union revival" led by the colorful evangelist and pastor of the Cosmopolitan Baptist Temple, Simon P. W. Drew, and for the

Homecoming Week at the Galbraith AME Zion Church, pastored by Rev. S. L. Corothers.[19]

A prominent activist in the political realm, Corothers led a campaign of "independent Negroes" and "insurgent Republicans" to withdraw traditional Black support from the Republican Party in the 1910 and 1912 elections unless the GOP dramatically improved its actual performance on civil rights and Black economic opportunity. To this effort Sheafe lent, at minimum, his singing voice at a rally on September 6, 1910, at True Reformers' Hall.[20] This movement registered discontent with the incumbent Republican president, William Howard Taft. But Sheafe, it appears, was not narrowly partisan in sharing his musical gifts, for at some point during the Taft administration he also sang for an audience that included the president.[21]

Judging from press coverage overall, though, Sheafe's prominence in the community during the years from 1907 to 1913 had diminished considerably from that of 1902 to 1904. The fact that he was no longer a new phenomenon accounts in part for this. Also, some may have cooled toward him as the radical nature of the Adventist message and his project of building up a congregation at the expense, to some degree, of existing churches became more apparent. Years of infighting in the Adventist community, as well as rumors of unbecoming conduct on the part of Sheafe and members of the church—though apparently unsubstantiated—also took a toll on his public image in the city and that of Adventism in general.[22]

CLARA AND ANNIE

The standard nursing treatment would only debilitate them further, said Drs. Daniel and Lauretta Kress, after examining Annie and Clara Sheafe in December 1907. Both mother and daughter, it was clear, had been afflicted with "consumption"—tuberculosis. The disease was that era's severest scourge on the health of the African-American population, inflicting a death rate three times that of the White population, according to Wilbur P. Thirkield of Howard University.[23]

For Annie and Clara the best hope now, humanly speaking, would simply be good food, warm clothing, and plenty of fresh air, said the health-reforming physicians who headed the new Washington Sanitarium in Takoma Park. K. C. Russell, in his role as chair of the District Evangelical Committee, did what he could for them. He found that $2 remained due to Annie from her employment as a Bible worker, and sent her an extra $10.

When Russell and his daughter stopped by the Sheafe home three days before Christmas, they found a scene too sad for words. Clara, whose voice only a year earlier rang out beautifully for a standing-room-only crowd at the Washington Conservatory of Music student recital,[24] now struggled painfully just to draw a breath. Earlier that day, her suffering unbearable, she had pleaded with her mother for something that would help her die.

After the Russells concluded their visit with a season of prayer and were about to leave, the father and husband came into the room, his demeanor quite kindly toward the visitors. He and Russell went into the parlor to talk. In a very deliberate manner, Sheafe stated the grim reality that his daughter was probably beyond hope, and that as the girl's need was the only thing holding Annie up, she would likely collapse after Clara died.[25]

Clara's suffering came to an end at 6:00 the next morning. The funeral for the 16-year-old whose musical gifts had contributed incalculably to the success of her father's meetings took place at the People's church the day after Christmas.[26]

For Annie the end came a little more than two months later, on March 4, 1908. "Her kind disposition and Christian life won many friends during her residence in Ohio," noted the *Columbia Union Visitor*, then published in Mount Vernon. The announcement expressed a prayer for the comfort of "sorrowing husband and son" and the hope "that when the Lord shall come for his people they may be an unbroken family in the everlasting kingdom."[27]

Though seven years younger than her husband, Annie had been Lewis Sheafe's teacher, both in the classroom and in many of life's practical realities. She bore him three children, raised them, and held the home together, particularly during the uncertain, absence-filled early years of his Adventist ministry. Indeed, she had made his ministry her cause, both as a Baptist and in the risky plunge into the "present truth" of Adventism.

Whether they ever fully reconciled as husband and wife is unknowable, but seems unlikely. Their shared grief must surely have brought some tender moments. Indeed, deep and powerful currents of emotion must have swirled through Sheafe at this double loss coming amid the seemingly unabated controversy that now marked his career. But the specifics of these emotions and how he handled them likewise eludes us.

Before ending the conversation with Sheafe that followed his visit with Annie and Clara, K. C. Russell appealed to the preacher to "return to the truth" and work once again in harmony with the denominational plan of organization. "Well, if God so orders, I will," Sheafe replied. Many in the denomination—and indeed, some in the People's church as well—felt, like Russell, that God was ordering just that, and sought to help bring it about. So while deploying workers to oppose Sheafe in Washington and warning Black pastors and churches throughout the South against his influence, church leaders also engaged in repeated efforts at reconciliation with the perplexing but richly gifted preacher.

SHEAFE'S "DEFECTION" AND SHARED GOALS

The unenviable assignment of going to Washington to build up a Black church in opposition to Sheafe, even as efforts to reconcile him proceeded, went to Matthew C. Strachan. Converted to Adventism from an Episcopalian background, Strachan studied theology both at Battle Creek College and at Fisk University in Nashville, and was working in the Tennessee River Conference. At the Southern Union office in Nashville, G. I. Butler and J. S. Washburn recommended Strachan slightly ahead of Sydney Scott, who was evangelizing in Alabama. Though Scott was more of a "driver" and his work seemed to be well received everywhere he went, he was somewhat impulsive, and they believed that the studious and diplomatic Strachan might be less vulnerable to Sheafe's influence.[28]

However, even though both preachers professed strong allegiance to the denomination and had repudiated Sheafe's course, the Southern Union brethren also knew that both had given Sheafe's account of the Washington saga a sympathetic hearing and could not be completely certain either of them would remain firm. Furthermore, they doubted that either had the capacity to be very effective in such a difficult situation. "Sheafe is too much for the ordinary colored man," Washburn opined. And even though Scott was the better preacher, he was "nowhere near equal to Sheafe."[29]

But Strachan determined to improve on the opportunity, even though he knew the difficulties would be enormous. He hoped to establish credibility with denominational leaders through diligent, loyal labor, and thereby help bring them to the realization that genuine and profound grievances lay behind Sheafe's "defection," and that these must be addressed in a meaningful way if the truly powerful Adventist work among Black Americans that all desired was to become a reality.

Strachan's tent meetings in the summer of 1907 drew modest crowds of about 150 to 175 on Sunday nights and 40 to 60 during weeknights. His efforts resulted in formation of the Fifth Seventh-day Adventist Church in Washington (the first four being First, Memorial, People's, and Takoma Park). At first the little assembly seemed barely viable, but they persisted. After a year they numbered 24. Half of them joined "from the world," while nine came from the People's church and three transferred from the First church (or "Northeast church," as Strachan referred to it).[30]

At the same time, Strachan saw about half of those won to the message through his efforts end up at either People's or First church. The combined influence of Sheafe and the First church, Strachan pointed out, created "an enormous tide to stem against." Sheafe's high-profile and powerful preaching made certain that new converts quickly became aware of the racial injustices in the denominational system.

From the First church, still dedicated to the ideal of mixed-race congregations, word went out that in raising up a Black church, Strachan was a tool the General Conference used in their "wicked designs" of segregating the races. The issue was of more than local significance in the minds of the believers at the "mother church" of Adventism in Washington, D.C. They believed that denominational officials intended to extend their plan throughout the nation and break up mixed-race churches wherever they might exist. Frustrating it in Washington, though, might thwart its spread elsewhere.[31]

The quality of worship facilities also played an influential role. Why meet with Brother Strachan's little group in a rented room on the second floor of a mortuary, inhaling the "sickly odors" of embalming fluid, when one could enjoy the comfortable pews, carpeted floors, and splendid music at either of two churches where essentially the same message was taught, reasoned some. Strachan also claimed that some in the People's church who thought the move to independence had been a mistake stayed with it nonetheless because of their deep investment in the building and its improvements as a labor of love.[32]

In February 1908 Strachan addressed an appeal to the General Conference, outlining in bold terms what needed to be done in order to build a strong base of loyal Black believers in Washington, D.C. The negative influences emanating from the People's and First churches could be countered only by solving the problems that prompted them to act, he maintained, however wrong the course of action they chose. Though by his own description and that of others cautious and utterly loyal, Strachan now made the substance of Sheafe's case as powerfully as it was ever made, in written form at least.

First, he insisted that in order for Adventism's mission to Black America to thrive, priority must be placed on Washington, D.C.—"the very seat of culture among the Negroes" and "the great mecca of Negro intelligence and refinement." Thus:

"If this denomination has a message for the Negro race, then, just now, surely, the city of Washington has a larger claim upon it than any other place for a more material representation of the truth in the form of a building of some kind.

"While money has been and is being raised to pay for schools, sanitariums, and churches in other places and for other people, how shall we excuse ourselves from the responsibility of establishing the same for the Negro in Washington, the metropolitan and cosmopolitan Negro city of the United States?"

Some, Strachan acknowledged, would point to the considerable resources and efforts already devoted to Washington and their unfortunate outcome in "a great apostasy, led by the strongest colored worker among us." But he urged the brethren not "to quail at the difficulties and embarrassments which confront them in the work among the colored people of the District of Columbia." Without using the cliché, he reminded them that "where there's a will there's a way," and provided a very telling illustration from recent experience:

"When Dr. Kellogg threw down the gauntlet to our leading brethren a few years ago, and told them to go and build them a Mrs. White Sanitarium, the brethren immediately accepted the challenge and came to Washington, and today, the sanitarium stands dedicated, and all was done notwithstanding the many difficulties and perplexities which have arisen since then. Now, why cannot other things be accomplished in the same manner? *They will be,* if they are backed up by a determination and purpose on the part of our leading brethren."

Now, it was Strachan's turn to throw down the gauntlet to "the leading brethren," urging that someone arise and "champion the cause of the Negroes in Washington," and work for the establishment of "a church, a school and a modest little treatment room."

The young preacher did not hesitate to hold the leaders accountable to the "Spirit of Prophecy." "How much longer shall the sin of 'neglect' rest upon our brethren," he asked, alluding to Ellen White's appeal for action in 1891. "You cannot be justified in expending money so lavishly in providing conveniences for yourselves and furnishing facilities for those who have been more fortunate," he quoted from *The Southern Work* (p. 34), substituting the "We" that begins the printed sentence with "You."

Then Strachan brought the matter home to Washington, D.C., pointing to the "painful contrast between the provisions which you have made for yourselves, and the crying lack among the colored people here in the District." With all due gratitude for that which had indeed been done on their behalf, it was this "painful contrast" that had "for a long time given the enemy of this cause a sword with which to cripple your prospects for a bountiful harvest among the Negroes."[33]

Strachan's eloquent appeal did not produce immediate results, though it had a significant indirect impact. About the same time, he drafted a similar appeal concerning the "Negro work" in general, now apparently lost, that he sent to Elmshaven, hoping to gain Ellen White's approval for discreetly circulating among church leaders as the basis for discussing the issues.[34] Strachan's appeals were one part of a process that led to a milestone at the General Conference session of 1909.

In the meantime they were not so much ignored as held hostage to pursuit of the other track in the denomination's response to the Sheafe crisis. A. G. Daniells, W. C. White, and others had, of course, for some time affirmed in principle the necessity of taking the action step for which Strachan called. But the actual commitment of funds that had previously been delayed because of mistrust of Sheafe was, paradoxically, now held up by the possibility that he might return to the organizational fold.

Rather than throw its resources into making the new Fifth church the center of the denomination's work for Blacks in Washington, D.C., the General Conference adopted a policy of what some in the Adventist community called "watchful waiting." As long as the grapevine hummed from time to time about the possibility of Sheafe's return to the fold, and the General Conference president did not slam the door shut, it made sense to wait awhile and watch. The People's church and the fine facilities it had already acquired might yet turn out to be the answer.[35]

---

[1] "Report by Elder Sheafe."

[2] SS to AGD, Feb. 8, 1907, GCA.

[3] The other two were C. M. Kinny and A. Barry, 1894 YB. Louis Reynolds writes that Harry Lowe, a Baptist minister, preached the Adventist message after joining the Edgefield Junction, Tennessee, church in 1883. Lowe apparently was never ordained, though, and it is not clear how long his ministry as an Adventist continued. Taswell Buckner joined the church in 1889, but did not become a minister until 1899. See L. B. Reynolds, *We Have Tomorrow,* pp. 108, 109, 112, 113, 122; "General Conference Proceedings," GCDB, Mar. 3, 1899, p. 138.

[4] Sydney Scott, "Work in the South," *Gospel Herald,* July 1907, p. 26.

[5] Strachan worked only against Sheafe, while Scott and Green led attempts at reconciliation even while firmly opposing Sheafe's course of action.

[6] "The World's Greatest Issues" flyer, GCA. The "Eastern Question" had to do with the protracted demise of the Ottoman Empire, which for decades held a prominent place in Adventist evangelistic preaching on biblical prophecy. "Church Federation" was a timely topic, as the Federal Council of Churches, later renamed the National Council of Churches, had just organized in 1906. Jones gave his account of the meetings in his lengthy letter of July 3, 1907.

[7] W. A. Colcord to E. W. Farnsworth, EGWE, Apr. 25, 1907.

[8] AGD to HWC, Jan. 20, 1907, GCA.

[9] GIB to AGD, Jan. 20 and Feb. 11, 1907, GCA.

[10] SS to AGD, Jan. 24, 1908, GCA.

[11] I. H. Evans to AGD, July 30, 1908, GCA.

[12] Sydney Scott gives the number in "Work in the South for the Colored," *Gospel Herald,* February 1907, pp. 6, 7.

[13] Untitled transcript of Dr. Howard's statement dated Mar. 30, 1907, GCA.

[14] See, among many works on the subject, Michal Kazin, *The Populist Persuasion: An American History* (New York: HarperCollins, 1995), pp. 1-4, 27-42.

[15] W. A. Colcord to E. W. Farnsworth, 1907.

[16] Matthew C. Strachan, who, as will be discussed below, was called to Washington to build up a Black congregation loyal to the denomination, made this observation with reference to Sheafe's preaching on Adventism and the color line in general; MCS to AGD, Aug. 20, 1907, GCA. In a subsequent letter to Daniells, dated Dec. 2, 1907, Strachan reported in greater detail Sheafe's proclamations on race as the foremost test of Christian integrity and the necessity of reform in Adventism on this matter.

[17] AGD to SS, Feb. 4, 1907, GCA; MCS to AGD, Apr. 9, 1908, GCA.

[18] "YMCA Notes," *Bee,* Mar. 4, 1911, p. 4.

[19] "Dr. Drew Will Preach at the Union Revival," *Bee,* Nov. 23, 1907, p. 5; "Special Notice," *Bee,* Dec. 7, 1907, p. 4.

[20] "Great Mass Conference of Independent Negroes and Insurgent Republicans," *Bee,* Sept. 3, 1910, p. 1.

[21] "Noted Negro Minister Speaks in This City," San José *Mercury News,* Mar. 14, 1914, p. 3. The brief news note states simply that "L. C. Sheafe, the famous negro evangelist of Washington, D.C., who has preached before members of congress and sung for President Taft, lectured at the AOUW hall on First Street at three o'clock this afternoon."

[22] In a statement written to denominational leaders in the Washington area, probably in late 1912 or early 1913 (GCA), W. H. Green wrote that "vile heresies have been taught, gross immoralities charged against the elder and others, so that Seventh-day Adventists as to color stand in the eyes of the public generally as a stench and byword." It is not clear, though, whether Green believed such charges had any truth. The statement, discussed further below, is critical of Sheafe, but in the context of setting forth criteria that Green believed should be met in order for Sheafe and the People's church to be reintegrated into denominational organization. Green does not give any specifics on the alleged "vile heresies" and "gross immoralities." Whatever else he may have thought about the allegations, though, it is clear that he did not see them as a bar to the readmittance of the elder and his church, provided they demonstrated repentance on the matter of church organization.

[23] "Need of Negro Physicians," *Bee,* Dec. 26, 1908, p. 4. The story "Negro Congress on Tuberculosis" at Tuskegee, Alabama, in the same issue of the Washington *Bee,* reported that an exhibition on tuberculosis, the first health exhibit ever "devoted wholly to the welfare of Negroes," was soon to travel around the nation.

[24] Berenice Thompson, "Music and Musicians," WP, June 10, 1906, p. A5.

[25] KCR to AGD, Dec. 23, 1907, GCA.

[26] "Died," WP, Dec. 24, 1907, p. 3.

[27] "Funeral Announcement," *Columbia Union Visitor,* Mar. 18, 1908, p. 4. The reference to the sorrowing "son" should have read "sons."

[28] GIB to AGD, Mar. 3, 9, 17, 1907, GCA.

[29] JSW to AGD, Feb. 14, 20, 1907, GCA

[30] MCS to AGD, Aug. 20, 1907, GCA; MCS to WCW, June 25, 1908, EGWE.

[31] MCS to AGD, Dec. 2, 1907, GCA.

[32] Strachan mentions the embalming fluid odor in an appeal addressed to the General Conference, Feb. 26, 1908, GCA. He refers to "carpeted floors," "comfortable pews," and the church building as the decisive factor for some in remaining with the People's church, even though they would have preferred the denominational connection, in MCS to AGD, Apr. 9, 1908, GCA. I added the part about music, inferring from numerous sources in references scattered throughout the book.

[33] MCS to General Conference Brethren, Feb. 26, 1907, GCA.

[34] MCS to WCW, June 25, 1908; WCW to MCS, June 7, 1908, EGWE.

[35] A. F. Ballenger quotes the phrase in reporting on conversations he had in 1914 with members of First church, who filled him in on developments regarding People's and Fifth churches since 1907; "Notes by the Way," *Gathering Call,* May 1914, p. 4.

CHAPTER XXIX
RECONCILIATION INITIATIVES

SYDNEY SCOTT INITIATED THE FIRST OF TWO MAJOR ATTEMPTS in 1908 by Black Adventist ministers to reconcile Sheafe with the General Conference. One of the earliest graduates of ministerial training at the Oakwood school, Scott kept close tabs on the burgeoning Adventist movement among African-Americans, filing frequent reports in church publications. He corresponded frequently with key individuals, including Sheafe, with whom he had been in contact for several years.

SYDNEY SCOTT'S INITIATIVE

After hearing about the move to independence by the People's church, Scott began corresponding with Daniells. Sheafe "will give trouble if he is not carefully handled," warned Scott, offering his assistance in the hope that "we can save him to the cause." At the same time, Scott assured Daniells that he was in complete harmony with church organization and the General Conference administration, and denounced Sheafe's recent action as "a big mistake."[1] Favorably impressed, Daniells initially leaned toward calling Scott to Washington,[2] but then yielded to Butler's recommendation of Strachan.

Scott elaborated on his criticism of Sheafe's course of action in response to Daniells' report of the defiance he encountered at the People's church on February 13. Scott felt certain "the Sheafe movement" would sooner or later end in confusion, for a "muscle that jumps out of the body because the other muscles are sick" will die because it is cut off from the blood supply. He agreed with Sheafe, by implication, that the body was sick, but saw that as "a good reason . . . all the muscles should have a closer union."

Most telling was Scott's difference from Sheafe on the role of race in the Adventist message and identity. Sheafe linked race with Adventist faith in a way that left little room for tolerance of an Adventism that failed to meet a high standard of racial justice. By placing greater distance between the two, and subordinating racial identity to Adventist identity, Scott's approach gave greater scope for gradual resolution of racial problems in the framework of unswerving adherence to the Adventism of the general church body:

"Color and truth are two different things. Color is skin deep; truth is everlasting. Any movement which hath color as its reason *for separating from the body has a foundation too shallow to stand the test.* Color is color and truth is truth."[3]

Having won Daniells' confidence with assurances on church organization, Scott remained in friendly contact with Sheafe. He hoped to position himself in this way to help Daniells with the "careful handling" needed to bring Sheafe back into line.

In so doing, Scott endeavored to help Daniells gain a better grasp on how Black Adventists viewed the situation. A "proper adjustment" was crucial to the prosperity of the "colored work" as a whole, because the perception of racial injustice pervaded even the large majority who had no thought of following Sheafe in the path of independence.

In his first letter to Daniells inquiring about the Sheafe situation in January 1907, Scott relayed to the General Conference president the story going around the Southern Union: "It is claimed that the General Conference helped Washburn in his church but would not put one cent in the People's SDA Church building and that this unjust treatment has driven Elder Sheafe to take the course he has."[4]

Toward the end of a six-page reply defending his course, Daniells made a brief and rare acknowledgment that at least an element of legitimate grievance lay behind Sheafe's action. In a backhanded way he confirmed the essential accuracy of the story Scott mentioned. "I firmly believe that the only complaint Elder Sheafe can justly make against us," Daniells wrote, "is that we have not as a General Conference Committee arranged for him to have a large gift for the payment of the church building."[5]

With at least this sliver of recognition from Daniells that the blame did not lie entirely on Sheafe's side and that a genuine problem in need of attention existed, Scott continued doing "missionary work" with Sheafe by correspondence. By early 1908 Scott felt fully confident that his efforts had paid off.

By staying in touch with both sides, he informed Daniells in January, "I have the field clearly before me as to the real situation." And now he had very promising correspondence before him indicating that Sheafe and his church could be "won back in line with our organized work" if the situation was "properly managed." A month later Scott was even more confident: "If Sheafe is properly dealt with, he will abandon his course and return to the body with a right confession. I have no other doubt he will do otherwise."[6]

With reassurance to Daniells of his own full commitment to "this message and the plan which God has chosen to carry it" Scott sketched the actions that he believed Sheafe would find amenable to clearing the way for his return to denominational work:

- Assumption of the People's church building debt by the General Conference
- Placement of the church property in a trust held by the local or union conference
- A "proper confession" from Sheafe
- Relocation of Sheafe to Chicago or "some humble branch of the Lord's work"

Scott also proposed to bring his "missionary work" for Sheafe to culmination with a personal visit to Washington. Sheafe had been looking for him to come since October, he said, but other urgent matters had interfered, and he now hoped to make the visit in May.[7]

Sheafe had fueled Scott's optimism with a letter of January 14 declaring full agreement to the terms Scott proposed. In a letter of December 19 Scott had asked Sheafe three things: (1) whether he would consent to retrace his steps, if the conference would "agree to do everything in their power to make things right on their part"; (2) if he would make a confession if shown where he was mistaken; and (3) if he was willing to go to Chicago or St. Louis.

"I can answer these questions in the affirmative," Sheafe declared unequivocally. However, he went on to state that these things were what he had been contending for already, and that he had proposed something essentially similar at the height of the crisis in February 1907, but to no avail. This comment and further elements of the construal he placed on the terms did not bode well for significant change in his position.

His willingness to confess error shown him on the basis of Scripture indicated openness to change. If he had not been genuine about that, he would never have become an Adventist in the first place. But again, it represented no substantive change since his break with the denomination: "My standard in doctrine and work is the Bible. This has always been my position. It was Bible truth that convinced me, and there I stand. So, show me from God's word wherein I have done wrong, and I will bow at once."

Sheafe also had some specific stipulations for what the General Conference would need to do as "its part to make things right":

First, "establish and equip an [all-around] training school in this city, to which the members of the People's church may have access."

Second, "in no way interfere with the present status of the People's SDA Church" so that it would "always be for the people who will meet Bible requirements."

Third, make an immediate payment of $5,000 to clear the remaining indebtedness on the church property, with the People's church agreeing to return the $5,000 in the event that it ever again left the denominational connection.

Fourth, "agree to give me a living wage."

Having run down the specifics, Sheafe added that tangible action on them would be necessary. "Brother Scott," he declared, "promises will not do; I must see these things done." This insistence, of course, derived from his frustration over a long pattern of failure to match words with deeds. "I am thankful if you have found the side of fairness in your dealings with the conference brethren, and that they have not put you off with promises," he told Scott, adding, "My experience has not been as happy."

Furthermore, the provisions he stated were nonnegotiable. If Scott felt his requests were unreasonable, said Sheafe, "then kindly let the matter drop."

Scott thus probably overestimated the degree of change and flexibility represented by Sheafe's statement. Also, in his letters to Daniells, Scott seems to have glossed over the fact that Sheafe nowhere agreed that the church property be held in trust by the local or union conference—an important point in enhancing the appeal of the arrangement to conference officials.

Yet Scott may not have been too far off the mark in sensing an element of real desire on Sheafe's part to restore connection with the denomination. At minimum the statement makes clear that congregation-centered authority rather than conference-centered authority was not a matter of dogma for Sheafe. His desire that the present status of the People's church not be interfered with touches on the issue, but more as a general spiritual principle than a rigid formula for denominational governance. He did not regard independence in itself as an ideal state.

Nor did Sheafe make demands concerning the racial integration of church institutions, which might have been expected on the basis of some of his more radical sermons. Despite his inclination toward immediatism, he was willing to work in the framework of separate but equal institutions—an accommodation to deeply ingrained social sin—in order to be part of the Seventh-day Adventist body and its mission to all peoples.

Also, Sheafe's expression of "hearty thanks" to Scott "for what you have done and are now trying to do" seems more than perfunctory. "I truly enjoyed your letter," he wrote. "It breathed the spirit of a Christian. Thank you."[8]

SHEAFE AND DANIELLS, FACE TO FACE

In late February another initiative toward reconciliation took place closer to home. Joseph Gillis of First church phoned Daniells, inviting him to a meeting with Sheafe that same evening at Gillis' home. Though apparently unrelated, Scott's efforts at mediation by mail engendered some hope in Daniells, and probably Sheafe as well, that such a meeting might be productive.

But it did not go well. Daniells, whose account is the only one that survives, came looking for signs of penitence on Sheafe's part, but saw none. The two men talked for nearly three hours, but mainly rehashed and defended their previously held positions and actions.

In fact, though a tone of civility was maintained, Daniells left the meeting in a cold fury at Sheafe's attitude of arrogance and "base ingratitude." Replaying the dialogue in his mind during the ride home that evening, Daniells formulated Sheafe's position as follows: "If our denomination feels that it has lost enough by their separation from us and are willing to correct [our] wrongs, and take the right positions on these questions upon which we have differed, he will consider the question of reuniting with us."

As he thought of all that the denomination had sacrificially devoted, not only in funds but in human lives, to work for Colored people in the American South, in Africa, and in the West Indies, Daniells told Scott, "I am made to blush with shame for Sheafe and other persons claiming to be Seventh-day Adventists, who cruelly and wickedly charge this denomination with prejudice toward individuals and to the colored people."

Daniells also completely rejected the terms Sheafe proposed as a basis for reunification. It was not so much the specifics of Sheafe's proposal that aroused the General Conference president's ire, but the very notion of making a congregation's connection with the organization dependent on terms that would bind the conference. In Daniells' thinking that connection had to be a commitment based on faith that the organization represented God's church with the decisive message for the last days, not a negotiated settlement. He compared the commitment to that of marriage. In today's terminology Sheafe wanted a prenuptial agreement; Daniells wanted a more traditional union, entered into without contemplation or calculation of the unthinkable possibility of divorce.

"We found no basis of agreement whatever," Daniells concluded, leaving them, at the end of the meeting, as far apart as ever.[9]

An assessment equally emphatic, at the least, on Sheafe's part can be inferred from his falling out with Scott over the latter's continued support for the denominational leadership. In a letter written after the meeting with Daniells, Sheafe "blew me to the moon for the course I took," said Scott.[10] After nearly four years of writing letters trying to urge Sheafe "into line," Scott now resolved to waste no more stamps and stationery on the man, for he is "joined to his idols." Then located in South Carolina, Scott also related his efforts to counter Sheafe's influence throughout the state. It was stronger there, he said, where Sheafe himself had labored successfully some eight years before, than anywhere else in the South.[11]

WILLIAM H. GREEN'S INITIATIVE

The rancorous reverberations from the February 1908 meeting at the Gillis home had a tone of finality. Yet when one of Sheafe's protégés, W. H. Green, initiated another attempt at mediation later that same year, he found both parties receptive. Now pastor of the Second Seventh-day Adventist Church in Pittsburgh, Green drew on his legal skills to facilitate a resolution.

Sheafe and the People's church, he stated, "would like to be united in full fellowship with the conference on [a] fair and just basis to all, with no sacrifice on the part of any, or any part of this great truth." Seeking to build common ground, Green contended that in the year since the separation, the People's church had "made no fight on the denomination" and had continued regular use of Seventh-day Adventist literature.

Green also cited evidence of essential harmony on Ellen White's prophetic ministry—an important element in the conflict, even though it had been kept in the background of the discussions earlier in the year. Green had talked personally with Sheafe about "the Testimonies," and reported that "he has no fight on them and is willing to lay them more plainly before the members of the church." According to a member who was well read in Ellen White's writings, he added, some of Sheafe's sermons did in fact already draw heavily upon them.

Green's proposal moved beyond the earlier effort by Scott in another way that was of considerable potential significance. It pointed a way forward through compromise and gradual steps, showing that Sheafe's trenchant insistence in January that he must see things *done*, not just promised, need not be an obstacle.

"I am informed and believe that Elder Sheafe and the church stand ready to render to the conference every consideration that is justly due it under high heaven, even though they may not receive all that they think they are entitled to, if the conference will only begin to do something in good faith for the 100,000 Negroes there in the way of education and sanitariums, etc."

The former attorney then put into legal terminology a proposed action step based on essentially the same concept that Sheafe and Scott had put forward at the beginning of the year: the General Conference would pay the remaining debt on the People's church property and the church would return the money if it ever withdrew from the conference in the future.[12]

Daniells was again both willing to listen and unwilling to yield on his principles of organizational authority. He pointed out to Green that the People's church had stated their rejection of "the plans of organization held by us as Seventh-day Adventists" as the reason for their withdrawal from the denomination. The letter of January 1907 notifying the General Conference of their decision made no charges about neglecting or failing to give them financial support. Thus, the path to reunifying with the denomination had to begin with "an entire change of views" on the organization question, and then "coming back to us with repentance." Daniells portrayed the "disorganization theory" of A. T. Jones as the main motivation driving the People's church withdrawal. Without unconditional submission on this point, it would do no good even to take up the secondary disputes over funding.[13]

Once again, Daniells also flatly rejected the concept of making reconnection with conference organization conditional upon a financial consideration, calling it "too commercial." Sheafe and the members of his church "joined this movement because they believed it was established by the providence of God," and they did so "on the basis of the truths of the third angel's message," not any monetary inducement. Therefore, Daniells reasoned, they should return on the same basis and "trust the Lord and the brotherly cooperation of all the members to work out financial matters." He pointed to the investments that the denomination had poured into the school at Huntsville, in church buildings for Black believers throughout the South, and in African missions as "evidence to the members of the People's church that we are determined to do all we can to give the people of their race this message, and every advantage and blessing we possibly can to unite with it." With such evidence before them, he believed, "they ought to trust us to do the best we can in the future."[14]

Not having seen the letter in which the People's church declared independence from the denomination, Green requested and received a copy from Daniells. Duly noting the importance of the organization question, Green also sought to drive home the point that it was *not* the central concern in Sheafe's mind. Green had asked Sheafe to identify what he saw as the decisive issue in the dispute with the denomination. He responded that it was the matter "of assisting the church and doing a special work for the colored people here as the conference in its work was hindered on account of race prejudice in doing a joint work," and that so far as he knew, no point of doctrine was involved.

As for the assertion of independence on the part of the People's church, Green asked, if this were revoked, would the General Conference consider his original proposal of October 14? That was a matter that would best be discussed face to face, before any definite statements were committed to writing, Daniells replied. He was not dismissing the question. Whereas he had strongly advised Sydney Scott against his plans to come to Washington in May to engage in personal mediation, he now encouraged W. H. Green to do so, at General Conference expense.

FIRST CHURCH RECONCILIATION RAISES HOPES

Prior to his trip to Washington, scheduled for mid-December, Green received another letter from A. G. Daniells, this one about a different but related controversy in the capital city. The seemingly endless eruptions of conflict between the General Conference brethren and the First church had once again brought that congregation to the brink of severing its ties with the denomination.

The strong conviction prevailing at First church that recognition of racial distinctions in the church constituted a betrayal of Adventist faith stood at the heart of the matter, as it had since 1901. Though rooted in broad biblical principles, Ellen White's statement in 1891 that Black and White believers should hold membership together in the same congregation gave special tenacity to that conviction. It seemed to them that the Lord had spoken to the issue in a clear and definite way through Spirit of Prophecy, and conscientiously bound them to noncooperation with any efforts to segregate churches by race.

The precipitating incident in the summer of 1908 was the First church's refusal to recognize the authority of a newly appointed pastor, J. A. Strickland, because Strickland was also placed in charge of the Fifth church, which owed its very existence to the General Conference's truth-defying program of separating the races in Washington-area churches. Resistance to Strickland's pastoral authority by extension constituted resistance to the authority that appointed him—the General Conference's District Evangelical Committee.[15]

As the dispute roiled on through the July and August heat, Daniells was on a trip to the West Coast, part of which he spent at Ellen White's home in northern California. While there Daniells and W. C. White encouraged Ellen White to consider making a fresh statement on race relations that would speak directly to the situation in Washington. At the same time, they asked her literary assistants to compile relevant material she had written from time to time in recent years, most of it as yet unpublished.[16]

On October 19, 1908, Ellen White addressed a letter to "Our Churches in Washington, D.C.," counseling them on the issue that after years of severe struggle they still could not resolve. She warned that encouraging "the sentiment that the white and colored people are to associate together in social equality"—whether in the Washington area or "in other parts of the Southern field"—would bring hindrance beyond comprehension to the Adventist cause. Thus:

"If it should be recommended and generally practiced in all our Washington churches, that white and black believers assemble in the same house of worship, and be seated promiscuously in the building, many evils would be the result."

Though a clear rebuke to those at First church who insisted that racial integration be the policy for *all* Adventist churches in Washington, the letter did not deny the principle of racial equality or the propriety of racial mixing in one or more of the city's congregations. It also included a sharp warning to those who, on the other hand, would push segregation as a general principle and draw the color line in a hard and fast way:

"But who will press the question of entire exclusion? Both white and colored people have the same Creator, and are saved by the redeeming grace of the same Savior. Christ gave His life for all. He says to all, 'Ye are bought with a price.' God has marked out no color line, and men should move very guardedly, lest we offend God. The Lord has not made two heavens, one for white people and one for colored people. There is but one heaven for the saved."[17]

In his letter of November 23 to Green, Daniells did not refer to this message from Ellen White. Yet it was almost certainly the driving force behind the decisive breakthrough in relations between the General Conference and First church that he described. Along with K. C. Russell, he had spent the previous Sabbath with the First church, culminating in a meeting Saturday evening with the church board and other members of the congregation, including Dr. Howard. The joyous outcome was "complete reconciliation," Daniells told Green.

"The spirit of the Lord came into our meeting in a large measure, and showed us the way to settle our difficulties. . . . We all agreed to bury the entire past, and start together in full harmony and union. The General Conference will stand related to the church just as it does to every other church in the denomination, and the church will take its place with every other church on exactly the same ground, and we shall work together."[18]

At Sheafe's request Daniells had sent him a copy of Ellen White's letter of October 19.[19] Its positive impact at First church may have contributed to his hope that the reconciliation there would "pave the way for the return of Elder Sheafe and his church."[20]

But it was not to be. Whatever transpired during the mediation talks led by Green in December, they did not lead to the unity much desired by all.

Green followed up the discussions by declaring his confidence in Daniells "as the visible head" of God's "organized work" and that the General Conference had "taken a reasonable, fair, just and prudent stand" that left Elder Sheafe and his church without legitimate reason for remaining out of the organization.[21] It was such expressions of loyalty and trust that Daniells wanted to hear from Sheafe and that Sheafe could not bring himself to give.

Trust was the critical issue now, for on the substance of the conflict, the two were not far apart. Though not without complication, the issues of church organization and "the Testimonies" were manageable. Sheafe saw them as secondary matters on which he was willing to be conciliatory in order to achieve his central goal—a fair deal for his people in the Adventist system. In that regard Daniells acknowledged the justice and propriety of substantial General Conference help for the debt on the People's church building. And, all along he had pledged the denomination's support for a "colored training school" in Washington with a full curriculum.

But as to the timing and extent of that support, the General

Conference Committee had taken no concrete action and Daniells made no specific commitments. He believed the denomination had done more than enough to demonstrate the importance it placed on advancing the Adventist cause among Black people, so that with regard to the work in Washington, Sheafe should "trust us to do the best we can in the future." That Sheafe found impossible to do.

The layers of mistrust built up over the years, topped off by the glaring disparity between the denomination's treatment of Washburn's Memorial church project and his People's church project, and between the institutions developed for White people in Takoma Park and the lack thereof for Black people in Washington, made him adamant. He needed to see action before he would trust again. He could not even trust that, if he would make the first move, Daniells, who in the discussions surrounding the controversy had made much of his personal support for a $2,000 appropriation to the People's church prior to the break, would surely come through with at least that much.

For his part Daniells refused to trust that the practical terms of the Green and Scott proposals were intended to signal good faith in complying with the denomination's organizational principles. The provision for returning General Conference money—should a future rupture occur—might have been welcomed as a way out of a difficult impasse. It offered a guarantee against the suspicions on the General Conference Committee about Sheafe's intentions that Daniells said had blocked his efforts in 1906 for a major appropriation of funds to the People's church: in the unlikely, unforeseen event that something went wrong, the money would be returned with interest. At the same time, a General Conference Committee vote—in advance—guaranteeing at least some level of immediate, specific action, might have been seen as a way to build the trust of the People's church that the church's organizational system was geared toward biblical principles of justice and inclusion.

But Daniells, supremely certain of his righteous intent, his freedom from "one particle of prejudice,"[22] and his full ability, along with his White brethren, to manage affairs in a way that was equitable to all races, was likewise unwilling to bend. Though he could recognize an element of justice in Sheafe's protests, he could not or would not see how the pattern of events in Washington during the years of his administration made it appear that the interests of Black people were, to put it as charitably as possible, of lesser priority. Or that some tangible, out-of-the-ordinary gesture on his part to begin rectifying the situation might open the way to restoring genuine trust and loyalty to the denomination in the hearts and minds of the People's church and their pastor.

If Sheafe needed to see *action first*, Daniells needed to secure *trust first*, without being bound to specific terms. Then he would do his best to reward the trust.

THE NEGRO DEPARTMENT—A NEW ERA?

The specter of Lewis Sheafe looms unmistakably behind the establishment of the North American Negro Department at the General Conference session in 1909. He had originated the concept at the 1901 General Conference session, and saw his proposal referred to an all-White ad hoc committee that in turn recommended further study. Then the crisis surrounding him in 1907 served as backdrop and stimulus initiatives such as that taken by M. C. Strachan in 1908.

W. C. White questioned the necessity and prudence of circulating an appeal that Strachan drafted, suggesting that Strachan had overstated the difficulties and that the denomination's record measured up as well or better than any when it came to work on behalf of "the colored people of the Southern states."[23]

"But Brother White," Strachan insisted, "most assuredly a contrary wind is gaining strength on us." In view of that, Strachan felt it his duty "to arouse your pure minds to a realization of the fact; for it does not appear to me that you fully comprehend the situation as you might." He agreed with White's suggestion about the need for genuine conversion in individual hearts, but that experience, he proposed, should be "yoked up with the most healthy action, wise discretion, and judicious diplomacy on the part of our leading brethren."[24]

With a view toward the 1909 session Sydney Scott also called for far-reaching changes. Claiming to be the first Black delegate ever elected from the South, he suggested that the time had come for more advanced plans to be instituted for the work in the South that would "throw more of the responsibility on the colored constituents."[25]

By the time the conference opened in Takoma Park in May, the individual voices for change had become a united chorus. Twelve Black Adventist ministers affixed their signatures to "An Appeal in Behalf of the Work Among the Colored People." The appeal called attention to an urgent need for change "that will make for the more systematic and diligent spread of the third angel's message among the ten million Negroes in this country."[26]

In addition to Strachan and Scott the signatories were S. A. Jordan, J. W. Manns, J. K. Humphrey, Page Shephard, W. Hawkins Green, Leslie Munce, M. C. Strachan, J. Marion Campbell, U. S. Willis, W. H. Sebastian, and Thomas H. Branch. With so many of the most effective Black ministers expressing solidarity, it was an appeal that the General Conference leadership could ignore only at the peril of seeing the Sheafe defection replicate.

Accordingly, on May 28, at the twenty-sixth meeting of the 1909 session, A. G. Daniells proposed a new department of the General Conference—the Negro Department, declaring that it marked "a new era in our work in behalf of the Negro race." The "colored ministers" at the conference—the largest number ever at a General Conference, Daniells said, had requested establishment of the department, and the proposal had received the endorsement of the Southwestern, Southern, and Southeastern union committees as well as the General Conference Committee.

Daniells' introduction of the department came with the acknowledgment that although the church had expended considerable effort toward reaching the nation's Colored people, "we have not been meeting our own highest ideals, and we have not met the needs nor the instruction [from the Spirit of Prophecy] that has come to us." The new department would be the instrumentality for "a far greater effort, a more systematic effort, a more concerted effort."

Like other departments, Daniells said, the Negro Department would have a secretary—that is, an executive officer—and a committee.

"Their work will be to carry forward the evangelical work among the colored people. They will take up the question of mission schools, church schools, and higher schools, such as Huntsville, and will look after them. They will look after the publishing of such literature as will be best adapted to the people. In fact, they will take into consideration all branches of the work."[27]

In expressing his hearty support for creation of the new department, J. K. Humphrey of New York commented that it addressed a need he had begun thinking about four years before:

"It is a strange coincidence—yet it is not strange, because the time is near when we shall all see eye to eye—that four years ago I felt in my soul that something ought to be done in this line to advance the work among the Negro race. We have almost eleven million people. I am thankful to God that the time has come when the brethren are moving in this direction."[28]

It does not seem coincidental that it was about four years before, in 1905, that Sheafe suggested to him the possibility of breaking away from the denomination.

Other comments from the floor reflected strong majority support from those on the front lines of the Black work. Thomas H. Branch, for example, who had served in Africa as well as the United States, believed the department would remove the hindrances that had limited the church's growth among American Blacks. "Our hands have been tied," he said with reference to the fact that the extensive efforts of recent years had brought the Black membership to only about 1,000. "Now this department will loosen our hands so we can work for our own people, and if you do not pass it, you will tie up our feet as well as our hands."[29]

Sydney Scott, however, one of the primary drivers for change, now expressed serious reservations about whether the department would really place greater freedom and responsibility in the hands of Black ministers in conducting the work for their own people. He spoke frankly about why this was a crucial issue. "In the South our people are losing confidence in the white man," he said. "It is just as well to handle this question without gloves." Thus, he declared, "If this departmental work is carried out on a plan that will give a just representation to the Negro churches, then I say 'Amen' to the plan. If it will be one-sided, then I say 'No' in the loudest tone."[30]

If he had been allowed to peer nine years into the future but no further, Scott surely would have pronounced the North American Negro Department a sham. Not only did White ministers head the department during these years—they dominated the decision-making committees.[31] But he and the other Black preachers who cast their lot with the denomination had, with their eyes open, placed "truth" ahead of "color," while pressing forward with all vigor in the gradualist path to making the real truth about race relations a living reality. In time, the creation of the North American Negro Department would prove to be an important landmark in that long path.

---

[1] SS to AGD, Feb. 8, 1907, GCA.

[2] GCC minutes, Feb. 13, 1907, GCA.

[3] SS to AGD, Feb. 18, 1907, GCA.

[4] SS to AGD, Jan. 30, 1907, GCA.

[5] AGD to SS, Feb. 4, 1907, GCA.

[6] SS to AGD, Jan. 24, Feb. 27, 1908, GCA.

[7] SS to AGD, Feb. 27, 1908.

[8] LCS to SS, Jan. 14, 1908, GCA.

[9] AGD to SS, Mar. 2, 1908, GCA.

[10] SS to AGD, Jan. 14, 1909, GCA.

[11] SS to AGD, Feb. 4, 1909, GCA.

[12] WHG to AGD, Oct. 14, 1908, GCA.

[13] AGD to WHG, Oct. 28 and Nov. 4, 1908, GCA.

[14] AGD to WHG, Oct. 28, 1908.

[15] I. H. Evans to AGD, July 26, July 29, July 30, Aug. 2, Aug. 7, 1908, GCA.

[16] AGD to I. H. Evans, Aug. 3, 1908, GCA.

[17] "Our Churches in Washington, D.C.," Oct. 19, 1908, *Manuscript Releases*, vol. 4, pp. 32, 33.

[18] AGD to WHG, Nov. 23, 1908, GCA.

[19] LCS to AGD, Oct. 29, 1908, GCA.

[20] AGD to WHG, Nov. 23, 1908.

[21] AGD to WHG, Nov. 17, 1908, GCA; W. H. Green to AGD, Nov. 25, Dec. 20, 1908, GCA.

[22] AGD to WCW, May 25, 1906.

[23] WCW to MCS, June 7, 1908.

[24] MCS to WCW, June 25, 1908.

[25] SS to AGD, Jan. 14, 1909.

[26] "An Appeal in Behalf of the Work Among the Colored People," May 1909, GCA.

[27] "Twenty-sixth Meeting," GCB, May 30, 1909, pp. 209, 210.

[28] "Twenty-sixth Meeting," p. 210.

[29] "Thirty-fourth Meeting," GCB, June 1, 1909, p. 286.

[30] "Thirty-fourth Meeting," p. 286.

[31] Prior to the appointment of W. H. Green in 1918, the department was headed by A. J. Haysmer and C. B. Stephenson, respectively. Until 1913 the department had an all-White executive committee, with the other members of the full committee evenly divided along racial lines. After 1913 the committee size was reduced, and the executive committee eliminated. By 1915 the committee was evenly divided between Black and White members. See YB, 1910-1919 editions.

CHAPTER XXX

A MARRIAGE AND
AN OLIVE BRANCH

WITH THE DENOMINATION'S FIRST-EVER ministerial institute for Black workers scheduled to begin in just a week on the campus of the Oakwood Training School, A. J. Haysmer received disturbing news. As head of the North American Negro Department, Haysmer had overall responsibility for the institute that was to open on March 23, 1911. Now he learned that L. C. Sheafe was planning to attend.

"I am sure that his visit does not mean anything good for our work in its present stage and am perplexed to know just what to do," wrote Haysmer to A. G. Daniells. "You know [Sheafe] is a keen, slick fellow and can do a great deal of harm among our workers."[1]

Sheafe, however, had a loftier purpose for going to Oakwood than infiltrating the workers' institute. He was going to marry one of the workers. Lucy Parker Whetsel, a 35-year-old widowed schoolteacher and Bible worker from Florida, was one of six women out of a total of 34 participants appearing in a group photograph.[2]

LUCY PARKER WHETSEL

Sheafe's acquaintance with Lucy Whetsel began in Chattanooga, Tennessee, where he spent several weeks in 1898 and again in 1899 preaching in connection with the Helping Hand Mission. Lucy's husband, O. N. Whetsel, served as superintendent of the mission, which was connected with the Medical Missionary and Benevolent Association. The Whetsels then moved to Florida, where O. N. entered evangelistic ministry, leading to the establishment of at least three congregations. They had two children, Marguerite, probably born sometime between 1900 and 1904, and Arthur, born in 1905. When illness forced O. N. into retirement in the spring of 1906, George I. Butler credited his work with making the "colored work" in the Florida Conference "practically self-sufficient."[3]

Her husband died on Christmas Day 1906, after which L. P. Whetsel, as she identified herself in print, devoted herself to developing a mission school for impoverished children in Jacksonville under the auspices of the Southern Missionary Society. By the fall of 1910 the school that began with one pupil in her kitchen had grown to nearly 100 students, only a handful of them from Adventist homes.[4]

Daily attendance was not 100 percent, she acknowledged; if it were, some of the children would have to sit on the kitchen table. They had no desks and were dependent on donations for basic supplies. Even so, when M. C. Strachan paid a visit as field secretary for the Southeastern Union Mission, he was impressed with the educational pictures on the walls, as well as the "dainty little window curtains" and "running vines" that added "warmth and cheer."[5]

Despite the challenges and utter lack of personal means, Lucy, in language similar to that of her future second husband, declared "a perfect willingness to stand at my post of duty and help lift my people, whom I dearly love and for whom Christ died."[6] During the summer of 1910 she also assisted evangelist John W. Manns as a Bible worker for a tent series in Ocala that led to formation of a church of about 18 members.[7]

If Sheafe attended any of the institute meetings in 1911, or even came to the campus of the school on whose board he had served just a few years before, no surviving record so indicates. However, the *Gospel Herald*, now the publication of the Negro Department, did make brief mention of the marriage: "Our readers will be interested to read of the marriage of Mrs. L. P. Whetsel, recently of Florida, to Elder L. C. Sheafe of Washington, D.C."[8] The marriage certificate issued by Madison County, Alabama, bears the date March 27, 1911.

Brother Haysmer had to have known about the marriage plans, for it was a letter from L. P. Whetsel that alerted him about Sheafe's plans to be in Huntsville. His preoccupation with the potential dangers of Sheafe's presence among the ministers is understandable, though. The failure of the reconciliation attempts of 1908 left Sheafe and the People's church confirmed in the path of independence. In fact, their most significant attempt at forming a broader association of churches probably took place in 1910.

Sheafe issued a call to "all members and friends from the length and breadth of this land" to come to Washington, D.C., for the "First General Assembly of the People's SDA Church," to be held May 18 to 22. As a result of the expanding influence and work of the People's church, he explained, "we are beset on all sides by urgent calls for helpers and workers." The calls were coming, not just from the United States but from various points throughout North and South America as well as "the islands of the sea." Thus, he said, a general assembly was now "necessary for us in order to adjust our methods to the widening field."[9]

As evidence of a broadening work, Sheafe claimed that the People's church had already sent out 10 workers from its base. That was in addition to "those we employ at home," implying that the pastor was not the only one on the church payroll. Unfortunately, no records have been preserved of the general assembly itself or its impact on the efforts of the People's church to establish wider connections. If they had been carried through and sustained, it would have amounted to an alternative Black Adventist denomination.

Sheafe's decision to woo and marry Lucy Whetsel may in itself have diverted him from pursuing that possibility. Be that as it may, his second marriage did constitute at least a tilt toward the possibility of reuniting with the denomination. His new bride spoke openly and with confidence about her intention to encourage him back to the fold.

THE OLIVE BRANCH

K. C. Russell referred to Lucy's influence in explaining to A. G. Daniells his rather bold decision to accept an invitation to speak for the Sabbath worship service at the People's church on February 3, 1912. Russell no longer functioned as chair of the District of Columbia Evangelical Committee. That special instrument of direct General Conference oversight had gone out of existence in 1909 when the District of Columbia Conference was created to bring the Washington-area churches into the regular governance structure of the denomination. But, other than Daniells, Russell was the church official with whom Sheafe had worked most closely, and he remained at the General Conference as head of the Religious Liberty Association. So he was the one to whom Sheafe turned in extending, as Russell put it, an "olive branch."

Daniells was in Texas at the time, and though Russell had consulted with the other leading brethren before accepting the invitation, he expected that the president would be "a little surprised" to find out that he had preached at Sheafe's church. Along with L. P. Sheafe's pledge to influence her husband to rejoin the organized work, Russell cited in his explanation an example of how that influence was brought to bear on the foremost concern in Daniells' mind—A. T. Jones and his antiorganization doctrines. It seems that Sheafe had agreed to have the People's church choir sing for some meetings Jones was holding in the city, but, after consulting with his wife, called off the choir's participation.

More than that, Sheafe had repudiated Jones's "extreme views against organization." According to Russell, Sheafe "told Jones one time after a drastic sermon had been delivered in his church against organization that his sermon was no help to his people; for they obtained the idea that Jones taught that it was unnecessary to belong even to a local church." Russell made the obvious point that such teachings would be "suicidal even to Sheafe's organization."

At the Sabbath service Russell found a full church and a receptive spirit. The congregation's response had not been coached in advance, for they did not know he was to preach until he arrived. He felt the Lord's help with his preaching, and the hearts of the people "seemed touched," he reported, "as many were in tears."

Russell assured Daniells that he "did not fall all over" Sheafe, and was careful with his words. But he thought that Sheafe's "friendly advance is at least a cloud as large as a man's hand, indicating a desire to get back into line," and thus, "I tried to respond in a Christian and friendly way to his apparent desire to get closer to us."[10]

The promising breakthrough indeed led to no hasty action. It took more than a year to bring the protracted drama to a conclusion.

Meanwhile, Sheafe did not simply bide his time. He pushed forward with a slowly developing plan for broadening the wholistic ministry of the People's church that appears to have originated soon after the break with the General Conference. Early in 1908 Sheafe began acquiring property in Fairmount Heights, just east of the District line in Prince George's County,

Maryland. A cooperative project to establish a self-governing community in which Black families could acquire reasonably priced land and homes had been underway in Fairmount Heights since 1903. Some of Washington's most accomplished Black citizens joined in the venture, including the educator Francis P. Cardoza and architect William Sidney Pitman, whose wife, Portia, was the daughter of Booker T. Washington.[11]

According to the Washington *Bee*, Sheafe envisioned "extensive improvements" on the church's Fairmount Heights property and made several visits to the community in 1912. More specifically, the paper, crediting the preacher with "doing excellent Christian service in Washington and elsewhere," reported that he intended to establish a home for the aged. Lucy joined her husband for at least two of these visits, providing piano accompaniment with "telling effect" when "great crowds" came out to hear him sing and preach for an afternoon service at the community's Methodist Episcopal Church on Sunday, August 18.[12]

Before he could carry them much further, though, Sheafe's plans for Fairmount Heights were overtaken the following spring by rather rapid developments that finally restored his connection with the General Conference.

W. H. GREEN'S CAUTIONARY MEMORANDUM

W. H. Green took an important role in bringing the process to culmination, having won confidence from the General Conference brethren by his handling of the mediation attempt in 1908. But now, four years later, Green held a quite different view of his former mentor, and looked upon the prospect of Sheafe's return to the denomination with considerable skepticism. At least two and half of those years he had spent in Washington, engaged in direct battle against Sheafe's influence, and that experience shaped his new perspective.

Green returned to the city in October 1909, taking up the work M. C. Strachan had begun at the Fifth church. In the year since Strachan's departure in 1908, the congregation had grown considerably through the efforts of interim workers. Under the circumstances, it is impressive that under Green's leadership the membership increased to approximately 50. This was despite, in his words, the "errors that have been and are still being proclaimed by the enemies of our message."[13]

That opposition could easily refer to Sheafe and his church. This was difficult, but he expected it. However, he may also have had First church in mind as a source of opposition. His assignment from the conference put him in charge of the "colored work" throughout the District, but since First church still resisted the racial classification, they did not acknowledge his pastoral authority.

Still, the problems that First church was creating were small compared to the continued resistance from within the General Conference Committee to making the major investment in the work for Washington's large and influential Black population so thoroughly warranted by the multiple challenges and vast opportunity. The only fully loyal Black Adventist congregation in the nation's capital still, after five years, had no church building.

Green's perplexities, of course, stemmed in part from the General Conference's "watchful waiting" policy with regard to Sheafe. Now, just at the time Green's work in Washington was coming to an end in 1912, Sheafe's return suddenly became a much-rumored possibility once again, and with it, many questions about what would happen to the project called Fifth church, to which he had just devoted two and a half years of extraordinarily difficult labor.

This near-Byzantine backdrop brings out some of the remarkable features in a statement that Green addressed to denominational leaders sometime in 1912 or early 1913 at the latest, concerning the possibility of Sheafe and the People's church returning to the denominational fellowship. His unsparing depiction of Sheafe contrasts sharply with the portrayal he gave four years previously.

Green charged Sheafe with implementing a sinister strategy as soon as he built a strong following "wedded more to himself than to the real message (with a few exceptions)." He designed to "prejudice them against the brethren and the Spirit of Prophecy," and thereby "more firmly hold them in his wiles," so that if and when the time came for him to withdraw from the denomination, they would be well disposed to follow him. Furthermore, far from the receptivity he reported four years earlier, Green now stated that Sheafe had "branded" the Spirit of Prophecy "as a fraud," adding with emphasis, "I *do not think he has changed that view.*"

In cultivating this antagonism toward the organizational and charismatic pillars of authority in the Adventist Church, claimed Green, Sheafe had produced in the People's church "children of hatred to the organized work and the Spirit of Prophecy, twofold more children of hell than himself." Then he passed on, without substantiation, lurid allegations of "vile heresies" and "gross immoralities" circulating about "the elder and others." As for the second Mrs. Sheafe's efforts toward reconciliation, Green believed that in this she was motivated more by personal desires than by "real love of truth."

Before getting to his final assessment as to what should be done about the renewed possibility of Sheafe's return, Green made one more point: Sheafe was not the denomination's main problem in regard to the "colored work" in Washington. The problem was failure to devote the needed attention and resources to developing a positive work. Since the beginning of his work in the city, said Green, he had not feared Sheafe's influence. And the denomination need not fear it either, provided "it acts wisely toward the colored people." The church's "greatest foes are now in our own ranks," he added. And, by implication, he attributed to these the "most lamentable situation" that obtained in Washington. In other words, the key to success was truly to get behind the kind of work that he, and Strachan before him, had attempted to do.

By castigating Sheafe and his church in quite pejorative terms and contending that the denomination did not need to win back his favor in order to succeed in Black Washington, Green appeared to be building toward a resounding recommendation against moving forward with reconciliation. After the charges of evil conspiracy, outright opposition to the Spirit of Prophecy, and worse against "the elder," the logical conclusion would be a sharp warning against the possibility of good-faith negotiation with such a duplicitous, manipulative character. Better to resist the suspicious overtures from the Sheafe camp and throw everything into making the Fifth church, to which Green had devoted such patient, arduous labors, the center of the work.

A smaller-minded man might have proceeded to just such a conclusion. But W. H. Green's statement undergoes a striking change in tone as he proceeds to recommendations on what should be done if Sheafe and his church desired to return to the denomination. It is as if he has set aside the personal feelings of righteous indignation engendered by the struggles of the past two years to consider the matter in the light of the wider interests of the cause. Nothing, it turns out, that he has said about Sheafe in the rest of the document need stand in the way of receiving him back into the denominational fellowship if he will "come in good faith." To give evidence of genuine "good faith," Green proposed three criteria that Sheafe should meet:

He should acknowledge "that his course was wrong in leaving the organized work"; "that he returns because he believes such a course was and is wrong, which means finally eternal ruin and death to him and his followers"; "that being thus fully convinced, he returns to fully live out and proclaim the whole message in harmony with the organized work and the Spirit of Prophecy, and that he will firmly declare the same to others."

Green added a recommendation that Sheafe move to another field so that a new pastor could give the People's church "wise and patient instruction" in "the real *message*."

In sum, despite his skepticism about the motives of both Sheafe and his wife, Green urged that "every effort should be put forth for them and all the church to have them return to the organized work."[14]

---

[1] K. C. Russell, "The Huntsville Ministerial Institute," *Gospel Herald*, May 1911, p. 34. A. J. Haysmer to AGD, Mar. 16, 1911, GCA.

[2] *Gospel Herald*, May 1911, p. 36.

[3] George I. Butler, "An Occasion of Great Regret," *Gospel Herald*, June 1906, p. 24; George I. Butler, "Camp Meetings in the Southern Union," *Review*, Nov. 9, 1905, p. 18; YB 1907, p. 167.

[4] Mrs. L. P. Whetsel, "Letter and Appeal From Florida," *Gospel Herald*, January 1908, pp. 2, 3; "An Encouraging Report," *Gospel Herald*, July 1909, p. 3; "Jacksonville, Florida," *Gospel Herald*, December 1910, p. 84.

[5] M. C. Strachan, "Southeastern Union Mission News and Notes," *Gospel Herald*, February 1911, p. 10.

[6] "An Encouraging Report."

[7] J. W. Manns, "Orlando, Florida," *Gospel Herald*, August 1910, p. 52.

[8] T. H. Jeys, "Oakwood School Notes," *Gospel Herald*, May 1911, p. 35.

[9] Lewis C. Sheafe, "The First General Assembly of the People's SDA Church," circular letter, 1910[?], GCA.

[10] KCR to AGD, Feb. 5, 1912, GCA.

[11] Real Estate Transfers, Washington *Times*, Feb. 12, 1908, p. 12; Fairmount Heights municipal Web site, http://www.mdmunicipal.org/cities/index.cfm?townname=fairmountheights (accessed Dec. 31, 2009); "United Citizens' Association Officers Installed," *Bee*, Aug. 24, 1912, p. 5.

[12] "Fairmount Heights," *Bee*, June 1, 1912, p. 5; "Liberty! Freedom!! Union!! Now and Forever—One and Inseparable," *Bee*, June 22, 1912, p. 5; "Churches," in the "Fairmount Heights" column, *Bee*, Aug. 24, 1912, p. 8.

[13] W. H. Green, "Washington, D.C.," *Review*, Jan. 12, 1911, pp. 16, 17, and "Work Among the Colored People of the District of Columbia," *Review*, Jan. 25, 1912, pp. 16, 17.

[14] W. H. Green, "Brief Statement of the Situation Among Colored Seventh-day Adventists in Washington," c. 1912, GCA.

CHAPTER XXXI

RETURN FROM MIDIAN

A DRAMATIC, EMOTION-FILLED SCENE unfolded as the work of a committee giving final consideration to the teachings of A. T. Jones during the General Conference session of 1909 reached its conclusion. According to one observer, A. G. Daniells, pleading with Jones to set aside the past and reunite with the movement, extended his hand across the table, saying, "Come, Brother Jones, come." Jones haltingly moved his hand toward Daniells' before finally pulling it back, declaring, "No! No!"[1]

At the 1913 General Conference session, Lewis Sheafe grasped the proffered hand of the General Conference president. Documentation is sketchy for the process that led to an agreement prior to the public scene of reconciliation, but it proceeded roughly along the lines of Green's proposal.

"I can honestly say that I have always deplored the separation," Sheafe wrote to the General Conference Committee on April 12, 1913. After six years the letter finally signaled a decisive change in direction. Rather than free his church to spearhead the advance of Adventism in Black America, he recognized that independence generated conflict crippling to both sides.

"I am convinced that the cause in which we are interested, for which we have labored, has suffered by the separation. The effort of the People's SDA Church in this city has been neutralized, to a great extent, and no doubt this has been true of the work of the conference. I am sure that a united effort could avail much, and would testify to the power and glory of our God."

Whatever transpired since he extended an "olive branch" through

K. C. Russell 14 months before remained behind the scenes. His congregation, Sheafe said, knew nothing about his decision. He thought it better first to meet with the General Conference brethren, "not to discuss our differences, but to drop the tangle, and lock heart and hand in the work of closing up the message, and to decide on the best and most feasible way of bringing about the union."[2]

Daniells responded with a note assuring him "that we feel most friendly, and we rejoice that there is prospect of our all being united again in this great cause."[3] Soon afterward Daniells, along with W. T. Knox, vice president for North America and General Conference treasurer, and J. L. McElhany, president of the District of Columbia Conference, met with Sheafe to work out the details. Sheafe would present a public apology, along with a petition from the People's church to reunite with the denomination at the General Conference session scheduled to open the following month in Takoma Park. The preacher would also accept a call to work in another city, yet to be determined.

Sheafe in effect conceded to Daniells' preconditions that he had adamantly refused to consider in previous discussions. He no longer demanded to see action before pledging renewed loyalty to the organized work. He was now willing to trust first. However, as he understood it, advance promises were made, specific promises upon which he based his willingness to "drop the tangle" and reunite with the denomination so that the promises could be fulfilled.

In an account published four years later Sheafe recalled that early in 1913 an elder "high in authority" at the General Conference implored him to reconnect with the denomination and thereby remove the obstacle that stood in the way of the expenditure of the $7,000 currently on reserve for "work among the colored people of the District of Columbia." The church leader, said Sheafe, presented to him a rationale that contained assurances:

"We are planning to do with this money just what you have wanted us to do all these years. By your standing out of the conference connection, you are defeating the very thing you want for your people; that is, schools and treatment rooms. Now if you would return, we stand ready to go right ahead with the work in Washington for your people, using this money to further the work."

Later a conference president told him that $1,600 was on hand toward providing a building for the Fifth church. But if the People's church building with its abundant room could be incorporated into the conference work, it made little sense to invest in a new one. "So, Brother Sheafe," he said, "if you were with us we would pay the sixteen hundred dollars on the debt of the 10th and V streets church property, thereby doing what you have been asking us to do."[4]

In Sheafe's mind, then, his return to the denomination was more than a simple act of contrition and submission. The element of quid pro quo remained, even though he was now willing to do his part without first having the "payoff" in his hand.

Regardless of these considerations, the proceedings on the morning of May 30 at the twenty-fourth meeting of the 1913 General Conference session must have been moving. L. R. Conradi, vice president for the European Division and chair of the meeting, called Elder Daniells forward to make a statement. After briefly summarizing the events of the past decade involving Sheafe, People's church, and their decision to withdraw from the organization, Daniells declared, "I am very happy to tell you this morning that our brethren, after these years of observation and experience, have concluded that they do not want to stand apart any longer."

He also spoke of the "assurance" felt by denominational representatives who had met with the People's church during the past month. Later in the proceedings he would also assure those assembled that the church would be coming into "conference relationship" just as any other church and that Sheafe, returning to service on the same basis as other ministers, stood ready "to labor anywhere as the providence of God might indicate." At this point he asked Sheafe to come forward and read the letter sent by the People's church to the General Conference Committee a few days before.

Before doing so, Sheafe gave a personal testimony that both acknowledged his failure of leadership and expressed renewed confidence that God was leading the denominational cause. In the Adventist message he had seen, and still saw, the path to the liberation of his oppressed people. Like the youthful Moses, he had acted rashly, trying to jump ahead of God's plan.

"I want to say this morning that I feel I am in the house of my friends.

It has been eighteen years since this blessed message came to me. I believed it then to be the message of God, and I have believed it ever since to be the message of God. I saw in it wonderful possibilities for my people. I had no special personal aims or ambitions, but I felt that this message could do so much for my people; and in the various conferences that I have been privileged to attend that has been the one fact and thought before me. I feel that possibly this has been true—that, like Moses of old, when he came out and saw the Egyptian ill-treating the Hebrew, you remember he took off his coat and rolled up his sleeves and pitched in to deliver Israel himself. He was forty years ahead of God, and therefore God had to put him in the mountains tending sheep to teach him a lesson. God had a thought for Israel and for the Hebrews deeper, grander than Moses had, and afterward God called him out and used him wonderfully in leading his people forward."

Even during the time of separation, said Sheafe, as he pondered the situation he realized, "This message of truth has made us what we are. It will not pay for us to depart from its principles." So he had continued all along trying to proclaim the Adventist message. But now, he said, in a thorough and serious reevaluation of their status, the People's church voted on May 21 to send the following message to the General Conference Committee:

"After more than six years of separation from conference connection, having prayerfully reconsidered our action, we are convinced that the separation was a sad mistake, for which we are heartily sorry. We have earnestly sought and obtained forgiveness from our heavenly Father, and do here and now acknowledge our fault to you.

"We are in full accord with the teachings, doctrines, and polity of the Seventh-day Adventists of the United States of America. Therefore we desire to unite with you to help close up this glorious message of love and mercy. Our earnest prayer is that Heaven may continually smile on this union."

Here was the unequivocal expression of repentance and affirmation of denominational *polity*, alongside doctrines, that Daniells and mediators such as Scott and Green deemed essential. After a motion was introduced in favor of the General Conference Committee's recommendation to receive the letter "with joy" and refer it "for definite, formal action to the

District of Columbia Conference," Sheafe again rose to speak:

"I wish to express my hearty appreciation and thanks to the brethren for this cordial acceptance of our word, and we hope to be able in the future to demonstrate by our lives and actions the sincerity of the step that we have taken in asking for a place with you in this great work. And our earnest and sincere prayer shall be that God may further his cause and may hasten the glad day when all these differences and misunderstandings shall have passed away, and God himself will wipe the tears from the faces of his people and gather them into one family, where there will be no more separation, no more severed ties, no more misunderstandings arising to wound our hearts nor his people. May God ever guide us."

After further remarks from Daniells and a congregational singing of "Praise God, from whom all blessings flow," several of Sheafe's ministerial brethren testified to their joy and pledged their support. "I believe this move of Brother Sheafe has lifted the cloud over of the camp of Ham," said Sydney Scott, who pledged to unite with Sheafe "as a brother, and pull with him in the same traces to carry this glorious gospel to its full triumph."

Sheafe's stand "will be a means of raising a song of jubilee throughout the Negro constituency of this denomination," added W. D. Forde, under whose leadership the Shiloh church in Chicago was making rapid advances.

John Manns, then laboring with similar results in Savannah, Georgia, noted that he frequently encountered questions about Sheafe in his work, and was therefore "glad . . . [to be] able to carry the good news back to the state of Georgia."

J. K. Humphrey, not for the first nor the last time at a General Conference session, but in the most direct way ever, spoke briefly of the profound impact that the Sheafe crisis made on him, as well as its broad significance for the Adventist cause.

"No one present, probably, felt more keenly than I did when Brother Sheafe and his church separated themselves from the conference connection, and no one felt more keenly the influence and impress it had over the entire country. I believe this step will be one of greater spiritual advancement. And I believe it will mean greater impetus to our work among the Negroes in this country."

W. H. Green, J. O. Miller, H. W. Cottrell, and others also registered their approval, as did A. J. Haysmer, who welcomed Sheafe "with open arms" on behalf of the North American Negro Department. When question on the motion finally was called, it received approval from the entire congregation "by a rising vote."[5]

Sheafe warmed hearts further with musical solos at the conference, including two at the "Farewell Missionary Service" on Sabbath afternoon, June 7. After one of these, Daniells drew "Amens" by commenting that while the convocation was rejoicing in the reports coming from all around the world, "we should not forget to rejoice that Brother Sheafe and his people are united with us today." He was praying, Daniells added, that the preacher "will be baptized with the Holy Spirit, to reach thousands of the colored people in this country."

Sheafe responded:

"I am truly glad to be in this assembly of this people throughout this conference session. My heart and mind go back to the early days of my experience in this message, and to the kindly attitude the people held toward me in unfolding this word to us. I see men and women here from the North and the South, from the East and the West, to whom God has permitted us to break the bread of life; and my heart goes out in praise and thanksgiving to our Heavenly Father for his loving-kindness and his tender mercy that that he has spared us to again mingle our hearts and voices, and our activities, and consecrate our energies with yours, in the proclamation of this message, that it may be hastened to the close."

Granted the mixture of motives and likelihood of only partially suppressed suspicions all around, who, at that moment, could have doubted that great things lay ahead as Lewis Sheafe resumed his fully Seventh-day Adventist apostolate to Black America?

---

[1] G. R. Knight, *From 1888 to Apostasy*, p. 247.

[2] LCS to GCC, Apr. 12, 1913, GCA.

[3] AGD to LCS, Apr. 17, 1913, GCA.

[4] *Experience of the People's SDA Church*, pamphlet, n.d., Document File 53, EGWE. Though undated, the content solidly establishes that the pamphlet was issued in 1917.

[5] "Twenty-fourth Meeting," GCB, June 1, 1913, pp. 212, 213.

SECTION SIX:
"One Minister Who Thinks for Himself"

"Reverend Sheafe is one of the greatest Bible scholars in the United States, and one minister who thinks for himself."

—W. CALVIN CHASE, EDITOR
WASHINGTON *BEE*
AUGUST 26, 1916

"Mr. Lewis Sheafe is an apostate of the most dangerous sort."

—CIRCULAR LETTER ISSUED FROM
SEVENTH-DAY ADVENTIST
WORKERS' INSTITUTE
HUNTSVILLE, ALABAMA
JANUARY 9, 1917

CHAPTER XXXII

SHIFTING GROUND
IN SOUTHERN CALIFORNIA

LOS ANGELES BOOMED WITH OPPORTUNITY that beckoned Americans of all stripes in the early twentieth century with the bright promise of a new beginning. They came by the thousands every year, swelling the population from a little more than 100,000 at the turn of the century to 575,000 by 1920.[1] The Sheafe family became part of the tide after a North American Division committee vote at the Fall Council held in October 1913 confirmed that the elder's work would begin anew in southern California.

Coinciding with the hopeful turn to a new phase of ministry, new life blessed the Sheafe family. Lucy gave birth to a daughter, Doris Elizabeth, on October 14, 1913.

During the transitional period between the close of the General Conference in June and the move west in December, the details of reconnecting the People's church to the conference system had to be worked out. Because the sources of past conflict did not disappear overnight, this became a contentious matter.

The local conference into which the church was to be incorporated did not exist when the People's church withdrew in 1907. The procedural challenge for the small District of Columbia Conference, formed in 1909, involved bringing a new congregation into its fellowship, most of whose members had been baptized as Seventh-day Adventists and still thought of themselves as such, even though the church had repudiated conference governance. Some had been baptized after the separation.

Even more difficult, what should be done with the smaller Fifth church when the reason for its existence—the withdrawal of the People's church—no longer existed? It had no church building, but did have a sense of identity as loyalists, as contrasted with the formerly rebellious People's church.

The General Conference brethren stood nearby, of course, to guide and assist the local conference. They almost certainly took a strong role in this matter, not only because of its importance and unique history, but also because the D.C. Conference president, J. L. McElhany, resigned at the end of June, taking a call to New York, leaving the conference without a president for the next three months.[2]

Given the stand that the members of the Fifth church had taken, and the criticism directed at them both from the People's church and the First church, they were not likely to look favorably on simply dissolving and being absorbed into the People's church. Of even greater concern to denominational leaders, the attitudes that contributed to the separation remained alive to some extent in the People's church, and could be the source of future trouble, even with Sheafe off the scene. The fact that 11 of the members present on May 21 voted against rejoining the denomination (with 82 in favor)[3] made simply accepting the congregation back en masse problematic.

The best solution, it seemed to them, was to disband both churches at the same time. Then, a single new congregation, housed at the property on Tenth and V streets, would be formed, with a 15-point affirmation of faith used as the basis for membership.

Sheafe opposed the plan. If followed, the People's church would cease to exist, with admittance to membership and selection of officers in the new entity effectively controlled by conference officials. It smacked of the hierarchical "lordship" over the flock of God to which he objected. "I do not propose to let the leaders drive an ice wagon over my congregation," someone reported him saying.

Apparently unaware that Sheafe had warned his congregation against the plan, two teams of leading brethren set out on the same day, one to the Fifth church and one to the People's church, to implement it. The Fifth church, though not without some resistance, duly voted itself out of existence. The People's church, however, refused to cooperate, turning down the proposal by a vote of 55 to 25.[4]

It is not clear exactly how matters developed from there. Cooperation between Sheafe and J. Marion Campbell, who replaced Green at the Fifth church, may have helped smooth things over. The two preachers conducted an evangelistic series together that summer. A *Review and Herald* report mentioned it as a "strong . . . effort," giving no further details other than that it was the only Adventist tent series in the city during 1913.[5]

When Sheafe left for California, Campbell became pastor of the People's church. The congregation's return to denominational connection was not finalized until February 15, 1914, at the sixth annual session of the D.C. Conference. Campbell reported that "the Fifth church had very generally combined its membership with that of the People's church." He then presented the church's request for membership in the conference; by a unanimous vote it was "received into fellowship with the sister churches."[6]

A GOOD WORK ALREADY BEGUN

Rarely, if ever, did anyone take the Adventist medical missionary ideal to urban America as successfully as Jennie L. Ireland did to the Black population of Los Angeles during the first two decades of the twentieth century. That population, according to U.S. Census figures for Los Angeles County, grew from more than 6,000 in 1900 to nearly 19,000 in 1920.[7] Many settled in an ethnically diverse section of land between Watts and downtown Los Angeles known as the Furlong Tract. Jennie Ireland's initiative found favorable response there, beginning with postal worker Theodore Troy, who agreed to her giving a Bible study in his home.

A nurse trained at Battle Creek Sanitarium as well as a Bible worker, Sister Ireland led home classes in "hygienic cooking" and basic nursing treatments in addition to Bible studies. After two years of work along these lines, a church was organized in 1908 with 28 members. The Furlong church was the first Black Adventist congregation established west of Kansas City; from the families that formed its core came people who made stellar contributions both to the Adventist cause and the wider society.[8]

Troy's son, Owen, building on Jennie Ireland's methods, became one of the premiere leaders of Adventism in the twentieth century as a pastor, evangelist, radio broadcaster, musician, scholar, and administrator. His equally talented wife, Ruby, and her brother, Arna, were the children of a former jazz musician and brick mason from Louisiana, Paul Bontemps, and his wife, Maria (who died in 1908). Paul helped construct Adventist church buildings in California and then entered the ministry to build up the congregations as well. Arna became an educator and celebrated author, one of the leading figures in the Harlem Renaissance. Ruth Temple, who joined the new church with her mother and sister, became the first Black female physician in Los Angeles and a noted pioneer of public health measures for the city's neediest classes.[9]

The new converts joined in the small group evangelism, and Amy Temple, Ruth's mother, became a Bible worker alongside Jennie Ireland. By 1913 the membership neared 100. All this had been accomplished without an ordained minister or public tent effort, so hopes ran high for even greater progress through Sheafe's ministry. As the opening of Sheafe's first series of meetings neared, Sister Ireland wrote *Gospel Herald* editor T. H. Jeys with almost palpable anticipation: "The church has been working for years, getting the truth before the people by means of tracts and papers, and now all is ready for this public effort."[10]

On their way west the Sheafes stopped for nearly a week of ministry and visitation in the Chicago area. Sheafe spoke at the Shiloh church and two other Adventist churches, and at the sanitarium in suburban Hinsdale, headed by Dr. David Paulson. From Hinsdale Paulson led a network of city missions that at one time included the Helping Hand Mission in Chattanooga, with which both Lewis and Lucy had been connected.[11]

After spending their first Sabbath in California with new friends in San Francisco, the family arrived in Los Angeles on December 7, taking up residence at 1723 E. 51st Street. "Had we not known it was winter, we would have called it April or May," the elder commented.

The church was eager for public meetings to begin as soon as possible, and quickly found "an almost ideal hall" at 1207 Central Avenue, near downtown, convenient to two street car lines and close to a large concentration of the city's Black population. The meetings ran from January 11 to March 8, with good attendance, despite a stretch of bad weather. "Fifty signed the covenant to keep all God's holy law," Sheafe reported.[12]

As he had in Washington, Sheafe gained opportunities to speak in churches of other denominations and at other settings of importance in the Black community, such as the colored branch of the YMCA and the Forum, "an organization of progressive colored people." Much like Washington's Bethel Literary and Historical Society, the Forum was Black Los Angeles' leading venue for presentations on the issues of the day and high-class musical performances. Sheafe and Amy Temple "furnished the usual large gathering of citizens . . . with a splendid program," said the *California Eagle*, the major Black newspaper in Los Angeles, regarding the February 8 meeting of the Forum. Such speaking engagements, Sheafe pointed out to readers of the *Review and Herald*, help "advertise our work" and gain friends for the cause.[13]

Occasional references to Sheafe in the pages of the *Eagle* suggest that indeed he rapidly became widely known and well regarded in the community, though he did not draw the kind of coverage that he did from Washington's Black newspapers in 1902-1903. He was, for example, one of several ministers that editor Charlotta Bass called upon to help "save the flowers of our race" by supporting a petition against allowing women into clubs that serve alcoholic beverages. Another passing reference in a notice about an upcoming event mentioned that Sheafe was "said by many to be the ablest minister in Los Angeles County."[14]

NEW CONGREGATIONS: BEREAN AND WATTS

Sheafe began a summer evangelistic series in Los Angeles on May 31, 1914, in a tent located on West 36th Street. A young schoolteacher who was completing ministerial training at Pacific Union College, Frank L. Peterson, "rendered good service" as tent master and in assisting with the music. After two months interest was just building to its height, but the meetings had to be suspended for the annual Southern California Conference camp meeting.[15] Reluctantly Sheafe closed the tent down and headed for Alhambra to join the other conference workers and meet his assignments in what the Los Angeles *Times* called "the largest tent city ever constructed in this part of the state."[16]

The crowd at the main "auditorium tent" surpassed the seating capacity of 5,000 at a temperance rally held on Sunday, August 9. Sheafe sang an original temperance song written by the Southern California Conference president, F. M. Burg. Then the speakers—among them Guy W. Wadsworth, superintendent of the California Dry Federation, and

WCTU lecturer Julia Phelps—summoned the audience to action against the evil forces of the liquor traffic in the upcoming November election.[17] On Wednesday Sheafe preached for the evening service, giving an "impassioned" message entitled "The Judgment," which "held the attention of the vast congregation," according to the Los Angeles *Times*.[18]

After camp meeting Sheafe and his coworkers attempted, with partial success, to regain the momentum of interest that had been generated by the summer evangelistic campaign by holding some follow-up meetings. Despite the schedule-related setback, the effort led to formation of a substantial new congregation. The Berean Seventh-day Adventist Church was organized on January 30, 1915, and formally admitted to the Southern California Conference the following month with 30 members.[19]

A new tent series in the fall of 1914, this one held at 9th and Hemlock streets, led to 15 new church members. John King, the first Black nursing graduate from the Adventist medical college in Loma Linda, assisted Sheafe in this effort, both with the music and, along with another nurse, Mildred Anderson, in health education. Through the exposure provided by these meetings, Sheafe gained opportunity to speak in the city and county prisons, much as he had in Washington, D.C.

Sheafe concluded this series, as he had the one in the summer, in a distinctive fashion that gives another brief glimpse of the special attention he paid to children in his ministry. He devoted the final service in each campaign to a program presented by children from the church and the neighborhood surrounding the tent. Both occasions, he said, brought much delight to "the many who packed the tent."[20]

In January 1915, as he reviewed these developments over the past year and looked to the year ahead, Sheafe declared, "I am wonderfully encouraged to 'go forward,' believing fully that the coming King *is* at the door, and that very soon the 'faithful unto death' shall receive the overcomer's reward."[21]

Along with his endeavors during 1914 in the heart of Los Angeles proper, Sheafe also began building on the very successful work of Jennie Ireland and Amy Temple in Watts, some six miles to the south. In 1915 Watts received greater priority in his evangelistic work.

A "branch" Sabbath school was already meeting on Sabbath afternoons in Watts when Sheafe arrived. He organized the group into a church of 17 members. They proceeded to build a house of worship, doing much of the construction themselves; Sheafe helped them bring the building project to completion. On Sabbath, May 8, 1915, the new conference president, B. E. Beddoe, and other leading ministers in the area joined Sheafe for a service dedicating the new sanctuary.[22]

With the building completed, Sheafe set out to build up the congregation. He baptized five new members on Sunday evening, June 6, and began a series of meetings a week later, using the recently completed church rather than a tent.[23] However, other matters soon overshadowed that effort.

TRIED OVER THE TESTIMONIES

After spending Sabbath, June 19, at the Berean SDA Church in Los Angeles, C. J. Boyd, the principal and business manager of the Oakwood Manual Training School, sent back a glowing report for publication in the *Gospel Herald*. At the church, which now had 37 members, Boyd saw much evidence of "good work being carried on" under the leadership of Elder and Mrs. Sheafe. He found "a room well filled with earnest and smiling faces, and a neat little house of worship, located in a nice residential district of the city." Then he gave a brief summary of Sheafe's overall work since coming to southern California, rejoicing at "the many evidences of God's care for his work in this growing city."

Boyd's cheerful observations betray no hint of the shadows of renewed controversy beginning to darken around the Sheafes. Perhaps he had not heard. Or perhaps he had, and tried to do something constructive by publishing a positive report.

A month later, 400 miles to the north, Ellen G. White died in her Elmshaven home. Enfeebled and bedridden after a fall on February 13 that fractured her hip, the 87-year-old visionary leader breathed her last on July 16, 1915.[24] Meanwhile, Lewis Sheafe's relationship with the Seventh-day Adventist denomination was beginning to unravel barely two years after its much-celebrated restoration. The same set of three connected issues that caused the split in the first place resurfaced. But this time, in the minds of denominational leaders, the authority of the recently deceased prophet's writings superseded church organization as the foremost issue.

It is difficult to pinpoint how and when the difficulty began. In part it involved conflict between Lewis and Lucy Sheafe on the one hand and the Bible workers, Jennie Ireland and Amy Temple, on the other. This probably began cropping up in mid-1914, for in an article written in December 1915 Ireland refers to "difficulties met during this past year and a half." Neither she nor the Pacific Union Conference president, E. E. Andross, who charged the Sheafes with inciting the antagonism, provided further detail.[25] It is not difficult to imagine, though, conflict between an existing female leader who had accomplished much and a strong-minded new minister used to taking full charge.

The far more explosive aspect, though, was Sheafe's inability to reconcile passages on race relations published in volume 9 of Ellen White's *Testimonies to the Church* with biblical principles, or indeed with things she herself had written previously on the topic. The material placed in the section of volume 9 entitled "Among the Colored People" (pp. 199-226) brings together portions of counsels written by Sister White at various times and under varying circumstances. The general thrust of the section is toward the necessity of adapting the church's work to racial segregation, where it was rigorously enforced. Individual statements along these lines, particularly when read in isolation from the contexts in which they were written, became the subject of considerable perplexity and misunderstanding.

However, volume 9 was not a new problem in 1915. It was published in 1909, well before 1913, when Sheafe must have in some way satisfied the leading brethren about his attitude toward the Spirit of Prophecy. Why it suddenly became a problem in 1915, when it wasn't one in 1913, is a question that the extant sources leave unanswered.

It takes very little stretch of the imagination, though, to see how passages from volume 9 could be the source of serious pastoral and evangelistic problems for the Sheafes as they sought to broaden the Adventist work in Los Angeles' progressive Black community. How to explain such statements as: "The colored people should not urge that they be placed on an equality with white people" (p. 214) and "Let white and colored people be labored for in separate, distinct lines, and let the Lord take care of the rest" (p. 210)?

These and other statements, if taken as eternal principles of divinely revealed truth, would be problematic in distinctive ways for Black Angelenos. They lived, as historian Douglas Flamming puts it, in "an oddly half-free environment." They found much greater freedom there than in the segregated South, and many greater opportunities than in the large Northern cities. Yet even in southern California they faced "patterns of everyday racism." Moreover, the relative advantages they enjoyed were continually vulnerable to demographic and political shifts brought about by rapid population growth. Though Southerners were a minority in the transplanted White population, their influence was strong, and the imposition of a more Southern model of segregation an ongoing danger.[26]

Almost all of the material on racial matters included in volume 9 was written in response to the harsh reality of the consolidation of hard-line White supremacist control throughout the South. Insistence by White Adventist leaders on the application of everything in volume 9 of the *Testimonies* to southern California could thus be seen as supporting a very real threat that Southern policies on race relations would gain strength in California. Such a linkage would surely create a formidable barrier to winning and holding the allegiance of Black Californians to the Adventist movement.

The specific chain of events that prompted Lewis and Lucy Sheafe to speak out on the matter is unknown. At any rate, in 1915 they took the controversial public stand that certain portions of volume 9 did not harmonize with biblical teaching on racial equality, and thus could not be regarded as inspired by the Holy Spirit.

Before the crisis reached the breaking point in September, a committee of Southern California Conference leaders met with the Sheafes on at least eight occasions. "We stated plainly that we believed in Sister White as having the gift of prophecy," said Sheafe. But he and his wife could not accept "those statements in the book [vol. 9] which to us do not at all harmonize with God's Word." In fact, they expressed doubt as to whether Ellen White herself even wrote them.[27]

To the conference leaders, this must have looked like the "pick-and-choose" approach associated with A. T. Jones that the denomination had decisively rejected just a few years before. A pamphlet issued by the General Conference Committee in 1906 had compared Jones's claim that *some* of Mrs. White's writings could not be regarded as inspired to the modernist "higher criticism" that subjected the Bible to similar dissection. The outcome of such an approach, said the pamphlet, would be to "break down all faith in all inspired writings."[28]

In line with this rationale, the conference leaders confronted the Sheafes with a stark choice: either "accept all of Mrs. White's testimonies as inspired of God, or reject all as error." Their acceptance of "the testimonies" insofar as they "could understand them to be in harmony with the Bible" but not as "infallible interpreters of the Scriptures" was unsatisfactory.[29]

In view of that, Sheafe proposed that he and his wife go on with their work and say nothing further about volume 9. But the conference leaders "objected to our silence," he said.[30]

While the authority of Ellen White's writings now became the flashpoint of controversy, that issue remained closely tied to the authority of church leadership. As in 1907, it was not so much a theory or model of church organization that Sheafe protested as the perception of heavy-handed authoritarianism on the part of church leaders—in particular an all-White hierarchy that he felt was using the Ellen White of "volume 9" to buttress patterns of racial discrimination throughout the denomination. The Sheafes felt that some of their meetings with conference officials were so devoid of "the spirit of brotherly kindness" that they "almost wondered if 'Ichabod' were not written over some of their heads."[31]

The mounting crisis reached a defining moment at a meeting, apparently organized by the Sheafes or those sympathetic to them, on September 1 at Conference Hall on 417 West 5th Street. Mrs. L. P. Sheafe took the podium and boldly declared, "From this night on no longer shall any man or set of men stand between me and my God. I am a Free Seventh Day Adventist."[32]

With the Sheafes thus having raised the banner of public protest, to what extent would the fledgling Black Adventist community in Los Angeles rally behind the charismatic couple? The three churches— Furlong, Watts, and Berean—were called together for meetings the following week with conference leaders, including E. E. Andross and E. W. Farnsworth, president and vice president, respectively, of the Pacific Union, and B. E. Beddoe, Southern California Conference president. After the first meeting, which did not conclude until well after midnight, the prospects did not look good to Andross, who observed that "the situation was very serious indeed." Toward the end of a second meeting of similar length, though, "we made some headway in uniting the hearts of the people," he said.

Then, after the Sabbath ended on September 11, L. C. and L. P. Sheafe met with the committee once again. The time had come for a final decision, Andross told them. The Sheafes felt a greater measure of "brotherly kindness" at this meeting than some of the others, for which they thanked the brethren. But they believed that the "conference authorities" had forced them "into a position where we had to withdraw or give up righteous principle." They tendered their resignations that night from employment in the Southern California Conference. They saw it as a step of faith into an uncertain future—to move ahead "as God directs and opens the way and hope to finally obtain the crown promised to those who are *faithful*'—not 'successful.'"[33]

It was not a sheer leap into the dark. Sheafe could be confident that the Berean congregation, the one formed as a direct result of his own evangelistic work, would back him up. The following Wednesday evening, September 15, that congregation voted resolutions to withdraw from the Southern California Conference and invite Sheafe to pastor them as an independent church.

"Whereas, We, the members and friends of the Berean Seventh Day Adventists of Los Angeles, California, accept the Bible alone as our supreme rule of faith and practice, and accept only such other writings as harmonize with the Bible; and whereas, the Southern California Conference of the Seventh Day Adventists teaches that to question or disbelieve any part of the 'Testimonies' grieves the Holy Spirit and will lead to the utter destruction of those who doubt or question them; and whereas the same 'Testimonies' teach discrimination against the colored race, to wit, 'So long were they [the colored people] under the curse of slavery that it is a difficult problem to know how they should now be treated' [vol. 9, p. 213]. 'It is Satan's plan to call minds to the study of the [color] line.' . . . 'The colored people should not urge that they be placed on an equality with white people' [pp. 213, 214]. 'White and colored people should be labored for in separate and distinct lines, and let the Lord take care of the rest' [p. 210]. 'Opportunities are continually presenting themselves in the southern states, and many wise

Christian colored men will be called to the work. But for several reasons white men should be chosen as leaders' [p. 202]; and whereas, the said denomination makes marked discrimination in school and sanitarium advantages against the colored people; and whereas Elder Lewis C. Sheafe and wife have resigned from the employ of the Southern California Conference of Seventh Day Adventists because they could not conscientiously accept the position taken by the denomination; therefore, be it resolved that the Berean Church of Seventh Day Adventists withdraw its membership from the conference, Seventh Day Adventists, because the denominational position of discrimination in teaching and practice is contrary to the plain teaching of Christ and His apostles.

"Resolved, That we extend to Elder Lewis C. Sheafe and wife our confidence and love, and that we cordially invite Elder Sheafe to accept the pastorate of the Berean Church of Free Seventh Day Adventists, pledging him our loyal support spiritually and financially to carry forward the great work of the third angel's message as God shall direct. And resolved, that we invite Christians of all and any nation or race to examine our position in the light of God's word, and that if they find us to be on good, safe and sane basis, to feel free to unite with us. Resolved, that equal rights, personal and religious, be accorded to all men of every race."[34]

---

[1] Historical Resident Population, City & County of Los Angeles, 1850 to 2000, Los Angeles Almanac, http://www.laalmanac.com/population/po02.htm (accessed Aug. 10, 2009).

[2] "Sixth Annual Session of the District of Columbia Conference," *Columbia Union Visitor,* Mar. 18, 1914, p. 1. Officers of the Columbia union conference, of which the D.C. Conference was a part, may also have been involved. However, the Union Conference, formed in 1907, was itself relatively new, and at that time more physically remote, with headquarters in Mount Vernon, Ohio.

[3] "Twenty-fourth Meeting," GCB, June 1, 1913, p. 213.

[4] A. F. Ballenger relates a sketchy account of the episode in "Notes by the Way," *Gathering Call,* May 1915, pp. 4, 5.

[5] T. E. Bowen, "Washington, D.C.," *Review,* June 25, 1914, p. 18.

[6] "Sixth Annual Session of the District of Columbia Conference (cont.)," *Columbia Union Visitor,* Mar. 25, 1914, p. 2.

[7] Historical Census Records of Ethnic Groups in Los Angeles County 1850 to 1960, Los Angeles Almanac, http://www.laalmanac.com/population/po20.htm (accessed Aug. 10, 2009).

[8] Jennie L. Ireland, "The Colored Work in Los Angeles," *Pacific Union Recorder,* Dec. 23, 1915, pp. 3, 4; W. S. Lee and Owen A. Troy, Sr., "Evangelistic Origin and Expansion in the Southern Area," *North American Informant,* September-October 1961, pp. 4, 5; L. B. Reynolds, *We Have Tomorrow,* pp. 175, 176.

[9] Reynolds, pp. 176-183; Douglas Flamming, *Black Los Angeles in Jim Crow America* (Berkeley: University of California Press, 2006), pp. 24, 25.

[10] "Note and Comment," *Gospel Herald,* Feb. 1914, p. 16.

[11] "News Here and There," *The Life Boat,* Jan. 1914, p. 28.

[12] "Two Good Reports From California," *Review,* Apr. 2, 1914, pp. 16, 17; "Note and Comment."

[13] "Two Good Reports"; untitled local news note, *California Eagle,* Feb. 14, 1914, p. 3.

[14] "Let Us Save the Flowers of Our Race," *California Eagle,* June 12, 1915, p. 3; "To Celebrate Abraham Lincoln's 106th Birthday," *California Eagle,* Jan. 23, 1915, p. 3.

[15] Lewis C. Sheafe, "Work for the Colored Population of Los Angeles, California," *Pacific Union Recorder,* Jan. 28, 1915, pp. 17, 18.

[16] "Big Tent City for Convention," Los Angeles *Times,* July 29, 1914, p. II8.

[17] Ernest Lloyd, "Camp Meeting Temperance Rally," *Pacific Union Recorder,* Aug. 27, 1914, pp. 5, 6.

[18] "Education Theme of Adventists," Los Angeles *Times,* Aug. 13, 1914, p. II8.

[19] "Work for the Colored Population of Los Angeles," p. 17; C. J. Boyd, "Los Angeles. California," *Gospel Herald,* August 1915, p. 7; "Southern California Conference Session," *Pacific Union Recorder,* Mar. 11, 1915, pp. 10, 11.

[20] "Work for the Colored Population of Los Angeles," p. 17.

[21] *Ibid.,* p. 18.

[22] *Ibid.,* p. 17; "Two Good Reports," p. 16; B. E. Beddoe, "With the Workers," *Pacific Union Recorder,* Mar. 25, 1915, p. 4; untitled news note, *Pacific Union Recorder,* May 13, 1915, p. 8.

[23] B. E. Beddoe, "Southern California News Items," *Pacific Union Recorder,* June 10, 1915, p. 3.

[24] Arthur L. White, *Ellen G. White: The Later Elmshaven Years* (Washington, D.C.: Review and Herald, 1982), vol. 6, pp. 418-431.

[25] Jennie L. Ireland, "The Colored Work in Los Angeles," p. 3; E. E. Andross to AGD, Sept. 14, 1915, GCA.

[26] Flamming, pp. 2-5, 10-14.

[27] LCS and wife to AGD, Oct. 26, 1915, GCA.

[28] See G. Land, *Adventism in America,* pp. 156-161.

[29] This paragraph is drawn from a brief article by A. F. Ballenger, who in turn drew on an account published in a short-lived newspaper, the Los Angeles *Post.* Ballenger saw parallels between the Sheafes' experience and his own expulsion from the Adventist ministry 10 years before, and thus was biased in their favor. But there does not seem to be any compelling reason to discount the accuracy of his summary of the newspaper article. "Elder Sheafe Outside the 'Organization,'" *Gathering Call,* October 1915, pp. 5, 6.

[30] LCS and wife to AGD, Oct. 26, 1915.

[31] *Ibid.*

[32] Lewis C. Sheafe and J. W. Manns, "Free Seventh Day Adventists Are Not Aunt Hager's Children," Savannah *Tribune,* May 27, 1916, p. 6.

[33] E. E. Andross to AGD, Sept. 14, 1915; LCS and wife to AGD, Oct. 26, 1915.

[34] Charles Alexander, "Seventh Day Adventist Lose Race Elder," Chicago *Defender,* Oct. 9, 1915, pp. 1, 5. The quotations from *Testimonies,* volume 9, are reproduced here as they appear with minor inaccuracies in the newspaper quotation of the Berean church resolutions.

CHAPTER XXXIII

THE "VOLUME 9" PUZZLE

THE "CHINESE PUZZLE TO THE FAIR-MINDED CHRISTIAN"—that is how Lewis Sheafe characterized volume 9 a few months after his resignation from the Southern California Conference.[1] Something similar could well be said of the overall status and function of Ellen White's writings in the Adventist Church at the time of its publication. A critical issue of defining significance throughout Adventist history, the nature and authority of those writings became a matter of particularly intensive and often confusing controversy during the first two decades of the twentieth century.

Satisfactory analysis of the issues revolving around race relations in volume 9, let alone the broader tangles over the authority of the Ellen White writings, would range far beyond the scope of this book.[2] Yet a responsible telling of Sheafe's story requires, at the least, drawing attention to the complexity surrounding his reaction against volume 9.

Though it was, of course, a defense of the authority of the Spirit of Prophecy, the "all or nothing" position of the aforementioned pamphlet of 1906 refuting A. T. Jones came close to some of the abuses of her writings that both Ellen White and W. C. White tried to combat, but with limited success. The latter took issue, for example, with one of his parents' closest associates, Stephen N. Haskell. Some church leaders, White wrote Haskell, "feel that one of the most serious difficulties in holding their brethren loyal to the Testimonies is the fact that a few men of age and experience insist upon pressing on them the theory of verbal inspiration which Mother does not stand for, which the General Conference does not stand for, which my father never stood for. Some have expressed the opinion to me that the extreme and extravagant positions taken by a few men, including yourself, are doing more to bring the shaking over the Testimonies than any other one element in the work."[3]

The "verbal inspiration theory" viewed all of the statements in Ellen White's writings as propositions produced by divine revelation, and thus infallibly true. W. C. White characterized this view as being held by "a few men," and not that of the General Conference. While it is true that carefully measured statements in official sources stopped short of attributing infallibility to Sister White's writings, treatment of them as such predominated in the actual practice of church life. Dr. David Paulson, for example, surpassed by few Adventists in intellectual sophistication, put it this way in 1906: "I was led to conclude and most firmly believe that *every* word that you ever spoke in public or private, that *every* letter you wrote under *any* and *all* circumstances, was as inspired as the ten commandments."[4]

This despite the fact that Ellen White had addressed abuses associated with the "infallible propositions" extreme 25 years earlier. In 1881 she wrote:

"We see those who will select from the testimonies the strongest expressions and, without bringing in or making any account of the circumstances under which the cautions and warnings are given, make them of force in every case. Thus they produce unhealthy impressions upon the minds of the people. There are always those who are ready to grasp anything of a character which they can use to rein up people to a close, severe test, and who will work elements of their own characters into the reforms. This, at the very outset, raises the combativeness of the very ones they might help if they dealt carefully, bearing a healthful influence which would carry the people with them. They will go at the work, making a raid upon the people. Picking out some things in the testimonies they drive them upon every one, and disgust rather than win souls. They make divisions when they might and should make peace."[5]

Addressing herself specifically to overzealous health reformers, Ellen White here rebukes at least three widespread tendencies in the use of her writings that seem quite pertinent to Lewis Sheafe's struggles in relation to volume 9: (1) arbitrary or unbalanced selectivity; (2) treating counsels given in particular, distinctive conditions as fundamental principles of general applicability; (3) heavy-handed, authoritarian application.

An article in the Chicago *Defender* that reported on the actions of the Berean church in 1915 provides a glimpse—though not much more—at the substance of Sheafe's case. His critique of volume 9, as it appears here, is rather strained and superficial. That may be in part because of the pressure—even then—of reducing complex matters to "sound bites" for the press. More fundamentally, though, it mirrors the widespread extremes and distortions in the use of Ellen White's writings noted above.

The article attributes to Sheafe the claim that the "Testimonies teach racial discrimination," with the following excerpts cited as evidence:

- "From Australia, across the broad waters of the Pacific, cautions were sent that every movement must be guarded, that the workers were to make no political speeches, and that the mingling of whites and blacks in social equality was by no means to be encouraged" (vol. 9, p. 206).
- "In regard to white and colored people worshiping in the same building, this cannot be followed as a general custom with profit to either party—especially in the South. The best thing will be to provide the colored people who accept the truth with places of worship of their own, in which they can carry on their services by themselves" (p. 206).
- "But for several reasons white men must be chosen as leaders" (p. 202).

The "the doctrine of separation" here set forth, Sheafe commented, was "diametrically opposed to the author's teaching in earlier of her writings."

Here and elsewhere, Sheafe took particular umbrage at the statement about the necessity of White men being chosen as leaders. "This means that, however capable, no colored man can lead in this denomination," he declared.

The most obvious flaw here was Sheafe's failure to recognize—or acknowledge—that none of these counsels were set forth as "doctrines" or "principles" of truth, but as temporary expedients in order for the church to be able to carry out its mission in the Southern states where segregation was being enforced in increasingly violent, absolute ways. When the material is understood against that background, it can be seen that virtually everything in the controverted section of volume 9 was intended as provisional—"until the Lord shows us a better way" (Sheafe left this phrase out of his quotation of the passage on separate churches on pages 206 and 207). Such recognition, of course, would not necessarily mean agreement that the expediency measures were just and right, but it would weaken the claim that these passages show that the Testimonies as a whole teach racial discrimination.

In a somewhat more telling criticism made months later, in 1916, Sheafe reflected awareness that accommodation to a specific set of circumstances is at work in volume 9. Even here, though, his reasoning was based on the "infallible propositions" conception of inspired writings. In one passage Ellen White advised against actions that, rightful in themselves, in some settings might provoke a racist backlash against the church's cause: "If you see that by doing certain things which you have a perfect right to do, you hinder the advancement of God's work, refrain from doing those things" (p. 215). In reaction, Sheafe declared:

"Here is the most flagrant submission to prevailing prejudices in a writer who claims inspiration that we have ever seen. It appears that the writer would accommodate principles of right and justice to any kind of subterfuge in order to catch the popular breeze."[6]

Along with its rhetorical overkill, the criticism ignores Ellen White's allusion, in the same paragraph as the quoted sentence, to the apostle Paul's teaching about giving up certain liberties for the broader interests of the church and its mission: "All things may be lawful, but not all things are expedient" (see 1 Corinthians 10:23 and the context in chapters 8-10). Yet it does get at the fundamental, difficult question of what distinguishes an appropriate expedient from sheer compromise with sin. Was racial equality not, at some level, a truth worthy of a costly stand?

Granted, then, that Sheafe was on to an important point, the insights of C. S. Longacre, head of the denomination's religious liberty work, regarding prominent men who ran afoul of "the Testimonies" also seem pertinent to Sheafe's experience. In 1929 Longacre wrote to W. A. Colcord:

"You . . . set up your standards of infallibility for her writings and what she said from time to time, which she never set up for herself or her writings, and because she did not measure up to those standards which you set up for her, you naturally throw her overboard and try to make her out as a false prophet."[7]

Sheafe did not brand Ellen White's writings as a whole or her exercise of the gift of prophecy as false. But somewhat like the men such as Jones and Ballenger, whom Longacre had in mind, Sheafe did construct a "straw man" from the widespread conceptions of her infallibility. When statements excerpted from counsel given to meet very difficult conditions in very specific situations failed to meet that standard, his solution was to say that those portions of her writings were not inspired.

These observations about Sheafe's failure to be balanced and recognize context in criticizing the writings of Ellen White should not be accompanied by similar failures in interpreting *his* experience. From today's perspective, when a Black man has served as president of the denomination's North American Division, and it is no longer unusual when African-Americans are elected to such top leadership positions as the presidencies of union conferences and of church-operated colleges and universities, it may seem easy to dismiss Sheafe's vehement denunciation of a single passage about the necessity of White men being chosen as leaders. In 1915, though, that counsel seemed to be enforced with thorough rigor. The head of the North American Negro Department was White, and its executive committee was controlled by White ministers. The same was true of every denominational institution and organizational entity for conducting the church's work among African-Americans.

Moreover, it must be said that the relevant section of volume 9 of the *Testimonies* was not organized in a way that made it easy to apply Ellen White's admonition that "time and place must be considered" in the use of her published testimonies.[8] The section stitches together passages from various letters and manuscripts, and for the first 13 pages of the section these are not even identified. Thus, other than what can be inferred from the text itself, the reader is provided no information for bringing "time and place" into consideration. No guidance helps the reader reconcile or balance apparent clashes between the counsel given in volume 9 and that given in earlier publications, such as volume 7 of the *Testimonies* and *The Southern Work*.

Additionally, though the details are sparse, the evidence that does exist points to the likelihood that the conference officials who sought to bring the Sheafes into conformity followed procedures very much like the ones Ellen White herself criticized in 1881. They selected, out of a much larger body of writings on the topic, most of which would contain contrasting or "balancing" emphases, the particular set of statements collected in volume 9, and insisted that each statement must be accepted as a proposition inspired by God.

This seems very much like selecting from the *Testimonies* "the strongest expressions and, without bringing in or making any account of the circumstances under which the cautions and warnings are given, make them of force in every case." And, particularly in view of the acute sensitivity and complexity of the race problem, it seems indeed to have been done in such a way as to raise "the combativeness of the very ones they might help if they dealt carefully."

The evidence is insufficient to ascribe accountability with certainty or precision for the unfortunate turn of events between the Sheafes and the Southern California Conference in 1915. Yet particularly in view of the fact that at other times Sheafe acknowledged the logic if not rectitude of the "expediency" policy, and was prepared to live with it if carried out fairly on its own terms, the question remains, Why, in 1915, in southern California, did it become so divisive? Was Sheafe using it as a pretext for some self-interested agenda? Or were he and Lucy in fact driven into a corner by overzealous administrators intent on making the writings of the Spirit of Prophecy a tool for enforcing submission to tightly drawn, racially defined authority? Might Sheafe have been able to carry forward with loyal, productive labor in the denominational cause if allowed to put honest doubts and questions on the back burner of ongoing study and reflection rather than being forced into the choice of either denying conscientiously held views or leaving the ministry?

Whatever the answer to these questions, the outcome of the matter was that when confronted with propositions in volume 9 that they believed contradicted the Bible, Sheafe and his Berean congregation saw no other choice than to deny the inspiration of those propositions. They did not wish to deny the authenticity of Ellen White's spiritual gift. The *Defender* article reflected recognition that "she has written many excellent things about the Bible." But the refusal to recognize a portion of the writings as inspired would indeed put them, in the minds of would-be guardians of the Spirit of Prophecy, among those grieving the Holy Spirit and thus on a course toward eternal destruction. No way of transcending the "either/or" framework seemed open to them. To be free, they had to withdraw.

It would be a simplistic distortion to view Sheafe as a martyr of untainted virtue, victimized by a hopelessly tyrannical, racist ecclesiastical hierarchy. His own choices and character traits—for good or ill—directed his course of action. And his was not the only course forward for Black Adventists of integrity and race consciousness; indeed, most made very different choices.

But the perception of him as a sinister manipulator who made it his mission to seduce innocent believers away from church organization guided by altogether altruistic men and righteous policies completely free of prejudice would be equally distorted. Sheafe's unique background, training, and experience, his Christian conviction, and his driving passion for the advancement of his people brought him up, once again, against a situation he found intolerable. He made the choice he thought was right, the choice he thought the Word of God mandated.

Sheafe lost much through his separation from the Seventh-day Adventist denomination. But the denomination paid a heavy toll, as well, for its inability, in the end, to make room for this volatile, strong-willed, independent-minded convert who was so powerfully equipped to take the third angel's message to Black America, and who for so many years gave his all to do just that.

---

[1] L. C. Sheafe and J. W. Manns, "Free Seventh Day Adventists."

[2] The indispensable starting point for dealing with the racial issues raised by volume 9 remains Ronald D. Graybill, *E. G. White and Church Race Relations*. Regarding the turmoil of the use of Ellen White's writings in general, the following discussion relies heavily on George Knight's highly informative treatment in *Reading Ellen White: How to Understand and Apply Her Writings* (Hagerstown, Md.: Review and Herald, 1997).

[3] WCW to S. N. Haskell, Jan. 15, 1913 (quoted in Knight, *Reading Ellen White*, pp. 107, 108).

[4] Dr. David Paulson to EGW, Apr. 19, 1906 (quoted in Knight, *Reading Ellen White*, p. 105).

[5] Ellen G. White, *Selected Messages* (Washington, D.C.: Review and Herald, 1980), book 3, pp. 285, 286 (portions quoted in Knight, *Reading Ellen White*, p. 90).

[6] Sheafe and Manns, "Free Seventh Day Adventists."

[7] Quoted in Knight, *Reading Ellen White*, p. 112.

[8] Ellen G. White, *Selected Messages* (Washington, D.C.: Review and Herald, 1958), book 1, p. 57.

<h1 style="text-align:center">CHAPTER XXXIV</h1>

<h2 style="text-align:center">FREE SEVENTH DAY ADVENTISTS</h2>

"SEVENTH DAY ADVENTISTS LOSE RACE ELDER" ran the headline of the Chicago *Defender* article. It was right on the front page, top and center, of one of the nation's most widely circulated African-American newspapers. A subheading drew attention to endorsement of Sheafe's action by the NAACP's Los Angeles chapter, underscoring the public and decisive character of the breach. This time there would be no talk of reconciliation. Both sides risked action on fragile trust in 1913, and now both felt betrayed once again—twice burned.

In an important sense, though, the *Defender* headline was misleading. As far as Sheafe was concerned, his "loss" to the denomination by no means entailed loss of Seventh-day Adventist belief or identity. He would once again seek to sustain these in some alternative organizational form. But how?

His pastorate of the independent Berean congregation was an essential foundation but not the complete answer. A strong majority of Black Adventist Angelenos in the Furlong and Watts churches chose to stay with the denomination, and the short-term prospects probably did not seem strong for the kind of growth at the small Berean congregation that would be necessary to meet Sheafe's aspirations and financial needs. He applied for a position with the YMCA in Los Angeles,[1] which he could add to his pastoral role at Berean. But that did not work out.

Sheafe did have a strong base of support at the People's church in Washington, but at present that was a full-fledged member congregation of the District of Columbia Conference, pastored by J. Marion Campbell.

So he and Lucy began exploring the possibility of a new venture in her previous arena of labor—Jacksonville, Florida. They had in mind establishing a school, much as she had a few years before, but of broader scope. Some of their initial inquiries to potential supporters were rebuffed, but they did not give up on the idea.[2]

Meanwhile, another development in that region of the country raised intriguing possibilities. In the months just preceding the renewed turmoil surrounding Sheafe in California, John W. Manns and the strong church he established in Savannah, Georgia, withdrew from the denomination's jurisdiction.

A BLACK ADVENTIST DENOMINATION

John W. Manns began conducting tent evangelism and raising up Adventist churches in Florida no later than 1906.[3] Impressive results attended his preaching, and nowhere was this more true than in Savannah, where he set up his Beacon Light Gospel Tent in April 1912. The meetings led to formation of a church with approximately 100 members later that year. In November they secured a lot at 36th and Burroughs for a church building, and by 1914 had completed "a commodious house of worship" at a cost of $5,000.[4]

This seemingly standard progression of events was actually quite unusual in important ways. For one thing, Manns—more an itinerant evangelist than a settled pastor—usually did not stay long in one location. It was also unusual in the Adventist work for a new congregation to handle the building of a sanctuary completely on its own resources. Typically smaller than the one in Savannah and comprised of mostly poor people, new congregations usually depended on the conference to provide the assistance necessary for construction or purchase of a church building.

However, Black believers began to see a pattern of racial inequity in the expenditure of funds for worship facilities, which was under the complete control of White administrators. One denominational leader pointed out that "the poor colored people do not feel that they have had fair treatment," that we "always give them some cheap-john proposition."[5]

Thus, when conference officials instructed Manns and the Savannah church to turn the title to their property over to the conference, in accordance with denominational policy, they refused. The demand to cede control of property that they had financed on their own to the White leadership of a discriminatory system seemed outrageous. They formed a corporation to hold the property called the Christian Negro Seventh-day Adventist Church, with J. W. Manns as chair of the board of trustees.[6] The Savannah church also established a school and grocery store, attempting to implement Adventism's wholistic program for Christian development and all that it could mean for racial progress.[7]

Standing firm in their position, Manns and the Savannah church severed their connection with the Georgia Conference in the same year that Sheafe and the Berean church seceded from the Southern California Conference. The following year, the two dissident preachers made a joint cause.

When Sheafe traveled to Savannah to begin a tent series with Manns in May 1916, the two announced formation of a new denomination, the Free Seventh Day Adventists. An article on the front page of the May 13 edition of the Savannah *Tribune* stated that "Elder Sheafe found it necessary to leave the Regular SDA denomination last fall . . . because of the oppressive and unjust discrimination against the Negro by the officials of the denomination." Thus, Sheafe was depicted as the founder, his action paralleling that of the great pioneer of independent Black denominations, Richard Allen, who led in the formation of the African Methodist Episcopal Church in 1817. J. W. Manns, "the fearless champion of religious liberty," along with his church, had come to the standard thus raised, and the two men stood "united heart and hand in the work for extension throughout this country."[8]

A joint manifesto published in the same paper two weeks later announced the formation of "a new denomination." The name "Free Seventh Day Adventist" was inspired by Mrs. L. P. Sheafe's bold declaration at the meeting held on September 1, 1915, in Los Angeles. The authors grounded their action in the history of the church—both Christian history in the broad sense and the Adventist experience. The religion of Christ is "immutable," but it is administered by "mutable men" and thus "readjustment to the original standard" becomes necessary from time to time. Conditions requiring such "readjustment" may have to do with purity of doctrine or individual freedom of conscience.

The problem Sheafe and Manns saw did not have to do with the church's doctrines. Rather, it was a case in which "the stronger element of a religious body stands for and supports intolerance and ecclesiastical error." In such a situation the minority should undertake "persistent efforts for a remedy." But, the authors said, that had "been tried repeatedly in the past with but little or nothing accomplished." The only viable option now before them as a "powerless minority" was withdrawal. And in so doing, they were following the precedent of the great Protestant Reformers.

"The love of truth, freedom and righteousness that actuated Luther of Germany, Knox of Scotland, and Wesley of England glows in the heart of every Free Seventh Day Adventist; therefore, we are determined to enjoy the priceless boon of freedom purchased by Christ the Lord, for all mankind."

It was, of course, suppression of freedom along racial lines that Sheafe and Manns protested in the Adventist Church. The church had begun a "definite work among colored people of the South" about 25 years before, they said. For the first 10 years "the two races experienced no difficulty in the north and west, in the equal enjoyment of religious privileges." But then "race prejudice" and "Negro proscription" began to increase for two reasons: the denomination's growth in "influence and popularity," and the growth of Negro membership.

Referring back to the division of the Washington church in 1902, the Free SDA manifesto charged that denominational leaders "began, in a deceptive and unchristian way, the work of segregation of the Negroes in all of their churches, east, west, north, and south." While the leaders could accurately deny the existence of any such national policy, the statement about the general trend toward segregation wherever Black members existed in substantial numbers rang essentially true.

"All of this was contrary to their former profession and teaching," Sheafe and Manns continued. It was because of their inability to defend their actions on the basis of the Bible that the White leaders turned to Ellen White's writings. "They issued in 1909 volume 9 of the *Testimonies*," says the Free SDA manifesto, hinting that it was more a production of the leaders than Ellen White herself. The document's critique of the section on race relations in volume 9 proceeds, for the most part, along the lines of the Berean church statement of 1915.

The protesting Black leaders' case for "coming out" to form a separate organization concludes with a complaint against the recent policy requiring that "all church property must be signed over to the conference." It was a "device" that denominational leaders had "applied especially to church property held by colored congregations," they claimed.

The document outlined principles of organization for the new Free Seventh Day Adventist denomination similar to that of Baptist denominations, with no hierarchical authority above individual congregations.

"The organization of the church is such as the New Testament describes, a congregation of baptized believers, who trust in Jesus alone for salvation, taking the Holy Scriptures as their only rule of faith and practice. Each separate church or congregation is its own sovereign under God."

State or district assemblies and a general assembly would meet annually, but their role would be quite different from the conferences in the Seventh-day Adventist system.

"These assemblies are not legislative bodies; they do not exercise ecclesiastical authority of any kind over any of the churches. Their object is cooperation."

Sheafe and Manns called upon those dedicated to a "square deal for the Negro" to join them. But this was not simply about advocacy for civil rights in a general sense. Rather, the "square deal" would be in the context of carrying forward the same mission as the Seventh-day Adventist denomination they had left. The Free Seventh Day Adventists invited "all Christians who are keeping the commandments of God to unite with us that we may press the work to its final close and hasten the glorious kingdom of our Lord and Savior Jesus Christ."

At the time of the document's publication, only two other pastors and their congregations had rallied to the Free Seventh Day Adventist banner: Thomas DeFreeze of Dallas, Texas, and J. E. Brice of Lexington, Kentucky, where the church that Sheafe briefly pastored 18 years before was itself divided over a dispute with the Kentucky Conference concerning the church property issue.[9] More were expected, though, especially from Manns' sphere of influence in Georgia and in South Carolina, where the church in Lincolnville, near Charleston, soon did join.[10]

EARLY MOMENTUM

Sheafe was the principal speaker for the meetings conducted with

Manns in Savannah during May and June. Articles in the June 3 and June 10 issues of the Savannah *Tribune* give some glimpses on the proceedings, though they are not straightforward reports. Rather, they take the form of an imaginary and rather lopsided dialogue in which "Uncle Dudley" relates his impressions of the meetings to his friend "Browne."

"He done tore up a lot of old trash notions I had, I didn't want to let go, but who can stand out against the word of God[?]" Thus wrote "Uncle Dudley," who, without precedent or introduction, suddenly appeared in the June 3, 1916, issue of the Savannah *Tribune*, commenting on Sheafe's preaching at the "Banner of Truth Gospel Tent" meetings on the corner of Gwinnett and Magnolia streets. As he thus moves from curiosity to conviction to the brink of baptism, it becomes evident that Uncle Dudley's folksy persona has been created to promote the evangelistic effort. He models the progression the evangelists hope their listeners will make (and one that, in a composite sense, was arguably true to life).

Despite this inventive structure, the content of Uncle Dudley's narratives appear to have some value in adding texture to the picture of Sheafe as a preacher, and gives the impression that the Free Seventh Day Adventist movement indeed showed some early momentum. The stories also suggest that the content of Sheafe's messages differed little if at all from what he preached as a Seventh-day Adventist.

Among the many things "the preacher man" had proven from "the Bible alone," said Uncle Dudley, was that "it was Christ who gave the moral law on the mountain." Yet he also made clear that though these commandments thus were binding upon the Christian, no one could gain salvation through commandment keeping. "The saved man will work because he is saved, not to be saved," the preacher explained. "Then, sir," the writer continued, "he shows from the Bible the rise and fall of nations and kingdoms, in a wonderful way, bringing us clear down to this day and time and clear over till Christ comes again to gather His people unto himself."

At the same time Dudley's narratives further develop the picture of Sheafe as a preacher of vigorous, practical holiness, not merely proving doctrinal points but relating the biblical message to the issues his hearers faced day to day. At a time when the decades-long struggle for woman suffrage had reached the front burner of national issues, Sheafe spoke to much-discussed issues of gender as well as with race relations through the prism of a biblical story.

"What was his subject? Lands, I forgot to tell you. It was 'The woman of Destiny,' or 'The Life and Times of Esther.' Fine? Why, man, you will have to go back and get some more words to describe that sermon. Why, he just set Esther and all them folks of hers over against the Negro and his day and time. Say man, it was inspiring and encouraging, but he paid the women of the Negro race a finer tribute. This, he said, is woman's day; she can mold things as she wants them, and the future of this race depends on its noble women, of whom there are not a few, and a good woman with God using her is a mighty factor in any race."

Uncle Dudley cancelled a planned trip to Beaufort, South Carolina, implying that readers should make similar adjustments to their plans in order to be around for the upcoming week at the meetings, which promised to be "special."[11] Sure enough, "my preacher man struck fire this week, he sure did," he declared the following week. Sheafe's sermon on the law of God as "the standard of righteousness for all mankind" and "the standard in the judgment," testified Uncle Dudley, persuaded him "to cling to Jesus and drop the beer and whiskey."

Now, "wanting to see how my preacher would do indoors," Uncle Dudley found his way to the Free Seventh Day Adventist meetinghouse on West 36th Street the next Saturday—"that's the Sabbath of the Lord according to the commandments, you know," he took pains to make clear. Uncle Dudley didn't try to summarize the content of the Sabbath sermon, reporting instead on its powerful effect:

"Tears and moans were plentiful on every side. The people were moved to lay aside every weight and the easily besetting sin. Then the preacher drew in his net, just like a skillful fisherman, and she was loaded. He called for all who wanted to break with sin of all kinds and were now ready to confess and forsake them to come forward. There were about 200 present, and as true as I am sitting here, the whole congregation arose and pressed to the front. Here was enacted again the Pentecost of old. Such earnest prayers and deep testimonies as went up there, man, I've not heard in many a year, and you know I'm no boy."

Uncle Dudley related feeling a desire to linger in the sanctuary, even to present himself as a candidate for membership. Nonetheless, he slipped out around 3:15, just before the service, which began at 11:45, came to an end.

Still, he said, "the thing had such a hold on me" that he could not miss the baptism announced for the next day at the Thunderbolt River. A streetcar, crammed beyond capacity, conveyed 110 people from the church to the river. The cloudy skies cleared as Sheafe, clad in rubber boots and baptismal robe, immersed 12 in the "watery grave." Uncle Dudley also noted that "a large appreciative audience of both races" witnessed the proceedings, adding to the evidence that Sheafe possessed an unusual ability to reach beyond the racial barrier, even in the South. More were said to be preparing for the next baptismal service scheduled for two weeks later. Uncle Dudley felt that he must be among them—he too must "go down to the river and be baptized" (again, with unmistakable implications for the reader).

He also described meeting Sheafe personally. Despite the likelihood of creative license in its structure, the anecdote seems worth noting as an impression of how Sheafe came across in personal interaction. When Browne asked if he had gotten acquainted with the preacher yet, Uncle Dudley reported that after the meeting one night Sheafe had intercepted him before he could get away, seeming to have flown to the door of the tent. The preacher's penetrating gaze made Uncle Dudley a little uncomfortable, yet on the whole he felt drawn to him.

"Why sir, he caught my hand and gave me a kindly clasp, and he looks you right in the eyes, and it seemed to me he was looking clear through me. I wondered if the collar button on the back of my neck was all right or was he looking to see if my suspenders were on all right in the back. But I somehow rather like him, he puts you at your ease at once, and I felt at home with him."[12]

Uncle Dudley concluded his June 10 column by reminding Browne to look for him again next week. But just as abruptly as he appeared, Uncle Dudley disappeared from the pages of the Savannah *Tribune*, never to be seen again. Did the columns stop coming into the paper, or was it that the *Tribune* refused to publish any more of them? It seems impossible to know which or, in either case, why. Over the next few years the *Tribune* gave respectful coverage both to the Free Seventh Day Adventists and a reestablished Seventh-day Adventist congregation. Yet it is plausible that reaction from the established Black churches in the city somehow worked to discourage further publication of Uncle Dudley's creative narratives promoting the Adventist cause. Whether it influenced the newspaper or not, the inevitable reaction came. Surely it was no coincidence that on Sunday evening, June 18, at St. Philip AME church, one of the largest churches in the city, Rev. Singleton began a series on the Ten Commandments.[13]

Concern about the apparent momentum of the Free Seventh Day Adventist movement also registered at Seventh-day Adventist denominational headquarters, where I. H. Evans, vice president for North America, received word that "Sheafe and Manns are doing everything they can to tear down our work." Disaffection was growing around the claim that "when the colored people break away from us and handle their own business" they provide for themselves churches as good as the White people's, rather than the inferior facilities that came with conference assistance and control. The plea from the South was that funds to help secure two or three churches would be needed in order to "hold the work in South Carolina and Georgia."[14]

---

[1] Andross to AGD, Sept. 14, 1915.

[2] MCS to T. E. Bowen, Dec. 8, 1915, GCA.

[3] J. W. Manns, "The Work in South Florida," *Review,* June 13, 1907, p. 18.

[4] J. W. Manns, "History of the Seventh-Day Adventists in Savannah," Savannah *Tribune,* Dec. 5, 1914, p. 2.

[5] I. H. Evans to W. T. Knox, June 21, 1916, GCA.

[6] R. C. Jones, *James K. Humphrey,* p. 23; "Petition for Incorporation," Savannah *Tribune,* Mar. 27, 1915, p. 7.

[7] "Seven Day Adventist Grocery Store," Savannah *Tribune,* Sept. 1, 1914, p. 8; "Seventh-day Adventist Returned to Church," Savannah *Tribune,* Oct. 2, 1915, p. 7.

[8] "The Man and His Work," Savannah *Tribune,* May 13, 1916, p. 1.

[9] L. C. Sheafe and J. W. Manns, "Free Seventh Day Adventists."

[10] "Local Happenings," *California Eagle,* July 22, 1916, p. 5.

[11] "The Banner of Truth Gospel Tent," Savannah *Tribune,* June 3, 1916, p. 7.

[12] "The Banner of Truth Tent Meeting," Savannah *Tribune,* June 10, 1916, p. 7.

[13] "St. Philip Church," Savannah *Tribune,* June 10, 1916, p. 7.

[14] I. H. Evans to W. T. Knox, June 21, 1916, GCA.

CHAPTER XXXV

REVERSALS AT THE PEOPLE'S CHURCH

A NEW DRAMA UNFOLDING at the People's Seventh-day Adventist Church in Washington, D.C., raised prospects that Sheafe's former stronghold might also join the Free SDA movement. After the reconciliation of 1913 the church strove to show itself a dedicated, cooperating part of the Seventh-day Adventist organization. Its pastor, J. Marion Campbell, was thoroughly loyal to the denomination and gave effective leadership both in reviving the congregation after the years of controversy and in evangelistic efforts.[1] The church duly submitted tithes, Sabbath school missionary offerings, and contributions for special campaigns to the conference treasury.

THE COLORED TRAINING SCHOOL: A RENEWED APPEAL

At its first opportunity, which came at the annual District of Columbia Conference meeting in May 1915, the People's church issued an appeal regarding Christian education. In contrast to the confrontational style of the 1906 petition, they now worked through the regular, designated channels, presenting the following petition:

"Whereas, we have in our churches a large number of young people who could develop into Christian workers if they were provided with the facilities for proper training, and,

"Whereas, our young people are deprived of training school privileges in our conference, we, the delegates from the People's church, respectfully beg to submit the following request:

"That this conference take immediate steps toward the establishment of a training school near Washington, for our young people.

"We feel that the support which such a school would receive from the Atlantic and Columbia unions justifies its establishment."

In discussion of the petition some conference officials suggested that in light of heavy indebtedness on existing institutions, it would not be feasible to start a new one. However, Elder Campbell and others spoke fervently on the need for the school. So the delegates voted to request that the conference executive committee give favorable consideration to the petition and, since its scope was broader than the local conference, refer it to the appropriate entities.[2]

As the months rolled by with no response to the petition, frustration began to mount once again. Though there had been no formal agreements in advance of the congregation's return to the denominational fold in 1913, Sheafe had been made to understand that it would remove the obstacle to expending already-designated funds to reduce the church debt and begin development of a training school. Now, as 1915 drew to a close, two and a half years had elapsed, and despite the congregation's best efforts to play by the denominational rules, they saw no sign of action.

News of Sheafe's travails in California no doubt also had a disquieting effect, yet the church made no moves to jump into his footsteps and withdraw once again. When J. Marion Campbell transferred to First church, Fred Seeney was called from Wilmington, Delaware, to the pastorate of the People's church in December 1915.

At the next District of Columbia Conference session in April 1916 Seeney presented an optimistic report.[3] Meanwhile, though, events were confirming the disillusionment in his congregation over failed promises about funding for a school. At the same conference session the First church submitted a new petition for the school. Having already submitted a petition without reply, the People's church delegation declined to join in presenting the new proposal, but of course closely observed the response to it.

R. T. Dowsett, secretary-treasurer of the Columbia Union Conference, stated that the requested funding could not be provided, but proposed that if the Colored members would raise funds on their own, then the White constituency would come in with some assistance. Yet just a month before, the Columbia Union Conference committee voted to raise $25,000 for new buildings at Washington Missionary College in Takoma Park, an institution open to White people only. "The partisan injustice of that procedure is so plain that no comment can be needed," stated a pamphlet published by the People's church in 1917, narrating its troubled history with the denomination.[4]

In and of itself the training school issue would not have inevitably led to a new crisis jeopardizing the church's denominational connection. But it helped create the frame of mind that led the church and its pastor to take a course with regard to another matter that eventually did trigger an explosion.

A. T. JONES REDUX

In 1915 no name was as certain to grab the concerned attention of denominational leaders as that of Alonzo T. Jones. The fact that he continued to preach the church's main doctrines and traveled on the fringes of denominational circles made his influence more dangerous than that of an out-and-out apostate. In November Jones moved to Washington, near denominational headquarters, where he carried on publication of his independent periodical, the *American Sentinel of Religious Liberty*.

Renewing his old ties with the People's church, he began worshipping there on a regular basis, and soon was asked to speak for a Wednesday evening prayer meeting. The meeting drew a good many visitors, including the D.C. Conference president, R. E. Harter, and a ministerial colleague. The conference representatives arrived right on time and immediately took over the meeting, eventually dismissing it without allowing Jones to speak. Some church members, embarrassed and upset by the incident, urged Jones to join the church formally; as a member, his right to speak could not be denied. Jones cautioned them about the ramifications of such a move with conference leadership, but did not close the door. At that point the congregation was between ministers, but after Seeney arrived in January, he stood with the church board in a unanimous vote for inviting Jones into membership. When presented to the church as a whole on Sabbath, April 15, there was only one dissenting vote.

When Harter phoned Seeney that week, asking if it was true that Jones had been admitted to membership, his next question tapped on one of the ongoing sore spots between conference leaders and the People's church. "Don't you know that that is a colored church?" Harter asked rhetorically.

"It never has been," Seeney replied. Though in fact predominantly Black, and not so consistently resistant as the First church to being identified as such, the core of the People's church identity also had always been that it was a church open to all people. No governing authority would be allowed to impose racial or other invidious conditions on membership, as had been attempted in the 1902 division of the Washington church.

But the racial issue was not Harter's real problem, and that became apparent at a conference executive committee meeting to which he summoned Seeney that afternoon. It was the acute embarrassment, not just for Elder Harter but also for the General Conference leadership, that A. T. Jones had slipped into membership in a Seventh-day Adventist church under their watch. After serving notice throughout the nation against allowing Jones to speak at Adventist meetings or even going to hear him speak, now letters were coming into the brethren in Washington asking how it could be that "right there under your very eyes he becomes a member of the church!" And since, in the Adventist system, membership is a matter over which local congregations have complete authority, conference officials were powerless before the fait accompli.

Seeney could have blocked action and saved them a lot of trouble if he had done so, the committee told him. But the pastor of the People's church was unrepentant, and told the committee that the admittance of Jones to membership came with his full support.

Tensions escalated after another meeting with the conference committee in May, even though Seeney, accompanied by three leading members of the congregation, tried to make a constructive proposal for resolving the long-standing grievance about lack of funding for a training school. If the conference would donate the $1,000 remaining on the existing church property debt, the congregation would take responsibility for "a church school and treatment rooms." The committee responded that no funding would be provided unless the deed to the property was transferred to the conference. To this, Seeney would not agree.

At the same meeting, the committee refused the request of the People's church for a tent in which to hold a summer evangelistic series.

Jones's presence and other signs of discontent made the People's church one congregation that they had no interest in seeing grow. So when the church went ahead anyway, deciding to foot the bill on its own, R. E. Harter viewed the planned evangelistic effort as an intolerable act of defiance, most especially because Seeney called upon one of his members, A. T. Jones, to assist him with the series.

Harter ordered Seeney to "put your foot on that affair, or we will put our foot on you." Seeney stood his ground, and finally Harter shook his hand in parting with an expression of sorrow that made Seeney certain that his employment with the conference was over.

At a church business meeting on July 11, the fed-up pastor told his people that tithes and offerings were the only things that bound them to the conference. Inasmuch as they had been "put out of their councils, out of their schools, out of their sanitariums, and out of their business offices," he urged that they support an action voted by the church board intended "to awaken the conference officials to a sense of justice" but not sever ties with finality.

"Resting on our God-given rights as individuals and as a church, we most heartily protest against the unfair and unchristian treatment accorded us by the conference officials.

"Therefore, be it resolved that this church transact all its own business, handling its finances, as it thinks best, from the above date, and continue to do so until the conference accedes to our just requests."

The resolution passed by a large majority, though 21 voted against it.[5]

THE "CALIFORNIA ADVENTIST" RETURNS

Meanwhile the plot was thickening in connection with the evangelistic series just underway in a tent pitched on the lot next to the church building. Just days before the series began, Lewis Sheafe stopped in town. Having completed his meetings with J. W. Manns in Savannah, he was headed to Philadelphia and points farther north. In Washington he had an appointment to preach for the Sunday morning service at Walker Memorial Baptist Church. Seeney asked his former colleague to alter his plans and join in the tent meetings about to begin at the People's church, and the congregation's founding pastor agreed to do so.[6]

The Seeney-Jones-Sheafe meetings attracted good, sometimes overflow, crowds to the tent next to the church that remained, officially, Seventh-day Adventist.[7] The church's relationship with the District of Columbia Conference entered a state of suspended uncertainty after its announcement of July 11 that it would hold all its funds in protest against unjust treatment. No response came from the conference, and Seeney ceased sending in work reports, instead receiving his salary directly from the People's church treasury. Yet for the remainder of the summer, neither side took further steps toward finalizing a separation.[8]

Sheafe did not make an open, aggressive push in Washington for the new denomination he had just organized with Manns, though he clearly supported the moves made by the People's church toward renewed independence. A brief news item in the July 22 edition of the *California Eagle* stated that the Adventist church at 10th and V streets in Washington, where Sheafe was "conducting a big tent meeting," had just "voted itself independent of the Adventist conference." If this report technically stretched the truth with the word "independent," it did not claim that the Washington church had joined the Free SDA movement. This is significant because another item on the same page of the paper, which like the other one must have originated from either Lewis or Lucy Sheafe, reported that the Lincolnville, South Carolina, church had "joined the Assembly of Free [Seventh] Day Adventists last week."[9]

While Sheafe held back from trying to claim the People's church for the Free Seventh Day Adventists, the Seventh-day Adventist leaders in Takoma Park held back from cutting the very tenuous links with the denomination that remained. A group of about 30 members had withdrawn from the People's church out of loyalty to the denomination and were meeting in a private home. Even so, denominational leaders had not completely given up prospects of gaining control of the highly desirable property at 10th and V streets, and establishing a loyal congregation there. Nor had they completely given up on Fred Seeney as a minister with whom they might work in bringing this about. Having learned that Sheafe planned to return to California, they were waiting for him to leave town before making their move.[10]

Sheafe enjoyed a warm welcome from the broader community during his return visit to Washington. Washington *Bee* editor W. Calvin Chase still held him in highest regard. Noting the visit of the pastor of the Berean

Church of Free Seventh Day Adventists, Chase called him "one of the greatest Bible scholars in the United States, and one minister who thinks for himself."[11]

On his visit the "California Adventist," as one newspaper listing referred to him, touted the state as "an El Dorado for the enterprising Negro" and urged "the migration of goodly members of our progressive element to that section of the country."[12] In addition to his sermon at Walker Memorial Baptist on July 9, Sheafe's speaking engagements on this visit included an address to the Life Problem Club at the 12th Street YMCA on July 23 and the Sunday morning sermon at the Israel Methodist Episcopal Church on September 24.[13]

As summarized by a Washington *Bee* report of a farewell reception organized for him on September 25, Sheafe had both "rendered valuable service to the People's SDA Church" and helped "churches of other denominations, with his wonderful sermons, lectures and gospel songs" during his stay. The report described the reception as a thoroughly interdenominational and interracial gathering and commented, "This was as it should have been, for Elder Sheafe is the 'people's minister.'" With the elder on his way westward, said the author, "We still hear the echo as he sings, 'Keep Sweet.'"[14]

SEENEY REVERSES COURSE

It was not an easy time to "keep sweet" at the People's church. A week before Sheafe received his send-off, it became apparent at a meeting of the church board that Pastor Fred Seeney had come to see matters in a different light than he had on July 11 when he advocated the resolution to withhold funds from the conference. Board members, in anticipation of possible talks with the conference leadership, wanted to establish just what they would hold to as "just requests" that needed to be met. But Seeney opposed all that, and now urged them to take a conciliatory attitude toward the conference and express renewed loyalty, rather than set forth a list of demands.

At a subsequent meeting the pastor acknowledged that he had reversed course, and that he would explain why at a later time. Somehow, conference leaders had won him over, and now he would make one final effort to pull the People's church back from the brink and hold it and its property for the organized Adventist work. Against the advice of some board members to resign, Seeney gamely took the chair at the church's quarterly business meeting on October 9. When it became clear that, despite his vociferous opposition, a large majority favored a resolution to reaffirm and perpetuate the action taken on July 11, Seeney tried through various tactics to get the meeting adjourned without a vote being recorded. Finally, after failing in repeated efforts to get a motion for adjournment, he simply walked out of the church, never to return.[15]

After a 12-year saga of inspiring triumphs and debilitating conflict, of protests against injustice and heartwarming reconciliations, of hopes renewed and then dashed, the relationship between the People's church and the Seventh-day Adventist denomination was finally over for good. Through it all, the denominational leadership had not seen fit to put a single dollar into either the church building or development of a training school and sanitarium treatment rooms centered there. Now it was time to start again with the remnant from the People's church who left in protest against its return to independence. Within weeks the denomination put up $18,750 for the purchase of a sizable church building with a parsonage and adequate facilities for a school to house the Ephesus church, as the congregation of Black Adventists in Washington loyal to the denomination became known.[16]

---

[1] See, for example, his report "Washington Convention," *Columbia Union Visitor*, Dec. 19, 1914, p. 5.

[2] "District of Columbia Seventh Annual Session," *Columbia Union Visitor*, May 20, 1915, pp. 1, 2.

[3] "Minutes of the Eighth Annual Session of District of Columbia Conference, cont.," *Columbia Union Visitor*, May 25, 1916, p. 5.

[4] "Experience of the People's SDA Church," pp. 4-6. A. T. Jones authored a large section of this pamphlet, which sets forth his theory of church organization and narrates his conflict with the administration of A. G. Daniells. He may also have organized or edited the material in sections having to do with the experiences of Sheafe and the church in which he had no direct part. But his literary voice does not seem dominant in these sections, which seem to convey the firsthand experiences and observations of those involved. On the Columbia Union Conference commitment to raise $25,000 for Washington Missionary College, see "Resolutions Adopted at the Fifth Biennial Session of the Columbia Union Conference," *Columbia Union Visitor*, Apr. 17, 1916, p. 8. The union conference committee raised the total goal to $45,000 in July; see B. G. Wilkinson, "An Important Meeting of the Columbia Union Conference Committee," *Columbia Union Visitor*, Aug. 10, 1916, p. 1.

[5] "Experience of the People's SDA Church," pp. 6-13.

[6] "News of the Nation's Capital," Savannah *Tribune,* July 15, 1916, p. 1; "Experience of the People's SDA Church," p. 11.

[7] Untitled news item, *Gathering Call,* Aug. 1916, p. 8; "California Adventist Here," WP, Aug. 7, 1916, p. 10.

[8] "Experience of the People's SDA Church," pp. 12-14.

[9] "Local Happenings," *California Eagle,* July 22, 1916, p. 5.

[10] T. E. Bowen to MCS, Sept. 17, 1916, GCA.

[11] "Rev. Sheave," *Bee,* Aug. 26, 1916, p. 1.

[12] "News of the Nation's Capital," Savannah *Tribune,* July 15, 1916, p. 1.

[13] "Addresses Life Problem Club," WP, July 24, 1916; "Visiting Adventist Preaches," WP, Sept. 25, 1916, p. 10.

[14] "A Farewell Reception to Elder Lewis C. Sheafe," *Bee,* Sept. 30, 1916, p. 1.

[15] "Experience of the People's SDA Church," pp. 14-17.

[16] T. E. Bowen to MCS, Dec. 4, 1916, GCA; T. E. Bowen, "Another Memorial Church in Washington, D.C.," *Gospel Herald,* July 1917, p. 3.

CHAPTER XXXVI

"THE PEOPLE'S MINISTER"
OR "DANGEROUS APOSTATE"?

ESPITE LEWIS SHEAFE'S EXTENSIVE TRAVELS and far-flung connections, every indication in 1916 pointed to Los Angeles and the Berean Church of Free Seventh Day Adventists as his new home base. Speaking opportunities seemed plentiful as usual upon his return to the city in the fall. He spoke at the YMCA on October 22, giving what was billed as his "famous lecture" on "Conferences." The following Sunday he preached a "practical and forceful sermon" entitled "The Perils of the Strong" at Lincoln Memorial Congregational Church, and on November 19 it was another Sunday morning sermon, this one at Wesley Chapel.[1]

Rather soon, though, he and Lucy turned their attentions back East. Not (as rumor had it in the halls of the General Conference) to Washington, primarily, but to Jacksonville, where they pursued plans to establish a school. It is not clear exactly when and why they decided to leave Los Angeles. A brief news item about Sheafe's virtually annual series of meetings in Washington indicated the evangelist's headquarters to be Los Angeles as of July 1917,[2] but his activities there appear to have come to an end in December 1916.

Sheafe spent much of the winter of 1917 in Kansas City, Missouri, preaching for an extended revival series at the Allen Chapel AME Church. "Rev. Sheafe, the great evangelist, who has met with so much success during his stay here, preached his farewell sermon" on February 25, recorded the Missouri news section of Chicago *Defender* as the series, which began on January 14, drew to a close.[3]

DIVISION FROM MANNS,
DENUNCIATION FROM HUNTSVILLE

The plans for Jacksonville also included teaming up once again with J. W. Manns for a tent series in the spring. Anything attempted in Florida, though, would have to contend with determined opposition from the ever-vigilant Matthew C. Strachan, who headed the Negro Mission, as it was now termed, of the Florida Conference. After Sheafe purchased a lot in Jacksonville in December 1916, Strachan convinced the seller to back out of the deal and return the money. As for the impending meetings by the duo of renowned preachers, Strachan covered that threat by arranging for G. E. Peters, the Southeastern Union Conference evangelist who had developed a track record of success throughout the South, to conduct a strong tent effort at the same time.[4]

The Peters' series brought 64 new members into the Seventh-day Adventist church in Jacksonville,[5] but the anticipated competition never materialized. The Sheafe-Manns manifesto of May 1916 had declared, "The Free Seventh Day Adventist is here to stay," but the cofounders' alliance did not last a year. Before the meetings planned for Jacksonville got off the ground, the two men had gone their separate ways, unable to work together.[6] Though the Sheafes originated the name "Free Seventh Day Adventist" in Los Angeles, they left it with Manns, under whose leadership the group thrived for a time with a few congregations in the Southeast.[7]

In addition to his falling-out with Manns, Sheafe also reaped sharp denunciation in early 1917 from his former brethren in Seventh-day Adventist ministry. During a ministerial institute at Huntsville in early January, word came that Sheafe was preaching at various churches in Kansas City, and that some Adventists were going out to hear him. A circular letter, sent out from Huntsville on January 9, signed by some of the ministers attending the institute, including Sydney Scott and J. Marion Campbell, invoked the severest of spiritual sanctions in warning the faithful to have nothing to do with Sheafe:

"Mr. Lewis Sheafe is an apostate of the most dangerous sort. He is active and has a very pleasant tongue to divert souls in the wrong path. His efforts are desperate to tear down the organization which is divinely appointed to promulgate the third angel's message. He is fighting the Spirit of Prophecy and every other point of truth which cuts across his path. . . .

Our people should not attend his meetings, neither allow him to preach in our churches. He is sowing seeds of strife, division and confusion. A curse is left on the church that defies the scriptural injunction which reads as follows: 'Whosoever transgresseth, and abideth not in the doctrine of Christ, hath not God. He that abideth in the doctrine of Christ, he hath both the Father and the Son.' 2 John 9. The above-mentioned has departed from the doctrine of Christ. We should not spend our time in going to hear him; and if we do, it will be at the peril of our souls."[8]

Soon thereafter, on February 25 the People's church, 10 years after they had done so for the first time, unanimously adopted a public statement of congregational independence. Breaking denominational "fetters," they insisted, was not an act of apostasy but an assertion of freedom to carry forward the mission of their Adventist faith in a more faithful and genuine way:

"We are gratefully and devoutly thankful to God that we are now free from the ecclesiastical and denominational fetters that had been placed upon us, and that we are free in all things from molestation from the SDA General Conference system and denomination. Free to be Christians in having no respect of persons, as well as in all other things; and *in this* free to proclaim in *sincerity* in *Spirit* and in *truth* the third angel's message, which calls *all* people to the keeping of 'the commandments and the faith of Jesus.'"[9]

Sheafe was concluding his meetings in Kansas City when the church adopted the proclamation. It formally opened the way for him to resume the pastorate vacated by Seeney the previous October. He may have done so sometime in 1917, but it is not until 1918 that records show him to have once again made Washington, D.C., and the People's church his home base.

AN INDUSTRIAL SCHOOL FOR THE
"POOREST AND MOST NEEDY CLASS"

During 1917 and 1918 roughly coinciding with the period of American participation in World War I, Sheafe's main project was the industrial school that he and Lucy proceeded to establish in the suburbs of Jacksonville, Florida. He did conduct the annual summer tent series in Washington, drawing nightly the usual "large crowds."[10] At the same time, he was drumming up support, both monetary and "in kind," for the school. Lucy, who, presumably with the children, had located near Ocala early in the year, apparently joined her husband for at least a portion of his time in Washington. According to "News of the Nation's Capital" appearing in the Savannah *Tribune*, the couple left Washington together in October to open the new school in Florida.[11]

An open letter from the "Great Expounder of the Gospel and His Wife" appeared in the December 22, 1917, edition of the Washington *Bee*, in which the Sheafes expressed gratitude for the "pencils, paper, pictures, maps and funds" donated by their friends in Washington. The letter also reflected the idealism driving their project.

"In our attempt to establish this work we have in mind the conditions of the poorest and most needy, who are largely untouched. It is alarming to find that many dozens of children here who are of school age do not attend school.

"Education is not made compulsory, hence the necessity of making it attractive becomes evident."

The school had opened with an enrollment of 40, they said. And they appealed for continued support in the belief that "our effort here will grow and finally be numbered among the institutions that count for uplift among the truly needy class."[12]

THE PEOPLE'S MINISTER RESETTLES IN WASHINGTON

When Matthew Strachan learned that despite his efforts at obstruction, the Sheafes were moving ahead with plans to establish their school in Florida, he remained unperturbed. A man of Sheafe's makeup would never be satisfied living in the South, and his "cause is a lost one if he seeks to plant it where southern 'crackers' live," Strachan predicted.[13]

Sheafe, though, was no stranger to the South. So, while Strachan turned out to be correct about the brevity of Sheafe's sojourn in Florida, it cannot be assumed that he was right about the reason. At any rate, when the school term came to an end in May 1918, Sheafe returned to Washington, where he would reside for the remaining two decades of his life, serving as pastor of the church at 10th and V streets.

The details concerning the fate of the school in Jacksonville are unknown. It may simply have collapsed after one year, though Lucy may have kept it going for a while after the elder's departure. She apparently maintained a residence in Florida, for the 1920 census lists Lewis Sheafe, his 15-year-old stepson Arthur, and 6-year-old daughter Doris as renters in Washington, but it does not list Lucy or her daughter, Margaret. Soon thereafter, the family took up residence at 905 R Street Northwest, Washington, D.C. Lucy, however, spent the school terms back in Florida, for at some point prior to 1924 she joined the faculty of Fessenden Academy in Ocala, one of the many schools established for freedmen in the post-Civil War decades under the auspices of the American Missionary Association.[14]

Though the gulf between them and the denomination now stood fixed, Lewis Sheafe and his congregation continued, until 1926 at least, to be publicly identified as Seventh Day Adventist.[15] The People's church did not grow greatly—the number of full-fledged members was reported to be around 100 in the mid-1920s, with a total of about 250 adherents. Yet it was a vibrant part of the network of churches, civic organizations, and educational institutions that structured the city's Black community.[16]

The church constructed a 600-seat pavilion or tabernacle on the lot next to their building in 1921, which became the site for the annual summer series of nightly evangelistic meetings.[17] Amid the sharp combat between modernists and fundamentalists that raged in American Protestantism during the 1920s, Sheafe devoted some of his preaching to defense of the historic faith. He heavily advertised a sermon entitled "The Divinity of Christ Called in Question," presented along with a special musical program at the People's Tabernacle on March 9, 1924.[18] Three months later he returned to the prestigious pulpit of the Metropolitan AME Church to preach for the Sunday evening service on June 15.[19]

The very next evening the veteran evangelist rose to the defense of the seventh-day Sabbath at a widely publicized debate organized by Simon P. W. Drew, pastor of the Cosmopolitan Baptist Temple. A celebrated evangelist and enterprising activist with a flair for publicity, Drew claimed to have distributed more than 3,000 tickets to the event in Washington's Black churches. If all these were used, Dr. Drew's great "temple" would be filled to capacity, but visitors from Baltimore, Richmond, and Philadelphia were also anticipated.

The proposition up for debate would be: "Resolved: that Sunday, the first day of the week, is the Christian Sabbath according to the Bible." Dr. Charles S. Morris of New York was slated to argue in the affirmative, and Sheafe, "elder of the People's Seventh Day Adventist Church," in the negative. Twelve ministers were lined up as judges. Two weeks later, the same combatants engaged another aspect of the issue: "Resolved, that the seventh day is not binding on the Christian of today."[20]

Alas, no reports on what transpired at either meeting have turned up. But the previews themselves give indication that years after separating from the denomination, Sheafe continued to champion unpopular convictions that drove the great turning point of his life in 1896. And yet, in the fascinating duality already evident in his debut in the city in 1902, Sheafe's ministry also belonged to the people of Washington in a way that transcended doctrinal and denominational divisions. Despite the painful conflicts and tragic losses in his own life, and yet perhaps in part because of them, his words and music had an exceptional capacity to encourage and console.

A commentator on the music for the funeral of W. Calvin Chase bore striking if highly sentimental testimony to this pastoral quality. The mercurial and combative editor, who deployed mostly honey rather than stings in his coverage of Sheafe, died on January 3, 1921, after more than 35 years of publishing the Washington *Bee*, the city's most influential Black newspaper.

In what the writer described as his "clear and magnetic voice," Sheafe sang "Only Remembered for What I've Done" at the funeral. The Adventist pastor and his "estimable wife," continued the article, had "visited many sorrowing homes with prayer and sweet song, where he has been a panacea to their many woes."[21] In this sense, as well as in the church that was the most tangible achievement of his career, Sheafe was the "people's minister."

---

[1] "Local Happenings," *California Eagle,* July 22, 1916, p. 5; "What the Churches Are Doing," *California Eagle,* Nov. 4, 1916, p. 3, and Nov. 18, 1916, p. 2.

[2] "News of the Nation's Capitol," Savannah *Tribune,* July 21, 1917, p. 6.

[3] "Missouri," Chicago *Defender,* Mar. 3, 1917, p. 9; see also "Missouri," Chicago *Defender,* Jan. 20, 1917, p. 2.

[4] MCS to T. E. Bowen, Feb. 5, 1917, GCA; T. E. Bowen to MCS, Feb. 22, 1917, GCA.

[5] G. E. Peters, "Jacksonville, Florida," *Gospel Herald,* March 1918, p. 2.

[6] MCS to T. E. Bowen, Apr. 30, 1917, GCA.

[7] "Annual Business Meeting," Savannah *Tribune*, Jan. 31, 1920, p. 6.

[8] The letter, as printed in "Experience of the People's SDA Church," pp. 45, 46, bears the names of six signatories: J. W. Allison, [U].S. Willis, Sydney Scott, J. Marion Campbell, T. H. Branch, and R. L. Bradford, Jr. Though all were prominent ministers in the Black Adventist work, it is a matter of speculation as to why these six and no others among the considerably larger number of ministers attending the Huntsville institute signed the letter. In his report on the meetings in the *Gospel Herald*, the North American Negro Department periodical, I. H. Evans stated that "practically the entire colored working force" was in attendance at the institute, which was organized for "colored workers in that part of the [North American] Division Conference east of the Rocky Mountains. But Evans did not give a total number of the attendees ("The Huntsville, Alabama, Ministerial Institute," March 1917, pp. 1, 2). The total number of "colored ministers" in the division was reported to be 60 in 1918 (C. B. Stephenson, "North American Negro Department," *Review*, Apr. 25, 1918, p. 19). Since not more than 10 or so would have been located west of the Rocky Mountains, an attendance of 40-45 at the Huntsville meetings in January 1917 seems reasonable.

[9] "Experience of the People's SDA Church," pp. 42, 43. The heavy use of italics is an indicator of A. T. Jones's overall authorship/editorship of the pamphlet, and, quite possibly, a prominent role in the drafting of this statement.

[10] "News of the Nation's Capital," Savannah *Tribune*, Aug. 25, 1917, p. 7.

[11] "News of the Nation's Capital," Savannah *Tribune*, Oct. 20, 1917, p. 7. M. C. Strachan reported Lucy's location near Ocala in his letter to T. E. Bowen of Apr. 30, 1917.

[12] "Rev. L. C. Sheafe, Great Expounder of the Gospel, and His Wife Extend Thanks to the People and Friends," *Bee*, Dec. 22, 1917, p. 8.

[13] MCS to T. E. Bowen, Sept. 6, 1917, GCA.

[14] Kevin M. McCarthy, *African American Sites in Florida* (Sarasota: Pineapple Press, 2007), 149; "Minister's Wife Asks Support for Daughter," WT, July 30, 1926, p. 1.

[15] Since printed references to the People's church during this period used "Seventh Day Adventist" rather than the official "Seventh-day Adventist" in the church's name, the same rendering will be used here.

[16] A brief news note in the Washington *Post* concerning a celebration of the twenty-fifth anniversary of Sheafe's ministry in the city referred to his church as "one of the prominent colored churches of the District." "Sheafe Will Observe Jubilee as Pastor," WP, Apr. 30, 1927, p. 8.

[17] "People's Tabernacle," *Bee*, Sept. 3, 1921, p. 4; "Local News," WT, July 24, 1922, p. 5.

[18] Advertisement, WT, Mar. 1, 1924, p. 2.

[19] "Local News," WT, June 14, 1924, p. 2.

[20] "Debate on Authenticity of Christian Sabbath," WP, June 16, 1924, p. 2; "'Seventh Day' to Be Argued," WP, June 28, 1924, p. 12. In 1928 Dr. Drew ran for vice president of the United States as the running mate of 74-year-old "General" Jacob Coxey, who famously led an "army" of the unemployed in a march on Washington in 1894, on the ticket of the Interracial Independent Political Party; "Fifth Party," *Time*, June 18, 1928, at Time.com, http://www.time.com/time/magazine/article/0,9171,787279,00.html (accessed Aug. 13, 2009). On the 3,000-seat Cosmopolitan Temple building, see "Rev. Drew's New Church," New York *Age*, May 2, 1907, p. 1.

[21] "Editor Laid to Rest," *Bee*, Jan. 15, 1921, p. 1; "Impressive Music," *Bee*, Jan. 29, 1921, p. 1.

CHAPTER XXXVII

ADVENTIST GARVEYITE

ALONG WITH PROCLAIMING BIBLICAL TRUTH and giving pastoral comfort, the voice of the "people's minister" continued to register in the prophetic mode from time to time. One issue of righteousness that galvanized Washington's Black citizenry in 1919 involved danger to the quality of their public school system—a cherished bright spot within the city's segregated regime. During his lengthy tenure (1868-1900) as superintendent of District Colored Schools, George F. T. Cook had led the development of a stellar public educational system, at the top of which stood the academically rigorous M Street High School and the Armstrong Manual Training High School.

So important was Washington's Black school system in national perspective that the eminent scholar activist, W.E.B. DuBois, who stood second only to Booker T. Washington among race leaders, badly wanted to become assistant superintendent in charge of Colored schools when, in 1906, it appeared that the position might soon become open. However, to block his rival from getting the position, the "Wizard of Tuskegee" maneuvered to have his candidate, Roscoe Conkling Bruce, appointed.[1]

Bruce was the privileged son of the late Blanche K. Bruce, one of the two Black men to be elected to the United States Senate during the Reconstruction era. However, his support in the Black community became shaky over the years, mainly because he seemed too supportive of the efforts of White leaders to funnel Black students almost exclusively into trade schools, and thereby diminish the opportunities for professional and intellectual attainment represented especially by the M Street school.

In 1919 a scandal erupted after Bruce, with the support of other leading Black educators, permitted a White man named Professor H.M.D. Moens to photograph Black high school girls for "scientific research." Professor Moens' stated goal seemed appealing. He wanted to demonstrate physical similarities between Whites and Blacks. The appalling truth soon came out, though, that the subjects of the photographs were in various stages of undress. In the court case that followed, "Professor" Moens was exposed as a complete fraud.

The Moens scandal understandably fueled outrage, but the subsequent campaign, in which Sheafe participated, addressed a deeper matter: it was about removal of Bruce for being a tool of White discrimination, and, more basically still, about supporting policies making the school system a strong, comprehensive means for race advancement.[2]

On the evening of April 26 enthusiastic crowds filled two churches for rallies in support of a parents' league being organized "to reform the condition of the colored public schools," starting with the ouster of Roscoe Conkling Bruce. Though the limelight belonged to editor Calvin Chase and Nannie Helen Burroughs of the National Baptist Training School for Girls, Sheafe followed their speeches at the meeting in First Baptist Church by presenting a resolution for action in taking the campaign forward.[3] The parents' movement quickly gained broad popular support—more than 14,000 signed on in less than a month. The People's Seventh Day Adventist Church was prominent on a relatively short list of institutions—civic organizations and churches—that early on endorsed the purposes of the parents' league.[4] Though Bruce survived in the short term, relentless opposition, especially in the pages of the Washington *Bee*, finally led to his resignation in 1921.

The Bethel Literary and Historical Society remained unsurpassed as a setting in which race leaders spoke to the issues of the day, and Lewis Sheafe gained at least two more opportunities to make his voice heard there. The 1918-1919 season was a particularly brilliant one. It opened on November 12 with an address by Rev. Reverdy C. Ransom of Chicago, described by historian Ralph Luker as "the foremost black spokesman for the social gospel in his generation."[5] It concluded on May 20, 1919, with a rising star in race leadership, A. Philip Randolph, coeditor of the *Messenger* magazine, speaking on "Bolshevism, a Promise or a Menace." Three weeks before that, an "immense throng" packed the auditorium and gallery of the Metropolitan AME Church to hear W.E.B. DuBois, just returned from the historic Pan-African Congress in Paris.[6]

In the midst of these and other luminaries, Lewis C. Sheafe addressed the society on January 21. "Elder Sheafe is a forceful speaker, and you should hear him," said a notice advertising the meeting. His title, "The Black Diamond," which may have alluded to the Black Diamond Express, a fast-running mail train on the route between New York City and Buffalo, doesn't disclose the substance of his message. But surely he did not waste the opportunity on anything of secondary significance.[7]

Just a little more than two years later, on April 15, 1921, Sheafe gave "one of the most inspiring addresses the society has ever listened to," according to a brief report in the Washington *Bee*. The title, "Man and His Investment," once again was too general for concluding much about the content. The newspaper report's praise has a ring of generality—the sort of thing often said of well-received speeches. Yet that by no means entirely discounts its significance, and the report's notation that the meeting was held in the main auditorium of the Metropolitan AME Church implies that it drew a relatively large audience.[8]

The most remarkable of Sheafe's public causes in the 1920s was that of the controversial Marcus Moziah Garvey and his Universal Negro Improvement Association (UNIA). Though he launched the UNIA in his Jamaican homeland, Garvey's radical message of racial dignity and solidarity in the world struggle against the oppression of European peoples caught fire in Harlem just after World War I. Garvey mobilized the masses with unprecedented genius. He inspired them with militant rhetoric about the power of uniting 400 million people of African descent, but also involving them with meaningful tasks and offices in social, benevolent, and commercial lines of endeavor. Claims of 4 million followers may have been exaggerated, but no other movement could draw 25,000 people to a monthlong convention in Madison Square Garden, as did the UNIA in 1920.[9]

Albeit independent, Sheafe still identified himself as a Seventh Day Adventist minister, and was widely recognized as such, when he became one of Washington, D.C.'s leading Garveyites. He must have heard Garvey speak on one or more of the leader's several visits to Washington. A Washington division of the Universal Negro Improvement Association and African Communities League (UNIA-ACL) was organized in 1921, and Sheafe was one of three ministers cited by name in a historical sketch of the division as having been an officer.[10]

Almost as quickly as they sprang up, Garvey's business enterprises began to break down in 1921 under the combined weight of internal division, mismanagement, and federal government surveillance. A Justice Department investigation, directed by J. Edgar Hoover, led to Garvey's arrest on charges of mail fraud in January 1922. Interestingly, it was just after the federal indictment of Garvey that Sheafe demonstrated tangible support by investing $100 in a UNIA bond promising a return of 5 percent interest, dated February 6, 1922. The money was to be used for "the furtherance of the industrial, commercial and agricultural purposes of the association in its construction plans in the interest of the race."[11]

As Garvey's troubles compounded and he came under sharp attack from other major Black leaders, Sheafe remained a vocal supporter. While Garvey was incarcerated in a federal penitentiary in Atlanta, the Washington UNIA-ACL held its third convention beginning August 16, 1926, at Walker Memorial Baptist Church. Sheafe was the principal speaker for the opening night. It was the eve of Garvey's birthday, which was celebrated the next day with presentations on his achievements and his "persecution and imprisonment." Subsequent sessions dwelt on "the need for establishment of schools and universities for the 'independent education of the Negro race.'"[12]

Sheafe's support for the UNIA supplemented rather than replaced his other commitments. He remained first and foremost a minister of the gospel of Jesus Christ. He did not repudiate his membership in the NAACP because of its ideological differences with the UNIA. But the Garvey movement offered one more lever—and an especially audacious one—for lifting the race out of oppressive circumstances that showed little sign of letting up. In ways not altogether dissimilar to Adventism, it offered wholistic redemption through formation of separate, alternative institutions, uniting the race across national boundaries and leading it toward the promise of a glorious destiny.

---

[1] Lawrence Otis Graham, *The Senator and the Socialite: The True Story of America's First Black Dynasty* (New York: HarperCollins, 2006), pp. 268-287; J. M. Moore, *Leading the Race,* pp. 86-106.

[2] Graham, pp. 295-298; Moore, p. 107.

[3] "Two Meetings Held in Two Churches," *Bee,* Apr. 26, 1919, p. 1.

[4] Preston H. Harris, "Under the Capitol Dome," Chicago *Defender,* May 1919, p. 18.

[5] R. E. Luker, *The Social Gospel in Black and White,* p. 174; "Bethel Literary," *Bee,* Nov. 2, 1918, p. 4.

[6] "Bethel Literary Season to Close," *Bee,* May 17, 1919, p. 1; "Bethel Literary," *Bee,* May 3, 1919, p. 4.

[7] "Bethel Literary," *Bee,* Jan. 18, 1919, p. 8.

[8] "Bethel Literary," *Bee,* Apr. 19, 1921, p. 5.

[9] Among the plethora of works on Garvey and the UNIA, this summary draws on Cary D. Wintz, ed., *African American Political Thought, 1890-1930: Washington, DuBois, Garvey, and Randolph* (Armonk, N.Y.: M. E. Sharpe, 1996), pp. 10-14; Albert J. Raboteau, *Canaan Land: A Religious History of African Americans* (New York: Oxford University Press, 2001), pp. 86-89; and, impressionistically, on Colin Grant, *Negro With a Hat: The Rise and Fall of Marcus Garvey* (New York: Oxford University Press, 2008).

[10] "UNIA Celebrates 87 Years in Banneker City (D.C.)," *The Blackman* 31 (June 29, 2008), at The Negro World, http://www.angelfire.com/electronic/negroworld/black31.html (accessed Aug. 14, 2009).

[11] Copy in author's files, graciously provided by Mr. Mwariama D. Kamau.

[12] "Negro Associations Will Honor Garvey," WP, Aug. 17, 1926, p. 13.

ChAPTER XXXVIII

THE QUEST FOR
BROADER CONNECTIONS

While the People's church retained the name "Seventh Day Adventist" into the mid-1920s, it is also true that Sheafe was becoming less attached to it. This does not seem to have been a matter of changing theology. Rather, the reality was setting in that no viable options existed for connecting with any broader association generally recognized as Adventist. Separation from the Seventh-day Adventist denomination was now entrenched, and the possibility of reconciling with Manns and connecting with the Free Seventh Day Adventists does not appear to have come up for consideration. Despite the strong-willed independence of his temperament, and the fact that he favored a denominational polity that preserves congregational sovereignty, Sheafe did not regard congregational independence as an ideal state. He recognized the value of associations beyond the congregation; indeed, everything about his experience, training, and instincts pointed in the opposite direction of withdrawal and insularity.

A "DIVINE HEALING" MINISTRY
AND THE CHURCH OF GOD (SEVENTH DAY)

The People's church apparently did form a new denominational affiliation in 1923, though it was too short-lived to become a matter of permanent public record. Soon after the Seventh-day Adventist denomination formally organized in 1863, the opposition to James and Ellen White's leadership raised in Iowa by B. F. Snook and W. T. Brinkerhoff led to the formation of a group of seventh-day Sabbath observers who took the name Church of God. Though subject to numerous divisions and permutations that make its institutional history exceedingly complex, the groups of seventh-day observers taking the name Church of God collectively came to constitute a lasting religious movement.[1]

One of its evangelists, Milton Grotz, brought revival to the Stanberry, Missouri, based Church of God in 1923 with a "divine healing" ministry associated with a Pentecostal outpouring of the Holy Spirit. Health reform went hand in hand with instantaneous healing in Grotz's ministry, as he preached against eating pork and the use of tobacco, coffee, tea, and whiskey. The health angle likely was an important factor influencing Sheafe to welcome Grotz's "divine healing ministry" into the People's church.

According to *The History of the Seventh Day Church of God,* by Richard Nickels, many were healed at Grotz's revival in August, and the People's church as a whole came into the Church of God. Sheafe's name did appear in 1924 on the Church of God (Seventh Day) list of licensed ministers, and as associate editor of the *Advocate*, the denomination's "official organ." But the affiliation proved to be transitory, and the People's church continued to be identified in newspapers as Seventh Day Adventist.[2]

A "NEW AND WONDERFUL SCIENCE"

Even as Milton Grotz conducted his divine healing revival at the People's church, Sheafe was becoming a practitioner of the healing arts using a different methodology. The 63-year-old preacher was in school again, two thirds of the way through the course at Central Chiropractic College, and thus bringing to culmination a long-standing interest in health care extending back to his brief course in basic treatments at Battle Creek Sanitarium in 1896.

The Central Chiropractic College in Washington claimed to be the first duly incorporated school established "to teach colored people this new and wonderful science."[3] The Washington "Church News" section of the June 28, 1924, edition of the Chicago *Defender* announced that "Rev. [Lewis] C. Sheafe, the eminent preacher of the SDA religious faith, and lecturer" had completed the three-year course and set up his practice at 1850 8th Street NW. Soon afterward a local guild of the emerging profession organized, with Dr. Lewis C. Sheafe elected treasurer.[4] A newspaper advertisement listing Sheafe and three other chiropractors proclaimed that "acute and chronic diseases of all kinds, such as: rheumatism, lumbago-neuritis, constipation, incontinence of urine, female disorders and head troubles, are all greatly relieved by chiropractic treatments."[5]

Sheafe developed a successful practice, and ever the progressive, incorporated advances in the field as he neared the end of his seventh decade. After spending part of the summer of 1929 conducting research in Chicago, he took out an advertisement in the Washington *Tribune* announcing that his "already well-equipped office" now had a "Recto-Pelvo-Thermo-Phore, which is a wonder for the relief of high blood pressure, piles, constipation, urinal troubles, and all prostatic diseases."[6]

ANOTHER SEPARATION

As Lewis pursued chiropractic training, distance between him and Lucy grew. Lasting harmony eluded Sheafe in marital relationships just as, it seems, in denominational affiliations. Since the break with the Southern California Conference in 1915, they had spent long periods of time apart. In recent years her employment at Fessenden Academy meant that she was in Florida more than in Washington.

Lucy secured a teaching position closer to home at the State College in Dover, Delaware, for the fall of 1924. But by then renewed intimacy between the couple no longer seemed possible. They entered a formal separation agreement on May 15, 1924. He deeded to her the house in which they had been living at 905 R Street NW. She, in turn, discharged him from any future responsibility for supporting their daughter Doris, who by then was 10 years old. The elder, and now doctor, ended up at 1509 5th Street Northwest, where he set up his chiropractic office.

Less than a year later, though, a serious complication to the arrangement with Lucy arose when illness forced her to leave her teaching position in February 1925. Her only steady income now came from renting rooms in the house. Her son Arthur, who honed his skill as a cornetist at the Berean church in Los Angeles, was just beginning a successful career in popular music,[7] but neither he nor her daughter Margaret were able to help on a regular basis. So Lucy could not make ends meet for her and Doris.

She told her husband of her plight, but he refused to help, Lucy claimed. Finally she hired the law firm of Houston and Houston and took him to court in July 1926. Lucy contended that in addition to his salary from People's church, still at $100 per month, Lewis averaged $150 per month from his "lucrative practice" as a chiropractor, and $50 from rooms he sublet. Thus, he was more than able to support his daughter.

True to form when it comes to the failings of a preacher or politician, the press seized on the story. The Washington *Tribune* put it on the front page under the title "Minister's Wife Asks Support for Daughter," while the Baltimore *Afro-American* put the same story on page 2 with a somewhat more sensational headline—"Chiropractor-Pastor Sued by His Wife."[8]

Lewis' perspective was not included in the article, but apparently he was willing to support Doris if she was in his custody. Lucy, however, characterized her husband as "overbearing and irascible" and said that he "possesses an ungovernable temper." Thus, he was "temperamentally unfit" to have custody of their daughter.[9]

The court's ruling, reported a week later, largely went in Lucy's favor. She was given temporary custody of Doris, and the pastor was ordered to pay her $30 per month alimony.[10]

Lucy Whetsel remained married to Lewis Sheafe until his death in 1938. She moved with Doris to New York City sometime before 1930.[11]

CONNECTING WITH AN
"ESTABLISHED FAITH OF SABBATHKEEPERS"

The unflattering public exposure of domestic strife came at a particularly awkward time for Sheafe, for it coincided with a major change at the People's church. The church had continued for nine years as an independent Adventist congregation but had for quite some time recognized their "need for an alliance with some established faith of Sabbathkeepers." In a public statement that appeared in the July 9, 1926, issue of the Washington *Tribune*, Sheafe explained their decision to affiliate with the body of Sabbathkeepers established longer than any other, with origins stretching back to the seventeenth century.[12]

"We have decided to seek a connection with the Seventh Day Baptists. Their church polity is the same as the regular Baptist Church, each church its own sovereign. Its doctrines are simple; the Bible and the Bible only is the rule of faith and practice. They have gone farther than this and interpreted the New Testament as teaching the freedom of individuals to approach God through Christ directly, to interpret the Scriptures for themselves, to formulate their own beliefs, and to worship God according to the dictates of their conscience. Seventh Day Baptists have no creedal statements to which their members must adhere, and their covenants are most simple.

"The Bible with its Christ, faith and repentance, forgiveness of sins, immersion, the Sabbath of Christ, godly living, the fatherhood of God, and the brotherhood of all men, is the only creed they recognize.

"Therefore, we the members of the People's Seventh Day Adventist Church, located at Tenth and V streets Northwest, Washington, D.C., have unanimously voted to change our name to that of People's Seventh Day Baptist. We will be governed accordingly."[13]

If George I. Butler had still been alive, he might well have said, "I told you so!" When the People's church first withdrew from the denomination in 1907, Butler voiced his suspicion that Sheafe "never was a Seventh-day Adventist heart and soul" but was instead "just a Seventh Day Baptist."[14] On the matter of denominational polity, Butler probably was right. The Adventist system of organization probably never became, for Sheafe, a matter of conviction based on Scripture. At points of conflict he reverted to the Baptist "congregational sovereignty" system with which he was familiar and which he continued to regard as more in accordance with the Bible.

Yet the overall narrative thus far has established that Sheafe's connection with the Seventh-day Adventist message and mission went far deeper than that of the "Baptist seventh-day observer" of Butler's imagination. Had Sheafe experienced the Seventh-day Adventist system of governance as open and fair—particularly along racial lines—he would not have left the denomination over the matter of church organization.

In the July 9 statement Sheafe cited the Seventh Day Baptists' rejection of creeds and simplicity of covenants by way of implied contrast with what he had come to experience in Seventh-day Adventism. But these characteristics were as true to Seventh-day Adventist roots as Seventh Day Baptist. Membership in the earliest Seventh-day Adventist congregations was based on affirming a covenant simply to "keep the commandments of

God, and the faith of Jesus."[15] So in this regard Sheafe's change of affiliation in 1926 may represent changes in Adventism by the 1910s and 1920s as much as or more than a break on Sheafe's part from the Adventism he embraced in the late nineteenth century.

If Lucy's lawsuit came to the attention of the Seventh Day Baptists meeting in Alfred, New York, for the annual conference that summer, it did not sway them from a favorable response to the petition for affiliation submitted by the People's church. Rev. Robert B. St. Clair came to Washington on September 12 to convey the Seventh Day Baptist General Conference's official recognition and welcome to the People's church and its pastor.[16] It was not until the following year, though, that a council of ministers meeting at the People's church conferred on Sheafe official public recognition as an accredited minister of the denomination.[17]

Sheafe's new denominational connection seems to have been a happy one, for several years, at least. The Seventh Day Baptists' predominantly White membership proved no barrier to holding a national convention at the People's church in 1929.[18] Sheafe served as moderator for the Washington Union Association of Seventh Day Baptists, and as a member of its national board of education beginning in 1933. He conducted evangelistic meetings under the denomination's auspices in White Cloud, Michigan, north of Grand Rapids. And, in a council that met in Plainfield, New Jersey, in 1932, he probably took a special satisfaction in offering the motion to approve the credentials of a new candidate for Seventh Day Baptist ministry. That candidate was Ludwig R. Conradi, by far the most influential figure in establishing Seventh-day Adventism in Europe, and for many years leader of the work there as vice president of the General Conference's European Division. Toward the end of a long career, his conflicts with the other leading brethren led him, like Sheafe, to withdraw and connect with the Seventh Day Baptists.[19]

Something happened, however, to disturb the status quo of the People's Seventh Day Baptist Church around 1936 or 1937, for which a change in listing is our only clue. Whatever the cause, it prompted the elder, now in his late 70s, to move one more time in the direction of independence. A key word was added to the church's listing in the 1937 edition of the city directory to make it read "People's Seventh Day Baptist Independent."[20]

THE "NATIONALLY KNOWN EVANGELIST" HONORED

It was attorney Thomas L. Jones, a classmate of Sheafe's at Wayland Seminary, and not one of the participating ministers, whose oratory truly caught fire at the twenty-fifth anniversary celebration of Sheafe's ministry in Washington, D.C. The five-night affair had been filled with superb music and fine tributes from journalists, lawyers, college professors, and ministers of various denominations. Even the New York *Age* had taken note of the celebration of the ministry of the "nationally known evangelist." The outgrowth of the tent meetings Sheafe began in Washington in 1902, said the report, was "his present commodious temple," valued at $40,000, all but $2,000 of which had been paid.[21]

The fact that William H. Ferris authored a report on the affair for the Washington *Tribune* further reflects the esteem that continued to be accorded the aging preacher by prominent African-Americans. Ferris, an author, lecturer, and editor who held degrees from both Yale and Harvard, had been a close ally of W.E.B. DuBois in the Niagara movement and more recently editor of the UNIA newspaper, the *Negro World*.[22] According to Ferris, no "thrill" charged the audience until Jones's address on the final evening. One of Washington's most distinguished and experienced Black attorneys, Jones began his career as partner of John Mercer Langston, who was elected to the U.S. House of Representatives from Virginia in 1888. In 1925 President Calvin Coolidge appointed Jones assistant district attorney for the District of Columbia.

The lawyer preached on May 5, and his message of "protest against the decadent tendencies of the hour and the pernicious drift of modern civilization" had an Adventist ring to it. In addition to calling the church out of its lethargy in view of the crisis, he invoked an outline of history pointing to impending judgment.

"Two thousand years from creation and the flood came. Two thousand years more wing their way to the realms of a nameless oblivion, and the Christ was born.

"At the expiration of 2,000 years more, what will happen? Something is going to happen if the Bible is true, and God's word is true. Are you getting ready for it, church? Church, awake! Leaders of the race, awake! If you are asleep, awake! If you are standing, move! If you are moving, run! If you are running, fly! Watchman, what of the night? Where are we bound? We look, and the stars that once guided our course by night have faded from view. Strange theories come with the night, established ways are lost, and widening fields obscure the vision and point of view! But you have a safe pilot in Elder Lewis C. Sheafe, my schoolmate in Wayland Seminary years ago.

"Press on, press on, achieve, achieve, until you stand on Pisgah's summit, the monarch of the hour and the master of eternity!"[23]

The elder himself pressed on for another 11 years. He was said to be in failing health for several years before his death, though no specifics were disclosed. Nevertheless, Sheafe kept at his pastoral duties until 12 days before he passed away on June 24, 1938, at the age of 78.[24] He was still involved in public issues as late as December 1936, coming out in favor of a proposal to the District Board of Education that in the hiring of teachers, preference be given to total abstainers from alcohol, tobacco, and "other narcotics."[25] He was still taking guest speaking engagements at least as late as August 1937, when he was on the program for the quarterly meeting of the Woman's Convention Auxiliary to the Baptist Church of the District of Columbia.[26]

FELLOWSHIP AMONG SEVENTH-DAY OBSERVERS

Along the way Sheafe made at least one more concerted effort at reaching out to his Seventh-day Adventist brothers and sisters. In the summer of 1934 he initiated a move to build fellowship between the various seventh-day-Sabbath-observing Christian groups in Washington. One factor likely behind the initiative was the recent growth in Christian Sabbathkeepers in the area brought about when a branch of the Church of God and Saints of Christ (CGSC) moved its headquarters from Pittsburgh to Washington, D.C., in September 1933.

The CGSC, according to the 1936 U.S. Census of Religious Bodies, had more than 37,000 members. That represented phenomenal growth over the previous decade, at the beginning of which it reported less than 7,000 members. If the figures are anywhere close to accurate, the CGSC had surpassed the Seventh-day Adventist Church by a considerable margin as the American denomination with the largest number of Black seventh-day Sabbatarians.[27]

The movement originated in Kansas during the 1890s through the colorful ministry of William Saunders Crowdy. Prophet Crowdy, as he became known, was inspired by a vision in which he saw several tables covered with filth and then a table covered with pure white linen on which lay seven keys. The filth-covered tables represented the corrupted denominations of American Christendom, while the pure table represented restoration of the true church. Among the special points of truth represented by the keys was the observance of Sabbath on Saturday, the seventh day of the week.[28]

While similar to Seventh-day Adventism in obvious ways, Crowdy's CGSC also differed in important ways, the most obvious being observance of the Old Testament festivals, such as Passover and the Feast of Tabernacles. Indeed, it was these remarkable convocations and the unusual practices associated with them that drew the greatest notoriety to the CGSC.

During the final years of Crowdy's life (1903-1908) the CGSC made its headquarters in Washington, D.C.[29] Thus, Sheafe surely became familiar with the group at that time, if he had not previously. After Crowdy's death, the CGSC divided between those for whom being "black Jews" was the main emphasis and thus looked almost exclusively to the Old Testament,[30] and those, represented by the group that returned to Washington in 1933, who affirmed belief in Christ and the New Testament.

The Washington CGSC met at the Pythian Temple, 12th and U streets Northwest, and was led by Bishop Abel S. Dickerson, who was held in high regard as an "orator." Over the next few years they became a well-recognized part of the Black church scene in Washington, D.C.[31]

The idea of encouraging Christian unity among seventh-day observers "crystallized" in 1934 when Sheafe issued a call to all "Sabbathkeeping Christians . . . who desired a closer fellowship" to meet at the People's Seventh Day Baptist Church. The intention was "to emphasize the spirit of brotherly love and Christian unity, without abandoning any of the peculiar tenets that may characterize any of the various groups."

The initial results of the effort were "surprisingly successful," said a report in the Washington *Tribune* that probably originated with Sheafe. In addition to the People's church, three groups were represented at the first meeting, which probably took place in August or September: The Church of God and Saints of Christ; the Gathering Call Mission of Undenominational Sabbathkeepers, which was loosely associated with the *Gathering Call* periodical published by E. S. Ballenger, the brother of the late founding editor, A. F. Ballenger;[32] and the Fairmount Heights Seventh-Day Christians, led by G. W. Steele, who previously had been an elder at the People's church.

The CGSC hosted the second meeting. For the third meeting, scheduled to take place on October 13 at the Gathering Call Mission's place of assembly at a hall on T Street Northwest, members of the Ephesus and First Seventh-day Adventist churches were expected to attend. The meeting was to be "devoted only to worship, praise, and testimonies."[33]

The very brief follow-up report gave no specifics on whether or how many members of these congregations participated. None of the subsequent reports of the subsequent Christian fellowship meetings of seventh-day Sabbath groups gave definite indication of Seventh-day Adventist involvement, either. At least seven monthly meetings took place in 1934 and 1935, with evidently enthusiastic support from the groups who initially responded.[34] Diminished capacity to lead on the part of the aging Sheafe may have been a reason the effort to promote Christian unity among Sabbath observers without seeking doctrinal uniformity faded away.

The effort represents a central paradox of Sheafe's career. He was, on the one hand, a consummate joiner and activist. He eagerly connected with any group or association that could contribute to the two great purposes that animated his journey—liberation for his oppressed people and uncompromising faithfulness on the part all who would respond to the preaching of the gospel. Republicans, Odd Fellows, Afro-American League, NAACP, UNIA, countless local and short-lived organizations for civil rights and racial uplift, Baptists, Christian Endeavor, YMCA, Seventh-day Adventists, Free Seventh Day Adventists, Church of God (Seventh Day), Seventh Day Baptists—hopeful connections all, but valuable only to the extent that they served those purposes.

On the other hand, he also had a progressive's discontent with the status quo, a reformer's passion for truth and righteousness, a gifted striver's impatience to do great things for God, and a combative, impulsive, and sometimes volatile temperament. The connections he formed often were short-lived, falling short of their promise. Even where his attachments remained relatively long-lasting, the intensity or degree of his involvement fluctuated.

And yet, amid the frequent and sometimes turbulent shifts in organizational affiliation that marked Lewis Sheafe's career, he remained steadfast in his commitment to "the commandments of God, and the faith of Jesus"—the heart of the third angel's message (Rev. 14:12).

---

[1] The best historical account seems to be Richard Nickels, *The History of the Seventh Day Church of God* (Neck City, Mo.: Giving & Sharing, 1999). Full text online at Giving & Sharing, http://www.giveshare.org/churchhistory/historysdcog/ (accessed Aug. 14, 2009).

[2] *Ibid.*, chap. 9, http://www.giveshare.org/churchhistory/historysdcog/history9. html (accessed Aug. 14, 2009).

[3] Advertisement, WT, Feb. 3, 1923, p. 8.

[4] "Church News," Chicago *Defender,* June 28, 1924, p. A6; "Local Chiropractors Form Organization," WP, July 8, 1924.

[5] Advertisement, WT, Aug. 9, 1924, p. 7.

[6] Advertisement, WT, Sept. 20, 1929, p. 4.

[7] Arthur, 21, was touring in South America with his "music box orchestra" at the time of the lawsuit ("Society," Baltimore *Afro-American* [Oct. 16, 1926], p. 2). Later he performed with Duke Ellington and his Cotton Club Orchestra (Louis B. Lautier, "Washington, D.C.," Chicago *Defender,* Oct. 17, 1931, p. 19).

[8] "Chiropractor-Pastor Is Sued by His Wife," Baltimore *Afro-American,* July 31, 1926, p. 2.

[9] "Minister's Wife Asks Support for Daughter," WT, July 30, 1926, pp. 1, 4.

[10] "Court Directs Minister to Pay $30 Per Month Alimony," WT, Aug. 6, 1926, p. 4.

[11] The 1930 U.S. Census shows Lucy and Doris residing in Manhattan. Like her mother, Doris Sheafe (Lynk) went into the educational field. She graduated from Hunter College in New York in 1935, and earned an M.A. from Columbia University in 1939. She became a vocational and educational guidance counselor and producer and host of the WNYE-TV series *Guidance* in the 1970s (1970-1971). See *Marquis Who's Who in the East,* 18th ed. (Chicago: Marquis Who's Who, Inc., 1981), p. 482.

[12] Don Sanford, "A Brief History of Seventh Day Baptists," Seventh Day Baptist Historical Society Web site, http://www.sdbhistory.org/7.html (accessed Aug. 24, 2009).

[13] "Adventist Congregation Affiliates With Baptist," WT, July 9, 1926, p. 3.

[14] GIB to AGD, July 7, 1907, GCA.

[15] See, for example, the organization of the Michigan Conference, reported in "Doings of the Battle Creek Conference, Oct. 5 & 6, 1861," *Review,* Oct. 8, 1861, p. 4.

[16] "Washington Baptist Church Recognized," Washington *Evening Star,* Sept 13, 1926, p. 17.

[17] "Seventh Day Baptist Church," WT, Dec. 12, 1927, p. 6.

[18] "Seventh Day Baptist Church," WT, July 12, 1929, p. 2.

[19] Albert N. Rogers, *Seventh Day Baptists in Europe and America* (Plainfield, N.J.: Seventh Day Baptist Publishing House of the American Sabbath Tract Society, 1972), Vol. III, pp. 84, 85, 92.

[20] Paul Kelsey Williams, "Scenes From the Past . . . ," *The InTowner,* July 2006, p. 13.

[21] "Citizens of Washington Honor 25th Anniversary of Rev. Lewis C. Sheafe," *New York Age,* Apr. 30, 1927, p. 2.

[22] D. L. Lewis, *W.E.B. DuBois,* p. 513; C. Grant, *Negro With a Hat,* pp. 247, 260.

[23] Wm. H. Ferris, "Atty. Jones Praises Elder Sheafe," WT, May 27, 1927, p. 5.

[24] "7th Day Adventist Elder Is Buried," Washington *Afro-American,* July 23, 1938, p. 8.

[25] "More Clerics Favor Dry Teachers in 2nd Poll," Baltimore *Afro-American,* Dec. 19, 1936, p. 11.

[26] "Third Quarterly Meeting Held by Baptism Women," Baltimore *Afro-American,* Aug. 7, 1937, p. 21.

[27] "Census Shows Baptist Gains Lead All Others," WT, Aug. 24, 1940, p. 17. The Church of God and Saints of Christ should not be confused with the Church of God in Christ—a much larger Pentecostal denomination.

[28] Charles E. Bradford, *Sabbath Roots: The African Connection* (Ministerial Association of the General Conference of Seventh-day Adventists, 1999), pp, 171-175.

[29] Beersheba Crowdy Walker, *Life and Works of William Saunders Crowdy* (Philadelphia: Elfreth J. P. Walker, 1955), pp. 46-62.

[30] Elly M. Wynia, *The Church of God and Saints of Christ: The Rise of the Black Jews* (New York: Garland Publishing, Inc., 1994), pp. 68, 69.

[31] "Church of God to Start Sabbath Meetings Here," WT, Sept. 7, 1933, p. 10; "Seventh Day Observers in Fellowship Matter," WT, Nov. 3, 1934, p. 10. The latter statement is based on the author's perusal of most issues of the Washington *Tribune* and Washington *Afro-American* during the 1930s and 1940s.

[32] A letter to the editor in the *Gathering Call,* Aug. 1923, reported the formation of the Gathering Call Mission in Washington, but the group does not appear to have stayed in contact with the periodical.

[33] "7th Day Churches Are Sponsoring Closer Unions," WT, Oct. 6, 1934, p. 7.

[34] "Seventh Day Observers;" "Christian Fellowship Union," Washington *Tribune,* Feb. 9, 1935, p. 7.

CHAPTER XXXIX

LEGACY

YOU THINK YOU CAN PREACH? You should've heard Sheafe," a senior member of the Dupont Park Seventh-day Adventist Church in Washington, D.C., once told Charles E. Bradford, who served as president of the denomination's North American Division from 1979 to 1990 and in numerous other capacities before and since.[1] Readers who have heard Bradford preach will appreciate the significance of the comparison, even if it wasn't intended to be taken with absolute literalness.

When Alma Blackmon, the renowned Adventist musician and choral director, was about 5 years old, she had an encounter with Sheafe that she never forgot. She grew up in the First church in Washington, where her father, James Montgomery, was the head elder and a Sabbath school teacher. Young Alma was sitting on the front row when she heard Sheafe sing—and her memory was clear that it was the First church, even though the incident would have been several years after his separation from the organized work. He sang "The Pearly White City" with a beautiful tonal quality that registered in the musician's memory more than 80 years later. Even more memorably, in the middle of the song he stepped down from the podium, picked her up, and held her until he finished singing.[2]

Since his death Sheafe has made only a few flickering appearances in Adventist historical writing. Yet these anecdotes suggest that in segments of the Black Adventist community the memory of his extraordinary gifts and contribution lived on more powerfully than it did in written accounts.

The Dupont Park (formerly Ephesus) church has indeed maintained through the years recognition of Sheafe as a founding pastor. In 1947, 30 years after its formation amid conflict, when a number of the earliest members would still have been active and bitter memories still vivid, a feature article on the Ephesus church in the Washington *Afro-American* newspaper stated that the congregation had been organized in 1916 by "Elders Harter and Sheafe."[3] If the literal inaccuracy of the implied picture of Harter and Sheafe working cooperatively to found the church seems almost amusing, the statement's deeper level of truth is even more striking. Whoever provided the paper's religion reporter, Irene M. Waugh, with information for the article did not disown Sheafe as a founder, even though the congregation was born out of a traumatic controversy in which denominational leaders denounced him as a dangerous apostate. While the article collapsed the chronological gap, it is true that Ephesus was the child both of the church Sheafe organized and of the loyalty to the denomination, represented by R. E. Harter, that made it a distinct body.

Nearly 60 years later, the Dupont Park church held a centennial anniversary celebration, taking the year 1905, when the People's church acquired its own building at 10th and V, as its date of origin. Along with better awareness of the congregation's rich heritage in general, another purpose of the anniversary celebration, said planning committee chair Maurice Parker, was "to recognize Lewis C. Sheafe," who was "a major player and the church's first pastor."[4]

In Los Angeles the Berean church has also held its controversial founder in honored memory, even after restoring its connection with the denomination he left. Though its numbers gradually diminished after Sheafe's departure, the Berean church remained as an independent congregation in the 1940s, when Frank L. Peterson, who assisted Sheafe in the evangelistic meetings of 1914 that led to the church's formation, returned to Los Angeles. While serving as pastor of the large Wadsworth (formerly Furlong) church, Peterson shepherded the Berean group back into the Southern California Conference. Forty-five years later, though, when it was one of the churches included in a sociological study of congregations conducted by Professor Nancy Tatom Ammerman, the Bereans still saw the protest over racial injustice in the denomination under Sheafe's leadership as the defining circumstance of their origin as a congregation.[5]

At the same time, a "Free Seventh Day Adventist" church now located in the Atlanta, Georgia, area claims lineage from the Berean Free SDA Church that Sheafe founded in 1916. Ironically, these Free Seventh Day Adventists of the twenty-first century identify with the "historic Adventist" movement that became prominent in the 1990s, critical of the denominational leadership for, among other things, failure to uphold the authority of the writings of Ellen White.[6]

The specifically Seventh Day Baptist phase in the history of the People's church also formed an important part of Sheafe's legacy as a church founder and pastor. It remained a vital community of worship and faith for about a quarter of a century after his death. During the 1940s and 1950s, a time when the presence of women in public roles of ministerial leadership was virtually nonexistent in the Seventh-day Adventist denomination, women took a strong role in ministry at the People's church.

Sheafe's successor, Rev. Clayton O. Mason, apparently divided his responsibilities with at least one other congregation, for he preached at the People's church only on alternate Sabbaths. When Rev. Mason was not there, Mrs. Annie Sampson frequently led a "missionary service" at the 11:00 hour. Also, the Rev. Mrs. Esther Smallwood was an occasional guest preacher.[7]

In 1946 the congregation installed a full-time pastor, Luther W. Crichlow, a scion of the church. After gaining a college degree from Howard University, he earned his graduate degree from the Seventh Day Baptist School of Theology at Alfred University in New York. He led the Seventh Day Baptist Mission in Jamaica and then served as a U.S. Army chaplain in the Pacific theater during World War II.[8] However, the Rev. Mrs. Smallwood (Gales) still preached on occasion, as she did on June 26 and 27, 1954, at the annual memorial services for Elder Lewis C. Sheafe.[9]

Crichlow died in 1958, just 48 years old. In 1964 the handsome house of worship at 10th and V streets changed hands, becoming the Morning Bright Baptist Church. The People's church, "The Church That Elder Lewis C. Sheafe Made Famous," as it occasionally billed itself, passed into memory.[10]

Sheafe's historical significance, of course, extends well beyond the individual churches he founded and pastored. Despite spending his final years as a Seventh Day Baptist, the title of the brief newspaper article re-

porting on his funeral services—"7th Day Adventist Elder Is Buried"[11]—
points accurately, whether by design or not, to the fact that his largest and
most lasting imprint belongs to the Seventh-day Adventist movement as a
whole.

Though Sheafe spent just 12 of his 50 years of ministry with the organized Seventh-day Adventist work, his impact rivals that of J. Edson White in introducing Adventism to Black America. Charles Kinny, the first African-American to be ordained an Adventist minister, also blazed trails with proposals for handling race relations in the church and methods for presenting the message to individuals and small groups. Yet it was through the work of those who soon followed Kinny into the ministerial ranks during the late 1890s and first decade of the twentieth century that the numbers of Black Adventists mounted into the hundreds, then thousands, rather than dozens. And among these apostles Sheafe held clear preeminence.

He took the Adventist message to the great center of Black American culture, Washington, D.C. In so doing, he galvanized the attention of a major American city with an evangelistic ministry that reached beyond racial barriers as few—Black or White, before or since—have succeeded in doing. The People's church that eventually resulted was the first major Black Adventist congregation formed in a large city.

Another partial gauge of his impact comes in the form of people that his work, in one or more ways, influenced to engage in some form of ministry themselves. Their influences would in turn ripple out broadly in expanding and shaping the Adventist work among Black Americans down to the present day. Mary Senator, for instance, assisted Sheafe's evangelistic efforts in Washington as a Bible worker. When Sheafe disconnected from the denomination, she left for Chicago, where she worked with W. D. Forde in building up the Shiloh church, which became the bastion of Adventism in the Windy City, its membership eventually in the range of 3,000.[12]

One of the earliest converts through Sheafe's evangelism in Washington, attorney W. H. Green, became, in 1918, the first Black minister to head the North American Negro Department, and he led it with tireless zeal and unwavering fidelity for the next 10 years.

When he baptized a talented youngster named John H. Wagner,

Sheafe was independent of the denominational work. But, recognizing abundant gifts for ministry in the young man, Sheafe encouraged him to go to Oakwood for training. Like Sheafe, Wagner became noted as a singer as well as a preacher. Before the era of E. E. Cleveland and his son-in-law, C. D. Brooks, Wagner was Adventism's most successful Black evangelist in the cities of the Northeast and Mid-Atlantic. When the Allegheny Conference, one of the denomination's initial Black-led conferences, formed in 1944, it elected Wagner as its first president. In that office he led in the founding of Pine Forge Academy near Pottsville, Pennsylvania. Located within a few hours' travel from Washington, Baltimore, Philadelphia, and New York, Pine Forge finally brought partial fruition to Sheafe's long-standing goal of an Adventist training school, open to Blacks and well located for young people from the great cities of the North and East.

Beyond such lines of direct impact, the story of Lewis Sheafe, as told here, invites readers to reflection on its significance for broad themes in Adventist history. The fact that a man of Sheafe's ability, training, relative prominence, and high level of involvement in struggles for racial justice cast his lot with the movement, and stayed with it as long as he did, despite compounded frustrations and disillusionment, bears intriguing witness to the appeal of Adventism during America's progressive era. Because he did so, his ministry in turn helped bring out the movement's potential for being a transforming social alternative by virtue of fidelity to its mission of preparing a people for the reign of Christ in the new world soon to come. The work he led in Washington brought Adventism to the threshold of an enormous opportunity for becoming widely known as a source of hope and help to African-Americans amid deepening racial oppression.

To be sure, the failures in realizing that opportunity say something about the movement's besetting weaknesses, as well as Sheafe's own. Expedient accommodations to segregation (theoretically, only temporary), paternalism, and shortsightedness compounded into an institutionalized racism that caused incalculable, long-term damage to the Adventist cause.

Not long after Sheafe affiliated with the Seventh Day Baptists, James K. Humphrey reached the limit of his long-persisting patience with the denomination's White leadership. The changes had been too slow and the reversals too great in addressing the fundamental inequities that Sheafe brought to light when he sought alliance with Humphrey nearly 25 years earlier. In 1929 Humphrey finally did what he had for so long insisted he would never do. The Harlem-based United Sabbath-Day Adventist denomination that he organized can be seen as the final and most powerful in a series of thrusts toward a separate Black Adventist denomination that began with Sheafe.[13]

Yet, though Humphrey's movement made by far the strongest thrust, it faded as a denomination after little more than a decade. Thus, even in its controversial dimensions, Sheafe's story is a crucial part of a much larger story of how it turned out that no lasting, separate Black Adventist denomination ever formed. That is a notable feature of Adventism, considered from the standpoint of American religious history. The pattern of separate Black denominations among Baptists, Methodists, and Pentecostals—the dominant forms of American Protestantism—did not replicate itself in Adventism. Though ugly stains mar its historical record, Adventism today stands out among American Protestant denominations for racial diversity.

Sheafe's costly confrontations with injustice, as well as his inspiring evangelistic triumphs, illuminate the pathway toward that outcome. The issues he raised could not be avoided, thereby prompting eventual responses to the benefit of the denomination from which he became alienated. His story sheds light on the workings of an amazing grace amid the pain, injustice, and missed opportunities by which Seventh-day Adventists remained one church.

What went through Lewis Sheafe's mind as he sat on the steps in front of F. L. Peterson's home at 621 8th Street, across from the First Seventh-day Adventist Church? During the years when Peterson was in Washington, serving as head of the Seventh-day Adventist Church's Negro Department, Sheafe, the notorious "defector" from the cause, with whom Peterson once worked, stopped by occasionally. He would visit with Peterson's mother, who had been one of his church members in Los Angeles. She greatly enjoyed the sermons of her beloved former pastor, and once in a while her son, out of filial duty, took her to services at the People's church.[14]

As the aging preacher sat there, visiting with Sister Peterson, looking across the street at First church, did he replay in his mind the dramatic events that took place there more than three decades before? Did he savor the memory of those exhilarating days when he stirred Washington by preaching the Seventh-day Adventist message?

Did he ever reflect on that poignant moment of reconciliaticn at the 1913 General Conference session in Takoma Park? At the farewell missionary service, he had sung "Only a Sinner Saved by Grace." When he'd finished, A. G. Daniells had come to the podium and said, "That's what we all are, dear friends—sinners saved by grace, and to God be the glory." And the record attests, the people said Amen![15]

---

[1] Interview, Jan 10, 2007.

[2] Interview, Aug. 5, 2008.

[3] Irene M. Waugh, "Seventh Day Adventists ...," Washington *Afro-American,* Jan. 25, 1947, p. 22.

[4] Beth Michaels, "Dupont Park Church: Celebrating a Century of Ministry," *Columbia Union Visitor,* Jan 2006, p. 10.

[5] Nancy Tatom Ammerman, *Congregation and Community* (New Brunswick: Rutgers University Press, 1997), pp. 93, 94; F. L. Peterson, "The Secretary's Itinerary," *North American Informant,* November-December 1956, p. 10.

[6] "Free Seventh-day Adventists" Web site, http://www.freesda.org (accessed Oct. 3, 2009).

[7] See, as one of several examples, the church's listing in "D.C. Church Frograms," Washington *Afro-American,* Nov. 29, 1941, p. 22.

[8] "People's 7th Day Baptist Elects Ex-Chaplain Pastor," Washington *Afro-American,* June 8, 1946, p. 22.

[9] Advertisement, Washington *Afro-American,* June 26, 1954, p. 13.

[10] "Rev. Luther Crichlow of Seventh Day Baptist," WP, July 3, 1958, p. B2; advertisement in Washington *Afro-American,* Sept. 14, 1946, p. 25.

[11] "7th Day Adventist Elder Is Buried," Washington *Afro-American,* July 23, 1938, p. 8.

[12] L. B. Reynolds, *We Have Tomorrow,* p. 214.

[13] See R. C. Jones's biography, *James K. Humphrey and the United Sabbath-Day Adventists.*

[14] Interview, Clara Peterson Rock, Aug. 6, 2007.

[15] "Special Midsummer Services," *Review,* July 3, 1913, p. 17.

INDEX

A

Adams, John Q., and St. Paul *Appeal*, 24, 30, 31, 49, 50, 63-66, 71, 220

Afro-American League/Council, 42, 43, 51, 59-62, 242, 431

Aiken, S.C., evangelistic effort, 160-162

Allee, N. W., 130, 131, 144-146, 152, 155, 170, 174

Allen Chapel AME Church, Kansas City, Mo., 410

Amadon, George W., 306

"An Appeal in Behalf of the Work Among the Colored People" (1909), 354

Anderson, Mildred, 377

Andross, E. E., 379-381

Anti-Saloon League, 87-94

apostate, Sheafe denounced as, 411, 412

Atlantic Union Conference, 185, 190, 195, 218, 270, 402

B

Ballenger, A. F., 148, 149, 152, 153, 158, 181, 183, 293, 331, 384, 389

Barry, Alfonso, 117, 124, 130, 131

Battle Creek Sanitarium, 114-116, 132, 165, 304-306, 310, 374

Battle Creek Tabernacle, 116, 165, 305, 306

Beddoe, B. E., 378, 381

Berean Seventh-day Adventist Church, Los Angeles, Calif., 377, 378, 381, 435

Bethel Literary and Historical Society, 239, 240, 376, 418, 419

Bethesda Baptist Church, Minneapolis, Minn., 64, 66

Beulah Baptist Church, Alexandria, Va., 27

Blackmon, Alma, 434

Bontemps family, 374, 375

Boyd, C. J., 378

Bradford, Charles E., 434

Branch, Thomas H., 354, 355

Brandon, William, 189, 199, 200

Brice, J. E., 396

Britton, Mary E., 131

Brooks, Walter H., 235

Bruce, Roscoe Conkling, 417, 418

Brunson, John L., 182

Burg, F. M., 376

Burroughs, Nannie Helen, and National Training School for Women and Girls, 272, 418

Bushnell, Asa, 104-106

Buster, James R., 115, 126-130, 137, 152, 154, 288

Butler, George I., 189, 199, 200, 308-310, 320, 323, 328, 335, 358, 426

C

California Eagle, 376

Camp Nelson, Ky., 155-157

Campbell, J. Marion, 276, 354, 374, 392, 401, 402, 411

Capehart, B. Ashbourne, 249, 254, 258

Central Chiropractic College, 423

Chapman, Walter Scott, 123

Chase, W. Calvin, and Washington *Bee*, 203, 220, 221, 236, 237, 242, 243, 406, 407, 415, 418

Chesapeake Conference, 187, 195, 202, 212, 214, 218, 224, 259, 263, 270

Chicago *Defender*, 387, 392

Chiles, J. Alexander, 131-133

Christian Endeavor (Young People's Society of the Christian Endeavor), 47, 48, 87-92, 134, 431

Christian Help work, 133

Christian Negro Seventh-day Adventist Church, 394

Church of God (Seventh Day), 422, 423, 431

Church of God and Saints of Christ, 429-431

Claflin University, 160

Cleveland *Gazette*, 71, 82, 83

Colcord, W. A., 324, 327, 331

Collie, J. W., 127, 130

Colored American newspaper, see Cooper, E. E.

Columbia Union Conference, 402

Connolly, W. S., 302

Conradi, Ludwig R., 142, 367, 427

Cooper, E. E., and the *Colored American*, 24, 178, 203, 221-223, 226, 235, 237-241, 288

Corothers, S. L., 240, 242, 333

Cosmopolitan Baptist Temple, Washington, D.C., 332, 414-415

Cottrell, H. W., 142, 167, 168, 190, 193, 214-220, 223, 224, 260, 328, 370

Crichlow, Luther W., 436

Crowdy, William Saunders, 429, 430

Curry, Elmer W.B. and the Curry Institute, 76, 84, 85